# IRISH POLITICAL THOUGHT AND THE UNION

Moving beyond binary nationalist and unionist narratives of nineteenth-century Irish history, this study instead explores political thought through ideological battles over government. Drawing on neglected pamphlets, political tracts, and polemical newspapers, Colin W. Reid reveals how Irish protagonists – unionists and anti-unionists, Catholic Emancipationists, Repealers, Tories, Fenians, and federalists – clashed over the meaning of representation, sovereignty, and the British connection. Reid traces how competing constitutional visions, rather than national allegiances, drove Ireland's political evolution. From the bitter Union debates to the birth of Home Rule, it recovers forgotten arguments about parliamentary reform, the 'Irish question' in imperial context, and the fraught experience of a small nation within a multinational polity. With fresh insights into figures such as Daniel O'Connell, Isaac Butt, and lesser-known polemicists, this study redefines Irish political thought as a dynamic struggle for representative government. This title is also available as open access on Cambridge Core.

COLIN W. REID is Senior Lecturer in British and Irish History at the University of Sheffield. He is the author of *The Lost Ireland of Stephen Gwynn: Irish Constitutional Nationalism and Cultural Politics, 1864–1950* (2011) and a number of articles and chapters on Irish political thought.

# IDEAS IN CONTEXT

*Edited by* DAVID ARMITAGE, RICHARD BOURKE, ADOM GETACHEW and JENNIFER PITTS

The books in this series will discuss the emergence of intellectual traditions and of related new disciplines. The procedures, aims and vocabularies that were generated will be set in the context of the alternatives available within the contemporary frameworks of ideas and institutions. Through detailed studies of the evolution of such traditions, and their modification by different audiences, it is hoped that a new picture will form of the development of ideas in their concrete contexts. By this means, artificial distinctions between the history of philosophy, of the various sciences, of society and politics, and of literature may be seen to dissolve.

*A full list of titles in the series can be found at: www.cambridge.org/IdeasContext*

# IRISH POLITICAL THOUGHT AND THE UNION

## *Visions of Representative Government, 1798–1879*

COLIN W. REID

*University of Sheffield*

CAMBRIDGE
UNIVERSITY PRESS

CAMBRIDGE
UNIVERSITY PRESS

Shaftesbury Road, Cambridge CB2 8EA, United Kingdom

One Liberty Plaza, 20th Floor, New York, NY 10006, USA

477 Williamstown Road, Port Melbourne, VIC 3207, Australia

314–321, 3rd Floor, Plot 3, Splendor Forum, Jasola District Centre, New Delhi – 110025, India

Cambridge University Press is part of Cambridge University Press & Assessment, a department of the University of Cambridge.

We share the University's mission to contribute to society through the pursuit of education, learning and research at the highest international levels of excellence.

www.cambridge.org
Information on this title: www.cambridge.org/9781009630184

DOI: 10.1017/9781009630191



First published 2026

Cover image: College Green, Dublin. Published 1816 by James Del Vechio, Dublin

*A catalogue record for this publication is available from the British Library*

*Library of Congress Cataloging-in-Publication Data*
NAMES: Reid, Colin, 1979– author
TITLE: Irish political thought and the Union : visions of representative government, 1798–1879 / Colin W. Reid, University of Sheffield.
DESCRIPTION: Cambridge, United Kingdom ; New York, NY : Cambridge University Press, 2026. | Series: Ideas in context | Includes bibliographical references and index.
IDENTIFIERS: LCCN 2025048031 (print) | LCCN 2025048032 (ebook) | ISBN 9781009630184 hardback | ISBN 9781009630153 paperback | ISBN 9781009630191 epub
SUBJECTS: LCSH: Ireland–Politics and government–19th century | Representative government and representation–Ireland–History–19th century | Home rule–Ireland
CLASSIFICATION: LCC JN1411 .R45 2026 (print) | LCC JN1411 (ebook)
LC record available at https://lccn.loc.gov/2025048031
LC ebook record available at https://lccn.loc.gov/2025048032

ISBN 978-1-009-63018-4 Hardback
ISBN 978-1-009-63015-3 Paperback

*For Caoimhe, Iseult, and Maeve*

# *Contents*

# *Acknowledgments*

This book took *slightly* longer than I anticipated, and I've incurred many debts along the way. It's a pleasure to acknowledge the people who have supported and challenged me, and helped shape this work in countless ways.

Vincent Comerford, Roy Foster, Ultán Gillen, Matt Kelly, Ian McBride, and Matt Roberts all generously read drafts and offered characteristically incisive feedback. They cannot, of course, be held responsible for any shortcomings in what follows, but anything of value in these pages owes much to them.

I'm grateful to the Arts and Humanities Research Council for awarding me a Leadership Fellowship in 2020–1 (AH/T00195X/1). That period of work unfolded against the grim backdrop of the COVID-19 lockdowns, and I'm especially thankful to Ann Marie O'Brien for her diligent research on my behalf at the National Library of Ireland when travel to Dublin was impossible.

My colleagues at the University of Sheffield have been a constant source of support. I thank successive Heads of History, Phil Withington and Adrian Bingham, for their patience and encouragement. Regular chats with Esme Cleall, Miriam Dobson, and Danica Summerlin – our convivial accountability group – offered more motivation than they know. Danica also assisted with Latin translations and enlivened discussions about legal history and sci-fi. For their collegiality and friendship, I salute Anna Barton, Kate Davis, Sebastian Gehrig, Andrew Heath, Eirini Karamouzi, Tom Leng, Tehyun Ma, Julia Moses, Caroline Dodds Pennock, and James Shaw.

This research was enriched by visiting fellowships at the Gladstone Library, Hawarden, the much-missed Moore Institute, Galway, and Marsh's Library, Dublin. My thanks to Dan Carey, Jason McElliott, and Amy Boylan for their hospitality and interest in my work. I was fortunate to meet Tadhg Foley – a fellow Isaac Butt enthusiast (a rare breed) – at the

Moore Institute. His encouragement led me to explore the 1830s and 1840s more deeply than I had originally intended.

I'm grateful to staff at the following libraries and archives for their assistance and guidance: the British Library, London; John J. Burns and O'Neill Libraries, Boston College; Marsh's Library, Dublin; the National Library of Ireland, Dublin; the Public Record Office of Northern Ireland, Belfast; and the Weston Bank Library, University of Sheffield. Digitised holdings on archive.org made much of this research possible from Sheffield.

Over the years, I've benefited from the friendship, insights, and generosity of Lauren Arrington, Guy Beiner, Eugenio Biagini, Gemma Clark, Michael Cullinane, Christian Dupont, David Gleeson, James Greer, Erica Hanna, Emily Jones, Matt Kelly, Catriona Kennedy, Katarzyna Kosior, Daniel Laqua, Patrick Maume, James McConnel, Simon Middleton, Marc Mulholland, Margaret O'Callaghan, Martin O'Donoghue, Senia Pašeta, Jennifer Redmond, Jennifer Regan-Lefebvre, Jay Roszman, Andrew Sanders, Rob Savage, James Stafford, Brian Ward, and Tim Wilson. My early interest in Irish history was sparked by the scholarship and distinctive seminar styles of Paul Bew and Alvin Jackson. Jackie Hill helped clarify my approach to the subject matter. All historians of Ireland owe a debt to Roy Foster, whose work and advocacy elevated the field; I'm deeply grateful for his friendship and support. Richard Bourke has been an indispensable supporter of this project, from its conception to completion. The friendship of Matt Roberts has made life in Sheffield brighter. And my fellow booker, Ultán Gillen, remains a constant source of camaraderie.

I've relished joining a growing network of scholars exploring Irish political thought. My thanks to participants in workshops at Sheffield (2022) and Aberdeen (2024), especially Michael Brown, for lively discussions of method and historiography. It's heartening to collaborate with those reimagining Ireland's political past in new and exciting ways. Long may the network flourish.

The team at Cambridge University Press has shown remarkable patience throughout this project. I've particularly enjoyed working with Liz Friend-Smith and Rosanna Barraclough, whose professionalism has been exemplary. Many thanks to the series editors and the anonymous peer reviewers, who helped me to sharpen the book.

I'm grateful that the *English Historical Review* and Oxford University Press granted me permission to revise parts of an article of mine from 2014 ('An experiment in constructive unionism': Isaac Butt, Home Rule and federalist political thought during the 1870s) in Chapter 6.

Thanks to Mum, Dad, Jenny, and all my family for their support over the years. I'm also proud to be part of the McDaid clan: thanks to Fergus, Bridie, Ailbhe, Róisín, Bríd, and Niamh for their love and loyalty. If only they'd heed music recommendations from John Morrissey, whose taste is immaculate. Jason Gordon and I have been blethering on about history, politics, and everything else for more than half our lives now. Here's to many more years of it; thank you, my friend.

This book is dedicated to Caoimhe and our daughters. Caoimhe has been my first reader for years, offering the kind of immediate, insightful feedback that every writer craves. Without her support, this book would not have been possible; it owes much to her inspirational example. And now that Daddy has finished his book, Iseult can finally reclaim the computer for her elaborate PowerPoint presentations, and Maeve's snacks will arrive with fewer delays.

# *Abbreviations*

| | |
|---|---|
| *BMM* | Belfast Monthly Magazine |
| *DUM* | Dublin University Magazine |
| IMCS | Irish Metropolitan Conservative Society |
| IRA | Irish Republican Army |
| IRB | Irish Republican Brotherhood |
| MP | Member of Parliament |
| NLI | National Library of Ireland |
| PR | Proportional Representation |
| PRONI | Public Record Office of Northern Ireland |
| RIC | Royal Irish Constabulary |
| TCD | Trinity College Dublin |

# *Introduction*

What was Ireland during the nineteenth century? A kingdom, a colony, or a clandestine republic: the answer was in the eye of the beholder. The Irish parliament existed until 1800 but lacked executive independence and represented a political nation that was exclusively Protestant. Ireland became an integral component of the United Kingdom from 1801 yet retained configurations of colonial government that intermingled with British domestic structures, creating a constitutional apparatus that lacked conceptual clarity. While Ireland was not unique in terms of its ambiguous constitutional framework – the 'state fragments' within the Habsburg Empire that the German jurist, Georg Jellinek, analysed offer parallel examples and terminologies – the tensions arising created uncertainty at the heart of the nineteenth-century British world.[1] The island was framed as a victim of unresponsive imperialism; at the same time, even sympathetic British observers such as John Stuart Mill believed that the Irish lacked the political maturity for independent statehood.[2] Province or nation, kingdom or colony, the deceptively simple question of what Ireland 'was' in the nineteenth century remains deeply contested.[3] By excavating the contested visions of government – from the dying embers of the parliament in Dublin to the origins of Home Rule – this book explores the ways in which observers and protagonists engaged with Ireland's puzzling constitutional position, and how Irish ideas concerning the structures of government were articulated and changed over time.

[1] Natasha Wheatley, *The Life and Death of States: Central Europe and the Transformation of Modern Sovereignty* (Princeton, NJ: Princeton University Press, 2023), p. 15.

[2] Bruce L. Kinzer, *England's Disgrace? J. S. Mill and the Irish Question* (Toronto: University of Toronto Press, 2001), p. 34.

[3] As the essays in the provocatively titled collection by Terrence McDonough suggest: *Was Ireland a Colony? Economics, Politics and Culture in Nineteenth-Century Ireland* (Dublin: Irish Academic Press, 2005). Also see Stephen Howe, *Ireland and Empire: Colonial Legacies in Irish History and Culture* (Oxford: Oxford University Press, 2000), p. 37.

Many Irish, British, and European observers grappled with Ireland's complex status as a kingdom within the Union state that was governed through colonial structures.[4] This has echoed through historiography, with a well-trodden debate asking whether it is paradoxical that the Irish acted as agents of British imperialism abroad while being a colonised people themselves.[5] Colonial and postcolonial models for examining the case of Ireland have become increasingly influential in recent years, inspired by the disciplinary rise of global history, the 'decolonising' moment within wider society, and the end of the 'Troubles' in Northern Ireland, the latter of which permitted a franker discussion of the applicability of terminology with polemic meanings.[6] Such frameworks can offer valuable insights, but caution is needed to avoid airbrushing the contradictions of Irish life away to 'fit' a colonial prism. The print culture that underpins the research of this book, for example, suggests that the Irish from the late 1790s through to the period of the Union did not necessarily view themselves as a colonised people. Colonial models of examining the Irish past are useful, but a flexible approach remains essential, one that prioritises historical actors' self-perceptions and avoids imposing anachronistic categorisations on Ireland's multifaceted relationship with empire.[7]

Regardless of the framework for interpreting the constitutional position of Ireland, Irish *distinctiveness* from Britain was clearly a defining feature of the period. Nineteenth-century British observers tended to position Ireland as an alien country with very different political and cultural assumptions than Britain.[8] Indeed, given the painful history of conquest, economic subordination, and religious divisions, integration into the British state was always likely to be a challenging feat. The distinctiveness of Ireland did not fade under the Union but was accelerated by Irish legislation that deviated from British 'norms' in law and order, education, and poor relief.[9] Far from

[4] See, for example, Séamus Ó Síocháin (ed.), *Social Thought on Ireland in the Nineteenth Century* (Dublin: UCD Press, 2009), and the early pioneering work of Nicholas Mansergh, *The Irish Question, 1840–1921*, 3rd ed. (Toronto: University of Toronto Press, 1975).

[5] This is outlined in Kevin Kenny, 'The Irish in the Empire', in Kenny (ed.), *Ireland and the British Empire* (Oxford: Oxford University Press, 2004), pp. 92–3.

[6] Caoimhe Nic Dháibhéid et al., 'Round table: decolonising Irish history? Possibilities, challenges, practices', *Irish Historical Studies*, vol. 45, no. 168 (2021), pp. 303–32.

[7] This chimes with the approach of Ian McBride, *Eighteenth-Century Ireland: The Isle of Slaves* (Dublin: Gill & Macmillan, 2009), p. 8.

[8] See, for example, K. Theodore Hoppen, *Governing Hibernia: British Politicians and Ireland, 1800–1921* (Oxford: Oxford University Press, 2016), p. 89.

[9] Roger Swift and Christine Kinealy (eds.), *Politics and Power in Victorian Ireland* (Dublin: Four Courts Press, 2006), p. 9; K. Theodore Hoppen, *Elections, Politics, and Society in Ireland, 1832–1885* (Oxford: Oxford University Press, 1984), p. vii.

erasing Ireland's uniqueness, the Union amplified separateness. This sentiment powerfully shaped Irish political thought throughout the nineteenth century. Indeed, the stark distinctiveness of Ireland was internalised by elements within unionism, which emphasised the need to ensure that 'English theories' of government were influenced by 'Irish facts'.[10] 'Union', to such unionists, meant empowering Irish distinctiveness, not eliminating it.

The French political scientist Gustave de Beaumont witnessed the distinctiveness of Ireland firsthand in his travels through the country during the 1830s. He noted that Irish differences with Britain had become more entrenched since the passage of the Union in 1800. The chief reason for this, according to Beaumont, was that the apparatus of government was imbued with the spirit of conquest, with Ireland treated not as an equal partner within a multinational state but as a conquered territory.[11] Alexis de Tocqueville, who toured Ireland with Beaumont, concurred, noting that the aristocratic British state provided the English with 'one of the best governments that exists in the world' while subjecting the Irish to 'one of the most detestable that could ever be imaged'.[12] Beaumont and Tocqueville positioned Ireland as a consequence of the absence of responsible government, linking misgovernment to the wretched poverty that blighted the countryside, the toxicity of sectarianism, and the distinctive Irish political culture that had flourished since 1800.

The ambiguities of Ireland's constitutional status and the problems of integrating the island into the United Kingdom spurred observers to craft imaginative solutions. The amelioration of Ireland through a more responsive and Irish-focused political economy, centring on the need for substantial land reform, was one such powerful reply favoured by European intellectuals.[13] This conclusion partly rested on the widespread belief among international observers (such as Beaumont and Tocqueville) that transferring political power to Ireland via the creation of an Irish parliament was a flawed answer to the question of misgovernment. The reasons for this judgement included the belief that the Irish lacked the necessary political character to govern a polity, that a self-governing Ireland would

[10] *Dublin University Magazine*, December 1835, pp. 682–96.

[11] Gustave de Beaumont, *Ireland: Social, Political and Religious*, ed. and trans. W. C. Taylor (Cambridge, MA: Harvard University Press, 2006; first published 1839), p. 191.

[12] Emmet Larkin (ed.), *Alexis de Tocqueville's Journey in Ireland, July–August 1835* (Washington, DC: Catholic University of America Press, 1990), pp. 80–1.

[13] This is the main theme of James Stafford, *The Case of Ireland: Commerce, Empire and the European Order, 1750–1848* (Cambridge: Cambridge University Press, 2022).

come into inevitable conflict with the imperial parliament, and that such an outcome was highly unlikely anyway, given the recent incorporation of Ireland into the Union state.[14] A transformation to political economy was, then, proposed as the soundest method to achieve a better, more legitimate government, while also copper-fastening the Acts of Union.

This diagnosis was not uniformly accepted in Ireland. The strain of 'misgovernment' prompted the rise of more overt constitutional solutions, especially in the reordering of the structures of government. The chief argument of this book is that Irish political thought from the debate over parliamentary union in the 1790s to the emergence of Home Rule in the 1870s was dominated by competing visions of *representative government*. The ideas considered in this book attempted to reconcile (or terminate) Ireland's unique constitutional status within broader British and imperial frameworks, with the aim of producing a more coherent sense of representative government. If the Union produced poor government, this fact prompted a wave of responses that reimagined the structures of power to create good government accountable (in differing forms) to the Irish (however defined).

The ideological disputes covered in this book owed less to ideas of national allegiance and more to the apparatus of power. Conceptions of government dominated Irish political thought, reflecting the contemporary importance of the question of political representation. Indeed, the ability of the institutions of government to positively shape the character of a society was a ubiquitous Enlightenment idea that lingered well into the nineteenth century. The classical Whig definition of liberty as the extent to which a people were governed by laws of their own also held a special resonance in the age of nationalism.[15] These intermingling conceptions of government had a problematic application in Ireland during the nineteenth century. Legislative programmes centring on Ireland were rarely consensual, with governing passions largely dictated by British moods, as apparent in the abrupt swings between conciliatory and coercive laws.[16] Equally corrosive were the lengthy periods of largely inactive and uninterested government, a political moratorium that left the Irish in limbo, unable to shape their destiny through the orthodox structures of parliamentary power.[17] While

14 Beaumont, *Ireland*, pp. 363–4; Mansergh, *Irish Question*, p. 90.

15 Quentin Skinner, *Liberty as Independence: The Making and Unmaking of a Political Ideal* (Cambridge: Cambridge University Press, 2025), p. 90.

16 Hoppen, *Governing Hibernia*, p. 3.

17 By this, I draw on the spirit of Ciaran O'Neill's framing of Ireland as a 'palliative state': *Power and Powerless in Union Ireland: Life in a Palliative State* (Oxford: Oxford University Press, 2024), pp. 4–7.

a number of observers from Ireland (and beyond) conceptualised the disturbed state of the country during the century primarily as a crisis of government, there was little agreement on whether the British constitution could accommodate the Irish desire for more representative forms of governance.[18]

The political history of Ireland has tended to be told through the drama of parliamentary crises, popular mobilisation, and agrarian unrest. This book shifts the focus to the realm of political thought, exploring how Irish thinkers, protagonists, and polemicists conceptualised Ireland as a polity.[19] Whether Ireland was imagined as fully integrated into the United Kingdom, a semi-autonomous administration, or an independent state, a key consideration was the provision of meaningful *representative government*, a constitutional form that enshrined the Irish demand to influence the direction of political power. Proposals to create representative government for Ireland implied a negotiation (or rejection) of British sovereignty, offering an Irish take on the design of constituent power within a centralised multinational state.[20] Irish political thought in the period covered by this book is, therefore, a window into how contemporaries from a small but strategically important island, with a complex history that mixed epochs of independence, kingdom, and conquest, imagined the ideal constitution to realise Ireland's potential within (or without) the Union.

The shape of competing forms of representative government offers critical insights into the historical Irish mind; but such thinking also problematises certain aspects of the British representative system. Take, for example, the notion of 'virtual representation'. Virtual representation was the theory that pre-reformed Westminster embodied the collective will of the people of all stations in life, regardless of their suffrage status. Members of parliament were believed to 'represent' the interests of the unfranchised, ensuring a connection between non-voters and the structures of power.[21] The exclusion of Catholics from public office under the penal laws was, however, denounced by the Irish-born Edmund Burke as a

18 Hoppen, *Governing Hibernia*, pp. 66–70; Jay R. *Roszman, Outrage in the Age of Reform: Irish Agrarian Violence, Imperial Insecurity and British Governing Policy, 1830–1845* (Cambridge: Cambridge University Press, 2022), p. 12; Stafford, *Case of Ireland*, p. 258.

19 Recent work has introduced this strand of thought into the revolutionary period. See Richard Bourke, 'Introduction', in Richard Bourke and Niamh Gallagher (eds.), *The Political Thought of the Irish Revolution* (Cambridge: Cambridge University Press, 2022), pp. ix–xli.

20 Lucia Rubinelli, *Constituent Power: A History* (Cambridge: Cambridge University Press, 2020).

21 J. C. D. Clark, *The Language of Liberty, 1660–1832: Political Discourse and Social Dynamics in the Anglo-American World* (Cambridge: Cambridge University Press, 1994), p. 98; Mónica Brito Vieira and David Runciman, *Representation* (Cambridge: Polity Press, 2008), p. 42.

bastardisation of this principle.[22] For virtual representation to function successfully, a commonality was required to tie together the representative and unfranchised group.[23] The explicit constitutional identification with Protestantism, however, rendered such a bond impossible. The result was that Ireland's denominational majority was cast adrift without *any* political representation, virtual or real – a subversion of a key constitutional doctrine. Burke's argument was that virtual representation was not compatible with the penal laws: the one merely highlighted the theoretical limitation of the other.

The experience of Irish MPs also complicated late Georgian and Victorian theories that parliament 'mirrored' society through the formal representation not of classes but of salient interests. This amounted to a defence of a limited but varied suffrage, which 'mirroring' advocates believed was essential for an inclusive parliament. Mass enfranchisement, in this scenario, created an expanded but potentially more uniform electorate, heralding the victory of crude majoritarianism over balanced deliberation.[24] As Gregory Conti has demonstrated, the 'ideal of the mirroring Commons was the polestar for a sprawling Victorian discussion about political representation'.[25] Ireland's reflection in this mirror was, however, troubling. The debate over parliament mirroring the social realities of society was problematised by the Irish experience of Westminster, particularly from the 1830s. A number of critics believed that parliament did not reflect the interests of Ireland, not because of the franchise but because of the inability of Irish MPs to shape the legislative agenda. The numerical dominance of British MPs in Westminster ensured that a distinctive Irish interest was stillborn in parliamentary terms, a frustration that contributed to the rise of self-government as an aspiration within Ireland. The franchise might have mirrored Irish society but, paradoxically perhaps, the parliament did not.

Irish ideas of representation, then, shed light on the limitations of the British model of parliamentary government and provide an important explanatory factor for the growing tensions within the Union state. Interpreting the difficulties in incorporating Ireland into the United Kingdom as a problem in governing structures and representation, rather than as an identity-driven national dispute, permits a more nuanced

[22] Richard Bourke, *Empire and Revolution: The Political Life of Edmund Burke* (Princeton, NJ: Princeton University Press, 2015), p. 796.

[23] David Judge, *Representation: Theory and Practice in Britain* (London: Routledge, 1999), p. 99.

[24] Gregory Conti, *Parliament the Mirror of the Nation: Representation, Deliberation, and Democracy in Victorian Britain* (Cambridge: Cambridge University Press, 2019), pp. 15–26.

[25] Ibid., p. 359.

investigation into political languages and ideas. There is a danger, as has been suggested in a different historiographical context, that 'the transition to freedom' appears as a linear nationalist narrative that flattens a range of constitutional, political, and economic ideas that waxed and waned during the journey.[26] In Ireland, the articulation of constitutional visions often invoked conceptions of the nation – Home Rule as a 'national' form of government, for example – but it was political power rather than identity formation that concerned many of the writers and protagonists covered in this book.

If we take seriously the constitutional and political arguments made by Irish polemicists, the differences in emphasis made by those broadly designated as 'nationalists' come into sharp focus. Nationalism has been the dominant paradigm for understanding the Irish political experience since the late eighteenth century.[27] If treated without care, however, the ubiquity of nationalism risks smothering a range of constitutional perspectives. The major work on the topic, for example, drifts towards grouping all political positions that championed forms of self-government together as nationalists. 'Eighteenth-century Protestant nationalists' appear alongside 'nineteenth-century Catholic nationalists', while the nineteenth-century Fenians and the twentieth-century Irish Republican Army (IRA) are unified as 'militant Irish nationalists'.[28] The term 'nationalist' is used here in such an elastic fashion that it is conceptually meaningless, echoing Partha Chatterjee's warning that 'as history, nationalism's autobiography is fundamentally flawed'.[29]

More precision and context are needed to understand the constitutional ambitions of an individual, group, or body of texts. Theoretically, Daniel O'Connell, the leader of the Catholic Emancipation and Repeal of the Union campaigns from the 1820s to the 1840s, James Stephens, the founder of the militant Irish Republican Brotherhood (IRB), and Isaac Butt, the first leader of the Home Rule movement, were all 'nationalists': they led movements seeking self-government for Ireland, one of the most obvious motifs of Irish nationalism during the period. But O'Connell envisaged self-government as the restoration of the pre-1801 Irish

[26] Vikram Visana, *Uncivil Liberalism: Labour, Capital and Commercial Society in Dadabhai Naoroji's Political Thought* (Cambridge: Cambridge University Press, 2022), p. 2.

[27] See, for example, D. George Boyce, *Nationalism in Ireland*, 3rd ed. (London: Routledge, 1995) and Brian Jenkins, *Irish Nationalism and the British State: From Repeal to Revolutionary Nationalism* (Montreal & Kingston: McGill-Queen's University Press, 2006).

[28] Boyce, *Nationalism in Ireland*, pp. 327, 388.

[29] Partha Chatterjee, *The Nation and Its Fragments: Colonial and Postcolonial Histories* (Princeton, NJ: Princeton University Press, 1993), p. 6.

parliament, a quasi-colonial institution with legislative but not executive powers; Stephens desired an independent republic based on the sovereignty of the people and dabbled in internationalist radicalism; and Butt devised a system of federalism to divide sovereignty equally throughout the United Kingdom, with Irish MPs continuing to serve in London to deal with imperial matters. These three examples personified radically different conceptions of Irish autonomy, suggesting that ideas of sovereignty in Ireland were multilayered and contested.[30]

An all-encompassing definition of nationalism, and its use as the primary political framework, fails to capture the stark differences in how these leaders imagined Ireland's future political status. The very different schemes proposed by O'Connell, Stephens, and Butt should not be fused together into an unchanging 'national question' based on the broad premise of self-government.[31] Likewise, enemies of Irish nationalism – chiefly unionists in Ireland – were far from monolithic in their political thinking. The character of debate shifted through time, and political languages and tropes evolved in certain contexts. The potential for prolepsis – imposing a political perspective on past actors that they would not recognise – is increased if constitutional ideas and their underlying rationales are not seriously considered, or if conceptions of Irish self-government are merely reduced to 'nationalist' programmes. Some opponents of the theory and practice of Union in Ireland from the 1790s to the 1880s were no more nationalists than Plato, in his attack on ancient democracy, was a sponsor of totalitarianism.[32]

In shifting the focus away from 'national feeling' and pointing towards political power and representation, the diversity of constitutional ideas that sustained Irish politics is unveiled. Accordingly, this book breaks with a narrowly high-political approach, which has tended to concentrate on the activities of a small elite involved in parliamentary affairs, and instead examines the ideas of what representative government looked like within Irish political thought. How a varied cast of pamphleteers and partisans conceptualised 'government' lies at the heart of the chapters that follow.

[30] This chimes with work on the operation of multiple ideas of sovereignty within the Austro-Hungarian Empire in Wheatley, *The Life and Death of States*.

[31] As an aside, while O'Connell is widely heralded as a founding father of modern Irish nationalism, Joep Leerssen has cast doubt on his nationalist credentials from a European perspective. *Remembrance and Imagination: Patterns in the Historical and Literary Representation of Ireland in the Nineteenth Century* (Cork: Cork University Press, 1996), p. 22.

[32] Plato as a proto-totalitarian thinker is, of course, a key component of Karl Popper's *The Open Society and Its Enemies* (Abingdon: Routledge, 2011; first published 1945).

Rival conceptions of government underpinned many of the constitutional ideas that emerged from across the political spectrum, from Tory notions of conditional unionism to the separatist ideal of the 'sovereign people'. The appropriate form of government for Ireland and the nature of its connection with the wider British world were acute questions for contemporaries, and provoked powerful and imaginative responses. Political conflict in Ireland thus derived from disputes about representative rights and left a deep imprint within the constitutional imagination of generations of Irish thinkers and activists.

## Representative Government

The idea of 'representative government' was a defining theme of Western political thought during the late eighteenth and nineteenth centuries, although its definition remained in flux.[33] Radical ideas of popular sovereignty erupted into the political mainstream with the revolutions in America and France, asserting the natural right of man to control his own political destiny, free from the arbitrary rule of hereditary aristocrats and monarchs, as well as (in the American case) colonial empires.[34] The most suitable constitutional apparatus to enshrine popular sovereignty was, however, fiercely contested.[35] The principle of representation was advocated by prominent radical thinkers (most notably Thomas Paine and Emmanuel Sieyès) as a bridge between the people and power.[36] That said, representative government did not necessarily equate to democratic government: the most common form that emerged gave the people *indirect* power, while their delegates participated in statecraft within fixed constitutional limits.[37]

The world typically could not be made anew within such a governing structure, but the key point was that the institutions of power gained legitimacy through popular participation. The ability of people to choose

[33] James T. Kloppenberg, *Toward Democracy: The Struggle for Self-Rule in European and American Thought* (Oxford: Oxford University Press, 2016), p. 655.

[34] Geneviève Nootens, *Popular Sovereignty in the West: Polities, Contention, and Ideas* (London: Routledge, 2013), p. 60.

[35] Jonathan Israel, *Revolutionary Ideas: An Intellectual History of the French Revolution from The Rights of Man to Robespierre* (Princeton, NJ: Princeton University Press, 2014), p. 346; John Dunn, *Setting the People Free: The Story of Democracy* (London: Atlantic, 2006; first published 2005), pp. 74–5.

[36] J. C. D. Clark, *Thomas Paine: Britain, America & France in the Age of Enlightenment and Revolution* (Oxford: Oxford University Press, 2018), p. 10; Rubinelli, *Constituent Power*, pp. 12–13; Israel, *Revolutionary Ideas*, p. 346.

[37] Rubinelli, *Constituent Power*, p. 20.

representatives to exercise power was framed by American revolutionaries as the appropriate constitutional apparatus to enshrine a form of popular sovereignty within a complex, modern state.[38] Writing in *The Federalist Papers*, James Madison stressed the theoretical positives of combining aspects of democratic and oligarchic rule. 'It may well happen', he reflected, 'that the public voice, pronounced by the representatives of the people, will be more consonant to the public good than if pronounced by the people themselves, convened for the purpose'. The accountability provided by the public would also restrict 'men of factious tempers, of local prejudices, or of sinister designs' from gaining office.[39] Madison presented representative government in a republican light as an open system that encouraged rule by the wisest. A vivid contrast was made with the limited representative nature of the British system, in which only the House of Commons was made up of elected members from a very restricted franchise.[40] The representative model of government emerged as a viable (and, from a certain perspective, subversive) alternative to the long-established governing norms in the 'old world'.

The representative system was held by advocates during the nineteenth century as one of the great achievements of the American Revolution. The model was depicted by adherents as the most logical means by which to bestow a government with the consent of the sovereign people.[41] Beaumont wrote that a lasting legacy of the American Revolution was the ongoing 'discussions of a free representative government', which he detected in Ireland in 1839.[42] As this suggests, application of the idea of representative government was not confined, as Madison imagined, to republican structures. European liberals were also attracted to the ideal of redesigning parliamentarianism to enshrine a representative component within what were mostly monarchical and oligarchical states across the continent.[43] There was, of course, much resistance from more autocratic

[38] Bernard Manin, *The Principles of Representative Government* (Cambridge: Cambridge University Press, 1997), pp. 1–3.

[39] James Madison, 'The Federalist No. 10', in Alexander Hamilton, James Madison, and James Jay, *The Federalist Papers*, ed. Ian Shapiro (New Haven, CT: Yale University Press, 2009), p. 51.

[40] Eric Nelson, 'Prerogative, popular sovereignty and the American founding', in Richard Bourke and Quentin Skinner (eds.), *Popular Sovereignty in Historical Perspective* (Cambridge: Cambridge University Press, 2016), p. 210.

[41] Richard Tuck, *The Sleeping Sovereign: The Invention of Modern Democracy* (Cambridge: Cambridge University Press, 2015), p. 238.

[42] Beaumont, *Ireland*, p. 81.

[43] William Selinger, *Parliamentarism: From Burke to Weber* (Cambridge: Cambridge University Press, 2019), p. 3; Wheatley, *The Life and Death of States*, p. 14.

interests; the inability to reshape such regimes contributed to Europe's revolutionary moments across the nineteenth century.

While the United Kingdom avoided a revolution akin to France in 1830 or 1848, it was not immune from the contagion of representative government. From a Whig perspective, the debate during the British 'Age of Reform' was concerned with incorporating wider interests – wealth, industry, and intelligence – into the Crown-in-parliament. Responsible government, the Whigs proposed, should be flexible: this was one of the key lessons learnt from the fate of the *ancien régime* in France.[44] Given the importance of successive reform acts in mapping the political evolution of the United Kingdom, historiographical ideas of representative government and modern citizenship in a British context are generally (and understandably) framed by debates over the franchise.[45] But the idea of representative government was much broader than possession of the vote, encompassing as it does the role of the representatives and the structures of power they operate within.[46] As two of the most significant European studies of representative government published during the nineteenth century reveal, contemporary understandings of *representativeness* were malleable and multifaceted.

François Guizot and John Stuart Mill published works written from a classical liberal perspective that attempted to provide a synthesis of the theory and practice of representative government. Guizot was a French liberal who served as Prime Minister on the eve of the revolutions of 1848. In the early 1820s, he delivered a series of lectures that were published three decades later as *Histoire des origines du gouvernement représentatif en Europe*. In 1852, an English translation – *History of the Origin of Representative Government in Europe* – was released. Guizot positioned representative government not as rule by a majority, but as a coalition between established institutions of a state and the interests of the people. He pointed to the early reforming impulse of the revolution of 1789, which he claimed attempted to create 'the alliance of free institutions with hereditary monarchy'. The political violence and oscillations from one regime to another that followed were fatal results of a deviation from this

44 Angus Hawkins, *Victorian Political Culture: "Habits of Heart & Mind"* (Oxford: Oxford University Press, 2015), p. 83.

45 For example, see Robert Saunders, *Democracy and the Vote in British Politics, 1848–1867: The Making of the Second Reform Act* (Farnham: Ashgate, 2011); Matthew Roberts, *Popular Movements in Urban England, 1832–1914* (London: Macmillan, 2009); Norman Gash, *Politics in the Age of Peel: A Study in the Technique of Parliamentary Representation, 1830–1850* (London: Longman's, 1966; first published 1953).

46 Hanna Fenichel Pitkin, *The Concept of Representation* (Berkeley: University of California Press, 1967), p. 227.

middle path. Guizot believed that there was not a singular blueprint for representative government and that its form should alter from state to state. While 'representative governments' looked very different across the map, the common goal of such a structure of power was to harmonise 'order and liberty'.[47] Guizot framed representation as the way in which the collective constructs of 'reason, justice, and truth' within society are incorporated into the body of the state. 'In other words', he reasoned,

> it is required to discover all the elements of legitimate power that are disseminated throughout society, and to organise them into an actual power; that is to say, to collect into one focus, and to realise, public reason and public morality, and to call them to the occupation of power.[48]

Representation was, therefore, in Guizot's reading, more than the sum of 'individual wills'; it was a 'natural process by which public reason, which alone has a right to govern society, may be extracted from the bosom of society itself'.[49]

Guizot advocated a conception of representation that stressed the importance of incorporating society's collective wisdom and judgement into political deliberation. John Stuart Mill's *Considerations on Representative Government* built on this premise but conceded that democratic politics were inevitable, meaning that the institutions of power had to change to contain its excesses. In Mill's reading, the role of the representatives was as crucial as that of the represented; the former should temper the instincts of the latter.[50] Mill defined the elements of 'good government' as the possession of the 'virtue and intelligence of the people' and the 'degree in which it tends to increase the sum of good qualities in the governed, collectively and individually'.[51] Like Guizot, Mill warned of the toxic dangers of majoritarianism in a democratic system: the principle of equality in terms of the franchise could result in 'one part of the people rul[ing] over the rest'.[52] Such an arrangement threatened to crush minority interests, consigning the representatives of any groups opposed to the majority consensus to political passivity. A wide and inclusive franchise was, therefore, not

[47] François Guizot, *History of the Origin of Representative Government in Europe*, trans. Andrew R. Scoble (London: Henry G. Bohn, 1852), pp. vii–viii.
[48] Ibid., pp. 347–8. Also see Jeremy Jennings, *Revolution and the Republic: A History of Political Thought in France since the Eighteenth Century* (Oxford: Oxford University Press, 2011), p. 175.
[49] Guizot, *Representative Government in Europe*, p. 348.
[50] Vieira and Runciman, *Representation*, p. 50; Selinger, *Parliamentarism*, p. 164.
[51] John Stuart Mill, *Considerations on Representative Government* (London: Parker, Son, and Bourn, 1861), p. 30.
[52] Ibid., p. 133.

in itself the path to a truly representative polity (and indeed, an expansive voting base was no guarantee of an inclusive form of government).[53] Mill proposed a range of constitutional safeguards to curtail the impact of majoritarianism, including replacing property with education and career status as the criteria for possession of the vote. The higher the 'intelligence' of the citizen, the greater the number of votes they should receive.[54]

The handling of representative government by Guizot and Mill demonstrates the diversity of the idea. 'Representative government' did not mean one thing; rather, its appearance altered according to the philosophical perspective of the observer. Given its multifaceted applications and the rich contemporaneous engagements it provoked, representation has emerged as a vibrant research area within the history of political thought.[55] At its core, the topic of representative government concerned questions of inclusion and exclusion from political power. But just as representation meant more than merely possessing the vote, political exclusion was experienced in different ways. The ideas of Mill and Guizot found a distinctive Irish inflection, where theories of representation collided with the realities of colonial governance, religious exclusion, and the difficulty of integration into the British state.

As the case of Irish political thought during the nineteenth century demonstrates, exclusion was felt by many people who enjoyed the suffrage. With the penal laws, the abolition of the Irish parliament, and the later perception of being a minority bloc within the English-dominated House of Commons, Irish engagement with ideas of representative government was profoundly shaped by a detestable sense of political impotence. While Ireland sent representatives to parliament, this was not the same as representative government. Irish Tories, naturally sympathetic to unionist aspirations, were often disillusioned by the realities of poor government from London. Such impressions did much to fuel the crisis of government that blighted the operation of the Union, underpinning periods of political instability, agrarian violence, and sectarian enmity.

'Misgovernment' was a perennial theme within Irish political discourse, but its manifestations need a careful contextual approach. Daniel O'Connell's

[53] Judge, *Representation*, p. 30.

[54] Mill, *Considerations*, pp. 173–4. Also see Chris Barker, 'Mass and elite politics in Mill's *Considerations on Representative Government*', *History of European Ideas*, vol. 41, no. 8 (2015), pp. 1143–63.

[55] For a historiographical review article, see Max Skjönsberg, 'The history of political thought and parliamentary history in the eighteenth and nineteenth centuries', *Historical Journal*, vol. 64, no. 2 (2021), pp. 501–13.

son, John, included 'misgovernment' as an entry in his *Repeal Dictionary* of 1845: he presented the example of the ambitions of Irish MPs being permanently 'swamped by the votes of English and Scottish members' in parliament as a definition.[56] While the Irish enjoyed representation in parliament, O'Connell asserted, they did not enjoy representative government. Tory unionist enemies of O'Connell also drew on the language of 'misgovernment'. A candid moment was captured in the pages of the *Dublin University Magazine*, an Irish Tory periodical, in 1833 when it noted that Catholic discontent with the Union was not the result of Anglophobia, but 'English misgovernment'.[57] As Ireland lurched through the Famine years, the conditional nature of Tory unionism became more visible, with prominent figures such as Sir Samuel Ferguson briefly calling for the restoration of the Irish parliament.[58] Irish Tory ideas about representation and the relationship between the individual and the state fluctuated according to circumstance, a fluidity that was shared by other ideological positions on the island.

## Thinking Politically

Irish writing during the nineteenth century was saturated with politics. Malcolm Brown has written that Ireland 'provides us with the classic case of an impressive literature brought to birth by politics', implying that an explicitly political narrative can be derived from the history of fiction, poetry, and creative autobiography.[59] But while Shelley's idea of the poet as 'legislator' found expression in generations of Irish creative writing from Young Ireland onwards, formal political writing, from a historiographical perspective, appears to be hiding in plain sight.[60] Studies of Irish writing rarely examine the vast array of political tracts, pamphlets, and treatises published throughout the nineteenth century. There are several ironies at play here, not least the prominent place of political prose and speeches in nineteenth-century literary anthologies, which placed politicians such as Henry Grattan, Daniel O'Connell, and Isaac Butt on the same intellectual

56 John O'Connell, *Repeal Dictionary, Part One* (Dublin: J. Browne, 1845), p. 249.

57 *Dublin University Magazine*, November 1833, p. 592.

58 Eve Patten, *Sir Samuel Ferguson and the Culture of Nineteenth-Century Ireland* (Dublin: Four Courts Press, 2004), pp. 128–9.

59 Malcolm Brown, *The Politics of Irish Literature: From Thomas Davis to W. B. Yeats* (Seattle: University of Washington Press, 1972), p. vii.

60 Percy Bysshe Shelley, *Essays, Letters from Abroad, Translations and Fragments*, ed. Mary Shelley, 2 vols. (Philadelphia, PA: Lea and Blanchard, 1840), i, p. 62.

plane as creative writers such as Maria Edgeworth, Thomas Moore, and James Clarence Mangan.[61]

A vast number of pamphlets were published in and about Ireland during the nineteenth century, but as a source, they seem to fall between the two chief methodological stools used to study political culture: the 'high' politics of parliaments, politicians, and institutions, and the 'low' politics of popular mobilisation, provincial newspapers, and regionalised activism.[62] Pamphleteering does not quite fit into either category, but remained a ubiquitous feature of Irish life in the period covered in this book.[63] In 1910, the ever-insightful *Irish Book Lover* recorded that pamphlets during the nineteenth century 'were the political educators of the time'.[64] Stephen Small's innovative study of late eighteenth-century Irish political thought expands on this point. Small records that 'political disputants, theorists, and propagandists saw pamphlets as the chief medium of serious, public political debate'.[65] The pamphlet was expansive enough to permit detailed discussion, while its ephemeral nature encouraged rapidly written responses. Pamphleteers were often not professional writers or politicians, ensuring that certain debates over pressing political questions contained a more diverse range of voices than a narrower methodological focus on, say, parliamentary speeches or newspaper editorials. Like the pamphlet debate over the French Revolution, some of the writers examined in this book are well known, but many remain obscure. All of them, however, are valuable for recovering the political values of their age.[66] To adopt Gregory Conti's

61 Margaret Kelleher, 'The Cabinet of Irish Literature: a historical perspective on Irish anthologies', *Éire-Ireland*, vol. 38, no. 3 (2003), pp. 68–89.

62 For recent examples of 'high' approaches, see Paul Bew, *Ancestral Voices in Irish Politics: Judging Dillon and Parnell* (Oxford: Oxford University Press, 2023); Paul Bew, *Enigma: A New Life of Charles Stewart Parnell* (Dublin: Gill & Macmillan, 2011); Patrick M. Geoghegan, *King Dan: The Rise of Daniel O'Connell, 1775–1829* (Dublin: Gill & Macmillan, 2008); Patrick M. Geoghegan, *The Liberator: The Life and Death of Daniel O'Connell, 1830–1847* (Dublin: Gill & Macmillan, 2010);Hoppen, *Governing Hibernia.* For 'low' approaches, see Paul Bew, *Conflict and Conciliation in Ireland, 1890–1910* (Oxford: Oxford University Press, 1987); Fergus Campbell, *Land and Revolution: Nationalist Politics in the West of Ireland* (Oxford: Oxford University Press, 2005);Marie-Louise Legg, *Newspapers and Nationalism: The Irish Provincial Press, 1850–1892* (Dublin: Four Courts Press, 1998).

63 A very brief overview of pamphlets and their prominence at times of crisis and controversy can be found in Charles Benson and Siobhán Fitzpatrick, 'Pamphlets', in James Murphy (ed.), *The Oxford History of the Irish Book, vol. iv: The Irish Book in English, 1800–1891* (Oxford: Oxford University Press, 2011), pp. 139–43.

64 *Irish Book Lover*, no. 9 (1910), p. 119.

65 Stephen Small, *Political Thought in Ireland, 1776–1798: Republicanism, Patriotism and Radicalism* (Oxford: Oxford University Press, 2002), p. 10.

66 Kenneth Margerison, *Pamphlets & Public Opinion: The Campaign for a Union of Orders in the Early French Revolution* (West Lafayette, IN: Purdue University Press, 1998); William H. Sewell Jr.,

mantra, nineteenth-century Irish political thought was 'an ensemble rather than a star-driven production' and is no less stimulating for this.[67] Such material introduces new voices into the study of political life and disrupts narratives founded on the affairs of high-profile figures.

The neglect of pamphlets and other apparently ephemeral printed materials also provides an explanation for the relative dearth of studies of the history of political thought in nineteenth-century Ireland. While some of the best recent work on Irish political history has engaged with ideas in a more sophisticated manner than hitherto has been the case, we still lack a sustained exploration of published polemical texts akin to Bernard Bailyn's pioneering study of the American Revolution.[68] Political engagement meant more than the affairs of parliamentary elites and the tactical considerations of ideologically motivated movements: the written word provided political legitimacy for actions, ensuring that authors were as essential to the functioning of politics as politicians. Writers of political texts had certain goals in mind, and they deployed particular vocabularies, tropes, and rhetorical justifications to achieve them. As such, the long-form essay that often lay at the heart of pamphlets and other published material stood at the interface between the development of political ideas and ongoing debate.[69]

Published political writings perform an essential role in mapping the languages used by contemporaries to write (and speak) about politics.[70] These political languages – the rhetoric, tropes, and vocabulary used to define ideological positions – evolved to articulate what was deemed legitimate in the realm of politics. This does not mean that political languages were deeply theorised; on the contrary, they were often constructed on a magpie-like basis, drawing on parts of political theory and

*A Rhetoric of Bourgeois Revolution: The Abbé Sieyès and What Is the Third Estate?* (Durham, NC: Duke University Press, 1994); Gregory Claeys, *The French Revolution Debate in Britain: The Origins of Modern Politics* (Basingstoke: Palgrave Macmillan, 2007).

67 Conti, *Parliament the Mirror of the Nation*, p. 6.

68 Bernard Bailyn, *The Ideological Origins of the American Revolution* (Cambridge, MA: Harvard University Press, 2017; first published 1967). For recent work on Ireland, see, for example, John Bew, *The Glory of Being Britons: Civic Unionism in Nineteenth-Century Belfast* (Dublin: Irish Academic Press, 2009); David Dwan, *The Great Community: Culture and Nationalism in Ireland* (Dublin: Field Day, 2008); Matthew Kelly, *The Fenian Ideal and Irish Nationalism, 1882–1916* (Woodbridge: Boydell Press, 2006). For works with a more explicit history of political thought methodology, see Richard Bourke, *Peace in Ireland: The War of Ideas* (London: Pimlico, 2003) and S. J. Connolly (ed.), *Political Ideas in Eighteenth-Century Ireland* (Dublin: Four Courts Press, 2000).

69 Amanda Goodrich, *Debating England's Aristocracy in the 1790s: Pamphlets, Polemics and Political Ideas* (Woodbridge: Boydell Press, 2005), p. 13; Bailyn, *Ideological Origins*, pp. 3–4.

70 Quentin Skinner, *The Foundation of Modern Political Thought*, 2 vols. (Cambridge: Cambridge University Press, 1978), i, p. xiii.

experience that legitimised – and delegitimised – particular perspectives. The choices made in the construction of political languages offer a window into the thinking of an age. Irish engagement with ideas of representative government was at times informed by theory, international parallels, or bitter experience. In understanding how contemporaries made sense of their political predicament, we move a step closer to excavating more of the historical world.

## The Structure of the Book

The book follows six episodes showcasing Irish engagements with ideas of representative government between 1798 and 1879. The chapters are sequenced broadly chronologically but focus thematically on important ideological debates or platforms that defined the Irish political world. Published texts, especially pamphlets, form my major source base, as political works provide a guide to the constitutional languages and mentalities of the age. This means that, for the most part, figures who played influential public roles but did not write political texts are not included in the book. For example, Bishop James Warren Doyle is discussed, while Cardinal Paul Cullen is omitted, because the former was the author of political treatises and the latter was not. Cullen was one of the most important figures in nineteenth-century Ireland, but it is Doyle's status as a writer that makes him of interest in a study of political thought. While Daniel O'Connell is usually not positioned as a 'thinker', he commissioned and wrote several texts that offer insights into Irish conceptions of government. It is this side of O'Connell that is explored here. Michael Davitt is covered not for his Land League activism, but for his writings on the failure to export the British constitution to Ireland. When the speeches of politicians are examined, it is usually because they were published in pamphlet form (as was common during the debate over an incorporating union between 1798 and 1800). The speechmaker became, therefore, an author.

As the footnotes reveal, the genre of political writing in Ireland was heavily dominated by men. As elsewhere across the world during the late eighteenth and nineteenth centuries, women were often excluded from inclusive-sounding notions such as the 'People', which tended to refer to a gender-defined political nation.[71] While Irish women at times subverted

[71] Susan Moller Okin, *Women in Western Political Thought* (Princeton, NJ: Princeton University Press, 1979), p. 5.

gender norms and carved out a place within political works, their contributions were often more literary-focused, as the example of Ellen O'Leary, the Fenian poet, testifies.[72] Women also found space within the politics of the crowd within O'Connellism.[73] But this is not the same, alas, as political writing – the primary means by which to assess thought. Maria Edgeworth is a rare example within this period of an Irish female writer who finds a place in a study of political thought. The richness of *Castle Rackrent* (1800) partly rested on its ambivalent political messaging, but Edgeworth also edited the works of her father, a former member of the Irish parliament. She stands, then, as a unique presence within the sphere of Irish political thought in this period. The source base to seriously assess the political thought of Irish women only manifested itself by the late nineteenth century; it is much more difficult to find examples earlier in the century relating to ideas of government.[74] The sources I have used reflect the unfortunate imbalance of political writing in Ireland, which was (in this period) a near-exclusively male space.

The starting point for the book is the aftermath of the 1798 rebellion, as a heated debate about Ireland's future constitutional status emerged from the mist of military suppression. The battlelines drawn in the resulting pamphlet war sketched the ideological skeleton of competing ideas of unionism and anti-unionism, which would gain momentum during the nineteenth century. Chapter 1 follows the contours of this pamphlet debate that broke out in 1798 over the utility of parliamentary union between Ireland and Britain. A central component of this debate was the clash between the proposal of incorporating union and rival Irish theories of political representation. Would Ireland be better served by retaining a domestic parliament, or by sending a much-reduced number of members to the imperial parliament in London? This question hinged on the definition of 'Ireland': should representatives serve the existing political nation (the Protestant minority, who sat in the Irish parliament) or be radically expanded to formally include the entire (mostly Catholic) population? The debate also highlighted competing ideas of sovereignty, as the act of transferring the jurisdiction of one parliament to another was fiercely

72 Rose Novak, 'Ellen O'Leary: a bold Fenian poet', *Éire-Ireland*, vol. 43, nos. 3–4 (2008), pp. 58–84.

73 Mary O'Dowd, 'O'Connell and the lady patriots: women and O'Connellite politics, 1824–1845', in Allan Blackstock and Eoin Magennis (eds.), *Politics and Political Culture in Britain and Ireland, 1750–1850: Essays in Tribute to Peter Jupp* (Belfast: Ulster Historical Foundation, 2007), pp. 283–303.

74 Senia Pašeta, 'Feminist political thought and activism in revolutionary Ireland, c.1880–1918', *Transactions of the Royal Historical Society*, vol. 27 (2017), pp. 193–209.

disputed. As the anti-union pamphlets reveal, many defenders of the Irish parliament had internalised that the institution was autonomous and free; their inability to appreciate the precarious nature of Ireland as a dependent polity was a striking but little-acknowledged aspect of the debate.

While the Union became the crucible of political conflict during the nineteenth century, its commencement in 1801 did not mark a decisive break with eighteenth-century frameworks. The 1790s were distinguished by the intensity of discussion about parliamentary reform and the shape of the political nation; the imperfections of Union, if anything, perpetuated this contestation. Political thought in Ireland, as in Britain, during the first three decades of the Union was dominated by the reforming and anti-reforming impulses. But there was no fixed meaning to the term 'reform', contributing to the seeming intractability of the issue. In addition, there were profound structural differences that resulted in rather different inflections in political language in Ireland. While reforming ideas in Britain centred on franchise expansion, especially providing representation for new centres of population, the situation in Ireland was rather different. Catholic Emancipation did not arrive at the same time as the Union, which was the intention of the Prime Minister, William Pitt. Irish reforming culture after 1801 thus retained a decidedly denominational character, with the resumption of the campaign for Catholic political rights. This had wider political ramifications, most notably the perpetuation of a distinct Catholic 'interest' in Ireland. Proponents may have championed the Union as a mechanism to import 'English liberties' into Ireland, but the reality of a politically sanctioned anti-Catholicism damaged the credibility of the constitution. Chapter 2 therefore considers the evolution of Irish political thought in the opening decades of the nineteenth century, which unfolded against the backdrop of a prolonged and heated debate over Catholic Emancipation. For many supporters of Emancipation, the question was viewed through the lens of political citizenship: inclusion in the representation of the polity was a right of the enfranchised. Opponents of Emancipation often connected political liberty to Protestantism, fearing a politicised Catholicism that stood outside this rubric. This was also an age when political citizenship was marked by ideas of 'character', and Irish debates were not immune to this.

The mass mobilisation that resulted in the achievement of Catholic Emancipation in 1829 overtly deployed the language of democracy. When Daniel O'Connell launched the movement to repeal the Act of Union on the back of the successes of the Catholic Association, the democratic impulse once again moved into the political mainstream in Ireland.

Repeal implied a restoration of the Irish parliament rather than a new departure, albeit with a franchise based on the recently expanded political nation. The fusion of democracy with this 'ancient constitutionalism' is a feature of Chapter 3, as are the classical republican theories of political representation of the Young Ireland group. The Young Irelanders were part of the Repeal movement, but their conception of representative government was more republican in nature than the mainstream O'Connellite organisation. Democratic and republican conceptions of government during the 1830s and 1840s did not exist in a vacuum but constantly evolved in reaction to rapidly changing circumstances, not least the trauma of the Famine. This chapter plots the shifting ideas of legitimate government within Repeal political thought before and after the horrors of the 1840s, probing the intellectual justifications for the restoration of self-government, such as natural right, contractarianism, and historical precedent. The varied arguments of the Young Irelanders – particularly relating to the idea of the 'nation' as a political entity and the idea of a distinctive *Irish* political economy – are also given prominence in this chapter.

From the perspective of the first half of the nineteenth century, the Union was a new constitutional experiment that had to prove its worth to Ireland. Chapter 4 explores Irish Tory political thought, which was grounded in unionism, during the 1830s and 1840s. Through the dilemmas faced by this grouping, a picture emerges of constitutional and national ideas that were much more fluid than those associated with their brethren later in the century. The Act of Union abolished the Irish parliament, the institution that had provided Irish Tories with an obvious platform to exercise national leadership. The new constitution was, therefore, something of a rupture for this group, who found themselves in an age of democratic uncertainty without a clear purpose beyond support for the British connection. Many Tories fell back on ideas of a Protestant constitution shared across the United Kingdom, connecting the idea of liberty to Protestantism. Still, Irish Tories were not oblivious to the changes that had occurred since the 1820s. A striking feature of political culture in the age of O'Connell was Irish Tory attempts to modernise their platform, mirroring the mass mobilisation tactics of the Repeal movement. Yet, with the coming of the Famine, some of the most profound criticisms of the Union came from these Tories, who were appalled at the lack of a credible response from the government. This chapter teases out these tensions to construct a picture of the complexities of Irish Tory political thought, and its conflicted visions of representative government against the backdrop of human tragedy.

Chapter 5 examines the political thought of the clandestine IRB. This secret society was established in 1858, with the aim of overthrowing the British state in Ireland through revolutionary means. While nineteenth-century republicans were notoriously coy in advocating a particular constitutional design for a future independent Ireland, the 'Fenians' (the term commonly used for the IRB) proclaimed themselves the Provisional Government of the Irish Republic. Fenianism was, therefore, a subversive manifestation of Irish popular sovereignty, a bold assault on the established parliamentary traditions of representation and deliberation. There were strong undercurrents of Rousseauian thought within the IRB, particularly its articulation of an Irish general will and its claim to the allegiance of the people of Ireland. Fenian political thought thus provided a radical alternative to the more mainstream ideological platforms that were rooted in a constitutional idiom informed by British and Irish precedent.[75]

Chapter 6 examines the origins of Home Rule. As a political slogan in the late nineteenth and twentieth centuries, 'Home Rule' was used by contemporaries to signify various schemes of self-government, from devolution to virtual independence. This chapter examines the genesis and evolution of the Home Rule idea in the context of the late 1860s and 1870s. The Home Rule label was first applied to a federal plan that aimed to perfect the Union by creating a United Kingdom-wide network of national parliaments to administer 'local' affairs. A central rationale of this was to create a stronger sense of representative government within the peripheries of the whole kingdom; but the scheme also explicitly expressed a desire to transform Westminster into a genuine 'imperial parliament' to administer the affairs of the Empire. The federalist Home Rule framework was, therefore, *unionist* in intention; but this detail became obscured under the weight of the more separatist-inclined rhetorical trappings that were added to the notion of Irish self-government. This chapter charts the fortunes of the unionist case for self-government, with particular attention paid to the languages used by pro-Home Rule thinkers to rationalise radical changes to the constitution, and the confusion it caused within wider Irish and British political life. Crucial to this chapter is Isaac Butt's pioneering *Irish Federalism* (1870), which, despite its name, presented the case for a United Kingdom federation. It quickly became apparent, however, that many advocates of Home Rule in Ireland were not federalists,

[75] For the constitutional idiom, see James Epstein, 'The constitutional idiom: radical reasoning, rhetoric and action in early nineteenth-century England', *Journal of Social History*, vol. 23, no. 3 (1990), pp. 553–74.

and conceived of self-government from a more radical, anti-unionist political mindset.

The book ends with the rise of Charles Stewart Parnell to the leadership of the Irish Parliamentary Party. With the collapse of federalist Home Rule and the fusing together of radical agrarianism and a vision of self-government that emphasised Irish national rights, political culture in Ireland became more rigid and polarised, resulting in less fluidity within the collective political imagination of the island. In response to the appearance of a more muscular and less compromising nationalist bloc in Westminster, unionism became increasingly unconditional and inflexible. The modern binary framework of Irish politics was established during the 1880s, ensuring that, as the subsequent histories were written, the nuances of the various Irish ideological perspectives in the preceding decades became increasingly obscured. Articulations of political exclusion, and the constitutional proposals that this grievance generated, became subsumed into an unchanging and static notion of *the* 'Irish Question'.

If the voices of the pre-1880s generations of political writers in Ireland are heard, if their rhetorical points are understood, and if their contexts are appreciated, it becomes clear that the Irish political imagination was more mercurial than hitherto recognised. The most important aspect of the debate about union during the late 1790s hinged on conceptions of government, not national identity. There was scope to imagine a successful Irish polity within and without the Union. The ideal of Catholic Emancipation was often articulated in a universal language of political inclusion and liberty, rather than a particular Irish discourse. The Repealers were not Parnellite Home Rulers, the Tories of the era of the Famine were not the unionist diehards of 1912, and the mid Victorian IRB were not the IRA of the twentieth century. We should listen with empathy to the various political languages articulated in Ireland to grasp how past generations grappled with the issues that shaped their world. In the end, Ireland's turbulent nineteenth century was not merely a battle over identity or national rights, but a reckoning with the most fundamental questions of political life: who are the people; who speaks for the people; and how are the people represented in a multinational state?

CHAPTER 1

# *Between Two Parliaments*

## *Visions of Representation in the Union Debates*

> An Union presupposes that when it is completed, the contracting states shall be bound together by the same Constitution, Laws, and Government; and by an identity of interests, and equality of privileges.[1]
>
> Edward Cooke (1798)

> Enter into no treaty of Union with Englishmen. They may hold out to you very fair and flattering promises, but trust them not.[2]
>
> 'Hibernicus' (1799)

To preserve the status quo in Ireland in the aftermath of the 1798 rebellion, Lord Clare, the Irish Lord Chancellor, concluded that the parliament in which he sat in Dublin must be destroyed. Clare was one of the most prominent advocates of a parliamentary union between Ireland and Britain during the 1790s.[3] In an age of French-inspired democratic ideas and the terrifying spectre of revolution spearheaded by the United Irish movement that had recently revealed itself in Ireland, Clare opined that the Irish Protestant 'Ascendancy', the bastion of order and privilege, could only survive as part of a greater British polity. Such a conclusion was reached partly through fear of the Catholic majority in Ireland, enthused by a new political vocabulary of popular sovereignty and civic equality. Advocacy of a parliamentary union with Britain was also an explicit criticism of the nature of Irish governance during the turbulent decades since the 1780s.

Inspired by the American Revolution, the Irish parliament, the representatives of which were restricted only to the Anglican minority, had

[1] [Edward Cooke], *Arguments For and Against an Union, Between Great Britain and Ireland, Considered*, 2nd ed. (Dublin: J. Milliken, 1799), p. 6.

[2] 'Hibernicus', *English Union is Ireland's Ruin! Or an Address to the Irish Nation* (Dublin: James Moore, 1799), p. 25.

[3] For an overview of his career, see Ann C. Kavanaugh, *John Fitzgibbon, Earl of Clare: Protestant Reaction and English Authority in Late-Eighteenth-Century Ireland* (Dublin: Irish Academic Press, 1997).

asserted its independence in legislative matters in 1782. More than a decade on, Clare sneered at the fallacy of an independent administration that had failed to pacify Irish discontent. The rebellion of 1798 was, he reasoned, as much a product of an ineffective parliament suffering from delusions of grandeur as it was a doctrinaire expression of Irish separatism or republicanism. As Ireland peered into the nineteenth century in the aftermath of the violence of 1798, Clare believed that the country had to choose between two competing conceptions of union: the protection of property, rule by the wise, and the upholding of the Protestant interest through the parliamentary fusion of Dublin and London; or a union of the masses offered by the Society of United Irishmen, which threatened to tear down the traditional structures that governed society. The democratic radicalism of the United Irish movement desired, in Clare's words, 'the grand project of Parliamentary Reform, or in other words, of Anarchy and Democracy'.[4] While the rebellion was suppressed by the state in 1798, Clare was concerned that the revolutionary genie would not go back into the bottle, casting a dark shadow over the Protestant political nation. To maintain its privileges, the shape of representative government had to be reimagined.

Clare's intervention came in the context of a sustained debate over parliamentary union between Ireland and Britain in the aftermath of the rebellion of 1798. Visions of union between the two countries had been articulated periodically since the seventeenth century and appeared to some observers as the logical destination of the journey that had begun with English unions with the Welsh and Scots.[5] Indeed, from a historical perspective, the idea of British-Irish union appears the logical culmination of the process that commenced with formal Anglo-Welsh integration in 1541, via the union between England and Scotland in 1707.[6] But in Ireland, any sense of inevitability about a union with Britain was fiercely contested.[7] At stake were two rival visions of the political status of Ireland.

[4] John Fitzgibbon, *The Speech of the Right Hon. John, Earl of Clare, Lord High Chancellor of Ireland, in the House of Lords of Ireland, on a Motion made by the Earl of Moira, Monday 19 February 1798*, 4th ed. (Dublin: J. Milliken, 1798), pp. 17–19.

[5] James Kelly, 'The origins of the Act of Union: an examination of unionist opinion in Britain and Ireland, 1650–1800', *Irish Historical Studies*, vol. 25, no. 99 (1987), p. 237. James Kelly, 'The Act of Union: its origins and background', in Dáire Keogh and Kevin Whelan (eds.), *Acts of Union: The Causes, Contexts and the Consequences of the Act of Union* (Dublin: Four Courts Press, 2001), p. 49; Douglas Kanter, *The Making of British Unionism, 1740–1848: Politics, Government and the Anglo-Irish Constitutional Relationship* (Dublin: Four Courts Press, 2009), p. 72.

[6] Kelly, 'The Act of Union: its origins and background', p. 49.

[7] John Bew, *The Glory of Being Britons: Civic Unionism in Nineteenth-Century Belfast* (Dublin: Irish Academic Press, 2008), p. 56.

Unionists promised access to imperial power and commercial prosperity through parliamentary fusion; anti-unionists warned of a surrender to colonial subjugation, invoking the spectre of a sovereign parliament committing political 'suicide'. These competing claims – rooted in Enlightenment theories of sovereignty, practical anxieties about Catholic inclusion, and bitter experience with British economic dominance – revealed Ireland not as a passive recipient of imperial policy, but as a battleground for defining representative government in the age of revolution.

In promoting a union, Lord Clare denigrated the Irish parliament as the seat of a provincial and inferior government, all too eager to bare its teeth in foolhardy assertions of independence from Britain to prove its 'patriotic' credentials. Despite the narrow definition of the Irish political nation as a Protestant one, such was the abysmal record of the Irish parliament that Clare 'should feel most happy to commit my country to the sober discretion of the British parliament, even though we had not a single representative in it'.[8] In Clare's reading, then, British political despotism was preferable to Irish representative vanity. Irish parliamentarians, the gentry, and supporters of the Protestant Ascendancy in Ireland, figures who were brilliantly satirised by Maria Edgeworth in *Castle Rackrent*, thus faced an existential crisis as the eighteenth century drew to a close. Union may have meant many things, but the phrase above all implied the destruction of *their* parliament.

## The Edgeworthian Connection: Unionism as Modernity?

When Maria Edgeworth published *Castle Rackrent* in January 1800, the constitutional future of Ireland was still clouded by uncertainty. From the final months of 1798 to the summer of 1800, when the Acts of Union were passed through the Dublin and London parliaments, the arguments for and against abolishing the Irish parliament and transplanting a portion of its representatives to London preoccupied political society in Ireland, triggering lengthy parliamentary discussions and a lively pamphlet war. While Edgeworth's novel preceded the Union, she astutely recognised that change was coming. Her 'Hibernian tale' was a satirised depiction of her own world, the Anglo-Irish landed gentry, albeit through the prism of one family – the slovenly Rackrents – and with a careful temporal positioning through the proclamation that the events of the novel occurred 'before the year 1782'. At the heart of the novel is the vulgarness of Irish life, chiefly

[8] Fitzgibbon, *Speech ... on Monday 10 February 1800*, p. 58.

through the rank abuses of the Protestant aristocracy and the illiteracy of the Catholic peasantry. Completed in the context of a wider political discussion concerning the future of Irish government, the story's central motif was the need to recalibrate the 'national' in Ireland to politically incorporate – and improve the condition of – the Catholic majority. This made *Castle Rackrent* an important intellectual intervention at a sensitive time. It positioned union as an enlightenment project, founded on the principles of moral and social improvement, the most logical vehicle to usher in the age of rationality to Ireland.[9] But 'union' implies a two-way direction of travel, and Edgeworth humorously cast doubt on *which* national character, Irish or British, would be most transformed through exposure to the other: 'Did the Warwickshire militia [who were stationed in Ireland during the 1790s] . . . teach the Irish to drink beer, or did they learn from the Irish to drink whiskey?'[10] Will Irish representatives bring enlightenment *to* Ireland, or poison the well of the imperial machine?

Several months after the publication of *Castle Rackrent*, Maria's father, Richard Lovell Edgeworth, was tormented by doubt about the political future of Ireland. A member of the Irish parliament only since 1798, Richard Edgeworth struck an unusual figure within Dublin political society. While he was the head of a landed estate in County Longford, Edgeworth was a progressive landlord, staunchly opposed to the absenteeism that blighted Irish rural life, and interested in the latest agricultural techniques. He was attracted to the radical educational thinking of Jean-Jacques Rousseau, which emphasised the importance of instilling the unselfish values of citizenship into young children, in order to prepare them for political – and, more to the point, republican – society.[11] He published several books on aspects of education, including a primer on how the young can enjoy poetry.[12] Edgeworth was half-English: his early life was spent in England, but the family moved to Ireland in 1782. Maria was constantly by her father's side as he travelled throughout his estate, experiencing the manners and customs of the Irish peasantry at first hand. The Edgeworths personified a latent unionism that straddled the two islands, which desired a greater role for the positive – and, more precisely, rational – influence of Britain in Irish cultural and intellectual

[9] Michael Brown, *The Irish Enlightenment* (Cambridge, MA: Harvard University Press, 2016), p. 466.

[10] Maria Edgeworth, *Castle Rackrent*, ed. George Watson (Oxford: Oxford University Press, 2008; first published 1800), p. 97.

[11] Richard Lovell Edgeworth, *Memoirs of Richard Lovell Edgeworth, Esq.: Begun by Himself and Concluded by his Daughter, Maria Edgeworth*, 2 vols. (London: R. Hunter, 1820), i, p. 177.

[12] Richard Lovell Edgeworth, *Poetry Explained for Young People*, new ed. (London: R. Hunter, 1821).

life. But the unionism of Richard Edgeworth was complex. 'I am a unionist', he confided to a friend after a particularly gruelling session in the Irish parliament in March 1800, 'but I vote and speak against the union now proposed to us'.[13]

The dilemma faced by Richard Edgeworth illuminates the ambiguous nature of the union debate and, indeed, the measure itself. Edgeworth may have been a self-professed unionist, but tensions inherent within nascent unionism came to the surface in his contributions to the debate in the Irish parliament. Edgeworth reflected that 'We are fond of imitating the British Constitution', but 'ours is but an imperfect imitation of it'. With a union, however, there is no need to rely on an imitation: 'we may have the original'. Given the inability of the Irish parliament to ameliorate itself – most glaringly in its continuing hostility to Catholic representation and wider franchise reform – Edgeworth reasoned that union might prove the only way to 'improve our present Constitution'.[14] Union offered, in other words, a path to parliamentary reform. Here, Edgeworth ironically echoed Clare and Lord Castlereagh, the latter the most fervent Irish champion of union, both of whom conceptualised the disenfranchising of the Irish boroughs in a newly merged parliament as a definite – and final – act of reform. Castlereagh couched the union as a progressive measure that offered constitutional change while securing political safety, ensuring such a measure was a reasoned reply to the question of parliamentary reform.[15]

Edgeworth agreed with the sentiment of change, but not Castlereagh's decidedly modest interpretation of reform. Edgeworth stressed the potential transformative impact of union on the public face of Irish politics, hypothesising that a reduction in the number of Irish members of parliament would 'weaken the force of aristocratic influence in elections', as fewer seats implied a more determined challenge from the 'popular power'.[16] He placed parliamentary representation at the heart of his contribution to the union debate. While he spoke the language of reform

[13] Richard Lovell Edgeworth to Dr Robert Darwin, 31 March 1800, in Edgeworth, *Memoirs of Richard Lovell Edgeworth*, ii, p. 252.

[14] Richard Lovell Edgeworth, *The Substance of Three Speeches, Delivered in the House of Commons of Ireland, February 4, March 6, and March 21, 1800, Upon the Subject of an Union with Great Britain* (London: R. Johnson, 1800), p. 5.

[15] Lord Castlereagh, *The Speech of the Right Hon. Lord Viscount Castlereagh, Upon Delivering to the House of Commons of Ireland, His Excellency the Lord Lieutenant's Message on the Subject of an Incorporating Union with Great Britain, with the Resolutions Containing the Terms on which it is Proposed to Carry that measure into Effect, 5 February 1800* (Dublin: J. Milliken, 1800), pp. 33–4. See John Bew, *Castlereagh: Enlightenment, War and Tyranny* (London: Quercus, 2011), p. 143.

[16] Edgeworth, *Substance of Three Speeches*, p. 8.

in challenging aristocracy and desiring commercial and trading interests inside parliament, his argument was also conditioned by the peculiar Irish setting. The 'true cause' that called for 'strong measures to restore us to security' was religious division, 'the real cause of all our evils'.[17] Deep-rooted sectarianism and the spectre of rebellion was the dual inheritance of Irish statesmen in Edgeworth's age, and he believed the political classes lacked the acumen and imagination to confront the problem, most obviously in the collective inability to bury the last of the penal laws by permitting Catholics into parliament. Instead, 'the force of England' was needed as a restrainer of the acrimony that permeated Irish political life. The *removal* of self-government would lessen the burdens on the Irish political classes, who stubbornly remained unrepresentative of majority opinion, while shielding them from the rancour that a religiously defined oligarchy inevitably produced. If nothing else, union held out the hand for 'the revival of better passions' in Ireland by the potential dilution of Irish grievances within a larger polity. Given the history of Irish domestic quarrels, Edgeworth believed that parliamentary independence – the concept stressed by anti-union champions of the 1782 constitution, which retracted the British right to enact laws over Ireland – was an intoxicating illusion. 'So long as the property of this country requires protection from Great Britain, we cannot be independent', he asserted. The failure to incorporate the various religious groupings into mainstream political life in Ireland ensured that the only progressive vision of the future centred on a legislative tie to the greater power across the Irish Sea.[18]

In highlighting the Irish parliament's refusal to reform itself, especially the continuing lack of Catholic representation, Edgeworth provided a coherent rationale for union. He was deeply sympathetic to the cause of unionism and offered a progressive case for union as a measure of parliamentary reform. Despite this, Edgeworth voted against the measure when it was introduced in the House of Commons in Dublin. Maria recalled that when her father rose to address the Irish parliament on the subject of union in 1800, he was uncertain as to the correct course of action, and only voted against the measure because of the scale of hostile speeches made by 'the men of sense and property in the nation'.[19] But this reading downplayed the extent of Edgeworth's criticism of the proposal, if not the principle, of union. He believed that equality should underpin any future constitutional connection between the two ancient kingdoms, but realised

[17] Ibid., p. 13. [18] Ibid., pp. 13–15.
[19] Edgeworth, *Memoirs of Richard Lovell Edgeworth*, ii, p. 244.

that the proposals for legislative union in 1800, as presented to the Irish parliament, were not sufficiently anchored in the ideal of partnership. '[E]verything which can be an object of Legislative exertion', he proclaimed, 'must be upon a perfect footing of equality'.[20] As it was, Edgeworth read the proposals as the burdening of Ireland with the rapidly accruing British war debt in a disproportionate and unfair manner. This was not the basis for equality between the two kingdoms: Edgeworth believed that the debt question would be the harbinger of a broader pattern of British dominance over Ireland, disguised behind the discourse of partnership.

This threat was amplified by the hostility to combining union with parliamentary reform. While Edgeworth pointed to Irishmen who flourished in Britain, such as Edmund Burke, Isaac Barré, and Richard Brinsley Sheridan, he questioned the general effectiveness of Ireland's representatives in London under the existing franchise. He suggested that William Pitt should combine union with reform by 'lopping off 100 English borough Members', thus producing Edgeworth's representative ideal, a 'considerable majority of county and city Members'. Union would have a restorative impact if accompanied with reform; this was the method, as Edgeworth colourfully put it, to 'pour better blood into the veins of the British Constitution, while an equal quantity of what was corrupted, was drawn out by another channel'.[21] For Edgeworth, union in itself was not the answer to the broader question of representative government. There was little point in sending Irish members to an unreformed imperial parliament that excluded mercantile and modern commercial interests: reform was needed alongside union to create a modern state deserving of both countries within it. He concluded sourly that the proposed measure fell far short of this ideal: 'We are to have alterations without improvements, and change without reform'.[22]

Just as Maria Edgeworth's *Castle Rackrent* was an appeal to liberate Ireland from its past,[23] so too did Richard Edgeworth's conceptualisation of union rest on a decidedly modernist ideal, stripped of historical sentiment. He drew on arguments rooted in the principles of national sovereignty, parliamentary reform, and political economy. At the heart of his contribution was a deep-seated concern for how Irish interests would be represented in a unified parliament. In an unreformed Westminster that maintained the existing number of British members but reduced the incoming Irish members to around 100, Edgeworth judged that Ireland

[20] Edgeworth, *Substance of Three Speeches*, pp. 18–19. [21] Ibid., pp. 6, 8. [22] Ibid., pp. 39–40.
[23] Brown, *Irish Enlightenment*, p. 467.

would not enjoy the benefits of representative government. Edgeworth believed that the British and Irish 'Constitutions are founded upon representation', but this principle was warped by the aristocratic stranglehold over power.[24] Edgeworth was prepared to support union only if such a measure won '*the consent of the nation*', but this was structurally impossible to secure in a political system that retained a narrow franchise.[25] Without explicit consent, union would be nothing less than an act of submission, which threatened to poison the well of British-Irish relations. Given the widespread animosity towards union from the propertied class and wider public opinion, Ireland's representatives, in Edgeworth's reading, had no choice but to reject it. Failure to oppose union, he reasoned, was a derogation of political duty.

To Edgeworth's chagrin, however, the incorporating union passed through the Irish parliament. The promise of improving security through strengthening the British-Irish connection in the face of a menacing international and domestic Jacobinism was a powerful incentive to ditch the Dublin legislature.[26] The 'compensation' to disenfranchised borough representatives that Castlereagh mentioned turned out to be a euphemism for bribes and rewards to support the union.[27] Parliamentary acts to clear the way for union were passed simultaneously in London and Dublin during the summer of 1800. The anti-unionists were horrified: rather than watch the indignity at first hand, Richard Edgeworth joined a walkout of most of the opposition from the House, never to return to College Green.[28] The eight articles of the Act of Union between Great Britain and Ireland came into effect on 1 January 1801. On that day, the two kingdoms of Britain and Ireland were united under one common legislature. Dublin lost its parliament, and 100 Irish members, several of whom had been staunchly in the anti-union camp, took up their seats in the newly unified parliament in London.

## Sabines and Romans

The passing of the Union is typically depicted as a high political tale, centring on the drama in the two parliaments and on key figures driving

[24] Edgeworth, *Substance of Three Speeches*, p. 21. [25] Ibid., pp. 32, 48. Emphasis in original.

[26] James Kelly, 'The failure of opposition', in Michael Brown, Patrick M. Geoghegan, and James Kelly (eds.), *The Irish Act of Union: Bicentennial Essays* (Dublin: Irish Academic Press, 2003), p. 128.

[27] S. J. Connolly, *Divided Kingdom: Ireland 1630–1800* (Oxford: Oxford University Press, 2008), p. 492.

[28] Patrick M. *Geoghegan, The Irish Act of Union: A Study in High Politics, 1798–1801* (Dublin: Gill & Macmillan, 1999), p. 116.

the project, such as the Prime Minister, William Pitt; the Lord Lieutenant for Ireland, Lord Cornwallis; and the Chief Secretary, Lord Castlereagh.[29] As a result, the details of how the Union became law are well known, but rather less understood are the competing constitutional visions of representative government that were debated at the time.[30] Broadly speaking, advocates of union made the case that Irish representatives would be empowered in London through access to imperial networks, shifting Ireland from the periphery to the centre of the empire. Anti-unionists, by contrast, stressed that a parliament in Dublin provided local accountability (often ignoring the exclusively Anglican nature of the parliament), and that Irish MPs in Westminster would have little influence over policy matters. This was, therefore, primarily an exchange concerning the nature of representative government.

The debate spilled out of parliament from the second half of 1798, with a dramatic upsurge in pamphlet material. Some 300 pamphlets were published between 1798 and 1800 on the question of union, the majority of which sided with anti-unionism.[31] The prospect of union carried existential hopes and fears for the future of Ireland, and thus engaged many people formally outside of the political elite. The pamphlet wars also suggest the contemporary importance placed on mobilising public opinion: unionism and anti-unionism needed legitimacy in the form of ideas and popular support.[32] While the financial and patronage corruption that underpinned the passage of the Union is well known, the importance of the vast sums set aside by the British government for propaganda work is underappreciated: that there was a secret service fund to hire writers, publish a plethora of pro-union materials, and potentially arrange for the wholesale purchase of opposition pamphlets to destroy them, tells its own story about the centrality of public opinion and debate.[33]

[29] Geoghegan, *Irish Act of Union*; and G. G. Bolton, *The Passing of the Irish Act of Union: A Study in Parliamentary Politics* (Oxford: Oxford University Press, 1966). A brilliant recent revision of the high political drama is Bew, *Castlereagh*.

[30] Kanter, *Making of British Unionism*, p. 98.

[31] W. J. McCormack, *The Pamphlet Debate on the Union between Great Britain and Ireland, 1797–1800* (Dublin: Irish Academic Press, 1996), p. 10; James Kelly, 'Popular politics in Ireland and the Act of Union', *Transactions of the Royal Historical Society*, vol. 10 (2000), p. 266.

[32] Jim Smyth, 'The Act of Union and "public opinion"', in Smyth (ed.), *Revolution, Counter-Revolution and Union: Ireland in the 1790s* (Cambridge: Cambridge University Press, 2000), p. 153; James Stafford, *The Case of Ireland: Commerce, Empire and the European Order, 1750–1848* (Cambridge: Cambridge University Press, 2022), pp. 141–2.

[33] Patrick M. Geoghegan, '"An act of power & corruption"? The Union debate', in John Gibney (ed.), *The United Irishmen, Rebellion and the Act of Union, 1791–1803* (Barnsley: Pen & Sword Books, 2018), p. 125.

Edward Cooke's innocuous sounding pamphlet, *Arguments For and Against An Union* appeared in the winter of 1798, kickstarting the war of ideas. Cooke was a talented English undersecretary at the Civil Department in the Irish administration.[34] Once William Pitt's preference for union became publicly known after the outbreak of rebellion in the early summer of 1798, Cooke identified that hostility to the idea in Ireland, not least from its ruling class, was a potential barrier to success.[35] He believed that union would only become a legislative reality if it were 'written up, spoken up, intrigued up, drunk up, sung-up and bribed up'.[36] Towards the end of 1798, he turned to the 'write up' himself by publishing anonymously his pamphlet. Despite its seemingly impartial title, *Arguments* presented a sustained case in favour of unifying the parliaments of Ireland and Great Britain. The pamphlet offered a coherent pro-union case, chiming with, and solidifying, much of Pitt's legislative thinking. Cooke anticipated many aspects of the union debate as it unfolded throughout 1799 and 1800, such as the competency of the Irish parliament to consent to incorporation with London and the question of Catholic inclusion into the political nation. But while *Arguments* sketched out a vision for union, its publication unintentionally gave anti-union writers a direct target, and they did not hesitate in joining the literary firing line in what became the most intense pamphlet war in Ireland since the early years of the French Revolution.

Cooke's underlying message was that union between Ireland and Great Britain promised a partnership of equals, bound by the same constitution, laws and government. Union was not subjection; the two countries would be tied together in a state of healthy interdependence. Given the obvious power imbalance in existing British-Irish relations, Cooke aimed to whet the appetites of his Irish readers, who had, in his reading, much to gain from a union with the stronger country:

> Equal liberty. Equal privilege with the people of Great Britain, guaranteed by a Parliament composed from the Representatives of both kingdoms, and upheld by the power of all the subjects of the two islands; in short, the consolidation of Great Britain and Ireland in one kingdom, with one Constitution, one King, one Law, one Religion, can never be the ruin of Ireland. It widens the foundation of our liberties.[37]

[34] Bew, *Castlereagh*, p. 110.
[35] Mansergh, 'The Union and the importance of public opinion', in Keogh and Whelan (eds.), *Acts of Union*, p. 127.
[36] Kelly, 'Popular politics', pp. 264–5.
[37] [Cooke], *Arguments*, p. 54.

It was a calculated appeal to Irish political pride. The Patriot campaign for Irish parliamentary independence, led by Henry Grattan and Henry Flood in the 1770s and 1780s, was based on the belief that Ireland should have the same (post-1688) constitution as Britain. In essence, this meant that just as the British parliament was subject to no higher legislative authority, the same principle should apply to the representatives of the Irish political nation.[38]

This idea was immensely influential within Irish political thought. For Patriots such as Grattan, Whigs such as Burke and, indeed, later advocates of Irish self-government, such as Daniel O'Connell and John Redmond, the British constitution was, in the words of the astute commentator, Stephen Gwynn, 'a kind of Holy Writ, marking the highest point of political achievement'.[39] Cooke fully understood this impulse: his case for union was constructed on an appeal to the very sentiment that achieved the constitution of 1782. But while Ireland may have secured an independent legislature, Cooke queried the calibre of the representatives that sat in it, suggesting that they were directed by the 'Cabals of British Party'. Given that the case for Irish legislative independence was founded on mirroring the British constitution, Cook asked the obvious question: 'might it not be a measure of wisdom to incorporate the Parliaments together, and that Ireland should accept the same Guarantee for its Liberty and Prosperity, as satisfies the people of England?'[40]

Certainly, this rationale had wider purchase. William Cusack Smith, an Irish lawyer and MP, in a public letter to Henry Grattan, stressed that union with Great Britain represented the ultimate realisation of the constitution of 1782, not its destruction. Irish representatives would be formally incorporated into the very British constitutional model that the Patriots advocated, completing the logic of 1782.[41] Smith, *pace* Grattan, believed that union did not imply the 'surrender' of political rights, as 'a legislative incorporation would leave the principles of the Irish Constitution unimpaired'.[42] He minimised the sense of disruption that union implied by suggesting that 'Union does not take away our Parliament: it merely

38 Stephen Small, *Political Thought in Ireland, 1776–1798: Republicanism, Patriotism and Radicalism* (Oxford: Oxford University Press, 2002), p. 46.

39 Stephen Gwynn, *Henry Grattan and His Times* (Dublin: Browne and Nolan Ltd., 1939), p. 106.

40 [Cooke], *Arguments*, p. 14.

41 William Cusack Smith, *Letter to Henry Grattan, Esq., MP* (Dublin: Marchbank, 1800), p. 23.

42 William Cusack Smith, *The Substance of Mr William Smith's Speech on the Subject of a Legislative Union Between this Country and Great Britain, Delivered in the House of Commons, Thursday, January 24th, 1799, and now Reduced to the Form of an Address to the People of Ireland*, 2nd ed. (Dublin: Marchbank, 1799), p. 18.

changes the residence of that body'.[43] Maurice Fitzgerald, the Knight of Kerry, concurred, telling the Irish House of Commons in 1799 that as Irish political rights were affirmed by 'the law of England', union copper-fastened the existing constitutional condition.[44] The notion that union 'preserved' Irish sovereignty by transferring it to a larger polity became an important feature within a number of unionist pamphlets.[45]

While Cooke's *Arguments* rejuvenated unionism within Irish political debate, it served as the rallying call for the articulation of the anti-union position. For Charles Kendal Bushe, the distinguished lawyer and outspoken critic of union, Cooke's pamphlet was 'the most audacious, profligate, and libellous production', a scandalous publication designed to 'insult the feelings of a nation'.[46] Richard Jebb, another lawyer and former friend of Theobald Wolfe Tone, attacked Cooke's conceptualisation of union as 'a wound in our national pride', which threatened to transform 'a powerful, growing kingdom to a small and petty member of the Empire'.[47] The language adopted by Bushe and Jebb gave the impression that the anti-unionist argument was founded simply on emotion.[48] Such a reading, however, overlooks the political and theoretical content of their contributions. While there was certainly not a unity of purpose within the anti-unionist ranks (a point that seriously weakened the cause),[49] there was a broad consensus that self-government was the greatest symbol of liberty that a political nation can possess. While some opponents of Cooke and the unionist programme criticised the unrepresentative nature of the Irish parliament, not least its exclusion of Catholics, the *right* of that parliament to continue to legislate was fiercely upheld.[50]

This line of thought united the various wings of Irish anti-unionism. While there were multiple arguments made against a legislative union,

43 William Cusack Smith, *Review of a Publication, Entitled,* The Speech of the Right Honourable John Foster, Speaker of the House of Commons of Ireland; *in a Letter, Addressed to Him by William Smith, Esq.*, 2nd ed. (Dublin: Marchbank, 1799), p. 36.

44 *A Report of the Debate in the House of Commons of Ireland, on Tuesday and Wednesday the 22nd and 23rd of January, 1799, on the Subject of an Union* (Dublin: James Moore, 1799), p. 17.

45 For example, 'A Barrister', *Letters on the Subject of Union, Addressed to Messrs Saurin and Jebb, in which Mr Jebb's* "Reply" *is Considered* (Dublin: J. Milliken, 1799), p. 7; Anon., *A Loyal Subject's Thoughts on an Union between Great Britain and Ireland* (Dublin: J. Milliken, 1799), p. 28.

46 [Charles Kendal Bushe], *The Union: Cease Your Funning, or the Rebel Detected*, 4th ed. (Dublin: James Moore, 1798), p. 44.

47 Richard Jebb, *A Reply to a Pamphlet, Entitled,* Arguments For and Against a Union (Dublin: William Jones, 1798), p. 20.

48 McDowell, *Irish Public Opinion,* 1750–1800 (London: Faber and Faber, 1944), pp. 210–11.

49 Kelly, 'The failure of opposition', p. 128.

50 Joshua Spencer, *Thoughts on an Union* (Dublin: William Jones, 1798), p. 21.

cutting across issues such as security, political economy and local responsibility, a common denominator was the centrality of the College Green within the political psyche of the anti-unionists. From this perspective, Ireland possessed and cherished separate constitutional rights from Britain: the idea that the Irish would surrender its parliament was insulting.[51]

Cooke attempted to reassure readers that Irish incorporation into the British state would not imperil the political status of Ireland. He drew a parallel with ancient Rome's foundation myth concerning the Sabines and Romans, which he believed provided a historical case study of the fusing of two peoples (and states). He suggested that the Sabines 'united' with the Romans to enhance 'their liberty, their happiness, and their power'.[52] The Romans-Sabine trope had a longer history, going back to Grotius's *On the Law of War and Peace* (1625). Daniel Defoe deployed the analogy during the English-Scottish union debate, suggesting that integration into the Roman state inferred equal rights to the incorporated peoples.[53] Given the pedigree of the comparison, Cooke seemed to be on firm ground; but it quickly provoked a hostile response. Where Cooke (like Defoe) saw the extension of rights, opponents saw the pretext for exploitation and domination. For anti-unionists such as Isaac Burke Bethal, the historical precedent for union lifted the veil on the implicit imperialism underpinning British intentions. Critics seized on the more brutal aspects of the analogy, chiefly the rape of the Sabine women by the Romans. A popular ballad from 1798 mocked Cooke's classical reference:

> The Clerk [Cooke] he informs us the Romans and Sabines,
> United, some thousands centuries ago?
> But the latter rememb'ring the flames of their cabins,
> And rapes of their daughters, would fain have said no.[54]

It was indeed a misguided analogy, as it generated more heat than light. Pemberton Rudd asserted chillingly that 'Roman greatness' was constructed on the eradication of the 'very name of Sabine'. Nevertheless, 'if the Author *will* have Sabine history', Rudd carped, 'why did he forget to hint at the fate of Sabine Tatius?'[55] Titus Tatius was the king of the

[51] 'Hibernicus', *English Union is Ireland's Ruin!*, p. 6. [52] [Cooke], *Arguments*, p. 7.

[53] Laurence Dickey, 'Power, commerce and natural law in Daniel Defoe's political writings, 1698–1707', in John Robertson (ed.), *A Union for Empire: Political Thought and the Union of 1707* (Cambridge: Cambridge University Press, 1995), pp. 88–9.

[54] *A New Song: Billy Pitt & The Union* (Dublin, 1798), Broadside Ballads Online, Bodleian Library, Oxford, http://ballads.bodleian.ox.ac.uk/search/roud/V8767 [last accessed 3 November 2023].

[55] Pemberton Rudd, *An Answer to the Pamphlet Entitled* Arguments For and Against an Union, *in a Letter Addressed to Edward Cooke* (Dublin: J. Milliken, 1799), pp. 9–10. Emphasis in original.

Sabines; he was co-opted as joint ruler of the expanded Roman kingdom following the Sabine war but was murdered a few years later. After his death, the Roman king, Romulus, assumed sole authority once again. Would-be 'Sabines' in Ireland, warned Rudd, should bear in mind the denouement of Cooke's ancient precedent.

A principal component of the anti-unionist platform was the belief that incorporating union would result in Irish servitude, not equality with the more powerful partner. This was the essence of the contributions made by writers as diverse as the United Irish radical William Drennan, the Patriot Henry Grattan, and the loyalist William Saurin.[56] The speaker of the Irish parliament, John Foster, professed to admiring Britain and British values, but was 'not ready to give up the Irish character' of high politics in Dublin.[57] The anti-unionist outrage at the potential encroachment of Irish liberties by Britain sprang from an inherent belief in the independence of the constitutional tradition in Ireland. Barry Maxwell, the first Earl of Farnham, held up the 'solemn recognition of her independent legislative power' in 1782 as Ireland's 'Magna Charta'.[58] The parliament in Dublin was a guarantor of liberty, as freedom was bound up with self-government. The union threatened to strip Ireland of its 'Magna Charta' and, as such, was condemned by anti-unionists as foreshadowing a new age of unresponsive government at best, or political slavery at worst. Given British parliamentary arithmetic, Farnham did not believe that transferring a portion of the Irish parliament to London in the aftermath of a union represented a continuance of self-government (as Cooke asserted), given that Ireland's MPs would be outnumbered by English and Scottish members. He argued that Ireland's lack of influence in shaping the future legislative agenda within a unified state would be so insurmountable that the Irish might as well not have any representation in London at all.[59] If there were a clash between representatives of Britain and Ireland in a

[56] William Drennan, *A Letter to the Right Hon. William Pitt* (Dublin: James Moore, 1799), p. 4; Henry Grattan, *An Answer to a Pamphlet Entitled,* The Speech of the Earl of Clare, on the Subject of a Legislative Union, Between Great Britain and Ireland, 5th ed. (Dublin: J. Moore, 1800), p. 6; William Saurin, *An Accurate Report on the Speech of William Saurin, Esq., in the Irish House of Commons, on Friday, the 21st of February, 1800, on the Question of a Legislative Union with Great Britain* (Dublin: J. Moore, 1800), p. 22.

[57] John Foster, *Speech of the Right Honourable John Foster, Speaker of the House of Commons of Ireland, Delivered in Committee, on Thursday the 11th Day of April, 1799* (Dublin: James Moore, 1799), p. 67.

[58] Right Hon. Barry, Earl Farnham, *An Examination into the Principles Contained in a Pamphlet, Entitled* The Speech of Lord Minto, *with some Remarks upon a Pamphlet, Entitled* Observations on that Part of the Speaker's Speech which Relates to Trade (Dublin: James Moore, 1800), p. 37.

[59] Ibid., p. 10.

post-union parliament, Thomas Goold told listeners at a debate of the Irish bar in December 1798, the British interest would inevitably triumph, not because it was inherently correct, but simply because it had weight of numbers.[60] William Saurin, the most distinguished Irish lawyer on the anti-union side, cynically concluded that the fusion of the two parliaments was intended to reassert 'the supremacy of the British legislature' and to reduce Ireland to a 'province' within a multinational state. This reduction in status would deprive Ireland of meaningful representative government.[61]

The vast bulk of the pamphlet material generated during the union debate was hostile to the proposed British connection. The case for union, while not as voluminous as its counterpoint, was, however, diffuse, but at heart it concerned the question of representation. Rebuffing the anti-unionist argument that the reduction of Irish representatives in a union state – the 300 MPs in College Green would become 100 MPs in Westminster – inevitably diminished Irish influence, unionists pressed the case that the *quality* of representation in London would be dramatically enhanced. The insular corruption of the existing Irish representative system, with its low-calibre members, rotten boroughs, and closed franchises, would terminate when Ireland's political centre turned towards London.[62] Another critical argument ran that Irish MPs would not sit in London as MPs *for* Ireland, because the competing regional interests would melt away in the face of the affairs of the greater imperial whole. The 'respectable representatives for Great Britain' would be as responsible for Ireland as Irish MPs.[63] William Johnson, a pro-union barrister, concurred, suggesting that if Irish affairs were governed by the same principles as the British applied to their concerns, political representation would be more effective in Westminster. He developed Cooke's idea of one common governing principle within the larger polity, stressing that in the new state, 'there cannot be one law for Ireland, and another for the rest of the united kingdoms'.[64] Experience would painfully disprove this point.

If a union held the promise of enhancing the quality of representative politics in Ireland, the proposed constitutional framework offered the

[60] *A Report of the Debate of the Irish Bar, on Sunday, the 9th of December, 1798, on the Subject of an Union of the Legislatures of Great Britain and Ireland* (Dublin: J. Moore, 1799), p. 43.

[61] Saurin, *An Accurate Report*, p. 22. [62] Edgeworth, *Substance of Three Speeches*, p. 8.

[63] Archibald Redfoord, *Union, Necessary to Security: Addressed to the Loyal Inhabitants of Ireland* (Dublin: J. Archer, 1800), p. 47.

[64] 'A Barrister' [William Johnson], *Letter to Joshua Spencer, Esq., Occasioned by his* Thoughts on an Union (Dublin: John Archer, 1798), p. 32.

alluring goal of addressing Catholic exclusion from the Irish political nation. Unionist writers were divided in their view of Catholic Emancipation, ranging from vocal advocacy to an existential dread of its inevitability. Regardless of perspective, the idea commonly floated was that with Ireland part of a larger, firmly Protestant, polity, the denominational Irish majority could be 'safely' brought into the political nation.[65] While the Irish parliament mirrored its British counterpart in slowly undoing the vestiges of the penal laws (a Catholic Relief Act was passed in Dublin in 1793, for example, which relieved a limited number of social and economic disabilities), there was little sign that full political emancipation was on the cards. One pamphleteer dismissed the 'independence' that the anti-unionists feted, given that political rights were denied to the majority of the population under the constitutional settlement of 1782.[66] This was the state of affairs that Edmund Burke sought to puncture in his *Letter to Sir Hercules Langrishe* in 1792, which appealed to British constitutional reasoning to alter the political position of Catholics in Ireland. Burke argued that in a mixed constitution with a popular component, it was not politically feasible to exclude the majority of the population from the rights of citizenship, as to do so was to undermine the idea of a commonwealth.[67] Burke made the distinction that Catholics were not excluded from the '*state*', but from '*the British constitution*'. Government continued to function despite the political bar on Catholics; yet the Irish majority were locked out of the rights and obligations that their Protestant fellow countrymen assumed as natural. Burke rejected any claim that Catholics were 'virtually' represented in the Irish parliament, as the 'sympathy of feeling' required between disenfranchised community and political delegates did not exist. 'As things stand', Burke claimed, 'the Catholic, as a Catholic and belonging to a description, has no *virtual* relation to the representative; but on the *contrary*'. This tension was potentially calamitous. 'Our constitution', Burke warned, 'is not made for great, general, proscriptive exclusions; sooner or later, it will destroy them, or they will destroy the constitution'.[68]

65 See, for example, 'A Mimber', *Unconnected Hints, and Loose Ideas Upon the Union, with Two Propositions* (Dublin: Marchbank, 1799), p. 25; Sylvester Douglas, *Speech of the Right Honourable Sylvester Douglas, in the House of Commons, Tuesday, April the 23rd, 1799, on Seconding the Motion of the Rt. Hon. The Chancellor of the Exchequer, for the House to Agree with the Lords in an Address to His Majesty, Relative to a Union with Ireland* (Dublin: John Milliken, 1799), p. 98.

66 'Atticus', *To the People of Ireland* (no publishing details, [1800]), p. 4.

67 Richard Bourke, *Empire and Revolution: The Political Life of Edmund Burke* (Princeton, NJ: Princeton University Press, 2015), p. 795.

68 Edmund Burke, *A Letter from the Right Hon. Edmund Burke, MP in the Kingdom of Great Britain, to Sir Hercules Langrishe, MP, on the Subject of Roman Catholics of Ireland, and the Propriety of*

Burke died in 1797, but his analysis of the political state of Ireland permeated the arguments of some on the unionist side. If the penal laws ensured that virtual representation did not operate for Irish Catholics, then parliamentary union could address this deficit. Pitt spoke openly in 1799 about a union state providing a 'safe' framework for Catholic participation in political life.[69] For Pitt, an act of union must be accompanied by legislation to formally end the penal laws, particularly the abolition of the bar on Catholics to enter parliament. Such a bold step would secure, in Pitt's calculation, the support of Irish Catholics and radical reformers, helping to unify the new 'United Kingdom'.[70] As Michael Brown has observed, the form of British government that Pitt was seeking to extend into Ireland simply would not work 'if the majority did not have access to it'.[71] With a parallel act of Catholic Emancipation, Pitt and his chief allies, Castlereagh and Cornwallis, hoped to secure a genuine union of the two countries by including the previously excluded.[72] Union was the path to a more inclusive sense of Irish representative government.

This argument was most prominently taken up in Ireland by Theobald McKenna.[73] McKenna, a leading Catholic lawyer, had, in the early 1790s, been an outspoken member of the Catholic Committee (he made the stringent case that the penal laws were a violation of natural right); the tide of radicalism in 1791 pushed him into the Dublin branch of the United Irishmen. His increasing despair at events in revolutionary France from 1792, and the parallel deepening of radicalism within the United Irish movement, however, led McKenna to advocate a more moderate reform agenda.[74] Radical reformers, such as Theobald Wolfe Tone, dismissed McKenna's gradualist arguments, in which Catholics were not granted full and immediate political rights, as 'bladdering stuff'.[75] But such 'bladdering stuff' was politically useful in pushing Catholic opinion towards

*Admitting Them to the Elective Franchise Consistently with the Principles of the Constitution Established at the Revolution* (Dublin: J. Byrne, 1792), pp. 5, 22. Emphases in original.

69 William Pitt, Speech of the Right Hon. *William Pitt, in the House of Commons, Thursday 31 January 1799, on Offering to the House the Resolutions which he Proposes as the Basis of a Union between Great Britain and Ireland* (Dublin: John Exshaw, 1799), pp. 39–40.

70 Eric J. Evans, *William Pitt the Younger* (London: Routledge, 1999), p. 70.

71 Michael Brown, 'The injured lady and her British problem', in Brown, Geoghegan, and Kelly (eds.), *Irish Act of Union*, p. 49.

72 Bew, *Castlereagh*, p. 132. 73 Stafford, *The Case of Ireland*, pp. 149–50.

74 Theobald McKenna, *Political Essays Relative to the Affairs of Ireland, in 1791, 1792, and 1793; With Remarks on the Present State of that Country* (London: J. Debrett, 1794), pp. 165–206.

75 T. W. Moody, R. B. McDowell, and C. J. Woods (eds.), *The Writings of Theobald Wolfe Tone*, 3 vols. (Oxford: Oxford University Press, 2001), i, p. 217.

union in the aftermath of the 1798 rebellion, or so the British government, at least, believed. McKenna was paid £300 per year for 'literary services' on behalf of the unionist cause.[76] Two substantial pamphlets appeared bearing his name during the union debates, and despite the less-than-wholesome motives for writing, McKenna's texts set out the clearest case why Catholics should support an incorporative union with Great Britain.

McKenna crafted an argument to appeal to national sentiment and a moderate reforming agenda by challenging the Irish status quo. He presented union as a transformative moment, which would allow Ireland to play a full and active role in the affairs of empire – an imperial right hitherto denied because of the myopic nature of Irish politics. While anti-unionists upheld the right to Irish self-government, the parliament in Dublin, with its 'mock independence', claimed McKenna, served only the 'vanity' of the small clique that sat in it. As such, the parliament was nothing less than a provincial distraction from the 'council of empire' in London.[77] He argued that the injudicious and ill-tempered nature of Irish politics stemmed from the stuffy narrowness of the parliament in Dublin. In setting a political agenda guided only by the interests of a minority, the parliament had damaged the 'manners' of the population.[78] The penal laws sanctioned the coercive power of 'little minds' from the Protestant Ascendancy, the leader of which 'studied manners and politics in an Orange Lodge'. The exclusion of Catholics from the political liberties of the state, McKenna rationalised, highlighted the bitter prejudices of the Protestant Ascendancy, who monopolised the state apparatus in Ireland. McKenna drew on Adam Smith's connection between prosperity and electoral privilege, suggesting that, in denying the franchise to an entire religious denomination, Ireland stood apart from wider Enlightenment trends.[79] 'Whilst the adjacent nations were resolving into civilised habits', McKenna declared, 'what has been the government of Ireland, but a perpetual scuffle between the state and the people?'[80] As with his calls for Catholic political relief from the early 1790s, McKenna rejected universal male suffrage, stressing that only propertied Catholics should be franchised. He explicitly rejected 'a Democracy' where 'population' was

[76] Geoghegan, *Irish Act of Union*, p. 128.

[77] Theobald McKenna, *A Memoire on Some Questions Respecting the Projected Union of Great Britain and Ireland* (Dublin: John Rice, 1799), pp. 4, 12.

[78] Theobald McKenna, *Constitutional Objections to the Government of Ireland by a Separate Legislature: In a Letter to John Hamilton, Esq., Occasioned by his Remarks on* A Memoire on The Projected Union (Dublin: H. Fitzpatrick, 1799), p. v.

[79] McKenna, *Memoire*, p. 22.

[80] McKenna, *Constitutional Objections*, p. 11.

'superior to property'.[81] McKenna called for the extension of political rights to Catholics as they existed for Protestants in Ireland; while this was not 'reform' in the radical sense of the term during the 1790s, he concluded that union offered an opportunity to subsume Irish differences within the larger British polity.

This line of thinking on the Catholic question also found a place in the thinking of Pitt and Cooke. Cooke speculated that the Irish parliament would never grant the denominational majority civil equality, as such a course would leave Protestants outnumbered by three to one. This consigned Catholics to a limbo state, with minimal hope of joining, or even influencing, the political nation. But the sting could be taken out of the issue if a new polity, spanning Britain and Ireland, enfranchised Catholics across the two kingdoms. This framework granted Catholics the rights they sought, while protecting the Protestant interest through the sheer scale of numbers.[82] The logic of Cooke's argument was that, in the aftermath of union, Irish religious demographics would cease to matter as a political issue. In his second pamphlet on the question of union, McKenna pushed the boundaries of Cooke's argument by reiterating his belief that contemporaneous notions of Irish political independence were false. He made the case that European powers recognised the British Crown's authority over Ireland, not a separate and independent Irish state; for all intents and purposes, the archipelago resembled a confederation.[83] The constitution of 1782 may have tinkered with the legislative relationship between Ireland and Britain, but it did not undermine 'the rights of the British Crown' in Ireland, nor withhold the 'obedience of the Irish people' to that Crown.[84] Irish unrest, McKenna asserted, was generated by a parliament in Dublin that perpetrated the worst excesses of denominational oligarchy.[85] As such, he positioned an irreformable Irish parliament as the chief barrier to a welcome extension of the 'British constitution' into Ireland. He concluded that incorporating union offered the means to harmonise the relationship between the kingdoms, while defusing religious tensions.[86]

Only a few anti-unionists questioned McKenna's and Cooke's trust in the British parliament to emancipate Catholics. 'Let the Catholic look to the political history of Great Britain', countered one of McKenna's critics, 'and he [*sic.*] will see a system of government that ought at one view to

[81] McKenna, *Memoire*, p. 35. [82] [Cooke], *Arguments*, pp. 23–32.
[83] McKenna, *Constitutional Objections*, p. 17. [84] Ibid., p. 22. [85] Ibid., p. 62.
[86] Ibid., p. 84.

convince him of the fallacy of such expectations'.[87] Richard Jebb suggested that in trying to reconcile Catholics and Protestants to a union with Britain, Cooke, in the end, satisfied neither group. Instead of union, he called for the Irish parliament to 'make one great effort of patriotism' in emancipating the Irish majority.[88] Cooke's critics also borrowed from classical republicanism to warn against union. An anonymous writer in a periodical called *The Anti-Union* channelled John Milton's seventeenth-century commonwealth ideal with the assertion that 'if you cannot be free without the patronage and protection of Britain, you cannot be free with it'.[89] This neo-Roman abstraction suggested that dependency on another nation was counterintuitive to notions of emancipation, as a free state was defined by its capacity for self-government.[90] This argument carried considerable purchase within anti-unionist circles. Thomas Goold, the industrious lawyer from Cork, for example, celebrated 'the independent parliament' in Dublin as the 'only guarantee of liberty'. To consent to the destruction of the seat of government in Ireland was to 'become a slave on terms of my own making'.[91]

The zeal of anti-unionism alienated certain observers. The Irish-born Lord Sheffield, speaking in the British House of Commons, could barely hide his annoyance at the leaders of 'an English colony', maintained by 'English arms and treasure', proclaiming their 'independence'.[92] Indeed, the anti-unionist celebration of '1782' overlooked that the Catholics of Ireland were locked out of self-government and forced to acquiesce in laws not of their making. As a result, only a handful of anti-unionists harnessed the Catholic question in framing their argument, as inclusion of a formally excluded segment of the body politic undermined the case to maintain the principled independence of the Irish parliament. A thoughtful pamphlet signed by 'A. N.' appeared in late 1798, for example, which made the case that union risked violating the contract between the representative and constituent. Yet for all the references to the political rights of the 'people'

87 John Hamilton, *A Letter to Theobald McKenna, Occasioned by a Publication Entitled A Memoire on Some Questions Respecting the Projected Union* (Dublin: James Moore, 1799), p. 27.

88 Jebb, *Reply to a Pamphlet*, pp. 21–3; quote on p. 23.

89 *Anti-Union*, no. 22 (14 February 1799), p. 86. For Milton, see Quentin Skinner, *Liberty before Liberalism* (Cambridge: Cambridge University Press, 2012; first published 1998), p. 30.

90 Philip Pettit, *Republicanism: A Theory of Freedom and Government* (Oxford: Oxford University Press, 1997), pp. 31–2; Skinner, *Liberty before Liberalism*, p. 26.

91 Thomas Goold, *An Address to the People of Ireland, on the Subject of the Projected Union* (Dublin: James Moore, 1799), p. 12.

92 Lord Sheffield, *Substance of the Speech of the Right Honourable Lord Sheffield, Monday, April 22, 1799, Upon the Subject of Union with Ireland* (Dublin: J. Milliken, 1799), p. 30.

and the importance of public opinion – 'Let Parliament be the organ, but give the people the will' – both of these concepts excluded Catholics. The 'people' and public opinion were often euphemisms for the existing (denominationally defined) political nation.[93] The use of the 'People' in anti-unionist tracts can read as apparent proclamations of Irish popular sovereignty, when it was in fact a synonym for the Anglican propertied interest that was represented in College Green.[94] That said, the pamphlet material represented a concerted effort – on both sides – to reach a broader constituent base than the political nation.[95]

The political economy of incorporating union was another pronounced theme within the pamphlet material.[96] That said, economic and fiscal issues were viewed primarily through the constitutional prism, with unionists holding the promise of commercial growth through integration with British markets, while anti-unionists fretted about an upsurge in the Irish tax burden within a large imperial polity at war with France. Cooke set the unionist tone in connecting political and commercial integration in an incorporated state, with Irish merchants placed on an equal footing with British traders, able to access a wider range of markets. Echoing Adam Smith's prediction in *The Wealth of Nations* (1776) that a union with Britain was the key to Irish economic improvement, Cooke argued that Ireland, as a separate political entity, risked economic marginalisation in a world dominated by large imperial states.[97] Union promised the creation of a free-trade zone between Britain and Ireland, which would prompt British capital and resources to circulate throughout the smaller island, materially improving Irish industrial and mercantile conditions.[98] Scotland was cited by McKenna as an illuminating case study: the Scots suffered religious clashes and economic hardship before 1707, but had found 'internal quiet' after the union, creating the foundations for increased prosperity within an imperial state.[99] Unionists conceded that the Irish

93 'A.N.', *Thoughts on the Constitutional Rights of Parliament, Respecting the Power of Surrendering the Legislative Independence of Ireland* (Dublin: V. Dowling, 1798), pp. 7–8, 10.

94 *The Speech of the Right Honourable Barry, Lord Yelverton, Chief Baron of His Majesty's Court of Exchequer, in the House of Lords of Ireland, on Saturday, March 22, 1800; in the Debate on the Fourth Article of a Legislative Union Between Great Britain and Ireland* (Dublin: J. Milliken, 1800), p. 9.

95 Smyth, 'Act of Union', pp. 157–8.

96 For wider contexts, see Stafford, *The Case of Ireland*, pp. 139–40.

97 [Cooke], *Arguments*, p. 39; Adam Smith, *An Inquiry into the Nature and Causes of the Wealth of Nations*, 2 vols. (London: W. Strahan, 1776), ii, p. 583.

98 'A Freeman of Dublin', *An Appeal to the Loyal Citizens of Dublin* (Dublin: John Milliken, 1800), p. 28.

99 McKenna, *Memoire*, p. 15.

would inherit British wartime debt in a union state, but taxes would be proportional to Ireland's (newly enhanced) ability to pay.[100]

This did not convince the anti-unionists, such as Henry Grattan, who adopted a more pessimistic view.[101] The extension of British taxes into Ireland threatened to cripple the smaller island, wiping out any material benefit that the union provided.[102] As the productivity of the Irish economy depended on cheap labour and low wages, the importation of a tax burden would devastate the natural order in Ireland.[103] *Pace* McKenna's use of Scotland as an example of economic improvement within the union state, a common trope in the anti-unionist literature was the imposition of the malt tax by the English on the Scots, a demonstration of the fiscal damage wrought by London on the Celtic periphery.[104] But more fundamentally, anti-unionists fretted about the power imbalance that would define Ireland's relationship with Britain inside an incorporated state, and how the commercial and fiscal equality talked up by Cooke was an illusion. Dublin manufacturers were concerned that the implementation of free trade would see a decrease in demand for Irish products in Ireland.[105] An anonymous Catholic pamphleteer questioned the idea of commercial equality, suggesting that it was not in the economic interest of the British to 'raise rivals' to their established industrial and trading towns and cities.[106] The fate of the Irish woollen trade, which was destroyed by English protective legislation in 1699, was frequently cited as an example of Irish economic interests being of little concern to the holders of power in London.[107]

Added to these fears about increased taxes and an economically subordinate role for the Irish within a union state was the threat of an increase in absenteeism. The absent landlord – the owner of Irish land who resided

100 Anon., *An Exposition of the Principal Terms of Union, and its Probable Effects on Ireland* (Dublin: J. Milliken, 1800), p. 15.

101 *The Speech of Henry Grattan, Esq, on the Subject of a Legislative Union with Great Britain...* (Dublin: J. Stockdale, 1800), p. 26.

102 'A Student of Trinity College', *Observations on a Pamphlet, Supposed to be Written by an Englishman, Entitled* Arguments For and Against an Union (Dublin: J. Milliken, 1799), p. 31.

103 John Collis, *An Address to the People of Ireland, on the Projected Union* (Dublin: James Moore, 1799), pp. 10–12.

104 'A Student of Trinity College', *Observations*, p. 15.

105 Cormac Ó Gráda, *Ireland: A New Economic History, 1780–1939* (Oxford: Oxford University Press, 1994), p. 44.

106 'An Irish Catholic', *An Argument for Independence, in Opposition to an Union, Addressed to all his Countrymen* (Dublin: J. Stockdale, 1799), p. 6. This has been attributed to the United Irishman W. J. MacNeven: McCormack, *Pamphlet Debate*, p. 28.

107 Robert Orr, *A Review of the Speech of the Right Hon. William Pitt, in the British House of Commons, on Thursday, January 31st, 1799* (Dublin: J. Stockdale, 1799), pp. 2–3.

elsewhere, usually Britain – was long held up as a contributing cause of economic distress, as rents were not spent in Ireland and the condition of estates could be neglected.[108] Anti-unionists warned that an increase in Irish absenteeism would follow the transfer of power from Dublin to London, suggesting that a further exodus of the landed interest would inevitably drain the country further of wealth.[109] Speaking in the British House of Commons in 1799, the Irish-born playwright, Richard Brinsley Sheridan, commented that absenteeism was one of the gravest evils that Ireland faced at the turn of the century. He could not resist scoffing that the proposed remedy was the creation of an 'Absentee Government' for Ireland.[110]

## Political Suicide: The Right of the Irish Parliament to 'Die'

The pamphlet war over the union was fought in an age when questions of imperial allegiance and sovereignty were at the fore of British politics.[111] The conflict with the American colonies shook notions of theoretical sovereignty within the empire, as the political authority of the imperial parliament was subverted by the emergence of the idea that power resided in those who deemed themselves 'the represented people'.[112] Just as the American colonists adopted a disparate range of legitimising languages in opposing British sovereignty, so too did anti-unionists in Ireland in opposing incorporating union. Anti-unionism found classical republican ideas of self-government nestling alongside notions of the liberties of the freeborn (Protestant) Irishman and assertions of the right to resist tyrannical encroachments of political rights by government. While incorporating union meant, constitutionally speaking, a fusion of the parliaments of Ireland and Britain, the stark symbolism of the abolition of College Green had an enduring appeal. Much of the anti-unionist case was wrapped in emotive rhetoric, such as Grattan's dire warning of the

[108] R. D. C. Black, *Economic Thought and the Irish Question, 1817–1970* (Cambridge: Cambridge University Press, 1960), p. 73.

[109] Matthew Weld, *No Union! Being an Appeal to Irishmen*, 4th ed. (Cork: J. Haly, M. Harris, and J. Connor, 1798), p. 14.

[110] *Speech of Richard Brinsley Sheridan, Esq., in the House of Commons of Great Britain, on Thursday, January 31st, 1799, in Reply to Mr Pitt's Speech on the Union with Ireland* (Dublin: James Moore, 1799), p. 22.

[111] J. C. D. Clark, *English Society, 1688–1832* (Cambridge: Cambridge University Press, 1985), p. 199.

[112] J. G. A. Pocock, *The Machiavellian Moment: Florentine Political Thought and the Atlantic Republican Tradition* (Princeton, NJ: Princeton University Press, 2003; first published 1975), p. 525.

'extinction of the Constitution' or William Drennan's apocalyptic vision of national 'destruction' following the loss of self-government.[113]

As such graphic imagery hints, the competency of the parliament in Dublin to legislate for union, thus ending its own separate existence, was a highly charged aspect of the debate. The British establishment could not simply *impose* union on Ireland; it was vital for Pitt, Castlereagh and other governmental figures that the parliament in Dublin passed legislation to bestow legitimacy on the new constitutional connection from the Irish side. This explains the systematic corruption that came with union, as Pitt's government doled out – illegally, in some cases – money to buy off votes and seats in College Green, as well as the use of peerages as bribes.[114] Set against the backdrop of the war with France, the stakes of national security were high at the time of the union, but an Irish blessing, even one gained through extortion, was needed for the proposed constitutional marriage.[115]

The question of parliamentary competence to legislate for union crystallised two contrasting conceptions of sovereignty. The anti-unionists pressed the case that the Irish parliament did not have the power to extinguish itself; if this was attempted, power would shift directly to the 'people' (however narrowly defined). While Sieyès went uncited in the pamphlet debate, this was an Irish version of his ideal of a constituent power, the inherent right of the nation to fix the boundaries of a constitution. Under this theory, a constituted body could not dissolve itself unilaterally.[116]

The unionists, on the other hand, saw no legal barrier in the way of the Irish parliament to decide the constitutional future of Ireland. These arguments tended to draw on Hobbesian interpretations of parliamentary sovereignty, stressing that a properly constituted assembly possessed the authority to enter into a union with another. This vision rejected the implicit (and at times explicit) popular sovereignty of the constituent power theory. Pitt, for example, derided the notion that there was, in the secular world, a higher authority than governments: the 'people' were not

113 Henry Grattan, in *A Report of the Debate in the House of Commons of Ireland, on Wednesday and Thursday the 15th and 16th of January, 1800 on an Amendment to the Address Moved by Sir Laurence Parsons, on the Subject of An Union* (Dublin: James Moore, 1800), p. 125; Drennan, *Letter to Pitt*, p. 46. Drennan was the only northern Dissenter to contribute to the union debate: see Ian McBride, *Scripture Politics: Ulster Presbyterianism and Irish Radicalism in the Late Eighteenth Century* (Oxford: Oxford University Press, 1998), p. 210.

114 David Wilkinson, 'How did they pass the Union? Secret service expenditure', *History*, vol. 82, no. 266 (1997), pp. 223–51; Geoghegan, *Irish Act of Union*, pp. 118–29.

115 Dana Y. Rabin, *Britain and Its Internal Others, 1750–1800: Under Rule of Law* (Manchester: Manchester University Press, 2017), p. 197.

116 Lucia Rubinelli, *Constituent Power: A History* (Cambridge: Cambridge University Press, 2020), p. 19.

sovereign. In Pitt's estimation, popular or national sovereignty, envisaged as an authority *over* parliament, was code for political factions expressing their grievances through extra-parliamentary agitation. 'In every Government', Pitt told the House of Commons in 1799, 'there must reside somewhere a supreme, absolute, and unlimited authority'.[117] Taking the legislative independence of the Irish parliament at face value, Pitt's message was that formal Irish sovereignty resided in College Green. There was, according to the Prime Minister, no legal authority that could stop Ireland from discussing, debating and ultimately consenting to union through its 'national' parliament.

Irish unionists deployed versions of Pitt's argument. Theobald McKenna pointed to the Irish parliament's past record in altering the 'laws, manners, religion, and property of this island' without recourse to debates about competency. On a more abstract level, McKenna also queried the notion of a higher authority than the Irish parliament. He defined the sovereign as the final arbiter in the decision-making process: if this was not College Green in the Irish case, McKenna asked, where did sovereignty in Ireland reside?[118] This constitutional question was echoed by Viscount Falkland, who published a pamphlet in 1799 on the issue of the competency of the Irish parliament to legislate for union. He suggested that College Green had the right to consent to the creation of a new, unified British-Irish state, as its members were granted by the electorate 'an unlimited confidence and independent authority'. A political nation chooses to exercise its liberties through its representatives, Falkland surmised, meaning that there is no higher authority than a parliamentary government.[119] The constitution was not an 'absolutely fixed' entity, according to the Irish MP, William Johnson, but malleable and able to agree to profound change.[120] Indeed, in a bid to transform the anti-unionist case into a straw man, several unionists hypothesised that if a parliament lacked the theoretical authority to enter into union, then the 1707 Act that bound England and Scotland together was constitutionally void.[121] Such thinking was, according to unionists, farcical.

[117] Pitt, *Speech of Pitt*, p. 61. [118] McKenna, *Constitutional Objections*, p. v.

[119] Charles, Viscount Falkland, *Considerations on the Competency of the Parliament of Ireland to Accede to an Union with Great Britain* (London: J. Wright, 1799), pp. 6–8.

[120] [William Johnson], *Reasons for Adopting an Union between Ireland and Great Britain* (Dublin: J. Milliken, 1799), p. 3.

[121] Lord Minto, *The Speech of Lord Minto, in the House of Peers, April 11, 1799, on a Motion for an Address to His Majesty, to Communicate the Resolutions of the Two Houses of Parliament, Respecting an Union between Great Britain and Ireland* (London: John Stockdale, 1799), pp. 146–7; [Cooke], *Arguments*, p. 42; Falkland, *Considerations*, p. 20.

If a parliament did not possess a legislative ability, the lawyer William Cusack Smith hypothesised, then the body in question was simply not a parliament. He argued that the 'law-giver must ever be the supreme power in the State'. To suggest that the Irish parliament could not authorise union, and thus admit that College Green was not the 'supreme power' in Ireland, was to 'degrade' the sitting representatives which collectively made up the country's political wisdom.[122] Smith, like a small number of other unionists, cited William Blackstone as an authority to suggest that the Irish parliament was competent to legislate for union. Blackstone was the eighteenth-century English constitutional theorist par excellence: his multi-volume *Commentaries on the Laws of England* were first published in 1765 and received numerous new editions through the rest of the century.[123] The *Commentaries* helped to popularise the concept of parliamentary sovereignty, emphasising the Hobbesian idea that the law-giver was the highest legal body in a state, at once absolute and omnipresent. As Blackstone contended, 'the power of making laws constitutes the supreme authority, so wherever the supreme authority in any state resides, it is the right of that authority to make laws'.[124]

Only a handful of pages in the *Commentaries* touched directly on Irish affairs, but unionists and anti-unionists clashed in their interpretations of the text.[125] Blackstone described Ireland as 'a distinct kingdom', though a 'dependent, subordinate kingdom'. While Ireland possessed a parliament, England retained a right to legislate for the smaller island. This political imbalance stemmed from the history of 'conquest' – Blackstone's term – the single most important aspect in shaping Anglo-Irish relations.[126] Blackstone believed that 'this state of dependence' was 'almost forgotten' and 'ready to be disputed' by the Irish.[127] Indeed, the analysis of Ireland as a conquered country was ignored by most

[122] William Cusack Smith, *Animadversions on the Speech of Mr Saurin and Mr Bushe etc.* (Dublin: Marchbank, 1800), pp. 9, 29, 31.

[123] For Blackstone's rather elusive life, see Wilfred Prest, *William Blackstone: Law and Letters in the Eighteenth Century* (Oxford: Oxford University Press, 2008).

[124] William Blackstone, *Commentaries on the Laws of England: Book the First* (Oxford: Oxford University Press, 1765; first published 1763), p. 52.

[125] Ultán Gillen, 'Blackstone and Ireland', in Anthony Page and Wilfred Prest (eds.), *Blackstone and His Critics* (London: Bloomsbury, 2018), pp. 97–115.

[126] Blackstone, *Commentaries*, bk. 1, pp. 98–101. See J. C. D. Clark, *The Language of Liberty, 1660–1832: Political Discourse and Social Dynamics in the Anglo-American World* (Cambridge: Cambridge University Press, 1994), p. 87.

[127] Blackstone, *Commentaries*, bk. I, p. 101.

anti-unionists, who nevertheless deployed Blackstone to argue that a parliament cannot surrender sovereignty to another body.[128]

So, Blackstone cropped up within Irish political debate to make a number of mutually exclusive points. He was most cited in the argument whether College Green possessed the power to legislate for union; but Blackstone was also deployed by both unionists and anti-unionists to make respective cases that union offered a path to either the perfection or usurpation of the constitution in Ireland. Less considered by both sides was Blackstone's depiction of the inferior status of the Irish parliament within the British constitution, which meant, in effect, that union was inevitable if the Crown-in-Parliament in London deemed it so.

This was a revealing blind spot of unionists and anti-unionists alike, as both sides appeared oblivious to the structural imbalance of the British-Irish relationship, presenting College Green as an independent and, at times, absolute, assembly. The Dissenting lawyer Robert Holmes, writing under a pseudonym, was a rare voice against this consensus, bluntly pointing out the subordinate relationship that Ireland endured with Britain. 'Had Ireland indeed an independent Parliament', he asserted, 'a Legislative Union between Great Britain and Ireland never could take place'.[129] In this sense, Holmes ruefully conceded that sovereignty in Ireland was indeed, as Blackstone testified, rooted in conquest.

It was William Cusack Smith who offered the most sustained engagement with Blackstone of all the participants in the union debate. For Smith, Blackstone had demonstrated that parliament possessed power to profoundly alter the constitution in order to perfect it, with the Act of Union between England and Scotland providing a ready-made example.[130] Smith also attempted to debunk Charles Kendal Bushe's questioning of the competency of the Irish parliament by asserting Blackstone's doctrine of the 'absolute, all-competent and uncontrolled' power of a lawfully constituted assembly.[131] Patrick Duigenan, the firebrand Protestant, also drew on Blackstone to demonstrate that it was not a union that threatened to undermine the constitution, but its potential pairing with Catholic

[128] P. Sheehy, *Union a Plague: In Answer to Counsellor McKenna's Memoire on the Projected Union* (Dublin: J. Hill, 1799), p. 22.

[129] 'A Philosopher' [Robert Holmes], *A Demonstration of the Necessity of a Legislative Union of Great Britain and Ireland, Involving a Refutation of Every Argument which has been or can be Urged Against that Measure* (Dublin: no publishing house, 1799), p. 17.

[130] Smith, *Substance of Mr William Smith's Speech*, p. 27.

[131] Smith, *Letter to Henry Grattan*, p. 78.

relief.[132] Other pro-union activists adopted a more conservative reading of Blackstone's mantra of parliamentary sovereignty to buttress the case that College Green was, from an Irish perspective, the final arbiter in settling constitutional questions.[133]

Another widely cited authority during the union debates was John Locke. Locke's *Two Treatises of Government* (1689) set out a social contract theory of sovereignty with, crucially, an in-built right to resist the sovereign if the supreme authority of a state became corrupted.[134] His influence was more keenly felt in late eighteenth-century Ireland than Britain, partly because of his privileged place within the curriculum at Trinity College Dublin and the United Irish movement's attraction to the potentially 'democratic' theory of sovereignty found in the second of the *Two Treatises*.[135] Locke's ideas regarding the ability or otherwise of an assembly to transfer sovereignty to another body were aired many times during the union debate.[136] But as the pamphlet war continued, the use of Locke's political philosophy, like Blackstone's, assumed a malleable quality, with friends and enemies of deepening the constitutional connection between Ireland and Britain studding their arguments with Lockean theory.

Locke's relevance to the debate over the union hinged on readings of chapter nineteen of the second of the *Two Treatises*, 'Of the Dissolution of Government'. In Locke's theory of sovereignty, civil government was created through a social contract with those seeking protection for 'property' (a term Locke defined broadly, including life and liberty as much as material goods or land). A sovereign power thus was constructed from, and legitimated by, the consent of the governed. If the sovereign failed to protect the property of political society, the people can withdraw their consent, and are 'absolved from any farther Obedience'. In such a

132 Patrick Duigenan, *A Fair Representation of the Present Political State of Ireland; In a Course of Strictures on Two Pamphlets, One Entitled* The Case of Ireland Reconsidered*; the Other Entitled Consideration on the State of Public Affairs in the Year 1799 – Ireland* (London: J. Wright, 1799), pp. 194–5.

133 'Author of the *Necessity of an Incorporate Union between Great Britain and Ireland*', *Competency of the Parliaments of Great Britain and Ireland to Incorporate their Legislatures; With Some Remarks Upon the Debate in the Irish House of Lords upon the Address* (Dublin: J. Milliken, 1799), p. 4.

134 David Wootton, 'Introduction', in John Locke, *Political Writings*, ed. David Wootton (Indianapolis, IN: Hackett Publishing Co., 2003), pp. 77–89.

135 Patrick Kelly, 'Perceptions of Locke in eighteenth-century Ireland', *Proceedings of the Royal Irish Academy*, vol. 89C (1989), pp. 17–35. For an example of Locke's influence on the United Irishmen, see Arthur O'Connor, *The State of Ireland*, ed. James Livesey (Dublin: Lilliput Press, 1998; first published 1798), p. 114.

136 Danny Mansergh, *Grattan's Failure: Parliamentary Opposition and the People in Ireland, 1779–1800* (Dublin: Irish Academic Press, 2005), p. 248.

circumstance, power reverts back to 'the People', who possess a right to 'resume their original Liberty' through the establishment of a new legislative assembly.[137] A parliament, in other words, was not considered the site of absolute and unbounded sovereignty; as legitimacy for political structures flowed from the consent of society, the people represented the higher form of authority *if* the sovereign became corrupted. But Locke made another observation that was also pertinent to the union debate in Ireland: 'The *Legislative cannot transfer the Power of Making Laws* to any other hands. For it being but a delegated power from the People, they, who have it, cannot pass it over to others'.[138] These Lockean tropes – the role of political representatives as delegates rather than final arbiters, the boundaries of formal sovereignty, the inability of power to be transferred to another assembly – were embraced by a number of anti-unionists eager to cast doubt on the right of the Irish parliament to terminate itself through an acceptance of incorporating union.

The most serious engagement with Locke during the union debates came from the anti-unionist lawyers, who wished to 'prove' that the Irish parliament did not possess the right to legislate for union. At a debate of the Irish bar in December 1798, Joshua Spencer cited Locke to contend 'that Parliament is utterly incompetent to such a measure [as incorporating union], without express authority from the people'.[139] Drawing on Locke, Spencer believed that College Green could not abolish itself for two reasons: the parliament lacked the consent of the people to do so, and the passing of political power from one body to another was unconstitutional.[140] The *Anti-Union* periodical, which was associated with the Irish bar, printed a letter in January 1799 confirming such a view, quoting directly from Locke to suggest that the delivery 'of the people into the SUBJECTION of a FOREIGN power' marked the 'dissolution of the government'.[141] In separate works, George Barnes and Matthew Weld, both prominent barristers, cited Locke while making the case that any attempt by the Irish legislature to (in Weld's words) 'annihilate the Constitution of the Lords and Commons of Ireland' would result in power returning to the people and (presumably) fresh elections returning a new parliament.[142]

[137] John Locke, *Two Treatises of Government*, ed. Peter Laslett (Cambridge: Cambridge University Press, 1988), p. 412.

[138] Ibid., p. 362. Locke's emphasis. [139] *Report of the Debate of the Irish Bar*, p. 8.

[140] Ibid., p. 9. [141] *Anti-Union*, no. 14 (26 January 1799), p. 55.

[142] Weld, *No Union!*, p. 23; George Barnes, *The Rights of the Imperial Crown of Ireland Asserted and Maintained, Against Edward Cooke, Esq., Reputed Author of a Pamphlet, Entitled* "Arguments For and Against an Union, &c." (Dublin: W. Gilbert, 1799), p. 72.

The Lockean argument also carried considerable weight among anti-unionist opinion formally outside the Irish bar. William Drennan, the United Irishman, claimed that 'the principles of John Locke' were the foundation stone of the 'republican part of the constitution'.[143] This implied that the Irish legislature – despite its considerable representative flaws in the eyes of Drennan – symbolised the proud virtue of self-government, with its removal threatening to plunge Ireland into 'provinciality and servitude'.[144] Drennan explicitly claimed that sovereignty rested within the Irish people and not College Green, meaning that the assembly did not possess legal authority to agree to union.[145] The right to resist any attempt by political representatives to 'destroy his Constituent' was vigorously asserted by another pamphleteer writing under the pseudonym of 'Irishman', who utilised the natural law theories of Locke, Hugo Grotius and Samuel Pufendorf to suggest that 'the form of Government' could not be fundamentally altered without first seeking the consent of the 'People'.[146] In this reading, the 'sovereign' was not the same thing as the 'government', providing a distinctive Irish engagement with Rousseauean ideas of power.[147]

Unionists combined a curious blend of respect for Locke and disdain for interpretations of his work that stressed the sovereignty of the people. The Lockean insistence of anti-unionists on an illegal transfer of power from one legislative body to another was condemned as a wilful distortion of the terms of incorporating union. The power of government was not being transferred 'to any other hands', as union presupposed an equal share of the spoils of sovereignty.[148] Sylvester Douglas, British lawyer, MP and former Chief Secretary of Ireland, published a pro-union speech through a Dublin printing house in 1799, which lamented that Locke's 'metaphysical principles have become the groundwork of the vain wisdom and false

[143] Drennan, *Letter to Pitt*, p. 43. By 'republican', Drennan was referring to the 'democratic' aspect of mixed government, thus adhering to the United Irishmen's advanced doctrine of imagining an Irish republic without monarchical or aristocratic elements.

[144] Ibid., p. 41. [145] Ibid., p. 46.

[146] 'An Irishman', *Reasons Against a Union, in which* 'Arguments For and Against a Union', *Supposed to Have Come From a Person in High Station, are Particularly Considered* (Dublin: G. Folingsby, 1798), pp. 3–4. The authorship of this pamphlet has been attributed to one John Kelly: McCormack, *Pamphlet Debate*, p. 73.

[147] This theme is the focus of Richard Tuck, *The Sleeping Sovereign: The Invention of Modern Democracy* (Cambridge: Cambridge University Press, 2015).

[148] 'Author of *The Necessity of an Incorporate Union*', *Competency of the Parliaments*, p. 15. Also see the same anonymous author's pamphlet, *Necessity of an Incorporate Union Between Great Britain & Ireland Proved From the Situation of both Kingdoms: with a Sketch of the Principles upon which it Ought to be Formed* (London: J. Wright, 1799), p. 83.

philosophy'. Chief among these was the 'mischievous principle of the direct sovereignty of the people'.[149] In the Irish House of Lords, Lord Minto condemned the 'juvenile refinements of political metaphysics' or 'the early puerilities of those who may have read their Locke without reading history, or in reading Locke have forgotten their history'. He believed that a constitution provided the legal framework for a state and society, setting out the ground rules to ensure the welfare of its people. The right to resist legitimate government, as advocated by anti-unionist readings of Locke, was equated with anarchy, and as such, Minto concluded, was incompatible with the 'tranquillity and peace of the people'. In Minto's reasoning, the primary duty of the sovereign was protection of the people.[150] While this was a direct Lockean inflection, Minto strongly opposed the more controversial idea that sovereignty resided outside of the sovereign.

Not all the contributions to the debate explicitly drew on, or rebuffed, constitutional authorities such as Blackstone and Locke when addressing the question of whether the Irish parliament possessed the ability to legislate for union. Edward Cooke dealt with the objection that the Irish parliament did not possess the competency to end its existence without recourse to such legal authorities. In every circumstance, governments should follow the mantra of 'the general good', even if it meant far-reaching constitutional reform. Union, Cooke asserted, came in the same vein as the Reformation, the Revolution of 1688 and the legislative connection between England and Scotland: major constitutional alterations that were opposed by many contemporaries, but ultimately vindicated by history.[151] Indeed, the logic of Cooke's stance was fleshed out and given a particular Irish cadence by Richard Edgeworth: if College Green was endowed with the right to embrace legislative independence in 1782 because it was 'useful to Ireland', then it followed that College Green possessed the ability to accept union in 1800 based on the same precondition.[152]

Anti-unionists scoffed at the idea that the loss of self-government was 'useful to Ireland' or promised to contribute to the 'happiness of the people'. One of the angriest yet most amusing denunciations of Cooke and the wider pro-union case came anonymously from Charles Kendal Bushe. Bushe was one of the most distinguished lawyers of the age, later rising to become Lord Chief Justice of the King's Bench for Ireland; but in his anti-union tirade, *Cease Your Funning*, he did not hold back in

[149] Douglas, *Speech of the Right Honourable Sylvester Douglas*, pp. 6–7.
[150] Minto, *Speech of Lord Minto*, pp. 129–30. [151] [Cooke], *Arguments*, p. 42.
[152] Edgeworth, *Substance of Three Speeches*, p. 4.

attacking British designs. In a later review of Bushe's career, Lord Brougham, the former Lord Chancellor, paid the Irish lawyer the highest compliment by comparing his pamphlet to Jonathan Swift's political satire.[153] In *Cease Your Funning*, Bushe ironically attacked Cooke for accidentally continuing the destructive agenda of the United Irishmen – in other words, conspiring to pull down the Irish parliament – in a bid to tarnish the unionist cause. Bushe also sank his teeth into Cooke's insistence that a parliament can terminate itself in the name of the 'general good'. Cooke, according to Bushe,

> repeats the sophism of Rousseau in defence of suicide – that reason being given to man to achieve happiness, he has a right to destroy himself whenever it tells him death is preferable to life. He knows that delusive argument was easily answered by Rousseau himself, and therefore urges it as a mock defence for what he hints to be political suicide.[154]

Bushe was drawing here, somewhat mischievously, on Rousseau's meditation on suicide found in his novel, *Julie, or the New Heloise*, which was published in 1761.[155] This conceptualisation of Cooke's case for union as an act of 'political suicide' had rhetorical traction, with several other anti-unionists deploying similar terminology.[156] Like the suicide of an individual, the notion of a parliament wilfully embracing oblivion could be depicted at once as deviant, illegal, and immoral. According to Bushe, the 'object of Parliament' is the 'general good'. How, then, he asked, was the 'general good' enhanced by the destruction of a parliament? 'This would be very schoolboyish', concluded Bushe, 'if it was not very wicked'.[157]

Most unionists ignored the 'suicide' analogy, reminding readers instead that incorporating union implied a fusion of the British and Irish parliaments, not the extinction of the latter.[158] Theobald McKenna was, then,

[153] Henry, Lord Brougham, *Historical Sketches of Statesmen who Flourished in the Time of George III, to which are added Remarks on the French Revolution*, third series (London: Charles Knight and Co., 1843), p. 229.

[154] Bushe, *Cease Your Funning*, pp. 42–3.

[155] See Daniel Gordon, 'From act to fact: the transformation of suicide in Western thought', *Historical Reflections*, vol. 42, no. 2 (2016), pp. 35–6.

[156] Charles Ball, *An Union Neither Necessary or Expedient for Ireland: Being an Answer to the Author of* Arguments For and Against an Union, Between Great Britain and Ireland, Considered (Dublin: William Porter, 1798), p. 22; 'An Irish Logician', *An Union to be Subjection, Proved from Mr C's Own Words in his Arguments For and Against. In Two Parts. Part I* (Dublin: J. Rice, 1799), p. 22.

[157] Bushe, *Cease Your Funning*, p. 43.

[158] [Cooke], *Arguments*, p. 14; 'A Freeman', *Observations on Mr Bousfield's Letter, etc.* (Cork: Cork Advertiser Office, 1799), p. 13.

something of an exception. In closing the preface of his second pro-union pamphlet, McKenna explicitly turned the notion of political suicide into a virtue. 'The power, which a man has over his own existence', reasoned McKenna,

> may serve to illustrate the capacity of a sovereign jurisdiction to make engagements for its extinction. The law of morality does not allow a man to commit suicide; but if the act be necessary, it is justified by the end. A man may not shoot himself capriciously; but he may go upon a mine, with a certainty of being blown up, and if he saves an army by exposing himself, his conduct is heroism.[159]

The demise of the Irish parliament thus was not a senseless act of self-destruction, but a sacrifice worth making for the greater good, for perfecting the constitution in Ireland. The alternative, McKenna reminded more reform-minded readers, was the maintenance of a political elite divorced from the non-Anglican majority in Ireland, and with it some of the most grotesque forms of 'Old Corruption'.[160] Union with Britain was not an act of political suicide; for McKenna, it was the path to national redemption and religious liberty.

## '... And for Ever After, Be United into One Kingdom ...'

The debate ended on 1 August 1800. On that day in the Irish House of Commons, a bill was passed sanctioning incorporating union with Britain, paralleling similar legislation that had completed its parliamentary journey in London the previous month. On 1 January 1801, the United Kingdom of Great Britain and Ireland came into being, with the first article proclaiming that the arrangement would last 'forever'. [161] The tonal emphasis of finality over flexibility was ominous.[162]

The Irish parliament was, in a legal sense, transferred to London (in terms of powers and a portion of its representatives). But in a more emotive political reading, as offered by Irish opponents of the Union before and after 1800, the termination of College Green heralded an age without the dignity of self-government. The final line of Jonah Barrington's explosive attack on the Union in *Rise and Fall of the Irish Nation*, published in 1833, captured this sentiment perfectly, the substance of which later provided

[159] McKenna, *Constitutional Objections*, p. vi. [160] Ibid., pp. 53–4.
[161] Article One, Union with Ireland Act (1800), 39 & 40 Geo. 3, ch. 67.
[162] Nicholas Mansergh, *The Irish Question 1840–1921*, 3rd ed. (Toronto: University of Toronto Press, 1975), p. 318.

an ideological justification for the political campaigns for repealing the Union, Home Rule and, indeed, independence. With the enactment of the Union in 1801, Barrington lamented, 'An independent country was thus degraded into a province – Ireland, as a nation, was EXTINGUISHED'.[163]

Union came without Catholic Emancipation, and this fundamentally damaged the measure's legitimacy in Ireland. Pitt's proposal to introduce a measure to eliminate the penal laws alongside the union legislation was blocked by George III, who believed that such a course was a violation of his coronation oath.[164] It was a watershed moment: the vision of the union state as a religiously neutral political space was lost.[165] Had the remnants of the penal laws been abolished at the same time as the Union became operational, as Pitt, Cooke, and a number of other unionists wished to see, the subsequent history of the United Kingdom – and Ireland's place in it – may have been fundamentally different. With Catholic representation in parliament from 1801, there would have been no need for the mass mobilisation spearheaded by Daniel O'Connell during the 1820s that did much to highlight the gap between Irish ideas of representative government and its practice. Devoid of the agitation that defined 'O'Connellism', the gifted O'Connell might himself have quietly taken a parliamentary seat in the 1810s or 1820s and dedicated himself to lobbying for parliamentary reform. Such were the consequences of delaying Catholic Emancipation for twenty-nine years.

The corruption and bribery that lubricated the passage of the Union through the Irish parliament became a staple in nationalist historiography throughout the nineteenth and twentieth centuries.[166] By the 1830s, the story of the Acts of Union, as told by Barrington and O'Connell, centred on the unsavoury image of parliamentarians lining their pockets with titles, favours, or riches. Yet there was much more to the origins of the Union than these depictions, not least the intellectual investment made by advocates and opponents of the measure before the summer of 1800, many of which were soon forgotten. The debate that raged in print culture from the end of 1798 to the summer of 1800 was unprecedented in scale within Irish political life and shed light on contemporaneous understandings –

[163] Jonah Barrington, *Rise and Fall of the Irish Nation* (Dublin: James Duffy, 1833), p. 479.

[164] Geoghegan, *Irish Act of Union*, p. 163.

[165] James Livesey, 'The fall of the Catholic cosmopolitan: Charles O'Connor and the Catholic debate on the Act of Union', *Britain and the World*, vol. 6, no. 2 (2013), pp. 152–70.

[166] James Kelly, 'The historiography of the Act of Union', in Brown, Geoghegan, and Kelly (eds.), *Irish Act of Union*, pp. 5–36.

and misunderstandings – of ideas such as sovereignty, representation, and the workings of the 'constitution'. While deeply polemic and partisan, the argument over incorporating union was a complex dispute over the nature of representative government.

Unionists pressed the case that the constitutional fusion of Ireland and Britain promised the Irish a share in the governance of a new and expanded state, with access to the levers of imperial power. Union, in this reading, extended the principle of self-government beyond the national boundaries. The anti-unionist case largely rested on the antithesis of this argument, that the destruction of the parliament in Dublin symbolised the end of Irish self-government. The fear of the anti-unionists was that incorporation with Britain would result in a more distant and remote governance of Ireland, with Irish representatives powerless to effect change. The anti-unionism of Charles Kendal Bushe was, in this regard, telling. While fearful that union would constitutionally sanction British dominance over Ireland, Bushe was also dismissive of the calibre of the Irish political elite in an unreformed parliament. Union could not improve Ireland's condition, Bushe bitingly concluded, as such a measure would simply 'remove these representative delinquents into a more remote theatre for the exhibition of their depravity'.[167] An incorporating union alone was insufficient to deal with wider Irish political problems.

For the authors of political texts written from 1798 to 1800, union between Ireland and Britain was a pathway to several imagined destinations. Union was the perfection of the British constitution in Ireland; union was the usurpation of the Irish constitution; union was the means to achieve parliamentary reform and Catholic relief; union was the bulwark of the Protestant and conservative interest. The sheer variety in the imagining of the potential of a union reflected the fractured nature of Irish political life at the turn of the century, with the measure attracting utopian – and dystopian – commentaries. The hopes and fears of the late eighteenth-century generation of protagonists who contributed to the debate over the union illuminate many aspects of Irish political thought in the final days of the Irish parliament in College Green, particularly contemporaneous understandings of the boundaries of sovereignty, the design of self-government, and the political rights of the 'people', however defined. From 1801, the experiment was finally operational, with the arrival of 100 Irish MPs to London. The theory of union could now be tested through practice.

[167] Bushe, *Cease Your Funning*, p. 7.

CHAPTER 2

# *Reform, Religion, and Radicalism*
## *Extending the British Constitution in Ireland*

> [Ireland] may fairly be said to be an anomaly in the history of government.[1]
>
> John Joseph Dillon (1810)

> The nation had become a nation of politicians.[2]
>
> Thomas Wyse (1829)

The quasi-colonial Irish parliament was consigned to history in 1801 when Ireland became an integral component of the United Kingdom. The Acts of Union of 1800 mimicked the 1707 Anglo-Scottish settlement; if history repeated itself, Ireland would replicate the 'success story' of Scotland in embracing its nearest neighbour, creating a mutually prosperous new polity.[3] But Ireland did not follow the Scottish script. The transition into a unitary constitutional entity from 1801 was blighted by the appearance of stubborn points of national difference that worked against the realisation of a truly 'United' Kingdom. The Irish executive in Dublin Castle, headed by the Lord Lieutenant, was retained, separate from and unaccountable to the Irish legislative members of parliament.[4] Article six of the Union legislation facilitated a free trade arrangement between Ireland and Britain, but this took several decades to implement in full. Mirroring the separate political executive housed in Dublin Castle was the maintenance of an Irish exchequer, ensuring that the national debt remained *Irish*: the two exchequers were only amalgamated in 1817, when

1 *Two Memoirs upon the Catholic Question, with an Essay upon the History and Effect of the Coronation Oath* (Bath: Meyler and Son, 1810), p. 54.

2 *Historical Sketch of the Late Catholic Association of Ireland*, 2 vols. (London: Henry Colburn, 1829), i, p. 340.

3 Richard Whatmore, *Terrorists, Anarchists, and Republicans: The Genevans and the Irish in a Time of Revolution* (Princeton, NJ: Princeton University Press, 2019), p. xiv.

4 Douglas Kanter, *The Making of British Unionism, 1740–1848: Politics, Government and the Anglo-Irish Constitutional Relationship* (Dublin: Four Courts Press, 2009), p. 78.

Ireland was close to bankruptcy.[5] Union provided legislative fusion between the Irish and British parliaments, but not executive or financial incorporation.

The Union of 1707 was much cleaner in managing the political and economic integration of England and Scotland. Indeed, on a comparative basis, the differences between the 1707 and 1800 Unions disadvantaged the Irish.[6] Scotland retained independence in the spheres of law, education and religion after 1707, whereas Ireland pined for similar institutions of national pride.[7] The Scots were co-opted into British expansionism relatively seamlessly during the nineteenth century, while the Irish found themselves on the receiving end of colonial-esque 'special' legislation (to use the contemporary euphemism). This was in keeping with the spirit of what Edward Wakefield, the respected English statistician, described as the 'separate colonial government' in Ireland, which contradicted the lofty ideals of the Acts of Union.[8] These were sizeable political and economic issues, but above all else, it was the political exclusion of the majority of the Irish population, on the basis of the remaining penal laws, that defined the antagonism at the heart of the Union during the early decades of the nineteenth century.[9]

Withholding full civic rights for Catholics undermined the reconciling potential of the Union from its inception. Reflecting on the passage of the Acts of Union in 1813, John Bernard Trotter, the Ulster-born former private secretary to Charles James Fox, highlighted that the new arrangement had merely perpetuated asymmetries of power in Ireland. 'The Minister of the day', Trotter recorded,

> in accomplishing his splendid but illusive object, treated only with the descendants of the English in Ireland, who surrendered their exclusive power in that Island, for the more extended and dazzling privileges of the Empire. The people at large however, which the Roman Catholics of Ireland may be without impropriety styled, were left out of the arrangement then made, and their rights and privileges long withheld, after the season of

[5] Cormac Ó Gráda, *Ireland: A New Economic History, 1780–1939* (Oxford: Oxford University Press, 1994), pp. 44–5. R. D. C. Black, *Economic Thought and the Irish Question, 1817–1970* (Cambridge: Cambridge University Press, 1960), p. 2.

[6] Alvin Jackson, *The Two Unions: Ireland, Scotland, and the Survival of the United Kingdom, 1707–2007* (Oxford: Oxford University Press, 2012), p. 187.

[7] Colin Kidd, *Unions and Unionisms: Political Thought in Scotland, 1500–2000* (Cambridge: Cambridge University Press, 2008), p. 5.

[8] Edward Wakefield, *An Account of Ireland, Statistical and Political*, 2 vols. (London: Longman, Hurst, Rees, Orme, and Brown, 1812), ii, p. 325.

[9] R. F. Foster, *Words Alone: Yeats and His Inheritances* (Oxford: Oxford University Press, 2011), p. 29.

English apprehension had passed away, were neither restored, adjusted or opened, for them.[10]

The persistence of religious discrimination from 1801 until the belated coming of Catholic Emancipation in 1829 profoundly shaped the Irish political imagination; the expectations for full civil inclusion into the new British-Irish state, an alluring feature of the union debates, morphed into frustration with the new structures and, very quickly, became a powerful grievance.

The penal laws were far from a codified constitutional tradition, and the impact of successive discriminatory legislation was varied.[11] Parts of the penal laws had been diluted through a suite of relief acts during the second half of the eighteenth century, which, for example, enabled Irish Catholics to purchase land (albeit with the proviso that the property in question should not be connected to parliamentary representation).[12] In 1793, Irish Catholics were enfranchised, a significant milestone which underpinned the later campaigns for full Emancipation and the Repeal of the Union from the 1820s through to the 1840s.[13] These concessions did not come willingly from the Irish parliament but were imposed by successive British administrations, often in the context of imperial crisis or military conflict with a foreign power, with a resultant need for (Catholic) recruits.[14] These reforms tacitly admitted the failure to 'Protestantise' Ireland and the limitations of the British state's control over Ireland; concessions were made to Catholics in an attempt to bridge the gap between the Protestant ethos of the constitution and the realities of Irish demography. Late eighteenth-century liberal commentators such as Adam Smith and Edmund Burke highlighted the counterproductive nature of the penal laws, which they believed entrenched Catholic alienation from the state apparatus in Britain and Ireland, inadvertently creating the conditions for political unrest to thrive.[15] Indeed, given the acceptance of Catholics into

[10] John Bernard Trotter, *Five Letters to an Eminent Character on Catholic Relief, the Affairs of Ireland, and the Conduct of the New Parliament* (Dublin: C. Crookes, 1813), p. 3.

[11] S. J. Connolly, *Religion, Law and Power: The Making of Protestant Ireland, 1660–1760* (Oxford: Oxford University Press, 1992), pp. 263–313. Thomas Bartlett, *The Fall and Rise of the Irish Nation: The Catholic Question, 1690–1830* (Dublin: Gill & Macmillan, 1992), p. 20.

[12] Stephen Small, *Political Thought in Ireland, 1776–1798: Republicanism, Patriotism and Radicalism* (Oxford: Oxford University Press, 2002), p. 137.

[13] Bartlett, *Fall and Rise*, p. 172.

[14] S. J. Connolly, *Divided Kingdom: Ireland, 1630–1800* (Oxford: Oxford University Press, 2008), p. 417. Ultán Gillen, 'Ascendancy Ireland, 1660–1800', in Richard Bourke and Ian McBride (eds.), *The Princeton History of Modern Ireland* (Princeton, NJ: Princeton University Press, 2016), p. 68.

[15] James Stafford, *The Case of Ireland: Commerce, Empire and the European Order, 1750–1848* (Cambridge: Cambridge University Press, 2022), p. 18.

property ownership and the electoral franchise, the maintenance of a bar on their right to sit as parliamentarians was condemned by early nineteenth-century observers such as William Parnell as more of an 'insult' than an 'injury'.[16] The remnants of the penal laws were, in other words, unjustified and irrational. If Irish Catholics were entrusted to vote *for* parliamentary representatives, the rationale for withholding the right to *serve* as representatives appeared illogical.

If the material consequences of the penal laws had diminished by the early nineteenth century, the psychological dimensions remained acute.[17] In 1812, Denys Scully, a prominent campaigner for Catholic Emancipation, emphasised the impact of this ongoing exclusion on Irish political mindsets:

> Now, the advantages flowing from a seat in the Legislature, it is well known, are not confined to the *individual representative*. They extend to all his family, friends, and connections; or, in other words, to every Protestant in Ireland ... Hence, every Protestant feels himself, and really is, more firm and secure in the favour of the Laws, more powerful in society, more free in his energies, more elevated in life, than his Catholic neighbour of equal merit, property, talents, and education. He alone feels and possesses the right and the legal capacity to be a Legislator, and *this consciousness is actual power*.[18]

The logic of Scully's argument was that the penal laws produced a constitutional oddity. Unfranchised Protestants enjoyed virtual representation in parliament by virtue of their denomination; Catholics, some of whom possessed the vote, were excluded from virtual representation because of the Anglican ethos of the state. Edmund Burke had warned of the corrosive constitutional damage of this exclusion in 1792; the passage of the Union, with the broken promise of Catholic Emancipation, newly intensified this feeling.[19] In essence, the British constitutional decree of an enlightened property order as the basis of representative government did not function in Ireland. The penal laws may have been petty, but this was

[16] 'An Irish Country Gentleman' [William Parnell], *An Inquiry into the Cause of Popular Discontents in Ireland* (London: J. Wallis, 1804), p. 14.

[17] Ian McBride, *Eighteenth-Century Ireland: The Isle of Slaves* (Dublin: Gill & Macmillan, 2009), p. 245.

[18] Denys Scully, *Statement of the Penal Laws, which Aggrieve the Catholics of Ireland*, 2 vols. (Dublin: H. Fitzpatrick, 1812), i, pp. 75, 77. Italics in original.

[19] Edmund Burke, *A Letter from the Right Hon. Edmund Burke, MP in the Kingdom of Great Britain, to Sir Hercules Langrishe, MP, on the Subject of Roman Catholics of Ireland, and the Propriety of Admitting Them to the Elective Franchise Consistently with the Principles of the Constitution Established at the Revolution* (Dublin: J. Byrne, 1792), p. 5.

not how notable Catholic political commentators such as Scully interpreted them. Instead, such Catholic discourse emphasised that exclusion from representation was one of the gravest political conditions that could befall a society.

## Character, Representation, and Revolt

The debate over the penal laws during the early nineteenth century intertwined with the wider question of 'character'. The idea that nations or peoples displayed certain character traits was a commonly articulated Enlightenment concept and was often used to demonstrate a global hierarchy of societies.[20] The 'wild' Irish, in contrast with the 'civilised' English, was a trope deployed countless times through the centuries.[21] Writing in 1748, David Hume insisted that the most important aspect in shaping national character was not the environment or climate, but the nature of political institutions. Hume held the English up as a special case: with governmental structures that fused 'monarchy, aristocracy and democracy', political power was shared, producing an unwavering commitment to 'liberty and independency' among the people.[22] A union between Britain and Ireland was, therefore, partly envisaged as a method to 'improve' the Irish, to export British constitutional liberties into Ireland.

Numerous engagements with Irish 'character' appeared in print during the early nineteenth century. These depictions were often reflected through the prism of the perceived rural lawlessness of the Irish countryside, with agrarian violence and secret societies carrying into the era of the Union. The notion that Ireland was different from Britain and required 'special solutions' (often based on coercive legislation and draconian policing) was widespread.[23] The English statistician Edward Wakefield left a detailed account of aspects of Irish character that he encountered in tours during the first decade of the century. His description of the 'poorer orders' stressed their barbarism and contempt for structures of British law

[20] For a provocative take, see Seamus Deane, *Strange Country: Modernity and Nationhood in Irish Writing since 1790* (Oxford: Oxford University Press, 1997), pp. 49–56.

[21] Roberto Romani, 'British views on Irish national character, 1800–1847: an intellectual history', *History of European Ideas*, vol. 23, nos. 5–6 (1997), p. 194.

[22] David Hume, 'Of national characters', *in Essays: Moral, Political and Literary* (New York: Longmans, Green and Co., 1898), pp. 249, 252. Notoriously, this essay also contains Hume's assertion that non-white people are 'naturally inferior' to white people (p. 252).

[23] K. Theodore Hoppen, *Governing Hibernia: British Politicians and Ireland, 1800–1921* (Oxford: Oxford University Press, 2016), pp. 48–9; Jay R. *Roszman, Outrage in the Age of Reform: Irish Agrarian Violence, Imperial Insecurity, and British Governing Policy, 1830–1845* (Cambridge: Cambridge University Press, 2022), pp. 17–28.

and justice. This regrettable trait was, he believed, partly caused by misgovernment. 'Notwithstanding that the inhabitants of this island have been for centuries under the nominal influence of British laws', Wakefield noted, 'yet few traces of happiness, arising from wise political institutions, are to be found in any part of the country'.[24] Ireland, particularly its recent history under the Union, represented a paradox: a place geographically close to the seat of British power (and thus a prime European 'civilising' force), but treated more as a 'distant province than as a component part of the British empire'.[25]

Similar sentiments on the relationship between Irish national character and the state of government shaped the work of the Scottish philosopher Daniel Dewar. Dewar's work on the question of character formation was steeped in Hume's thought. Dewar, an Irish speaker, travelled through Ireland and was appalled at the destitution he saw in the countryside. While the 'native Irish' were 'fond of knowledge', the majority, according to Dewar, 'are sunk in the lowest state of ignorance and degradation'.[26] The destructive vices of 'ignorance, superstition and barbarism' were rampant in Ireland.[27] Like Hume, Dewar emphasised the importance of political institutions in instilling moral virtue and purpose in a people. 'Character' flowed first and foremost from a 'free government'.[28] It stood to reason, then, that the wretched condition of the majority of the Irish was primarily the product of defective political institutions.[29] The penal laws were singled out by Dewar as the prime example of a state-sponsored project that retarded moral and civic growth in Ireland. Religious discrimination merely increased poverty in Ireland, strengthened the Catholic Church's authority over the majority of the people and encouraged a hatred of Protestantism. As a political project, Dewar affirmed, the penal laws had been disastrous.[30] He believed that Catholic Emancipation would not weaken the framework of the Protestant constitution. A 'few Catholic noblemen and gentlemen' in parliament were not a constitutional threat; indeed, Dewar cast the potential of their presence within the national assembly as a moment of reconciliation.[31]

The probing of the question of character intermingled with the politics of Catholic Emancipation. The notion that Catholics, because of the

[24] Wakefield, *An Account of Ireland*, ii, pp. 753, 836. [25] Ibid., ii, p. 326.

[26] Daniel Dewar, *Observations on the Character, Customs and Superstitions of the Irish; and on Some of the Causes which have Retarded the Moral and Political Improvement of Ireland* (London: Gale and Curtis, 1812), ii, p. 350. Dewar's book was published as one volume, but its pagination follows a two-volume model.

[27] Ibid., i, p. 25. [28] Ibid., i, p. 112. [29] Ibid., i, p. 5. [30] Ibid., ii, pp. 17–19.

[31] Ibid., ii, p. 56.

religious doctrines of their church, were 'unreliable fellow citizens' permeated the politics of anti-Emancipation during the period of the passage of the Acts of Union.[32] This impulse was bolstered considerably with the publication of Sir Richard Musgrave's history of the 1798 rebellion (1801). Musgrave was a former member of the Irish parliament and was well known for his virulent anti-Catholic views.[33] His *Memoirs of the Different Rebellions in Ireland* did much to propagate the view (which was embraced by nineteenth-century opponents of Emancipation) that the United Irish rebellion had a religiously sectarian motive, driven by Catholic hatred of the Protestant order. It followed that 1798 was not a republican rising, but a Catholic one, akin to the 1641 massacres. Musgrave divorced the rebellion from its French Revolutionary context, overlooking the influence of radical Presbyterian conceptions of republican liberty within the Irish melting pot, in favour of an account that stressed Catholic conspiracy as the motor of political revolution.[34] The origins of the rebellion, in Musgrave's reading, lay not in the rights of man or English tyranny in Ireland, but in bigoted Catholic secret societies such as the Whiteboys. The book was an unrepentant diatribe against Catholicism, seeing popish plots constantly lurking in the shadows of Irish society.[35] Musgrave sponsored the idea of Catholicism as an 'imperium in imperio', with two competing sovereigns, one civil, the other ecclesiastical, vying for authority in Ireland. The result was inevitable collision, producing the conditions for atrocity.[36] Barbarism in Ireland stemmed from popery, and Catholicism had warped the Irish character, affirmed Musgrave: the political exclusion of Catholics was thus not only warranted but necessary for the safety of the realm. In conjuring a history of 1798 which turned the Irish majority into secret agents of Rome, Musgrave foregrounded much of the argument over Catholic Emancipation after 1801. Indeed, Musgrave made his intention clear in dedicating the book to Lord Cornwallis: 'History, which is a mirror of past times, is the best guide to the statesman'.[37] The character of the Irish majority, as painted by Musgrave, justified their continuing political exclusion.

[32] J. C. D. Clark, *English Society, 1688–1832* (Cambridge: Cambridge University Press, 1985), p. 355.

[33] For Musgrave, see James Kelly, *Sir Richard Musgrave, 1746–1818: Ultra-Protestant Ideologue* (Dublin: Four Courts Press, 2009).

[34] Sir Richard Musgrave, *Memoirs of the Different Rebellions in Ireland, From the Arrival of the English* (Dublin: John Milliken, 1801), p. 305.

[35] Jim Smyth, 'Anti-Catholicism, conservatism, and conspiracy: Sir Richard Musgrave's *Memoirs of the Different Rebellions in Ireland*', *Eighteenth-Century Life*, vol. 22, no. 3 (1998), pp. 70–1.

[36] Musgrave, *Memoirs*, p. 4. [37] Ibid., p. v.

Even Cornwallis found Musgrave's book too relentless and disowned the dedication.[38] Musgrave's attempt to discredit liberal interventions in Ireland that might lead to further concessions to Catholics so concerned the Sidmouth administration (which assumed power following Pitt's resignation in 1801) that a reply was quietly commissioned.[39] In 1803, Francis Plowden, an English Catholic barrister and polemist, issued the quasi-official rebuttal to Musgrave. Plowden had published a number of weighty tomes on contemporary political questions, many of which stressed his 'love for the [British] Constitution'.[40] While Plowden celebrated the constitutional monarchy and mixed form of parliamentary authority that distinguished the British political and legal systems, the remnants of the penal laws – the Oath of Supremacy in particular – threatened to poison the Union. Irish Catholics were willing to recognise the monarch as 'the supreme head of the civil establishment of the Church of England', Plowden asserted, but their religious doctrine was incompatible with the King's proclaimed spiritual authority. He concluded with an appeal to parliament to address this 'cruelty' which actively discriminated against 'millions of well disposed, able and loyal subjects of his Majesty'.[41]

Even though Plowden's response to Musgrave was a commission, its message was very similar to his earlier history of the British constitution. 'This work is intended as an act of justice to the Irish nation', Plowden proudly pronounced. 'We are now one people'.[42] *Pace* Musgrave's depiction of barbarity and atrocity, Plowden's Ireland was one of a historic nation with a cultured past that stretched back to antiquity. Plowden's quest for 'historical justice' propelled him towards refuting Musgrave's (and others') portrait of the Irish as lawless. The contemporary problems that blighted Ireland were the product of gross misgovernment and constitutional neglect, not an inherently deviant national character.[43] English policy stoked the fires of religious difference in Ireland following the Reformation, instead of encouraging conciliation and fusion. While

38 Kelly, *Musgrave*, p. 122.

39 Stuart Andrews, *Irish Rebellions: Protestant Polemic, 1798–1900* (Basingstoke: Palgrave Macmillan, 2006), pp. 36–7.

40 Francis Plowden, *A Short History of the British Empire During the Last Twenty Months; Viz. from May 1792 to the Close of the Year 1793* (Dublin: P. Byrne, 1794), p. 3.

41 Francis Plowden, *The Constitution of the United Kingdom of Great Britain & Ireland: Civil and Ecclesiastical* (London: T. Sutton, 1802), p. 532.

42 Francis Plowden, *An Historical Review of the State of Ireland, from the Invasion of that Country under Henry II to its Union with Great Britain, on the 1st of January, 1801*, 2 vols. (London: T. Egerton, 1803), i, p. iv.

43 Ibid., i, pp. 20–2.

constitutional liberties spread through England from the revolution of 1688, conquest and coercion were its legacies in Ireland (or the 'perverted operation of the Revolution of 1688 in Ireland', as the Foxite John Bernard Trotter put it in 1813).[44] The rebellion of 1798 was not, as Musgrave asserted, a Catholic-inspired conspiracy, but a manifestation of the political and social problems that plagued Ireland through poor governance. Plowden was also at pains to remind readers of the cross-denominational appeal of the United Irish movement in certain parts of Ireland.[45] Regardless of the design of the revolutionaries, rebellion in Ireland was, for Plowden, a tragedy. He depicted union as a natural consequence of the political unrest of the 1790s, but one with the potential to ameliorate Ireland.[46] Plowden hoped that the 'most beneficial effects' would flow to Ireland as a result of 'this national incorporation', that the Irish would prosper with the eradication of the 'evil' that underpinned their former governing structures.[47] While Plowden's book was criticised by hostile reviewers for its long-windedness, its central thesis – that poor political institutions were the cause of Ireland's wretched poverty and social unrest – was abundantly clear to readers.[48]

The literary spat between Musgrave and Plowden was ostensibly about the rebellion of 1798, but in essence concerned the much larger question of the character of the Irish. For Musgrave, Catholic bigotry was the cause and consequence of Irish discontent; the rebellion of 1798 was a mask for an invidious form of sectarian cleansing. Plowden discounted the sectarian element as a driving force of the rebellion and highlighted the toxic consequences of state-sponsored persecution of Catholics. Disloyalty and the allure of separatism in Ireland sprang not from Catholicism, but from quasi-tyrannical rule. The quarrel continued for some time after 1803, with the arrival of new works by both men which repeated much of their earlier arguments.[49] Despite their profound differences, Musgrave and Plowden shared one key characteristic: both men were enthusiastic *unionists*, believing that the incorporation of Ireland into the British system was the path to political, social and moral improvement. While the character of the Irish was contested, 'unionism' had emerged as a consensus point

[44] Ibid., i, p. 190; Trotter, *Five Letters*, p. 12. [45] Plowden, *Historical Review*, ii, p. 708.
[46] Ibid., ii, p. 1076. [47] Ibid., i, p. 10. [48] Andrews, *Irish Rebellions*, pp. 38–9.
[49] [Sir Richard Musgrave], *Strictures Upon an* Historical Review of the State of Ireland*; by Francis Plowden, Esq. or, a Justification of the Conduct of the English Governments in that Country, From the Reign of Henry the Second to the Union of Great Britain and Ireland* (London: F. C. and J. Rivington, 1804). Francis Plowden, *The History of Ireland, From its Union with Great Britain in January 1801, to October 1810*, 3 vols. (Dublin: John Boyce, 1811).

across the political spectrum. Yet this was never quite unanimous: a few significant voices emerged advocating the resurrection of an Irish parliament, drawing on a particular interpretation of Hume's theory that a people's government defined the people themselves.

For Thomas Townshend, a former member of the Irish parliament, the passage of the Union was a double-edged sword. Townshend was an active pamphleteer during the French Revolutionary debate, issuing treatises that stressed the British constitution as the model of government par excellence.[50] In the year when the Union became operational, he published several political works which advocated Catholic Emancipation and British liberties on the one hand, while lamenting the loss of a distinctive Irish polity on the other. Townshend depicted government as a 'moral seminary' for a population, with a 'free government' heralded as the noblest prize in human history. 'It was not to the physical influences of sky or atmosphere that the erect Englishman of old times owed his glory', he observed, 'it was to his government'.[51] Misgovernment in previous ages had left Ireland in a wretched political, economic and social state. English (and later British) policy had crushed Ireland's commerce, largely to the advantage of the larger island; the feudal nature of Ireland's agrarian economy created a society with only two social classes, landlord and lowly tenant, without 'any active, intervening classes'. On top of this, the penal laws had a corrosive effect on the Irish mind. In discriminating against a people based on their denomination, the 'sacredness of property', a central motif of the British constitution, was undermined in Ireland.[52] Despite these seemingly grave conditions, Townshend believed that a 'free parliament' in Ireland could undo the damage wrought by centuries of misrule. This belief was rooted in his earlier conception of government as a moral force within a society:

> Of all nations, perhaps, there is not once to which a resident parliament was so essential as to Ireland. She had some weighty grievances to redress, and which wanted the confederation of a deliberative assembly ... She had two classes to amalgamate into one people and that people she had to raise from

[50] Thomas Townshend, *Consideration on the Theoretical Spirit of the Times: on the Inefficacy of Theory to the Formation of Civil Government; on the Doctrines of Liberty and Equality; on the different Kinds of Government; and also, on the Pre-Eminent Merits of the British Constitution* (Cork: A. Edwards, 1793); *A Summary Defence of the Right Hon. Edmund Burke* (London: A. Edwards, 1796).

[51] Thomas Townshend, *General Opinions on the Conduct of Ministers with Respect to the Past and Present State of Ireland, and Inculcating the Justice and Policy of Catholic Emancipation* (London: Oriental Press, 1801), p. 17.

[52] Ibid., p. 21.

> depression, without exposing her tranquillity to sudden and violent efforts.[53]

Townshend lacked confidence that an incorporating union, which did not provide a distinctive Irish space for national debate, could fill this remit. It was the British, after all, who upheld the poisonous penal laws, demonstrating to the Irish majority that the state was bigoted.[54] The penal laws, Townshend concluded, made 'the ministry everything, and the people nothing'.[55]

The second United Irish rebellion of 1803 appeared to confirm some of the fears of Musgravean interpretation of the lawless Irish. By the turn of the century, the United Irish movement was in a dreadful state, broken by the suppression of the rebellion of 1798 and haemorrhaging northern Presbyterian radicals.[56] Without the promise of French military backing, the insurrection in 1803 was confined to brief skirmishes in Dublin and Kildare. While the United Irish force was led by Robert Emmet, a Dublin-born Protestant, the episode was swiftly viewed as 'another popish rebellion' by many critics.[57] Yet, as with 1798, the ideals driving the revolt sprang from democratic radicalism and a desire to create an Irish republic based on principles of popular sovereignty and representative government. The extraordinary revolutionary blueprint published by Emmet – the manifesto of 'the Provisional Government to the People of Ireland' – was seized by Crown forces before it could be distributed. The radical document outlined a vision of post-revolution Ireland in which church lands became property of the nation, a parliament based on population representation rather than property, and significant power devolved to each county to preserve law, order and justice.[58]

Tellingly, the radical Presbyterian element that animated much of the United Irish activism of the 1790s did not rise with Emmet. Northern Presbyterianism initially opposed the Union in 1800, but swiftly became reconciled to the measure, in the hope that an alliance with British

53 Ibid., pp. 28–9. 54 Ibid., p. 73.

55 Thomas Townshend, *Part of a Letter to a Noble Earl: Containing a Very Short Comment on the Doctrines and Facts of Sir Richard Musgrave's Quarto; and Vindicatory of the Yeomanry and Catholics of the City of Cork* (Dublin: P. Fitzpatrick, 1801), p. 42.

56 James G. *Patterson, In the Wake of the Great Rebellion: Republicanism, Agrarianism and Banditry in Ireland after 1798* (Manchester: Manchester University Press, 2008), p. 75.

57 Marianne Elliott, *Robert Emmet: The Making of a Legend* (London: Profile, 2003), p. 66.

58 The Provisional Government's address is printed in full in R. R. Madden, *The Life and Times of Robert Emmet, Esq.* (Dublin: James Duffy, 1847), pp. 303–17.

radicalism would lead to a successful campaign for parliamentary reform.[59] The association between violent insurrection and democratic radicalism tarnished the political programme of the United Irish movement; the separatist republicanism of Tone and Emmet was noticeably absent in the public debates after 1803, until the emergence of the radical wing of Young Ireland in the 1840s. William Drennan, the most prominent former member of the United Irishmen in the north, believed that Emmet's attempted revolt was complete folly. Drennan was a critic of the Union proposals in 1800,[60] but he quickly reconciled himself to Ireland's place in the United Kingdom. The example of revolutionary France, the great beacon of hope for the United Irish movement during its halcyon early days, was destroyed by the turn to violence and Napoleonic despotism; after the failure of the rebellion of 1798, Drennan looked to the British constitutional tradition instead as a model to balance liberty and order. As Drennan and the strain of northern Presbyterianism that he personified adapted to the new world order after 1800, a tentative unionism was constructed and infused with aspects of the radicalism of the United Irish movement.[61] Even within this political constituency, the 'Catholic question' was inescapable. In this sense, the rebellion of 1803 did little to alter the trajectory of political thought, which remained fixated on the question of Catholic representative rights and the connection between representation and property status in the British constitution.

## Catholic Questions, Uncertain Answers

In 1804, William Parnell published the first of several powerful interventions on the problems confronting Ireland during the early years of the Union. Parnell came from a landed family with connections to the Patriot faction in the Irish parliament during the 1780s and 1790s; he was also the maternal grandfather to the future leader of the Home Rule party, Charles Stewart Parnell. In Roy Foster's estimation, William Parnell was 'as radical a theorist as it was possible for an Irish Protestant landlord to be' in the

[59] Gerard Hall, *Ulster Liberalism, 1778–1876* (Dublin: Four Courts Press, 2010), p. 59. Jonathan Jeffrey Wright, *The 'Natural Leaders' and Their World: Politics, Culture and Society in Belfast, c.1801–1832* (Liverpool: Liverpool University Press, 2012), p. 52.

[60] William Drennan, *A Letter to the Right Honourable William Pitt* (Dublin: James Moore, 1799).

[61] Ian McBride, *Scripture Politics: Ulster Presbyterians and Irish Radicalism in the Late Eighteenth Century* (Oxford: Oxford University Press, 1998), p. 211.

early nineteenth century.[62] Parnell's analysis centred on the historical problems that had blighted Ireland – dysfunctional government, state-sanctioned property confiscations and religious discrimination – which had, he believed, continued to plague the country. Written in the aftermath of Emmet's rising in 1803, Parnell suggested that 'we hear much of the effects of rebellion in Ireland, but very little of their causes'. He rejected the notion that the rising had a religious motive, chiefly the creation of a Catholic ascendancy, by highlighting the Church's unbridled support for state power in other European countries. The problems facing Ireland that Parnell identified were multifaceted, ranging from the Irish internalising that they were a 'conquered people' to the influence of 'a republican party'.[63] Despite the depth of the challenges, Parnell believed that solutions were, tantalisingly, within the reach of the government. The failure to 'blend all distinctions between the race of conquerors and conquered' was a disastrous consequence of the incomplete conquest of Ireland, but one that could still be reversed *if* political equality was the guiding principle of the Union. With the Irish 'entirely incorporated with the people of England', with the liberties enshrined in the British constitution spreading throughout Ireland, the 'conqueror' and 'conquered' distinctions would melt away.[64]

At the heart of Parnell's argument was the belief that the penal laws were a contemporary manifestation of the medieval and early modern English conquest of Ireland, and their continuing existence reinforced the colonial relationship between the two countries. A lack of civic equity reinforced the religiously defined political hierarchy in Ireland, which underpinned the profound sectarian differences and fostered revolutionary fervour.[65] For all the radicalism of Parnell's message, he could not escape the prejudices of his station, declaring that 'the Popish religion' was an engine of 'slavery and superstition'. But the penal laws were insufficient to destroy Catholicism's hold over the population; barring Catholics from certain political rights was a half-hearted attempt to maintain the appearance of a Protestant kingdom, while the United Kingdom was a multi-denominational polity. For Parnell, the solution was strikingly clear: either Catholicism was annihilated in Ireland, or (and this was the more attractive and straightforward option) the legislation that prohibited Catholics from taking seats in parliament was repealed.[66] Failure to incorporate Catholic representation into the state would empower future Irish rebellion.

62 R. F. Foster, *Charles Stewart Parnell: The Man and His Family* (Hassocks: Harvester Press Ltd., 1979; first published 1976), p. 16.
63 [Parnell], *An Inquiry*, pp. 1–3. 64 Ibid., pp. 6–7. 65 Ibid., p. 11. 66 Ibid., pp. 16–19.

Parnell injected more vigour into his argument several years later with the publication of his *An Historical Apology for the Irish Catholics*. This offered a striking defence of Catholic Ireland in the face of Musgravean slights on historical character, suggesting that instances of rebellion in the past sprang from political injustices suffered by the Irish majority. 'The Catholics, by being excluded from all offices of trust and emolument', Parnell argued, 'lose all political consequence in the country'.[67] The difficulties in Ireland were created not by Catholicism, but the zeal of Protestant persecution of Catholicism. Discontent within Catholic Ireland, which sporadically spilled over into violence, was the manifestation of exclusion from the political and social spheres. The absence of Catholics from the structures of parliamentary government was the most glaring form of exclusion; but Parnell also emphasised the corrosive effect of informal discrimination in operation within Irish Protestant 'convivial societies' and the yeomanry. Such bigoted social choices, which hampered cross-denominational cohesion in Ireland, were legitimised by the penal laws.[68] Parnell believed that it was in Protestant Ireland's interest for the penal laws to be repealed. Security for the Irish minority had not flowed from an unfair concentration of power and privilege; instead, the powerful grievance of Catholic Ireland created instability.[69]

Other advocates of Catholic Emancipation supported Parnell's assertion that Irish unrest sprang not from 'Popery' but from arbitrary laws. John Joseph Dillon, a prominent barrister, forcefully set out the case in 1801 that the penal laws were unconstitutional in British law, as a century of repealed test laws had enshrined the concept that citizenship was defined by property, not denomination.[70] The title page of Dillon's pamphlet bore a quote by William Blackstone to demonstrate that the 'laws against Papists' sprang from 'the urgency of the times which produced them', and should not be treated as 'a standing system of law'.[71] The penal laws were, therefore, a political relic from a different era.[72] While Dillon's primary aim was to promote the plight of English Catholics (who, in contrast to their Irish counterparts, remained wholly unfranchised),

67 William Parnell, *An Historical Apology for the Irish Catholics*, 2nd ed. (Dublin: H. Fitzpatrick, 1807), p. 135.
68 Ibid., pp. 137–8. 69 Ibid., p. v.
70 'A Barrister' [John Joseph Dillon], *The Question, as to the Admission of Catholics to Parliament, Considered, upon the Principles of Existing Laws* (London: W. & C. Spilsbury, 1801), p. 3.
71 Ibid. The quote was from Blackstone's *Commentaries on the Laws of England*, 4 vols. (Oxford: Oxford University Press, 1765; first published 1763), iv, p. 57.
72 [Dillon], *The Question*, p. 22.

the case of Ireland could not be ignored. Denying Irish Catholics the right to sit in parliament represented a breakdown in the social contract, with the state refusing to enshrine political rights for a portion of its citizens. As it was the duty of the sovereign to 'provide for the remedy of grievances', the maintenance of civic discrimination based on religion undermined the concept of political obligation and thus the legitimacy of the state.[73]

There was, then, a potent argument that the anti-Catholic legislation in place at the beginning of the nineteenth century was a constitutional aberration that undermined the political principle linking property to citizenship. In bringing a petition for the relief of Catholics to parliament in 1805, Lord Grenville, the Pittite Tory and future Prime Minister, condemned the denial of civic rights to Catholics based on their denomination, and not their property status. He pleaded that Emancipation was not an encroachment on Protestant rights, but rather a means to enable 'equal participation' and to spread the 'full benefits of the British Laws and Constitution' throughout the polity.[74] Henry Grattan, who made his return to Irish politics by winning a parliamentary seat in Dublin in 1806, instructed the Commons to 'complete' the revolution of 1688, the foundational moment for constitutional monarchy in the United Kingdom, by binding Catholics to the state through the granting of the same political rights as their Protestant countrymen. In the absence of equality before the law, that revolution was blighted by its connection to 'the principles of slavery'.[75] Grattan later expanded on this theme, conceptualising 1688 not as a victory of Protestantism over Catholicism, but 'civil and religious liberty over oppression'.[76] Reference to a 'Protestant constitution', in this reading, was misleading. In a pamphlet dedicated to Grattan, William Russell queried the legitimacy of an exclusive political system, suggesting that a 'well-ordered State' was founded on laws that were applicable to all; any deviation from this ideal threatened a descent

[73] Ibid., pp. 58–9.

[74] *Catholic Emancipation: An Accurate Report of the Speeches Delivered in both Houses of the Imperial Parliament of Great Britain, on the Subject of the Petition of the Roman Catholics of Ireland, for a Repeal of the Existing Penal Laws* (Liverpool: W. Jones, 1805), pp. 7–8.

[75] Henry Grattan, *The Speech of Mr Grattan in the House of Commons, on the Catholic Question* (Dublin: J. & J. Carrick, 1806), pp. 32–3.

[76] Daniel Owen Madden (ed.), *The Select Speeches of the Right Hon. Henry Grattan; to which is added his Letter on the Union, with a Commentary on his Career and Character* (Dublin: James Duffy, 1845), p. 421.

into political oppression.[77] Like a number of other Protestant writers (such as Parnell), Russell made the case for Catholic Emancipation while condemning the tyranny of 'Popery'. Indeed, Russell believed the 'Papal System' fed on Irish grievances; Emancipation thus had the potential to shatter it from within.[78] With this result in mind, Russell asserted that Protestant Ireland had nothing to fear from political equality. As he put it, 'are we afraid that immediately after the passing of such a bill in Parliament, the Protestants will generally lose their understandings, and take to sprinkling holy water, and fumbling over beads, and saying Ave-Marias?'[79]

In stressing the injustice of excluding a portion of the population from representation based on their denomination, a number of pamphleteers drew on a constitutional idiom. John Ryan, a priest in Cork, published a pro-Emancipation pamphlet in 1809 that queried the logic of withholding British constitutional values from 'four millions of the population of the empire', warning that the penal laws fuelled hostility to the present order. Only someone with the 'heart of a rebel', or the 'intellect of one of our modern no-popery bigots', claimed Ryan, could stand over the ongoing political exclusion of Catholics.[80] Catholics desired 'free participation of the blessings of the British Constitution', recorded one reflective (anonymous) writer in 1810.[81] In the same year, John Joseph Dillon stated that 'exclusion from parliament' was the main grievance of Irish Catholics.[82] In stripping representation from property, Ireland had become, in Dillon's phrase, an 'anomaly' in governing theory.[83] The continuing exclusion of Irish Catholics from the British political nation bred unrest within the majority population in Ireland, who looked to their 'fellow [Protestant] citizens ... enjoying their full measure of freedom, and basking in the sunshine of the Constitution'.[84] Pro-Emancipation writers strongly pushed for Ireland's integration into the British constitution through common representative rights; but that same constitution, the creation

77 William Russell, *Catholic Emancipation Contended for, and Justified from the Words of Eminent Statesmen, and the Plain Deductions of Justice and Common Sense* (London: the author, 1807), p. 9.

78 Ibid., pp. 28–9. 79 Ibid., pp. 10–11.

80 John Ryan, *Reflections on an Important Subject, Respectfully Addressed to the Roman Catholics of Ireland* (Dublin: R. Coyne, 1809), p. 7.

81 *State of Ireland Considered, with an Enquiry into the History and Operation of Tithe; and a Plan for Modifying that System, and Providing an Adequate Maintenance for the Catholic and Presbyterian Clergy*, 2nd ed. (Dublin: Downes and Reilly, 1810), p. 148.

82 Dillon, *Two Memoirs upon the Catholic Question*, pp. 5–6. 83 Ibid., p. 54.

84 [Scully], *Statement of the Penal Laws*, i, pp. 77–8.

of a parliamentary union between the two countries, perpetuated Irish distinctiveness by opting for continuing exclusion.

## The Demagogue and the Veto

In 1812, the Catholic Committee, the main body that lobbied for Emancipation, was replaced by the more assertive Catholic Board. The increasing belligerence of the Catholic Board was driven by frustration with the lack of success of the Committee and the emergence of the 'veto' controversy. The veto was a political initiative by proponents of Emancipation in parliament, which aimed to alleviate Protestant concerns about Catholic relief through a quid pro quo of a royal veto over episcopal appointments. Such thinking was a development of the long-established notion that the state should pay the priesthood to gain a degree of political control over Catholic Ireland. The young Irish Tory, John Wilson Croker, for example, believed that Emancipation was 'expedient' if the state's authority was enhanced over the Catholic Church.[85] Such compromise positions, especially the use of a veto over church appointments, however, inflamed sections of Catholic Ireland. This was a critical moment in the political organisation of the pro-Emancipation cause, as a number of politically active Catholics turned against the well-meaning (but ultimately ineffective) parliamentary lobbying of Henry Grattan and George Ponsonby. William Carey, a Catholic former member of the United Irish movement, rebuked the compromise position pursued by Grattan and Ponsonby in 1813, demanding that they remove themselves from leading the Emancipation cause.[86] While the majority of the Catholic movement acquiesced in the veto as a compromise to secure Emancipation, the anti-vetoists emerged as a vocal and increasingly influential minority.

Chief among the rising generation of restless Catholic leaders was the young lawyer, Daniel O'Connell. O'Connell had built a reputation as a critic of the Union for retarding the political ambitions of Irish Catholics; with his rejection of the veto compromise, he did much to discredit the old Patriot parliamentarians who favoured Emancipation. Increasingly, Catholic politics assumed a more popular form as O'Connell gained a

[85] [J. W. Croker], *A Sketch of the State of Ireland, Past and Present* (Dublin: M. N. Mahon, 1810), p. 56.

[86] [William Carey], *The Warning Protest of an Irish Roman Catholic, Against Every Interference, Change, or Arrangement in the Discipline and Constitution of the Roman Catholic Church in Ireland, as a Compromise or Barter for Catholic Emancipation, Respectfully Addressed to the Members of the Two Houses of Parliament*, 5th ed. (Dublin: Richard Coyne, 1813), pp. 15–16.

grip over the anti-vetoist wing of the Board, with public mobilisations becoming a weapon to influence parliament. In popularising the Catholic movement and seeking to weaken the influence of its aristocratic leadership, O'Connell was publicly testing the Convention Act of 1793, which prevented Irish Catholics from establishing their own representative organisation.[87] But the veto controversy was more than a clash over tactics and strategy within the pro-Emancipation movement. For O'Connell, the veto represented a microcosm of wider Irish conceptions of political liberty under the Union. Responding publicly to Grattan on the course to be taken regarding the Emancipation question in 1813, O'Connell denounced the veto compromise as an assault on Catholic freedoms. 'I hope the people of Ireland will show that they deserve to be free', he proclaimed, 'by evincing that they are acquainted with, and are resolved to assert the privileges of Freemen!'[88] In O'Connell's mind, the parliament in Dublin had been lost and the Irish majority were excluded from the legislature in London; the church of the people was all that remained. Suppressing the autonomy of the church thus risked crushing the last national institution in Ireland.

For the anti-vetoists, the ability or otherwise of the Crown to control the appointment of Irish bishops was a question of national independence from the state. When Denys Scully prefaced his forceful *A Statement of the Penal Laws*, published in 1812, with the declaration that the Catholics 'are emphatically the PEOPLE OF IRELAND', he put into words a growing self-reliance among the excluded majority that assumed the language of popular sovereignty.[89] The Foxite writer, John Bernard Trotter, an outspoken opponent of the veto, hypothesised a year later that 'the true question of Emancipation' was the 'distribution of political power in a divided Country'. Emancipation in exchange for the loss of independence in the nomination of Catholic bishops did not equate with civil equality.[90] This emerging consciousness was pushed further with the anti-vetoist rejection of several papal rescripts that (in line with wider European practice) advocated acceptance of a form of state oversight over the appointment of senior clergy. The authority of the Vatican in political matters was rejected by the anti-vetoists, just as the British Crown's right to make clerical appointments in Ireland was spurned. As the northern

[87] Oliver MacDonagh, *The Hereditary Bondsman: Daniel O'Connell, 1779–1829* (London: Weidenfeld and Nicolson, 1986), p. 108.
[88] *Freeman's Journal*, 22 November 1813.
[89] [Scully], *Statement of the Penal Laws*, i, p. ii.
[90] Trotter, *Five Letters*, pp. 27, 30–1.

radical, John Hancock, quipped in the *Belfast Monthly Magazine* (*BMM*), 'the Irish Catholics will suffer neither the Pope to intermeddle with his politics, nor the King with his religion'.[91]

The emergence of anti-vetoism within the Catholic Board marked the rise of a style of political activism unlike any seen before in Ireland. The Irish political imagination was widened to include (in the words of Cork writer, William Cooke Taylor) 'the passions of the priests and the prejudices of the people'.[92] When John Edwards, a Justice of the Peace in Wicklow, wrote a plea for British policymakers in 1814 to reconcile Catholics with the state through the deliverance of Emancipation, he did so with the knowledge that the 'lower orders' were increasingly embittered 'with a strong prejudice' that risked undermining Irish faith in the Union.[93] O'Connell, with his virulent language denouncing the veto and its chief advocate, Henry Grattan, personified this hardening of Irish opinion.[94] In a mischievous step, O'Connell equated Grattan's sponsorship of the veto to Lord Castlereagh's support for the Union. 'Does not Grattan know', O'Connell rhetorically asked, 'that Lord Castlereagh first dyed his country in blood, and then sold her'.[95] While Grattan later made his peace with Castlereagh, the comparison was jarring for the most prominent parliamentarian associated with anti-unionism and pro-Emancipation.[96]

Such an approach alienated as much as it electrified political opinion. One Protestant clergyman believed that unless the Catholics of Ireland 'disown the men who assume to be their leaders', the Emancipation question would languish in the depths of unrespectability.[97] 'Demagoguery' and 'zealotry' became staples of anti-Emancipation commentary on the Catholic movement.[98] Grattan's son (also called Henry), writing anonymously in 1815, voiced his irritation at the anti-vetoists' lack of

91 *Belfast Monthly Magazine* (*BMM*), vol. 12, no. 70 (May 1814), p. 425.

92 'A Munster Farmer' [William Cooke Taylor], *Reminiscences of Daniel O'Connell, Esq, MP, during the Agitations of the Veto, Emancipation and Repeal*, ed. Patrick Maume (Dublin: UCD Press, 2005; first published 1847), p. 36.

93 John Edwards, *Interests of Ireland: a New Method: with Confident Hopes to Attach the Lower Classes to the Laws and Constitution* (Dublin: William Watson, 1814), p. 29.

94 Patrick M. Geoghegan, *King Dan: The Rise of Daniel O'Connell, 1775–1829* (Dublin: Gill & Macmillan, 2008), pp. 139–40.

95 John O'Connell (ed.), *The Life and Speeches of Daniel O'Connell, MP*, 2 vols. (Dublin: James Duffy, 1846), i, p. 382.

96 Stephen Gwynn, *Henry Grattan and His Times* (Dublin: Browne and Nolan Ltd., 1939), p. 383.

97 Rev. William Thorpe, *An Address to the Protestants of Great Britain and Ireland on the Subject of Catholic Emancipation, Presenting Facts and Documents Illustrative of the Real Object of Irish Roman Catholic Leaders*, 3rd ed. (Dublin: R. Napper, 1815), p. vi.

98 Such as the anonymously published pamphlet, *Prudence, True Patriotism; or, an Exposure of the Arts, Views and Characters of the Catholic Directory* (Dublin: John Barlow, 1815), p. 30.

deference for his father. Grattan Jr's ire was particularly directed at O'Connell, who, in an astonishing passage, he positioned as a dangerous demagogue:

> His speaking is extravagant diction, a vulgar boast, a swaggering sentence, affected bombast and ludicrous composition; his liberty is not liberal, his politics are not reason, his reading is not learning, his learning is not knowledge, his rhetoric is a hyperbole, garnished with faded flowers, such as a drabbled girls would pick in Covent Garden, stuck on with the taste of a kitchen maid, and delivered in a barbarous dialect and Connaught declamation.[99]

Politically, Grattan Jr believed that the O'Connellites made a huge blunder in rejecting the 'securities' offered to the Protestant state of the veto, as it undermined the passage of a potential Catholic relief bill.[100] But this is to miss the point of the anti-vetoists' argument: in their eyes, the coming of Emancipation with a state veto over the selection of senior clergy was akin to snatching defeat from the jaws of victory. The principle behind the Catholic demand was noted by Robert Torrens, a Derry-born Royal Marine officer and future political economist, who asserted in 1813 that the 'Catholics of Ireland claim the privileges of the English constitution on the grounds of natural right, and on the principles of civil liberty'.[101] Any dilution of Emancipation was, in the eyes of O'Connell and the anti-vetoists, to diminish that 'natural right'.

## Turning the Clock: Backwards or Forwards?

While he reserved a particular disdain for O'Connell, Henry Grattan Jr was seething with anger more generally about the state of Ireland in 1815. 'It seems as if some evil genius possessed the land', he wrote,

> and with its brood of demons, either in the shape of desperate governors, and now of desperate leaders, walked out, doomed to deface and to destroy character and country, robbing one party of their privileges, and the nation of her Parliament; and leaving us, after this horrid sacrilege, the weeping prey to the worst passions, basest politics, and vilest leaders.[102]

99 [Henry Grattan Jr.], *Faction Unmasked: or a Letter to the Roman Catholics of Ireland, on the Conduct of Certain Men who Compose the Catholic Junta* (Dublin: Richard Milliken, 1815), pp. 22–3.

100 Ibid., p. 25.

101 Robert Torrens, *Thoughts on the Catholic Question*, 2nd ed. (London: Gale, Curtis, and Fenner, 1813), p. 29.

102 [Grattan Jr.], *Faction Unmasked*, pp. 42–3.

Poor government and the rise of the new 'vulgar' elite in Ireland were, therefore, in Grattan's eyes, a direct consequence of the loss of the parliament in Dublin. While many anti-unionists reconciled themselves to the Union after 1800, it remained more challenging for some. John Gamble, a Presbyterian writer from Tyrone, personified a form of Dissenting Protestant zugzwang in early nineteenth-century Ireland. He was ambivalent about the positive effects of the Union, while fearful of the direction of an increasingly assertive Catholic mobilisation; he idealised the theoretical virtues of the British constitution while critiquing its practice in Ireland. For Gamble, Ireland was trapped in a constitutional purgatory, an 'unnatural state' fostered by 'the melancholy spectacle of distrustful government and discontented people'.[103] Gamble looked to Emancipation to restore equilibrium in Ireland; but he was aware that others were attracted to more wholesale changes to the polity. By 1810, political dissatisfaction in Ireland began to manifest itself in a resurrected anti-unionism.

While the status of Catholics was the dominant issue in Irish political thought during the early years of the Union, discontent with Ireland's new constitutional status cracked through to the surface occasionally. In pressing the case for Catholic Emancipation, several prominent pamphleteers also voiced concern with the structure of incorporating union, with the fear that centralised power detached Irish opinion from the decision-making process and that the Irish debt was forced to absorb British military spending. William Parnell doubted the ability of the British political classes to formalise a method to consult Irish concerns when addressing government priorities. 'The English', he wryly noted in 1804, 'have the disposition of a nation accustomed to empire; anything that compromises their own dignity appears quite out of the question'.[104] Parnell lamented the lack of imagination in framing the Acts of Union, proposing that a system that maintained the Irish parliament while creating a shared executive with London would have squared the circle of imperial security and Irish sentiment for self-government.[105] Henry Dillon called explicitly for a 'federal Union' in 1805, with separate parliaments in Britain and Ireland tied together through the bonds of the Crown.[106] For Dillon, Catholic relief was, in itself, not enough to

103 'Protestant Dissenter' [John Gamble], *Brief Observations on the Present State of Ireland* (Dublin: Thomas Courtney, 1811), p. 16.

104 [Parnell], *An Inquiry*, p. 42. 105 Ibid., pp. 38–9.

106 Henry Augustus Dillon, *Letter to the Noblemen and Gentlemen, who composed the Deputation from the Catholics of Ireland, on the Subject of their Mission* (Dublin: H. Fitzpatrick, 1805), p. 4.

harmonise the Union: wider constitutional tinkering – with the Irish gaining control over their own government – was also required.

This impulse reinvigorated Irish political thinking in 1810. During that year, a pamphlet appeared in Dublin with the provocative title, *Repeal, or Ruin! Addressed to the People of Ireland.* 'Repeal' referred to the repeal of the Acts of Union, which would have (in theory) returned Ireland to its pre-1801 state. The tract was written by S. D. O'Mara, a minor literary critic; and while it hardly created a sensation at the time of its publication, it is one of the earliest pamphlets to deploy arguments that became mainstream within the O'Connellite campaign for Repeal from the early 1830s.[107] O'Mara presented a history of the passage of the Acts of Union which caricatured the personalities in the Irish parliament in 1800 as patriotic heroes (the anti-unionists) and treacherous villains (the unionists). The Union, O'Mara claimed, had crushed Ireland's national spirit, degrading its status from a self-governing 'Kingdom' to a 'minor province of the empire'. Irish wealth, in the form of increased absenteeism, was siphoned off to Britain. The loss of the parliament in Dublin ensured that 'everything is becoming foreign' in the capital city, as the Irish legislators were replaced by British administrators. O'Mara argued that ten years of Union had corroded Irish self-worth. He believed that the cause of Catholic Emancipation would produce positive changes in the Irish body politic, not least in strengthening reformist-minded politics; but national dignity could not be restored until a parliament was resurrected in Dublin.[108]

The publication of O'Mara's pamphlet coincided with the Dublin Corporation calling for a resolution for the Repeal of the Union. Against the backdrop of increasing economic hardship during the Napoleonic Wars, a number of Dublin guilds proclaimed their support for a restoration of the Irish parliament as a means to stimulate the city's mercantile life.[109] Invited to address the (Protestant) freemen and freeholders of Dublin in September 1810, O'Connell strenuously backed the cause of Repeal. 'We have been robbed, my countrymen, most foully robbed of our birthright, of our independence', O'Connell excitedly told the gathering. He concluded with a dramatic proclamation that put Repeal *above*

[107] Indeed, O'Connell owned a copy of O'Mara's pamphlet: *Catalogue of the Law and Miscellaneous Library of the Late Daniel O'Connell, Esq, MP, which will be Sold by Auction, by Order of the Executors, by John F. Jones* (Dublin: no publishing house, 1849), p. 351.

[108] S. D. O'Mara, *Repeal, or Ruin! Addressed to the People of Ireland* (Dublin: James Byrn, [1810]), pp. 6, 25, 30, 34.

[109] Jacqueline Hill, *From Patriots to Unionists: Dublin Civic Politics and Irish Protestantism Patriotism, 1660–1840* (Oxford: Oxford University Press, 1997), pp. 266–7.

Catholic Emancipation as a political ambition. 'Let us rally round the standard of Old Ireland, and we shall easily procure that greatest of political blessings, an Irish King, an Irish House of Lords, and an Irish House of Commons'. He went on to claim that he would accept the reenactment of the entire penal code if it were accompanied by the restoration of the Irish parliament, such was his desire to see Ireland regain the status of a self-governing country.[110]

While such an assertion was most likely posturing for the benefit of his Protestant audience, O'Connell's support for the Repeal of the Union was genuine. Such a prominent declaration of support from a leading figure in the Catholic movement did much, however, to sustain the notion that Repeal was a 'Catholic' cause, as John Gamble ascertained.[111] Other critics went further, accusing the O'Connellites of seeking a separatist Catholic kingdom in Ireland.[112] O'Connell was notoriously inconsistent in pressing for Repeal, with his campaigning for the restoration of an Irish parliament waxing and waning over the course of his long career. His tactical prowess should not, however, be read as a sign of a skin-deep commitment. O'Connell had been a critic of the Union since its passage, believing that it was disastrous for Ireland.[113] The *restorative* nature of his vision of a self-governing Ireland – the return to 'Old Ireland' – was a consistent thread within his anti-unionist argument.[114] Despite O'Connell's frustration with Grattan for his handling of the veto controversy, the O'Connellite blueprint for Irish self-government remained resolutely 'Grattan's parliament'.

The emergence of an anti-unionist political idea created the conditions for the articulation of its antithesis. One such example was found in the *BMM*, which was established in 1808 by William Drennan, John Hancock and Robert Tennent.[115] The *BMM* served as a vehicle for the evolving post-revolutionary political ideas of a number of individuals with ties to the United Irishmen in Belfast. Drennan's editorials revealed that his constitutional vision for Ireland had shifted towards a tentative unionism;

110 John O'Connell (ed.), *Select Speeches of Daniel O'Connell, MP*, 2 vols. (London: James Duffy, 1867), i, pp. 19, 24.

111 [Gamble], *Brief Observations*, p. 15.

112 Thorpe, *An Address*, p. 61; [Arthur Henry Kenny], *The Dangers with which Great Britain and Ireland are Now Menaced, by the Demands of Irish Roman Catholics* (London: F. C. and J. Rivington, 1817), pp. 4–5.

113 Geoghegan, *King Dan*, p. 85.

114 Indeed, O'Connell was a student of the pamphlet debate of 1798–1800: he owned a large number of the pamphlets, which are now housed in the Burns Library at Boston College.

115 Fergus Whelan, *May Tyrants Tremble: The Life of William Drennan, 1754–1822* (Dublin: Irish Academic Press, 2020), p. 273.

the independent Irish republic of the 1790s had been left behind.[116] Responding to the clamour over Repeal in 1810, the *BMM* retorted that Ireland's woes were not necessarily a symptom of the Union, but the lack of parliamentary reform to curb the oligarchic nature of power. The restoration of an unreformed parliament in Dublin would do little to address Ireland's hardships, as power would continue to be monopolised by the aristocratic classes. The problems facing Ireland were not caused by the Union, Drennan argued, but the costly war in Europe and, in political terms, the 'schism between the Commons and the people'.[117] He believed that radical reform – creating a more representative political system in terms of an expanded franchise, equal constituency sizes and empowering popular political delegates – was the path to the amelioration of Ireland.[118] The connection with Britain offered the best opportunity for radical reform, Drennan opined, as the larger political space offered by the United Kingdom had the potential to 'allay party feuds' and 'to relieve us from the rough riding of some of our unprincipled jockies'.[119] But the 'spirit' of union – paternal sovereignty, equality under the law, and reciprocal utility – needed time to permeate the institutions of the state.[120]

The *BMM* demonstrated that unionism could be articulated within the framework of radical political thought. Within the northern Presbyterian community that the *BMM* largely represented, Wolfe Tone's mission to sever the connection between Ireland and Britain seemed like a relic from a bygone age.[121] Drennan hinted at this break with the past when writing about Catholic Emancipation in 1813:

> We gloried, in our younger days, to see America resist Britain, upon British principles, and we now, on our declining years, glory, with equal rejoicing, that the Catholics of Ireland, by their conduct and thorough sense of the true principles of the Constitution, appear more Britons than the Britons themselves.[122]

Despite this optimism, the *BMM* folded one year later, despairing of the state of an Irish public opinion split by sectarian concerns.[123] The rhetoric

116 Wright, '*Natural Leaders*', p. 72; McBride, *Scripture Politics*, p. 215.
117 *BMM*, vol. 4, no. 22 (May 1810), pp. 387, 389–90.
118 *BMM*, vol. 3, no. 14 (September 1809), p. 230.
119 *BMM*, vol. 5, no. 26 (September 1810), p. 224.
120 *BMM*, vol. 1, no. 5 (December 1808), p. 385.
121 Marianne Elliott, *Wolfe Tone: Prophet of Irish Independence* (New Haven, CT: Yale University Press, 1989), p. 393.
122 *BMM*, vol. 10, no. 54 (January 1813), p. 67.
123 *BMM*, vol. 13, no. 77 (December 1814), p. 530.

of progressive unionism struggled to overcome the jagged politico-religious dimension within Irish life.

With the abdication of Napoleon in 1814, the *BMM* asserted that Europe could be remade with the 'principle of national representation recognised as the grand axiom worthy of universal assent'.[124] But significant aspects of Irish political opinion remained unconvinced that the United Kingdom was the appropriate framework for Ireland to achieve representative government. At the beginning of 1818, a new magazine with a provocative title – the *Anti-Unionist* – came into circulation. The *Anti-Unionist* rose from the editorial ashes of the *Dublin Examiner*, an accomplished but short-lived highbrow monthly that foreshadowed the rise of the better-known mid century Irish periodicals such as the *Dublin University Magazine*.[125] The *Anti-Unionist*, like its predecessor, did not last long – seventeen issues over a four-month period – but the magazine was an important vessel for the articulation of radical political ideas from what might be called a liberal Dublin Protestant perspective. While northern Presbyterians were articulating a form of unionism in the *BMM*, the *Anti-Unionist* reminded readers that radical Repeal sentiment remained a visible, if dissipating, element of Protestant political thought in the capital. The pages of the *Anti-Unionist* resolutely advocated a vision for the restoration of Irish self-government that was distinctive from the O'Connellite version.

The *Anti-Unionist*'s first editorial portrayed the Union as a moment of national disaster for Ireland, both politically and economically. The absence of the structures of self-government had undermined the dignity of the Irish since 1801, a debasing feature that perpetuated sectarian grievances. 'We are a nation of wretched traders, famishing peasants, and loathsome beggars', lamented the *Anti-Unionist*. The transformation of Irish political economy had not followed the Acts of 1800: the promised injection of English capital into Ireland had failed to materialise, as productive duties were retained in many cases. Indeed, it was English *debt*, from the imposition of high taxes in Ireland and the near bankruptcy of

124 *BMM*, vol. 13, no. 74 (September 1814), p. 252.

125 *Freeman's Journal*, 9 February 1818. The editor of the *Anti-Unionist* and *Dublin Examiner* was, according to the *Irish Book Lover*, 'a young man of the name of Woods, who had filled the office of private secretary to O'Connell'. *Irish Book Lover*, vol. vii, no. 1 (1915), p. 12. The present author has been unable to locate any other information on Woods. The editor of the *Dublin Examiner* is listed as 'anonymous' in Tom Clyde, *Irish Literary Magazines: An Outline History and Descriptive Biography* (Dublin: Irish Academic Press, 2002), p. 81, while the *Anti-Unionist* does not receive an entry at all.

the Irish exchequer, that dominated fiscal thinking in the pages of the *Anti-Unionist*.[126] Indeed, it was likely no coincidence that the *Anti-Unionist* appeared during a period of intense economic hardship for Ireland (and Britain more generally) in the years following the end of the Napoleonic Wars. The postwar fiscal crisis brought to the fore the structural economic problems that blighted Ireland, many of which stemmed from the implausibility of amalgamating two very different economic units at radically different stages of development.[127] One such issue raised by the *Anti-Unionist* was continuing gentry absenteeism, a practice that was long established in Ireland but unusual in England.[128] The magazine asserted that moving the Irish parliament to London had amplified the absentee problem, with money raised from rents in Ireland spent mostly in England and the solidifying of the image of the remote and disinterested landlord.[129] That the rot had set in only eighteen years after the Union disturbed the magazine. 'If half a generation has reduced us to this state, what must be our condition before the lapse of half a century?' Redemption, the *Anti-Unionist* believed, could only be achieved through the restoration of a parliament in Dublin. The *Anti-Unionist* conceded that this goal was not likely achievable in the short term, but the first step had been taken with the appearance of the magazine. 'One stage in the progress will be gained by making the Union and its effects the subject of every man's thoughts and the burden of his daily speech'.[130]

While the *Anti-Unionist* took its cue from the Grattanite Patriot faction's stance in 1799–1800 against the British connection, what is striking is the anchoring of Repeal as a measure of radical political reform. The desire for widening the franchise and removing the aristocratic grip over parliament was shared between the *BMM* and *Anti-Unionist*, but while the *BMM* argued that radical reform was achievable through the framework of the Union, the *Anti-Unionist* rejected this model. Under the Union, Ireland suffered a state of constitutional subjugation, which left 'the great body of the people' disenfranchised and poorly served by self-interested and remote representatives. 'Let us now look at the state of Ireland with respect to Representation', declared the *Anti-Unionist*:

126 *Anti-Unionist*, no. 16, 16 May 1818, p. 241; Douglas Kanter, 'The politics of Irish taxation, 1842–1853', *English Historical Review*, vol. 127, no. 528 (2012), p. 1125.

127 Ó Gráda, *Ireland*, p. 159; Black, *Economic Thought*, p. 2.

128 Ciaran O'Neill, *Power and Powerless in Union Ireland: Life in a Palliative State* (Oxford: Oxford University Press, 2024), p. 166.

129 *Anti-Unionist*, no. 12, 18 April 1818, p. 178.

130 *Anti-Unionist*, no. 1, 31 January 1818, pp. 1–4.

> What is the fact? At the lowest estimate five millions of people return one hundred members to sit along with five hundred and fifty-eight members returned by Great Britain. Ireland returns these hundred members once in seven years; and who in reality elects them? Is it the people? Alas! No. It is the aristocracy of the country.[131]

These factors, according to the magazine, ensured that Ireland occupied a passive constitutional space, deprived of the means of representation to effectively shape its own future.[132] With this analysis of the present state of Ireland, the *Anti-Unionist* posited that a Repeal of the Union did not imply a turning of the clock backwards to 1800: any parliament in Dublin must be 'reformed so as to give the great body of the people their real value'.[133] An expansive franchise was championed in the pages of the *Anti-Unionist*, as was the secret ballot.[134] While Repeal was the most eye-catching component of the *Anti-Unionist*, the magazine placed as high a value on radical reform as a means to representative government.[135]

The core message of the *Anti-Unionist* was thus grounded not on national sentiment or nostalgia, but a belief that the Union gravely weakened the link between the Irish people, political power and economic well-being. The magazine connected fiscal exploitation to a lack of effective political representation: Ireland 'must consequently expect to be imposed on', given its representatives had little influence on policy matters.[136] Such a spiteful constitutional set-up enabled sectarian differences to flourish unchecked in Ireland, as discriminatory laws were maintained by London. The message was stark: the new polity created in 1801, which promised so much from an Irish perspective – access to British capital, the lessening of religious divisions, the much-vaunted virtues of the British constitution – was, in fact, a tomb for political liberty in Ireland. Without a Repeal of the Union, 'the people of Ireland can never enjoy the advantages of representative government'.[137]

## 'A Sort of Political Pastorini'

The 1820s was the decade of mass Catholic mobilisation and the eventual – and begrudging – concession of Emancipation. After making a name for

[131] *Anti-Unionist*, no. 4, 21 February 1818, p. 51.
[132] *Anti-Unionist*, no. 11, 11 April 1818, p. 163.
[133] *Anti-Unionist*, no. 5, 28 February 1818, p. 65.
[134] *Anti-Unionist*, no. 4, 21 February 1818, p. 50.
[135] *Anti-Unionist*, no. 5, 28 February 1818, p. 68.
[136] *Anti-Unionist*, no. 11, 11 April 1818, p. 163.
[137] *Anti-Unionist*, no. 5, 28 February 1818, p. 68.

himself in the veto controversy, O'Connell's star began to wane in the post-1815 period. The formation of the new Catholic Association in 1823, with its innovative 'Rent'-based funding model and visibility via the medium of mass meetings, returned O'Connell to the forefront of Irish political consciousness, and on a scale never seen before. Foregrounding the establishment of the Catholic Association was a continuing defence of the 'Protestant constitution' by its defenders and assault on the 'Orange system' by its detractors. Henry Grattan Jr's attempt to retain the Dublin City seat of his recently deceased father in 1820 failed in the face of a concerted effort by Irish Protestant Toryism. Thomas Ellis, a prominent Orangeman, won Grattan's old seat and announced a drastic change of direction for the constituency. 'I shall oppose the unqualified demands of the Roman Catholics', he asserted, 'conceiving them to mediate the overthrow of the Constitution and the Protestant Religion'.[138] Sir Harcourt Lees, an Anglican clergyman and staunch opponent of Catholic Emancipation, issued two pamphlets in 1820 that asserted the primacy of what he called the 'Protestant constitution'. In Lees's argument, the Anglican Church and state were one; Protestantism and the idea of civil liberties in the United Kingdom were intimately bound together. Catholic relief was, therefore, unconstitutional. Lees also stressed that the 'bigots' who would inevitably represent Catholic Ireland in the event of Emancipation would destroy the state from within. Emancipation was thus, from Lees's vantage point, a revolutionary threat to the United Kingdom.[139]

Increasingly, however, such a perspective was difficult to maintain. The near-annual motions in the House of Commons on the question of Catholic relief were becoming extremely close, which gravely concerned Tories and other anti-Emancipationists.[140] There was also growing criticism of the structures of power in the Irish government and the judiciary, with the old wine of the Protestant Ascendancy appearing in the new bottles of nineteenth-century political and legal life. There was a flurry of pamphlets in the early 1820s critiquing the 'Orange System', a clandestine

[138] Anon., *Review of the Conduct of the Orange Party, during the Election for the City of Dublin* (Dublin: no publishing house, 1820), p. 57.

[139] Sir Harcourt Lees, *The Rehearsal: King and Constitution, or Pope and Catholic Emancipation. Recommended to the Attention of the Most Stupid of the Protestant Advocates for Unrestricted Civil Liberty* (Dublin: W. Underwood, 1820); *The Seventh Edition of the Antidote; or, 'Nouvelles à la Main.' Recommended to the Serious Attention of every Protestant in the Empire, in those days of Political and Religious Apostasy, Military and Naval Evangelicalism, Papal Intolerance, and Popish Bigotry* (Dublin: W. Underwood, 1820).

[140] Clark, *English Society*, p. 387.

faction associated with the Orange Order who enjoyed the tacit support of the state and continued to uphold the attitudes of the Protestant Ascendancy. A supporter of Grattan contrasted the harsh treatment of Ribbonmen, the oath-bound Catholic society, with the leniency that Orangemen received in the law courts in front of all-Protestant juries.[141] It was this explicit difference in how the law interpreted different Irish political and religious organisations that prompted several liberal Protestants, such as Thomas Wallace and the ubiquitous William Cusack Smith, to condemn the 'Orange System' in print.[142] Wallace believed that the power wielded by the Orange Order created a form of political apartheid that encouraged the anti-Protestant excesses of Ribbonism. 'What could be more natural for the Irish peasant', Wallace asked, 'when he saw or felt that a sworn confederacy was formed and in full operation against him, then he also should resort to a sworn confederacy for defence and protection?'[143] Smith believed that the perceived differences in how Protestants and Catholics were regarded by the judicial system, with Orangemen finding favourable treatment, was a festering sore within the Union. He warned that an increasing 'hatred of Orangemen' would ultimately result in 'their destruction'.[144]

There was a certain timeliness in Smith's words, given the popularity of the so-called Pastorini prophecies in Ireland during the early nineteenth century. 'Pastorini' was the pseudonym of Charles Walmesley, an English Benedictine who died in 1797. In 1771, he published a history of the Catholic Church which contained a commentary on the Book of Revelation, with a prediction about the destruction of Protestantism in the year 1825.[145] The book was hugely successful, running through numerous editions throughout the late eighteenth and nineteenth centuries. Numerous editions were published in Ireland, encouraged by the British government during the French Revolutionary Wars, to persuade Irish Catholics that France was the primary enemy of Catholicism.[146] The

141 *Review of the Conduct of the Orange Party*, p. 16.

142 'A Protestant' [Thomas Wallace], *The Orange System Exposed; and the Orange Societies Proved to be Unconstitutional, Illegal and Seditious, in a Letter to the Marquess Wellesley* (Dublin: Richard Milliken, 1823), p. 5. William Cusack Smith, *Recent Scenes and Occurrences in Ireland: or Animadversions on a Pamphlet entitled* 'One Year of the Administration of the Marquess Wellesley' (London: Longman, Hurst, Rees, Orme, and Brown, 1823), p. 183.

143 [Wallace], *Orange System*, p. 47.

144 Smith, *Recent Scenes*, p. 101.

145 *The General History of the Christian Church from her Birth to her Final Triumphant State in Heaven, Chiefly Deduced from the Apocalypse of St John the Apostle*, 5th ed. (Dublin: P. Wogan, 1812; first published 1771), p. 214.

146 Geoffrey Scott, '"The times are fast approaching": Bishop Charles Walmsley OSB (1722–1797) as a prophet', *Journal of Ecclesiastical History*, vol. 36, no. 4 (1985), p. 602.

irony was that the state sponsored a text dealing with religious apocalypse and the ultimate triumph of Catholicism, which circulated widely throughout Ireland.

At the end of the Napoleonic War, the sections from Walmesley's *History* dealing with the fall of Protestantism were reprinted as standalone small pamphlets and broadsheets.[147] The Pastorini prophecies formed part of the vocabulary of Catholic agrarian secret societies, such as the Ribbonmen and the Rockites, in parts of Munster during the early 1820s.[148] Given the fevered background, millennialism was projected by some onto the new Catholic Association. William Phelan, an Anglican clergyman, lamented the coming of 'a sort of political Pastorini', in which the state, through the maintenance of political exclusion, had abandoned the Catholics of Ireland to 'papal tyranny' and radical politics. Ireland was 'legally a member of the great British family' but was not 'morally' accepted as such. Opponents of the Anglican Church and state had flourished in Ireland, with fearful consequences inevitably to follow.[149] For unionist writers such as Phelan, the apparent widespread embrace of the Pastorini prophecies by sections of the Irish peasantry was a manifestation of the failure to meaningfully import the virtues of the British constitution into Ireland; moral authority in Ireland lay elsewhere, gravely weakening the institutions of the state and the Protestant Church.

The Pastorini revelations provided an unsettling backdrop for the inauguration of the Catholic Association. Such was the persistence of the prophecies that O'Connell felt obliged to appear in front of a House of Lords committee on the subject, where he claimed that they had 'no effect ... upon the lower orders of the Irish Catholics'.[150] O'Connell's utterance revealed his eagerness to downplay the lure of the 'prophecies' as he sought to build political respectability. On most metrics, he was successful. Through innovations such as the Catholic Rent, local organising agents and grassroots meetings, the Catholic Association became a

[147] Niall Ó Ciosáin, *Print and Popular Culture in Ireland, 1750–1850* (Dublin: Lilliput Press, 2010; first published 1997), p. 225.

[148] James S. Donnelly Jr., *Captain Rock: The Irish Agrarian Rebellion of 1821–1824* (Madison: University of Wisconsin Press, 2009), p. 4. Kyle Hughes and Donald R. MacRaild, *Ribbon Societies in Nineteenth-Century Ireland and Its Diaspora: The Persistence of Tradition* (Liverpool: Liverpool University Press, 2018), p. 77.

[149] [William Phelan], *The Case of the Church of Ireland, Stated, in a Second Letter, Respectfully Addressed to his Excellency the Marquess of Wellesley, and in Reply to the Charges of J.K.L.* (Dublin: Richard Milliken, 1824).

[150] C. M. O'Keeffe, *Life and Times of Daniel O'Connell, with some Sketches of his Contemporaries*, 2 vols. (Dublin: John Murray, 1864), ii, pp. 365–6.

mass movement from 1824, drawing people away from the violent Rockites; apocalyptic ambitions were tempered by a renewed and invigorating political agitation. Somewhat ironically, O'Connell was cast as the predestined deliverer of millennialism in Ireland, albeit a new age ushered in through the constitutional destruction of Catholic disabilities, not the fall of Protestantism.[151]

The connections between radical politics that challenged exclusion from representation and Catholicism unquestionably became more pronounced with the inauguration of the Catholic Association. This was personified by James Warren Doyle, who was one of the most prominent clerical figures in Ireland with an affiliation to the Association. Doyle became the Bishop of Kildare and Leighlin in 1819 and rose as one of the most significant political thinkers in Ireland during the 1820s. Through his pastoral addresses, appearances in front of parliamentary select committees and, most significantly, his political writings published under the pen name 'J. K. L.' (James of Kildare and Leighlin), Doyle's contributions to public debate embodied a form of Catholicism that cast off obeisance in religious and political matters, and demanded spiritual and civic equality within the Union.[152] At the heart of Doyle's thought was the dignity of Irish Catholics as a religious and political community.[153] The politicisation of Catholicism was, in his reading, a by-product of religious-based discrimination in secular matters:

> Not only politics, but education, and every right or franchise we possess or claim is resolved into or connected with our religion; and this religion being the apparent cause and the distinctive mark whereby we are separated from our fellow-subjects, it is found blended with all our privations and all our wrongs.[154]

The remaining cinders of the penal laws, therefore, created the conditions for the flourishing of a cohesive and confident Catholicism, with Doyle emerging as one of its indispensable mouthpieces.

Doyle came to prominence as a political commentator with the publication in 1823 of his pamphlet, *A Vindication of the Religious and Civil*

[151] Thomas P. Power, *The Apocalypse in Ireland: Prophecy and Politics in the 1820s* (Oxford: Peter Lang, 2023), p. 203.
[152] Thomas McGrath, *Politics, Interdenominational Relations and Education in the Public Ministry of Bishop James Doyle of Kildare and Leighlin, 1786–1834* (Dublin: Four Courts Press, 1999).
[153] Thomas McGrath, *Religious Renewal and Reform in the Pastoral Ministry of Bishop James Doyle of Kildare and Leighlin, 1786–1834* (Dublin: Four Courts Press, 1999), p. 212.
[154] William John Fitzpatrick, *The Life, Times and Correspondence of the Right Rev. Dr Doyle, Bishop of Kildare and Leighlin*, 2 vols. (Dublin: James Duffy, 1861), ii, p. 25.

*Principles of the Irish Catholics*. In addressing the Lord Lieutenant of Ireland, Richard, Marquis Wellesley, directly, 'J. K. L.' symbolically wrote as a critical citizen rather than a subordinate subject. The aim of the pamphlet was to refute four misconceptions of Irish Catholicism, which Doyle believed were promoted to copper-fasten the status quo: that the religion was slavish superstition; that the Catholic hierarchy desired to overthrow the Anglican Church; that the clergy stirred the minds of their flock to stoke rebellion; and that the Catholic Church was intolerant of other denominations.[155] While social injustices such as the continuing tithe system were condemned by Doyle, he powerfully stressed that such complaints should not distract policymakers from the real source of discontent in Ireland:

> When we speak of tithes, they may tell us we are the allies of Captain Rock, but we reject the imputation; and reply, that the savage and the philosopher have the same sensibilities, and that the language of pain which they utter, can scarcely be distinguished in its sound; let only the grievance arising from tithe, like the thousand grievances we suffer, be removed, and the savage will return to his rock, and the philosopher will retire to his books. Let us not be told it is the law; we know it is, and it is of the law we complain; but are the laws of a Draco always to continue? Are they not only to be written in blood, but also, like those of the Medes and Persians, never to be repealed. The penal laws, my Lord, will always, in Ireland, produce some Demosthenes or other, like O'Connell at present.[156]

The classical references suggested that Doyle framed Ireland in terms of a timeless political struggle between nascent ideas of popular liberty and the corrupt tyranny of a powerful state; the 'laws of Draco', referring to the vindictive Athenian lawgiver, was an evocative analogy. O'Connell, the new Demosthenes, was gratified by the *Vindication*, moving a vote of thanks to 'J. K. L.' on behalf of the nascent Catholic Association.[157]

Despite the sustained critique of the penal laws, Doyle (like O'Connell) was an enthusiastic advocate of the theory of the British constitution. His thinking was shaped by a conspicuous unionism, which imagined the United Kingdom as a political space that enshrined equality before the law for all citizens while incorporating Irish ideas into Irish policy. Once Britain and Ireland were bonded by the ties of equality, 'one solid empire'

155 'J. K. L.' [James Warren Doyle], *A Vindication of the Religious and Civil Principles of the Irish Catholics, in a Letter, Addressed to his Excellency, the Marquis Wellesley, K. G.* (Dublin: Richard Coyne, 1823), p. 19.

156 Ibid., pp. 45–6. 157 McGrath, *Politics, Interdenominational Relations and Education*, p. 18.

spanning the islands would be created.[158] Indeed, Doyle's understanding of the constitution was deeply influenced by English Whig political thought, such as the supremacy of parliament and the idea that 'corporate property' (such as land owned by the Church of Ireland) was held by the Crown as a trustee of the people.[159] He rejected the widely received notion held by such champions of the political status quo that the constitutional tradition established in 1688 was intrinsically 'Protestant', arguing that 'no civil constitution can be essentially either Catholic or Protestant'. Laws are made and unmade and constitutions continually evolve 'in Catholic and Protestant times'. The penal laws, in other words, were not a timeless component of the British constitution, but a legislative priority of a previous age that had lost its relevance in the early decades of the nineteenth century. The state had the right to suspend the political rights of a portion of its citizens 'in times of danger', but, as Doyle asserted, 'when the danger has ceased … the suspension of rights should cease also'. It was 'tyrannical' to maintain the penal laws when clearly there was no 'Catholic' plot against the state.[160]

Doyle rapidly became a popular and influential writer. His pamphlets were circulated widely throughout Ireland, and his writings were incorporated into Sunday Mass services.[161] In 1825, his standing as the political voice of Catholic Ireland was enhanced with the publication of his most engaging work and noted appearance as a witness to a parliamentary select committee. His *Letters on the State of Ireland* assumed the form of collected letters on a wide range of political and social matters, written from 'J. K. L.' to an unnamed friend in England. It was a tour de force of powerful polemic writing, offering a sweeping survey of the Irish political landscape. Opening the book with a letter on the character of the Irish government, Doyle deployed the analogy of Rome (one of many classical references that pepper the work) as a warning of the lurch into an unresponsive and unrepresentative state with highly centralised power, which would inevitably implode.[162] Doyle believed that Irish governance was not guided by a vindictive impulse, but 'bad laws', even if administered justly, were as damaging to Irish faith in the political structures of the United Kingdom as a despotic regime. Coercive legislation, such as the Insurrection Act of

158 [James Warren Doyle], *A Defence by J. K. L. of his Vindication of the Religious and Civil Principles of Irish Catholics* (Dublin: Richard Coyne, 1824), p. 97.

159 Ibid., pp. 57, 94, 104; McGrath, *Politics, Interdenominational Relations and Education*, p. 20.

160 [James Warren Doyle], *Letters on the State of Ireland; Addressed by J. K. L. to a Friend in England* (Dublin: Richard Coyne, 1825), pp. 239, 244.

161 Fitzpatrick, *Right Rev. Dr Doyle*, i, pp. 111–12.

162 [Doyle], *Letters*, pp. 9–10.

1822, had legitimate intentions – the aim of quelling rural unrest – but achieved this at the behest of Irish liberties. 'The spirit and the letter of almost all our laws', argued Doyle, 'are hostile to the people'.[163] While this state of affairs continued – while laws were passed without consideration of the needs of the Irish people – the Union was merely the modern manifestation of the 'spirit of conquest'.[164] At the heart of Doyle's commentary on the operation of governance in Ireland was a critique of its (from an Irish perspective) unrepresentative nature. Citing Montesquieu (from *The Spirit of the Laws* (1750)), Doyle queried whether the laws of one country could be 'transferred to another without regard to the temper, habits, trade, resources, modes of industry, or religion, of its inhabitants'.[165] His summary of British law in Ireland under the Union was that it retained a toxic colonialism from a previous age; the governing structures had not evolved to adequately incorporate Irish sentiment.

Doyle emphasised that the penal laws represented the most obvious weakness of the British constitution in Ireland. Deploying a somewhat tongue-in-cheek reference to the father of Scottish Presbyterianism to make his point, he recorded that John Knox 'would have it that Government should exist for the sake of the people, and not for the people for those who govern them'. As the Catholics were, as Doyle put it, 'morally speaking, the people of this country', the Irish majority 'should engross the principal attention of our rulers'.[166] He stressed that it was patently unjust in a modern state that a citizen's interaction with the law was dictated by their religious denomination.[167] In his evidence to the parliamentary committee on the state of Ireland in 1825, Doyle stated that if Emancipation was carried, 'the whole of the Catholic population would consider their grievances, as it were, at an end'.[168] Political equality for Catholics was the path to fully reconciling Ireland to the Union, argued Doyle; any other alternative options were disastrous. The political exclusion of Catholics underpinned, in Doyle's reading, 'an unnatural conflict between the people and the laws', with Irish society as a whole made to suffer through a lack of industry, agrarian tension and widespread poverty.[169] He voiced a desire to join Rousseau in a 'return to a state of nature', rather than accept the injustices inherent in 'the system in Ireland'.[170] Doyle posited an

163 Ibid., pp. 22, 25. 164 Ibid., p. 89. 165 Ibid., p. 88. 166 Ibid., p. 44.
167 Ibid., p. 86.
168 *Evidence of the Right Rev. James Doyle, DD. Roman Catholic Bishop of Kildare and Leighlin, given before the Committee of the House of Lords, on the State of Ireland, March 21st, 1825* (London: W. E. Andrews, 1825), p. 64.
169 [Doyle], *Letters*, p. 104. 170 Ibid., p. 105.

apocalyptic consequence if the penal laws were retained indefinitely, cautioning that 'we need no Pastorini to foretell the result'.[171] Continuing political exclusion was, he warned, turning the Irish into 'Reformers of the very worst description', driven in political matters not by hope but by 'revenge'. The logical outcome, Doyle believed, was the Repeal of the Union, achieved not through reasoned debate but politicised hatred.[172] Given Doyle's professed unionism, he believed that such a scenario was extremely dangerous. His gravest fear was rooted in a lesson from antiquity: 'My chief anxiety for Emancipation, after a sense of duty to my king, and attachment to my country, arises from my aversion – from my horror of civil war'.[173]

One of the major themes emphasised by Doyle was that there was no tension between the spiritual and temporal allegiances of Catholics. The charge of divided allegiance was part of the argument forwarded by champions of the ideal of an exclusively Protestant constitution. In such interpretations, Catholicism could be tolerated by the state, but could not gain a share in political power.[174] During a parliamentary debate on Emancipation in 1825, the Prime Minister, Lord Liverpool, asserted that 'Catholics were not entitled to equal rights in a Protestant country'. He believed that it was unconstitutional to concede 'the enjoyment of the same civil rights and privileges as the Protestant' to Catholic subjects, when their 'allegiance was divided between a spiritual and a temporal master'. The allegiance of the Protestant subject, in contrast, was undivided and 'acknowledged but one ruler', in line with the normative political theory of the state.[175] For Liverpool, this concept of divided allegiance emboldened the Catholic clergy, who eagerly spread their 'practical power' beyond the spiritual realm.[176] Doyle addressed Liverpool in his book, *An Essay on the Catholic Claims* (1826), stressing that the question of allegiance was not controversial. Doyle styled himself as 'Your Lordship's most obedient and most humble Servant' in the dedication to make his point.[177]

*An Essay on the Catholic Claims* presented a history of the papacy's secular authority from the Roman Empire to the medieval period, highlighting its waning influence as political power. Doyle's key argument was that the Pope's supremacy in spiritual matters was undisputed, but the Catholic Church did not sponsor papal dominion over the temporal claims

[171] Ibid., p. 49. [172] Ibid., pp. 284–5. [173] Ibid., p. 291.
[174] For this theme within anti-Emancipation thought, see Clark, *English Society*, pp. 350–2.
[175] *Hansard*, 17 May 1825, vol. 13, col. 741 [176] Ibid., col. 743.
[177] James Warren Doyle, *An Essay on the Catholic Claims, Addressed to the Right Honourable the Earl of Liverpool, K.G.* (Dublin: Richard Coyne, 1826), p. vii.

of monarchs and emperors.[178] While the bull *Unam Sanctam*, issued by Boniface VIII in 1302, was cited by opponents of Catholic Emancipation as evidence of papal aspirations for a universal monarchy,[179] Doyle offered a more temperate interpretation. Deploying an Irish form of Gallicanism, he suggested that 'no Bull of any pope can decide our judgement'. The imperial pretensions of *Unam Sanctam* were, in Doyle's view, 'odious', and could not be upheld in any legal (or even rhetorical) sense.[180] Claims that the papacy insisted on sovereignty over temporal matters were bogus, Doyle affirmed; such a doctrine was, in his view, never a pillar of Church teaching.[181] There was, thus, no barrier to Catholics pledging allegiance to a secular ruler, even a Protestant one. Catholics might not recognise a spiritual supremacy of the Crown in the United Kingdom, but as Doyle pointed out, neither did Protestant Dissenters.[182] The state was, in Doyle's reading, 'derived from God, and totally independent of the pope, or of any other authority whatsoever'.[183] The King was obeyed without question in temporal matters; his status as head of the Anglican Church was incidental to the practice of sovereignty. The Pope, on the other hand, 'has no arbitrary power over us' in worldly matters.[184] Doyle's powerful conclusion was, therefore, that the charge of divided allegiance made by opponents of Emancipation was unjust.

While Doyle was an important clerical advocate of Emancipation, he was prepared to deviate from the script set by the leaders of the Catholic Association. The year 1825 was a dramatic one for the Association, with its suppression in March, coupled with O'Connell actively working with English radical parliamentarians in drafting Emancipation legislation. Included in the text were several 'securities' to soothe Protestant fears – which became known as the 'wings' attached to the measure – including state payment of the Irish Catholic clergy and the disfranchisement of the forty-shilling freehold voters.[185]

O'Connell believed that there was a compelling case to abandon the forty-shilling freeholders as the price of Catholic Emancipation, as their

[178] Ibid., p. 20. For a discussion of this, see McGrath, *Politics, Interdenominational Relations and Education*, p. 49.

[179] See, for example, Henry Phillpotts, *A Letter to the Right Honourable George Canning, on the Bill of 1825, for Removing the Disqualifications of his Majesty's Roman Catholic Subjects*, 4th ed. (London: John Murray, 1827), pp. 115–16.

[180] Doyle, *Catholic Claims*, pp. 37–8. Also see Francis Oakley, *The Conciliarist Tradition: Constitutionalism in the Catholic Church, 1300–1870* (Oxford: Oxford University Press, 2003), p. 5.

[181] Doyle, *Catholic Claims*, p. 80. [182] Ibid., p. 4. [183] Ibid., p. 12. [184] Ibid., p. 17.

[185] MacDonagh, *Hereditary Bondsman*, pp. 217–18.

poor economic status rendered them electoral tools of the landlord interest.[186] Doyle, however, was at odds with this part of the O'Connellite compromise package. In the *Letters*, he mounted a robust defence of the small freeholder voters in Ireland. 'It is the natural right of man', Doyle pronounced,

> A right interwoven with the essence of our constitution, and producing, as its necessary effect, the House of Commons, that a man who has life, liberty, and property, should have some share or influence in the disposal of them by law. Take the elective franchise from the Irish peasant, and you not only strip him of the present reality, or appearance of this right, but you disable him and his posterity ever to acquire it.

Disenfranchising the forty-shilling freeholders was tantamount to falling from 'the image of a freeman' to the 'very essence of a slave'. Doyle utilised a classical analogy to depict the Irish peasant who had lost their voting rights: 'Like the Helot at Athens he may go to the forum and gaze at the election, and then return to hew his wood or fetch his water to the freeman'. The dignity of electoral rights was a central component of Doyle's political imagination; it was the ability to cast a vote that separated a 'citizen' from merely an 'inhabitant'.[187] Emancipation to him meant equality under the British constitution; disenfranchising a portion of the Irish population to achieve the rights of a citizen was an incongruous concept. The question of Emancipation was not solely about Catholic representative rights but about the definition of the 'people'.

Despite Doyle's defence of the forty-shilling freeholder, he was careful to avoid public criticism of O'Connell on the matter.[188] While O'Connell was increasingly confident of carrying Emancipation with the 'wing' of disenfranchisement, there was much discontent (and open hostility) within the re-established Catholic Association regarding the compromise.[189] Doyle's perspective certainly carried weight within Catholic Ireland; and in the election of 1826, it was the forty-shilling freeholder who delivered the incredible victory that the Catholic Association enjoyed in Waterford. Through a concerted campaign overseen by senior Catholic Association lieutenants, particularly Thomas Wyse, the small freeholders of the constituency abandoned the landed 'establishment' candidate, Lord

[186] William Fagan, *The Life and Times of Daniel O'Connell*, 2 vols. (Cork: John O'Brien, 1847), i, p. 399.
[187] [Doyle], *Letters*, pp. 295–6.
[188] McGrath, *Politics, Interdenominational Relations and Education*, p. 33.
[189] Geoghegan, *King Dan*, p. 218.

Beresford, in favour of the liberal, pro-Emancipationist, Henry Villiers Stuart. Underpinning the dramatic success was a disciplined organisation that mobilised the Catholic electorate, paid for by the renewed Catholic Rent. The clergy were central, as organisers and fundraisers, to these initiatives, although Doyle was hesitant in permitting priests in his diocese to become Catholic Rent collectors.[190] While Doyle believed that Emancipation would defuse religious antagonisms in Ireland and ultimately row back clerical involvement in politics, the figure of the priest was well entrenched in Catholic politics.[191] The triumph in Waterford demonstrated the potential of a mass democratic movement led by clerics, which ultimately created the conditions (via O'Connell's dramatic electoral victory in Co. Clare in 1828) to secure Catholic Emancipation. Despite Doyle's hopes for the post-Emancipation age, his politicised pulpit became normalised during the 1820s and continued long afterwards. While 'popery' signified backwardness to a British audience, Catholicism was cast by its adherents as the vehicle for liberty, justice and (ironically, perhaps, given its Protestant ethos) a share in the British constitution. As one pamphleteer, praising the role of the clergy in the Catholic Association, asked rhetorically in 1826, 'was it not to assert his right of citizenship that St Paul appealed to Caesar?'[192]

## 'The First Day of Freedom'

The pressure created by the spirited campaign of the Catholic Association soon paid dividends in the aftermath of Lord Liverpool's death in 1827. The crisis provoked by Daniel O'Connell's sensational victory at the Clare by-election in 1828, which prompted a panicked government led by Arthur Wellesley, the Duke of Wellington, to pass the Catholic Relief Act, is well known.[193] Writing to the secretary of the Catholic Association, Edward Dwyer, shortly after Emancipation received royal assent, a jubilant O'Connell saluted the dawning of 'the first day of freedom'. He praised the Association for instigating 'a bloodless revolution more extensive in its

190 Michael Keyes, *Funding the Nation: Money and Nationalist Politics in Nineteenth-Century Ireland* (Dublin: Gill & Macmillan Ltd., 2011), p. 40; McGrath, *Politics, Interdenominational Relations and Education*, p. 52.

191 *Evidence of the Right Rev. Doyle*, p. 41.

192 Anon., *Triumph of Justice and Liberty over Tyranny and Oppression, Through the Influence of the Catholic Clergy* (London: W. E. Andrews, [1826]), p. 7.

193 See, for example, the accounts in the two standard biographies of O'Connell: MacDonagh, *Hereditary Bondsman*, pp. 257–80; Geoghegan, *King Dan*, pp. 248–70.

operation than any other political change that could take place', and expectantly believed that the transformation would put an end to 'misgovernment' in Ireland. But he warned against Irish complacency and advocated the creation of a body – he used the phrase 'Society for the Improvement of Ireland' – to 'watch over the rising liberties of Ireland'.[194]

Several months later, a more despondent O'Connell bemoaned that the 'old system of government is in full force here'.[195] The unbridled optimism of the immediate aftermath of the passage of Emancipation had quickly evaporated, underpinned by O'Connell's guilt at paying the 'pound of flesh' in the form of the disfranchisement of the forty-shilling freeholder.[196] This 'wing' of the Catholic Relief legislation reduced the Irish electorate from 300,000 to 37,000, and damaged O'Connell's reputation as a political radical.[197] Still, O'Connell was emboldened by the concession of Catholic Emancipation and left disappointed by the resistance of the British state to reform itself. O'Connell now concluded that Ireland would be better served within alternative representative structures. The Repeal of the Act of Union became the next goal of his extraordinary political career.

Such a swift change in O'Connell's political mood spoke volumes for the confidence instilled within Catholic Ireland through decades of agitation in pursuit of Emancipation. The perception among Catholic political thinkers was that Emancipation would reorder the structure of politics based on the concepts of inclusion, equality and justice. Pro-Emancipation political literature often framed the eradication of the final penal laws as the path to Catholic empowerment. Once the full liberties promised by the theory of the British constitution became a reality in Ireland, Catholics would be on a par with the 'Established' denomination. With the majority population formally recognised as part of the political nation, improvement would inevitably follow. The Irish Catholic political mind connected the hardships that blighted Ireland not as symptomatic of unjust economic

194 Daniel O'Connell to Edward Dwyer, 14 April 1829, in Maurice R. O'Connell (ed.), *The Correspondence of Daniel O'Connell*, 8 vols. (Dublin: Irish Manuscripts Commission, 1977), iv, p. 45.

195 O'Connell to Pierce Mahony, 4 June 1829, in ibid., iv, p. 73.

196 K. Theodore Hoppen, *Elections, Politics, and Society in Ireland, 1832–1885* (Oxford: Oxford University Press, 1984), p. 1.

197 Laurent Colantonio, '"Democracy" and the Irish People, 1830–1848', in Joanna Innes and Mark Philp (eds.), *Re-Imagining Democracy in the Age of Revolutions: America, France, Britain, Ireland, 1750–1850* (Oxford: Oxford University Press, 2013), p. 167; Matthew Roberts, *Democratic Passions: The Politics of Feeling in British Popular Radicalism, 1809–48* (Manchester: Manchester University Press, 2022), p. 210.

structures, but as the formal exclusion from political power. This was a common interpretative framework in the first half of the nineteenth century. The *Anti-Unionist*, for example, stressed that the 'happiness' of populations rested on the 'introduction of representative governments'. The same issue explicitly explained the 'wretched condition of the poor' in Ireland as a 'consequence of their political degradation'.[198]

Emancipation was formally about the ability of Catholics to act as political representatives in the national parliament; but it also symbolised resentment at a post-1800 polity seemingly based, in terms of its Irish policy, on the principles of conquest and petty bigotry. O'Connell's frustration in 1829 at the lack of profound political change symbolised the advances of an organised Catholic politics that sought amelioration through the languages of political inclusion, equal rights and constitutionalism. These themes permeated Thomas Wyse's *Political Catechism* on Emancipation, published in 1829:

> Q: What are you?
> A: By religion, a Catholic; by birth, an Irishman and, by the constitution of the empire and the Act of Union, I ought to be a British freeman.
> Q: What do you mean by a British freeman?
> A: I mean the man who fully enjoys all the franchises and liberties, which of right belong to a freeborn Briton.
> [. . .]
> Q: Has an Englishman, then, any right to claim, in a national point of view, any superiority over an Irishman?
> A: None whatever, England is not more a portion of the British Empire than Ireland; nor an Irishman less a Briton than an Englishman.[199]

While the democratic base of the Catholic Association can be framed as a form of Irish constituent power that challenged Wellington's constituted power,[200] Emancipationists such as Wyse were explicit in framing Catholic relief as the means to import the British constitution into Ireland. The radicalism of the cause did not imply a radical constitution, despite O'Connell's drift towards Repeal of the Union.

Wyse was, of course, the able strategist who mobilised the forty-shilling freeholder in his native Waterford to take the seat for the Catholic interest.

198 *Anti-Unionist*, no. 5, 28 February 1818, pp. 65, 68.
199 Thomas Wyse, *The Political Catechism, Explanatory of the Constitutional Rights and Civil Disabilities of the Catholics of Ireland* (London: James Ridgway, 1829), p. 5.
200 Lucia Rubinelli, *Constituent Power: A History* (Cambridge: Cambridge University Press, 2020).

His great-grandfather, also Thomas, was a founder of the Catholic Committee in 1757.[201] As the Catholic Relief Act passed into law in 1829, Wyse published his *Historical Sketch of the Late Catholic Association of Ireland*, which offered an 'official' history of the O'Connellite campaign. It is a remarkable book, providing an insight into the ideas that permeated Catholic Ireland on the eve of Emancipation. 'In order to *be* free, there is one thing necessary', Wyse proclaimed, 'strongly, deeply, and perseveringly, to *will* it'.[202]

This 'will' was summoned into existence through the lengthy campaign for political equality. 'Catholic Emancipation', Wyse mused,

> Has not been achieved by a *coup de main*; liberty has not come to the Catholic by accident; nor is it, as has been falsely surmised, the gift of a few leaders; but its seeds have, year after year, been plentifully sown in the mind of a whole people, until the appointed moment for the sure and abundant harvest had fully arrived.[203]

Wyse depicted the eighteenth-century inheritance in colonial terms, explicitly labelling the Catholics of Ireland as the people of the nation who were excluded from political spaces. The 'revolution' of 1782 enhanced the status of the 'colony', but did nothing for the 'nation'.[204] The 'nation' was the people of Ireland, a familiar refrain in pro-Emancipation works; the potential for political change based on popular sovereignty represented, in Wyse's estimation, a break with eighteenth-century Irish thought. 'There was no People to appeal to', Wyse remarked of pre-1790s Ireland.[205] Born in 1791, Wyse was witness to a political revolution before reaching the age of forty. The Catholic Association, particularly in the contesting of elections from 1826, highlighted that 'the *people* had at last become important, and all future appeals were made to the *people*'.[206]

The democratic language and practical innovations of the Catholic Association are, of course, vital components of the political transformation that occurred in Ireland during the 1820s and have received due attention.[207] Wyse eagerly framed the campaign for Emancipation as part of a global struggle against tyranny, as Europe attempted to recover from the

201 For Wyse's remarkable biography, see James Johnston Auchmuty, *Sir Thomas Wyse, 1791–1862: The Life and Career of an Educator and Diplomat* (London: P. S. King & Son, Ltd., 1939).

202 Wyse, *Historical Sketch of the Late Catholic Association of Ireland*, 2 vols., i, p. 9. Emphasis in the original.

203 Ibid., i, p. 7. 204 Ibid., i, p. 110. 205 Ibid., i, p. 61.

206 Wyse, *Historical Sketch*, i, p. 270. Emphasis in the original.

207 For an arresting take, see S. J. Connolly, 'The limits of democracy: Ireland 1778–1848', in Innes and Philp (eds.), *Re-Imagining Democracy*, pp. 174–88.

Revolutionary and Napoleonic Wars. In his narrative, the British government attempted to 'conduct affairs on old principles' after 1815, but this was an age of a 'greater circulation of mind, greater freedom of thought and speech'.[208] He believed that a 'new alliance was formed between the Catholics and public opinion in every part of Europe'. The question was not merely whether Catholics in Ireland should obtain full political rights, but, as Wyse put it, 'whether in a free state there should not be recognised a regenerating power, capable of correcting ancient abuse, and of throwing off when necessary, in the progress of civilization, the slough and vice of its early corruptions'.[209] Echoing the words of the French travellers to Ireland during the 1830s, Alexis de Tocqueville and Gustave de Beaumont, Wyse believed that 'the cause of Ireland became the cause of Europe'.[210] The shared Catholicism of many European countries (especially France) and Ireland was an implicit theme of Wyse's framing; despite this, Irish Catholics were able to reach a seeming rapprochement with the 'Protestant state' of the United Kingdom in 1829. 'Catholic rights' were interpreted by their adherents as a share in existing 'Protestant rights'. As Wyse put it in his *Catechism*, for the Union to function effectively, genuine 'incorporation' was necessary. 'I mean by incorporation', he explained, 'a perfect mixing of one body with the other – a perfect identity of one country with the other'.[211] It was a political vision informed by liberal constitutionalism, in which the concepts of equality and popular sovereignty were held up as pillars within a just polity. Crucially, Emancipationists such as Wyse did not believe these political virtues were incompatible with the British constitution.

Wyse's account of the Catholic Association offers an illuminating snapshot of Irish Catholic political thought at its most brilliant victory. While O'Connell's pessimism about the limits of Emancipation set in quickly after the passage of the Catholic Relief Act, Wyse's history maintained a more optimistic vision for the future of Ireland. The *Historical Sketch* presented the end of the penal laws as the amelioration of historic grievance; with the creation of equal representative rights, a new age of political possibilities had begun. Wyse hoped that Emancipation would depoliticise religious identities in Ireland and that a political dispensation

[208] Wyse, *Historical Sketch*, ii, p. 80. [209] Ibid., ii, pp. 80–1.
[210] Ibid., i, p. 257. For Tocqueville and Beaumont in Ireland, see Hugh Brogan, *Alexis de Tocqueville: A Life* (New Haven, CT: Yale University Press, 2006), pp. 307–10.
[211] Wyse, *Political Catechism*, p. 11.

based on new interests would flourish. 'Matters of national improvement [now had] to be argued on their own intrinsic merits, and not on the fictions and prejudices of the past', Wyse hopefully declared.[212] While the 'Catholic question' was seemingly closed, Wyse anticipated that political argument would not cease but would build on the O'Connellite platform that had been created during the opening three decades of the Union:

> Catholic Emancipation has done this – it has given a just and national direction to the national efforts. It has done more than any other measure, since the period of the great laws of the Commonwealth, to make the country truly citizen. It has turned our faces to the right point. Its discussion has already given us activity, spirit, habits of thinking, or reasoning, of acting.

The Irish political mind had been transformed in the struggle for Emancipation. Wyse concluded with the plea to extend the British constitution into Ireland: 'all we now want is union'.[213] 'Union' indeed dominated the next phase of the Irish political experience, but not necessarily in the way in which Wyse hoped.

[212] Wyse, *Historical Sketch*, ii, p. 119. [213] Ibid., ii, pp. 120–1.

CHAPTER 3

# *Repeal*

## *Restoration, Democracy, and Revolution*

Our legislature is not dead, it only sleeps.[1]

Daniel O'Connell (1843)

What made the vast difference between Venice and Dublin and Cork? Was it not their institutions?[2]

Rev J. Godkin (1845)

In 1834, William Cobbett, the prominent English radical, arranged to spend time in Ireland to research a book on Irish political life. When Daniel O'Connell caught wind of Cobbett's intentions, he saw a momentous propaganda opportunity. Unable to host Cobbett himself, O'Connell asked – or rather, ordered – Edward Dwyer, the former secretary of the Catholic Association, to arrange a public dinner in Dublin for the visitor. In a revealing observation about Cobbett's status as a leader of radical political opinion, O'Connell admitted a wholesome admiration for the meritocratic nature of British public life. For O'Connell, that Cobbett started life as a farm labourer, enlisted in the army, and finally rose to national prominence as a writer and activist, spoke volumes for his work ethic, *and* the society that enabled such an upward trajectory. The 'democratic principle in British institutions', mused O'Connell, allowed Cobbett 'to make such an advance'. But Irish influence within these 'British institutions' was, in O'Connell's estimation, negligible – a fact more glaring in the post-1832 political world. O'Connell wished Cobbett to witness first-hand the gulf between Irish political ideas and the programme of the state, and the lack of good government in Ireland.[3] The broadcasting of

[1] John Levy (ed.), *A Full and Revised Report of the Three Days' Discussion in the Dublin Corporation, on the Repeal of the Union* (Dublin: James Duffy, 1843), p. 37.

[2] Rev. J. Godkin, *Third Prize Repeal Essay: The Rights of Ireland* (Dublin: James Duffy, 1845), p. 112.

[3] Daniel O'Connell to Edward Dwyer, 11 September 1834, in W. J. Fitzpatrick (ed.), *Correspondence of Daniel O'Connell: The Liberator*, 2 vols. (New York: Longmans, Green and Co., 1888), i, pp. 535–6.

Cobbett's Irish experiences would have, in O'Connell's words, 'the most beneficial effects'.[4]

Cobbett's visit to Ireland, which was his first and last, was notable for coming so late in his life. He was seventy-one years old when he made the crossing in the autumn of 1834; he died the following year, and the promised book on Ireland never materialised. He embarked on a tour of Ireland 'for the purpose of seeing with his own eyes the state of things in a country which had afforded so fertile a field for political controversy'.[5] Cobbett's radicalism was shaped by the centrality of the countryside in his political thought: his primary concern lay with the rural labourers, often exploited by large farmers, and threatened by the shift to mechanised agricultural techniques.[6] It was Ireland's rural poverty that Cobbett gravitated towards in a series of letters he wrote for his *Political Register* newspaper. The people were destitute, Cobbett observed, but the land was rich with livestock and crops; this was a different form of agrarian poverty from that found in more inhospitable rural parts of the wider United Kingdom.[7] Cobbett concluded grimly that Ireland needed the extension of the (old) poor law to provide relief to the paupers on the land, who were victims of an absentee landlord class that drained money from Ireland on an industrial scale.[8] This was a socio-economic problem, he surmised, but it required a political solution.

At a lecture in Dublin in November, Cobbett argued that 'a change there must be in the management of the affairs of Ireland'. Under the current constitutional setup, it was impossible for Ireland to influence government policy, which needed to tackle the destitution on the land:

> What is your number of representatives in the *imperial* Parliament? – for you are so lucky as to belong to an empire. Everything is now grand and imperial! Now, for my part, I would sooner have beer and bread, and live under a king, or even in a republic, than eat *lumpers*, and belong to an empire! (Hear, cheers, and laughter)... I say, as to the number of your representatives in the imperial Parliament, you can have no real

4 Daniel O'Connell to William Cobbett, 2 November 1834, in Lewis Melville (ed.), *The Life and Letters of William Cobbett in England and America: Based upon Hitherto Unpublished Family Papers*, 2 vols. (London: John Lane, 1913), ii, p. 256.

5 Robert Huish, *Memoirs of the Late William Cobbett, Esq., MP for Oldham*, 2 vols. (London: John Saunders, 1836), ii, p. 436.

6 See Ian Dyck, *William Cobbett and Rural Popular Culture* (Cambridge: Cambridge University Press, 1992).

7 *Political Register*, 27 September 1834.

8 *Political Register*, 1 November 1834. Cobbett was opposed to the 'new' poor law of 1834 (an act covering Ireland was passed in 1838) as it removed the right to relief.

> representation at all. There are your hundred of Irish members on one side, and 558 on the other.[9]

For Cobbett, Ireland had the trappings of representative government, but the spirit of government under the Union pitted the Irish against the British, effectively barring the former from wielding legislative power in a chamber numerically dominated by the latter. If political culture within the United Kingdom operated on a British-Irish binary, the Irish were locked out of the virtues of representative government.

John, Lord Russell, the leading architect of the Reform Act of 1832, defined the aim of expanding the franchise and altering the design of constituencies as the transformation of parliament into a 'mirror of the sentiments of the people'.[10] The 'mirroring' principle enabled reformers of the 1832 vintage to consent to maintaining a limited franchise, as a broader range of 'interests' (professional, industrial, middle class) were now represented in the Commons.[11] But the 'mirroring' principle struggled when confronted with Irish questions after Catholic Emancipation, partly because political culture in Ireland evolved on very different lines from Britain during the 1830s and 1840s. Against the backdrop of the structural 'colonial' aspects of Irish governance, which lacked legitimacy within the smaller island, Ireland challenged insular British debates about parliamentary reform and representation. The parliamentary 'mirror' held up during the nineteenth century contained reflections of Irish representatives, but their legislative and executive powerlessness was often unseen.

This critique of the operation of parliamentary government became a major part of the argument for the Repeal of the Union, made famous by O'Connell. The logic of 'Repeal' was that Ireland languished under the Union through political neglect: successive administrations governed Ireland without recourse to Irish ideas, resulting in a stagnant economy and political unrest. While the Union incorporated Ireland into the United Kingdom, in theory providing a role for the Irish within the imperial whole, the constitutional structures of the new state mitigated against such a vision. The Union state struggled to shake off the perception that it was the *British* who governed Ireland, rather than a genuine partnership. Repealing the Union posited that the solution to Irish woes

[9] Denis Knight (ed.), *Cobbett in Ireland* (London: Lawrence and Wishart, 1984), pp. 186, 190–1.

[10] Gregory Conti, *Parliament the Mirror of the Nation: Representation, Deliberation, and Democracy in Victorian Britain* (Cambridge: Cambridge University Press, 2019), p. 28.

[11] Ibid., p. 2.

lay in the restoration of an Irish parliament, which would bring balance to the relationship between Britain and Ireland, as both countries would enjoy meaningful self-government while sharing the same monarch. The articulation of the idea of Repeal also served as a declaration that Irish discontent with the structures of the United Kingdom was deeply felt.

The ideal of self-government was an intoxicating assumption. For O'Connell, the ability to control the destiny of a government was the supreme goal of a political civilisation. As he put it in a public letter in 1830, 'No man can undervalue self-government, but a man of low and grovelling mind'. The theory of Union offered the appearance of self-government within an expansive polity, but the perception of many in Ireland who flocked to the Repeal banner was that the constitutional experiment of 1801 merely furthered British domination over the smaller island. 'If an Irishman be equally fit to govern', argued O'Connell, 'to make laws, and to execute them, as the native of any other country, why should we give to others the power of making laws for us, or of executing them?'[12] Catholic Emancipation had addressed one powerful sense of political exclusion, while also crystallising another. The asymmetrical nature of the Union, the imbalance in the weighting of representatives, and their ability or otherwise to exercise power, came increasingly to the fore of Irish argument.

That said, O'Connell was famously inconsistent in his pursuit of Repeal. At times he was a ruthless advocate for the restoration of an Irish parliament; in other contexts, Repeal was quietly dropped in the pursuit of a meaningful relationship with the government. The rule of thumb during the 1830s with O'Connell is that he was a loud anti-Union activist while the Tories held power, and a constructive collaborator when the Whigs were in government.[13] O'Connell's critics, contemporary and posthumous, believed that such flip-flopping revealed a moral vacuum in his political outlook: the so-called 'Liberator' was willing to renege on Ireland's national demand for self-government if there was an opportunity for advancement on a more limited legislative front, such as tithe reform, or softening coercion.[14] O'Connell himself did not see any such inconsistency. He was a politician, after all, aware of the need to strike bargains to

[12] Daniel O'Connell, *Fourth Letter of Daniel O'Connell, Esq., on the Repeal of the Union* (Dublin: T. O'Flanagan, 1830), pp. 28–9.

[13] For the approaches of the two British parties and how they affected O'Connell's judgement, see Jay R. Roszman, '"Ireland as a weapon of warfare": Whigs, Tories, and the problem of Irish outrages, 1835 to 1839', *Historical Journal*, vol. 60, no. 4 (2017), pp. 971–95.

[14] James Quinn, *John Mitchel* (Dublin: UCD Press, 2008), p. 8.

secure political concessions.[15] But his tactical vision does not imply a lack of ideological commitment. At the heart of his approach was a consistent championing of 'justice' for Ireland. 'Justice', which O'Connell depicted as political equality for Ireland within the United Kingdom, rather than a parliament in Dublin *in of itself*, was initially the chief goal. The immediate origins of the powerful Repeal agitation of the 1840s, the age of the 'monster' meetings, lay in a campaign dubbed 'Justice, or Repeal'. Ever a man for establishing new political organisations, O'Connell founded the Precursor Society in 1838, which campaigned for parity in political rights between Britain and Ireland. This was to be the 'precursor' to a renewed struggle for Repeal if a transformation of the Union was not forthcoming. 'If Justice shall be done us, now we, of the present generation, are bound to submit to that Union', O'Connell announced in 1839.[16] There was no need to repeal the Union if all citizens across the United Kingdom enjoyed an equality of political rights and religious liberty. 'If we get the justice we require, then our Repeal Association is at an end', O'Connell announced at a mass rally in 1840. But O'Connell was also quick to add that he did not expect 'justice' to be done.[17]

O'Connellism was, then, not a straightforward 'nationalist' political platform based on the separate and distinct rights of the Irish people. O'Connell's primary aim was *good government* that provided redress to Irish grievances: if this could be achieved within the existing structures of the United Kingdom, all well and good; if not, the trial of the Union was over, and it was time for the restoration of a parliament in Dublin. For O'Connell, the fundamental problem at the heart of the Union concerned not clashing national identities but a lack of political and legal equality between the two islands. The period encompassing the campaign for Repeal, then, got to the crux of the issues of representative government and the Irish self-image. Were the interests of a small country best served as part of a globally powerful multinational Union, or as a separate political entity on the fringes of empire?

## The Repeal Imagination

With the achievement of Catholic Emancipation, O'Connell looked forward to Ireland's full incorporation into the British political system.

[15] Kevin B. *Nowlan, The Politics of Repeal: A Study in the Relations between Great Britain and Ireland, 1841–1850* (London: Routledge & Kegan Paul, 1965), p. 7; Oliver MacDonagh, *The Emancipist: Daniel O'Connell, 1830–1847* (London: Weidenfeld and Nicolson, 1989), p. 280.

[16] Edward Bullen (ed.), *Five Reports of the Committee of the Precursor Association* (Dublin: Richard Grace, 1839), p. vi.

[17] *Freeman's Journal*, 16 April 1840.

On entering parliament, O'Connell paraded his radical credentials by pressing for the expansion of the rights of voting (and thus of citizenship) to those who paid tax. Declaring himself a 'radical reformer' in the House of Commons in 1830, O'Connell lashed out at the aristocratic 'Old Corruption' that permeated the political hierarchy of the United Kingdom:

> Every day he lived, he was more and more convinced that nothing could be more debasing than the present system of Representation. When he saw Gentlemen otherwise of the highest honour, from the mere contact and association corrupted to the purposes of an oligarchical tyranny, he could not bring himself to speak of the system but with abhorrence and disgust. He raised his voice on behalf of the people; he called upon the House, which had shorn the talons of the Monarchy, to use its power to cut short the fell fangs of the oligarchical faction which lorded it over the land.[18]

Such sentiments were shared by many prominent radicals, such as Cobbett and Henry Hunt. Indeed, such was O'Connell's status that he was feted as one of the leading 'British' reformers of his day.[19]

The O'Connellites used their parliamentary platform to prove their universalist credentials in championing the abolition of the slave trade throughout the British Empire (which was achieved in 1833), and Jewish emancipation (which came, in a convoluted manner, in 1858). Underpinning these campaigns – and tying them to their core Irish cause – was the belief that 'justice' should drive all political action.[20] On entering the first reformed parliament in 1833, the O'Connellites sat on the same benches as the radical members of parliament, and fell in with Thomas Attwood, founder of the Birmingham Political Union.[21] Writing retrospectively, one of those Irish MPs, O'Connell's son John, was struck by the paradox of the British constitutional tradition that he observed firsthand. Unlike many of its European cousins, the British parliament appeared capable of reforming itself, and its role in the ending of slavery was a great victory for humanity. 'Why is it that a nation capable of acts

[18] *Hansard*, vol. 22, 18 February 1830, cols. 719–20.

[19] Laurent Colantonio, '"Democracy" and the Irish people, 1830–1848', in Joanna Innes and Mark Philp (eds.), *Re-Imagining Democracy in the Age of Revolutions: America, France, Britain, Ireland, 1750–1850* (Oxford: Oxford University Press, 2013), p. 166.

[20] Jeffrey R. Kerr-Ritchie, 'Black abolitionists, Irish supporters, and the brotherhood of man', *Slavery & Abolition*, vol. 37, no. 3 (2016), p. 605; U. R. Q. Henriques, 'The Jewish Emancipation controversy in nineteenth-century Britain', *Past & Present*, no. 40 (1968), pp. 138–9.

[21] John O'Connell, *Recollections and Experiences from a Parliamentary Career from 1833 to 1848*, 2 vols. (London: Richard Bentley, 1849), i, pp. 2, 5.

such as these', O'Connell mused, 'appears to be so utterly incapable of justice or reason' when Ireland was concerned?[22]

Traditionally, O'Connellite politics are viewed diachronically, as the origins of a modern Irish nationalism that was almost exclusively Catholic.[23] When examined synchronically, however, Repeal can be framed as an Irish response to the 'Age of Reform'. Repealing the Union envisaged a restoration of the Irish parliament, which O'Connell framed as a national demand; but this does not mean that Repeal was merely a preface to the later struggle for Home Rule. The assumptions that underpinned Repeal political thought were drawn from the rich well of contemporary parliamentary reform, chiefly the ideal of creating representative government, with democratic legitimacy at its heart. In 1830, at the height of the campaign for parliamentary reform, O'Connell triggered fresh agitation behind the Repeal banner. In the autumn of that year, he founded the (typically wordy) Association of Irish Volunteers for the Repeal of the Union. The Association did not last long – it was swiftly prohibited by Wellington's government, with the O'Connellites forced into staging 'Repeal breakfasts' in lieu of public meetings to get around restrictive laws – but it changed the nature of political debate in Ireland. The Repeal of the Union had become a mainstream political idea.

While the Tory government was successful in shutting down the Association of Irish Volunteers for the Repeal of the Union, it could not halt an avalanche of new pamphlets and printed material that framed Repeal as part of the wider reforming agenda. The language used in the early debate concerning Repeal in the aftermath of Catholic Emancipation, like that of parliamentary reform, was steeped in an appeal to constitutional traditions. Patrick Morris, a successful Catholic merchant, published a series of political and economic arguments in favour of Repeal in 1831, directed at liberal Protestants in his native Waterford. Morris proclaimed that the Irish had never known 'the advantages of a Government fairly representing their wants and interests'. Both the 'old' Irish parliament and the Union experiment excluded the bulk of the population and maintained aristocratic privilege in the face of the 'People'. This had resulted in a breach of the ethos of the Union, Morris surmised, with the passing of coercive laws for Ireland that did not apply to

[22] Ibid., i, p. 45.

[23] Lawrence J. McCaffrey, *Daniel O'Connell and the Repeal Year* (Lexington, KY: University of Kentucky Press, 1966), p. viii. Donal McCartney, *The Dawning of Democracy in Ireland, 1800–1870* (Dublin: Helicon Ltd., 1987), pp. 213–14.

Britain. Nothing short of a 'local Legislature', which enjoyed the confidence of the 'People', reasoned Morris, would raise Ireland 'from her present depressed and impoverished state'. Morris added that government rooted in the 'People' represented a return to the true nature of the British constitution, an idea that chimed with contemporary radical opinion.[24] 'All that the Irish want is good government', he argued, constructed on the pillars of representative legitimacy and justice. As it was, the 'free principles of the British Constitution', from Morris's perspective, did not extend to Ireland, leading to an arbitrary form of governance.[25]

Other political pamphleteers positioned Repeal within a broader radical framework. The noted Irish writer George Ensor described the British parliament as merely 'the echo of royalty', unable to cast off the corrupting hand of hereditary privilege.[26] William Joseph Battersby, in his *Repealer's Manual* (which went through three editions during the 1830s), imagined Repeal against the backdrop of other far-reaching constitutional reforms, such as the secret ballot, short parliaments, and an enlarged franchise.[27] Indeed, the connection between the idea of Repeal and wider parliamentary reform was also cited by enemies, who painted a scenario of a restored Dublin parliament captured by the excesses of radicalism, leading to mob rule and the destruction of property rights.[28] The anti-Repeal *National Magazine* (published in Dublin) feared a destabilising power struggle between a democratic parliament in Ireland and an aristocratic lower house in London, resulting in constitutional paralysis.[29] Repeal was thus strongly tinged – for some, tarnished – by its association with radical parliamentary reform.

This was no less true of radicals who valued reform above Repeal. In 1831, Luke Hope, the son of James 'Jemmy' Hope, the veteran of the 1798 and 1803 rebellions, launched *The Irish Rush-Light*, a short-lived

[24] James Epstein, 'The constitutional idiom: radical reasoning, rhetoric and action in early nineteenth-century England', *Journal of Social History*, vol. 23, no. 3 (1990), pp. 553–74.

[25] Patrick Morris, *Six Letters, Intended to Prove that the Repeal of the Act of Union, and the Establishment of a Local Legislature in Ireland, are Necessary to Cement the Connection with Great Britain and containing a short view of the Trade, Manufactures, and Agriculture of Ireland: Addressed to the Right Honourable Sir John Newport* (Waterford, 1831), preface, p. 5.

[26] George Ensor, *Anti-Union: Ireland as She Ought to be* (Newry: Morgan and Dunlop, 1831), pp. 16, 22.

[27] W. J. Battersby, *The Repealer's Manual or, the Union Reconsidered*, 3rd ed. (Dublin: T. & J. Coldwell, 1837), p. 6.

[28] Anon., *The Repeal of the Legislative Union of Great Britain and Ireland, Considered* (London: James Ridgway, 1830), p. 11; 'R. B. G.', *A Repeal of the Union: The Ruin of Ireland* (Dublin: William Curry, 1831), pp. 50–1.

[29] 'The Repeal of the Union', *National Magazine*, vol. 1, no. iv (1830), p. 631.

periodical that gave expression to the voice of non-O'Connellite radicalism in Ireland.[30] While *The Rush-Light's* central message sounded, to Irish ears, as a rekindling of the United Irishmen's democratic-infused politics, it chimed more with contemporary developments in radicalism in Britain, such as the establishment of Political Unions in major British cities, which self-consciously claimed to speak for 'the People'.[31] The first issue of *The Rush-Light* set out its radical agenda:

> We shall contend, under all circumstances, for universal suffrage and short parliaments but before all, for that great security for independence, that antidote to corruption, perjury, and crime – that sacred shield of freedom, and key to every other political right, the VOTE BY BALLOT.[32]

Universal suffrage, annual parliaments and the secret ballot were the mantras of British radicalism. *The Rush-Light* positioned itself within this milieu, to the extent that it frequently reprinted material from radical periodicals and newspapers across the United Kingdom. The Repeal of the Union was presented not as an 'Irish' demand, but as a manifestation of a right to enlightened self-government.[33] Giving notice of the impending general election in 1831, *The Rush-Light* called for candidates to commit to parliamentary reform and Repeal: 'The man who would contend for a radical reform in a British parliament whilst he will not demand a reformed legislature in his own country, cannot be a real patriot'.[34] With such a forceful assertion, *The Rush-Light* intimately connected the restoration of an Irish parliament with the cause of the franchise and ballot.

*The Irish Rush-Light*, like the Political Unions, faded away, but its radical agenda remained potent. In 1831, O'Connell eased off the Repeal message to grant the Whigs space to draft the Reform Bill. Marking the first attempt at an O'Connellite-Whig alliance, O'Connell confided in Lord Duncannon (John Ponsonby) that he had turned his followers 'from the overpowering question of the Repeal to the suitable one of Reform'.[35] But the genie was out of the bottle. On launching the campaign for Repeal in the autumn of 1830, O'Connell made a bold claim that periodically came back to haunt him:

[30] Tom Clyde, *Irish Literary Magazines: An Outline History and Descriptive Bibliography* (Dublin: Irish Academic Press, 2003), pp. 84–5.

[31] Nancy D. LoPatin, *Political Unions, Popular Politics and the Great Reform Act of 1832* (London: Macmillan, 1998), p. 5.

[32] *Irish Rush-Light*, April 1831, p. 2.

[33] *Irish Rush-Light*, November 1831, p. 231.

[34] *Irish Rush-Light*, April 1831, p. 8.

[35] O'Connell, *Correspondence of Daniel O'Connell*, iv, p. 370.

> In plain truth, the Union exists at this moment, only because men foolishly and childishly imagine that it is incapable of being abolished. Yet we have already demonstrated by practical experience, that a great majority of the Irish nation has only to demand, legally and constitutionally, but loudly and determinedly, civil rights – *the rights of nature* – and their demands will and must be complied with.[36]

The force of O'Connell's argument was immense, and it bestowed the ideal of self-government with its own momentum. By the end of 1830, 'Repeal' had become *the* clarion call of Catholic Ireland, and it proved difficult even for the Liberator to resist this.[37] After notable electoral successes in 1831 and 1832, for example, O'Connell, under pressure from young Turks in his ranks (such as Feargus O'Connor, the future figurehead of the Chartist movement), and against his own judgement, issued a Repeal motion in the Commons, which was soundly rejected by 523 votes to 38.[38] Despite the lack of progress at Westminster, Repeal framed the political outlook of many in Ireland during the 1830s and 1840s.

The rhetorical power of Repeal was unquestionable, but what did 'Repealing the Union' envisage? One contemporary critic of Repeal condemned its champions for deploying a 'mere delusive watchword': Repealers talked up the restoration of an Irish parliament, but there was 'a remarkable silence as to what sort of constitution we are to have'.[39] Indeed, Repeal legally implied the restoration of the *unreformed* Irish parliament, turning the political clock back to before 1801, with the resurrection of rotten boroughs, extremely restrictive franchises, and the exclusion of Catholics from the chambers.[40] Such an end result clearly contradicted the general view of a progressively led and fully reformed Irish parliament projected by Repealers. While O'Connell made much political noise about Repeal, he only sporadically sketched out details as to what a self-governing Ireland would look like, rarely straying from a vision based on radical staples of a secret ballot, household suffrage, and a fair distribution of seats throughout the country. He was vague on the ideal relationship between the Irish and British parliaments, but suggested that even a 'subordinate' legislative chamber would produce 'great advantages to

36 Daniel O'Connell, *Second Letter of Daniel O'Connell, Esq., on the Repeal of the Union* (Dublin: T. O'Flanagan, 1830), p. 17. Emphasis in original.

37 MacDonagh, *Emancipist*, p. 39.

38 William O'Neill Daunt, *Personal Recollections of the Late Daniel O'Connell, MP*, 2 vols. (London: Chapman & Hall, 1848), i, p. 18.

39 'Civis', *Thoughts on the Repeal of the Union* (Dublin: Richard Moore, 1831), pp. 5, 9.

40 Ibid., pp. 3–4

Ireland'.[41] It is telling that his five-hour speech during the parliamentary debate on Repeal in 1834 was dominated by a historicised account of the relations between Ireland and England.[42]

Still, the return of a parliament in Dublin represented a profound renegotiation of British sovereignty and the enshrining of Irish national rights within the constitution. The imagery of '1782' permeated Repeal political works and ephemeral materials, making clear that the termination of the Union would mark a restoration rather than a revolution. Michael Barry's prize-winning essay on Repeal from 1844 presented a narrative that emphasised the economic and cultural improvements in Ireland in the period of the 'independent' parliament between 1782 and 1800, in contrast to the 'miserable dependence' of the earlier part of the century.[43] The 'Volunteers of 1782' were revived in the 1840s (unarmed, it should be said), with elaborate membership forms that included the images of O'Connell and the Patriot MPs Henry Grattan and Henry Flood.[44]

The idealism of '1782' was, however, queried from an alternative historicised viewpoint centring on the record of the old parliament in Dublin. One pamphleteer expressed bewilderment at how the 'annals of the Irish Parliament' could be read as 'one favourable to the happiness of Ireland', noting that it was the London parliament that delivered (albeit belatedly) the Catholic Emancipation and Reform Acts.[45] The Dublin-born Robert Montgomery Martin, a historian of the British colonies, similarly attacked the notion that a 'restoration of the state in which Ireland was previous to the Union' would enhance Irish constitutional liberties. 'Ireland never was so truly and integrally a kingdom as she is at this moment', he argued in 1843.[46] It was a rhetorical paradox that the supporters of what became known as 'simple Repeal' could not quite overcome: the termination of the Union was presented as a liberal measure, but the historical record of the 'old' Irish parliament was far from progressive. Indeed, O'Connell occasionally conceded the existence of this

41 Bullen, *Five Reports of the Committee of the Precursor Association*, p. v.

42 *Repeal of the Union: Report of the Debate in the House of Commons on Mr O'Connell's Motion, and its Proceedings in the House of Lords on Earl Gray's Motion for Concurring in the Address of the Commons, April, 1834* (London: William Clowes, 1834).

43 *Essays on the Repeal of the Union, to which the Association Prizes were Awarded; with a Supplemental Essay, Recommended by the Judges* (Dublin: James Duffy, 1845), pp. 13, 41.

44 Loyal National Repeal Association of Ireland scrapbook, Thomas Ray papers, John J. Burns Library, Boston College, MS2007-019, file 1/4.

45 Anon., *Repeal, or No Repeal: Repeal of the Union Considered in its Practical Bearings* (London: James Ridgway and Sons, 1833), p. 21.

46 R. Montgomery Martin, *Ireland Before and After the Union with Great Britain* (London: Wm. S. Orr and Co., 1843), p. 36.

tension.[47] If the goal was the restoration of the Irish parliament, somehow this institution had to look very different to its eighteenth-century ancestor. The romanticised depictions of College Green with the text 'it was and shall be' that graced the membership cards of the Loyal National Repeal Association of Ireland during the 1840s did little to reconcile this problem, other than appeal to national pride and hazy memories of an 'independent' parliament.[48]

Some Repealers were drawn to more exotic constitutional ideas to resolve this perceived problem. Federalist ideas began circulating within Repeal circles from 1831 with the publication of several papers by a Catholic priest called Thaddeus O'Malley. Entitled *The Federalist*, the project was a self-conscious effort to appropriate the papers of the same name by Alexander Hamilton, James Madison, and John Jay in the 1780s.[49] O'Malley's work was not quite of the standard of its illustrious American namesake, but it nonetheless represented the first sustained engagement with federalist ideas from an Irish perspective since the passage of the Union. The Irish *Federalist* advocated a form of federalism based on the constitution of the United States. Under this model, Ireland would become a self-governing and sovereign 'state' within a federated United Kingdom, with England and Scotland enjoying equal powers.[50] While federalism quickly gained a reputation (and a largely negative one at that) in Ireland as a middle-of-the-road compromise position between the binaries of centralised Union and Irish self-government, it was, in fact, one of the most radical constitutional frameworks ever invoked for the United Kingdom.[51] Ireland would gain a parliament under the federal scheme proposed by O'Malley, but the price to be paid was the wholesale reimagining of the parliamentary system across Britain, and the likelihood of a written constitution to legally enshrine the rights of each 'state'. Federalism was at heart a *unionist* scheme, as it reconciled the ideal of national self-government with membership of the United Kingdom. O'Malley was explicit about the unionist underpinnings of federalism,

47 *Repeal of the Union: Report of . . . Mr O'Connell's Motion*, p. 13.

48 Loyal National Repeal Association of Ireland scrapbook, Ray papers, Burns Library, MS2007–019, file 1/3.

49 There are numerous modern editions. See, for example, Alexander Hamilton, James Madison and John Jay, *The Federalist Papers*, ed. Ian Shapiro (New Haven, CT: Yale University Press, 2009).

50 'A Minister of Peace' [Thaddeus O'Malley], *The Federalist: or a Series of Papers Showing how to Repeal the Union, so as to Avoid a Violent Crisis, and at the Same Time, Secure and Reconcile all Interests, no. 1* (Dublin: the author, 1831). O'Malley intended seven papers, but it appears that only two were published.

51 For context, see John Kendle, *Federal Britain: A History* (London: Routledge, 1997).

suggesting that such a perspective offered Repealers a trump card to play in the face of those who argued that Irish self-government threatened the Union. 'Federalists', O'Malley conjectured, 'would be a much better *nom de guerre* for the Repealers than "Anti-Unionists", since it expresses at once, that they are *for* a Union, not *against* one, and what sort of a Union it is they want'.[52] For some critics, this was precisely the problem.

The idea did not catch on in the early 1830s, but federalism became an enduring presence within Irish constitutional thought throughout the nineteenth and twentieth centuries.[53] Federalist ideas emerged again in July 1843, when the Ulster liberal William Sharman Crawford advocated such a scheme. O'Connell, reeling from the defeat of his 'monster meeting' strategy (which we'll discuss shortly), jumped on the proposal as a fresh idea to make a political impression. He attempted to woo liberal federalists into the Repeal camp, with some success: while Crawford declined O'Connell's advances (indeed, the relationship between the two had soured some years before),[54] Grey Porter, the sheriff of Fermanagh and the author of a pamphlet on federal union, joined the Liberator's ranks.[55] Porter was an eccentric character (a common trait within Irish federalist circles, it would appear), and his work on federalism was elusive in how he actually understood the concept, beyond occasional references to the 'American states'. For Porter, federalism represented a middle way between unresponsive Union and Repeal, the latter of which had become intimately bound up as a 'Catholic' cause. But Porter's argument for a federal union was underpinned by an assumption that all O'Connellites shared: discontent in Ireland was the consequence of a lack of 'any congenial national political institutions, of any bona fide self-government'.[56] O'Connell, in truth, saw little difference between federalism and simple Repeal, believing that both offered the fundamental goal of self-government.[57] But his courtship of the federalists concerned many in the Repeal movement, including his senior lieutenant, William O'Neill Daunt, who questioned

52 [O'Malley], *The Federalist*, no. 1, p. 29.

53 Alvin Jackson, *United Kingdoms: Multinational Union States in Europe and Beyond, 1800–1925* (Oxford: Oxford University Press, 2023), p. 254.

54 Gerald R. *Hall, Ulster Liberalism, 1778–1876: The Middle Path* (Dublin: Four Courts Press, 2011), p. 93.

55 B. A. Kennedy, 'Sharman Crawford's federal scheme for Ireland', in H. A. Cronne, T. W. Moody and D. B. Quinn (eds.), *Essays in British and Irish History in Honour of James Eadie Todd* (London: Frederick Muller Ltd., 1949), p. 246.

56 J. G. V. Porter, *Ireland: The Union of 1801 ... A Federal (The Only Fair) Union between Great Britain and Ireland Inevitable, and Most Desirable for Both Islands*, 2nd ed. (London: Fisher, Son & Co., [1844]), p. ix.

57 *Freeman's Journal*, 15 October 1844.

'the wisdom of expanding on the basis on which a struggle for local legislation could be made', and thus diluting the movement's aims.[58] Indeed, Crawford condemned O'Connell for 'trying to make the Repealers believe they are Federalists and the Federalists that they are Repealers', and in the end pleasing no one.[59] O'Connell's dabbling may have inadvertently discredited federalism before the premise of the scheme was seriously considered.

One thing on which O'Connell remained consistent was his downplaying of the revolutionary nature of Repeal. O'Connell repeatedly emphasised the *restorative* nature of Repeal, a *return* to a parliament in Dublin. In 1833, he told one of his most trusted confidants, P. V. Fitzpatrick, that repealing the Union meant '[i]n short, salutary restoration without revolution, an Irish parliament, British connection, one King, two legislatures'.[60] After the establishment of the Loyal National Repeal Association and the commencement of a fresh campaign in 1840, O'Connell chaired a committee to examine the shape of a self-governing Ireland, which advocated a lower chamber of 300 members (the same number who sat in the pre-1801 parliament), but without the boroughs disenfranchised by the Union. Counties, cities, and towns were to gain representatives based on population size. For Repealers, this genuinely marked a restoration, albeit with a constitution altered by more recent principles of parliamentary reform.[61]

While O'Connellism contributed to, and chimed with, developments in Irish anti-unionist thought, its underlying notion that 'justice' from Britain could reconcile Ireland to the Union provided the cause of Repeal with political flexibility. While O'Connell frequently advocated interpretations that implicitly or explicitly rejected the legitimacy of the Union, especially during more intense periods of the Repeal agitation, his political mind was not one of a simple binary between unjust *or* Irish government.[62] He held multiple and apparently contradictory beliefs at the same time: namely, the *process* of the Act of Union rendered the

[58] William O'Neill Daunt to O'Connell, 29 October [1844], in O'Connell, *Correspondence of O'Connell*, vii, p. 285.
[59] Quoted in Charles Gavan Duffy, *Short Life of Thomas Davis, 1840–1846* (London: T. Fisher Unwin, 1895), p. 186.
[60] O'Connell to Fitzpatrick, 21 February 1833, in O'Connell, *Correspondence of O'Connell*, v, p. 11.
[61] Daniel O'Connell, *Irish Parliament: Report of the Committee of the National Repeal Association of Ireland, to who, it was Referred to Suggest a Proposal, to be Converted into a Law, for the Reconstruction of the House of Commons of Ireland* (no publishing details, 1840).
[62] Daniel O'Connell, *Third Letter of Daniel O'Connell, Esq., on the Repeal of the Union* (Dublin: T. O'Flanagan, 1830), p. 26.

legislation illegitimate; self-government in the form of a restored parliament in Dublin offered the path to Irish liberty; but *if* a more sympathetic governmental machine in Britain was responsive to Irish sensitivities, offering reforms to address a series of perceived injustices – the tithe system, the status of the Church of Ireland, the rights to land ownership, the franchise – then Ireland could be reconciled to the Union. This latter approach became politically possible with the ascension of the Whigs to power in April 1835 on a platform of harmonising the Irish connection.[63] In September that year, O'Connell spoke at a public dinner in Edinburgh, delivering a striking pro-Union message: 'My object in this mission is to excite the people of England and Scotland in favour of my country, and so to render the repeal of the Union unnecessary, by making it a real Union instead of a parchment Union'. If Ireland were elevated to become an equal partner of England and Scotland, O'Connell told his enthusiastic audience, then 'hurrah for the Union'.[64]

How was the most pre-eminent critic of the Union able to embrace unionism? O'Connellism represented a balancing act between the ideal of Irish self-government and the reality of the power of the British state in an imperial age. Just as successive governments oscillated between coercion and conciliation in response to changing political contexts, so too O'Connellism swayed between repealing the Union and nascent unionism. The underpinning theory of Repeal political thought was that Ireland's social and economic problems – sectarianism, absenteeism, lack of industry, rural poverty – stemmed from a negligent government. A restored Irish parliament was the most eye-catching method to redress this, but it was not necessarily the only path.

O'Connellism, then, demanded a degree of political footwork from its adherents. The polemic literature produced on behalf of the Repealer cause, however, tended to lack O'Connell's more flexible approach. One such example was W. J. Battersby's *The Repealer's Manual*, which was first published in 1833. The second edition, which appeared in 1834, bore the vitriolic influence of Jonah Barrington in carrying the title *The Rise and Fall of Ireland: or, the Repealer's Manual.*[65] Battersby was a bookseller and writer of numerous works on aspects of Catholicism. His *Repealer's Manual* grew out of an essay contest in 1830 to highlight the problem of

63 Roszman, 'Ireland as a weapon', pp. 974–5.

64 *The Speech of Daniel O'Connell, Esq., MP, at a Public Dinner in Edinburgh, on Thursday, September 17th, 1835* (London: John Limbird, 1835), p. 8.

65 Barrington's *Rise and Fall of the Irish Nation* (1833) was a dramatic account that emphasised the role of bribery and corruption in the passing of the Union.

absentee landlordism and the Union, with Battersby's entry suggesting that such social grievances were created and maintained by misrule. It was through '*good government alone*', declared Battersby, that such evils would be removed. Battersby went on to expand on the Repealer logic that a parliament in Dublin represented the best means to secure '*native good government*'.[66] He equated self-government with nationhood; without formal political power, the Irish were a people of some eight million, but not a 'nation'.[67] So far, this was a standard Repealer interpretation, combining a sense of historic grievance with the perceived virtue of self-government. But Battersby lacked O'Connell's chameleonic ability to *reimagine* the Union to provide redress. *Only* an Irish parliament, in Battersby's reading, had the potential to deliver good government for Ireland. He picked up and ran with a favourite O'Connellite theme – the under-representation of Irish MPs in the House of Commons – but his conclusion offered little in the way of hope:

> Since if we had even our original 300 representatives [the number of MPs in the pre-1801 Irish parliament] against upwards of 500 [British MPs], *in a foreign legislature*, we never could expect the same measure of justice we would necessarily obtain, from half the number at home, under the eye, influence, and control of Ireland's own opinion?[68]

This argument had much currency. George Ensor critiqued the lack of influence that Irish representatives held in the House of Commons in the face of 'a supercilious overwhelming majority of foreigners'. Ensor lamented that even if the Irish members spoke with the rhetorical elegance of Pericles, they were doomed to be drowned out by sheer numbers.[69] In this analysis, the Union was structurally flawed: the levers of power were permanently out of the reach of the smaller country, and reliance on the sympathy of a British political party in government was debasing. 'Give the Irish people good government, and they will be peaceable', Battersby affirmed in his *Manual*.[70] But whether this was possible without terminating the Union was a question that separated O'Connell from many of his followers.

## Chartism, Democracy, and the Irish People

In 1838, disparate radical forces in England congregated around a political manifesto called the 'People's Charter'. This was the birth of the Chartist

66 Battersby, *Repealer's Manual*, p. 2. Emphasis in original. 67 Ibid., p. 11. 68 Ibid., p. 151.
69 Ensor, *Anti-Union*, p. 127. 70 Battersby, *Repealer's Manual*, p. 239.

movement, a popular organisation that campaigned for radical political reforms, including universal male suffrage, annual parliaments, and the secret ballot.[71] During the early 1830s, O'Connell was revered by some British radicals who later supported the People's Charter for his progressive support for measures to democratise the constitution. The Irishman's apparent volte-face – his support for the limited Reform Act of 1832 and formal embrace of the Whigs in 1835 – however, shattered any unity between the Repealers and working-class radicals in Britain.[72] An irony of this split was that one of the leading figureheads of Chartism, Feargus O'Connor, was a former Repeal MP for Cork County who publicly broke with O'Connell in 1836. The relationship between the two men remained antagonistic until O'Connell's death in 1847, which greatly damaged opportunities for cooperation between the Repeal movement and the Chartists. The personal grievances between O'Connell and O'Connor also encouraged later accounts to remain encased within their distinct national historiographical silos. Recent works have taken a more comparative approach, making a powerful case for viewing the two movements in light of each other, chiefly as expressions of radical ideology, passions, and organisation.[73] There is another point of comparison that is worth stressing: the shared sense within the Repeal and Chartist mind that the political and social woes suffered by their supporters stemmed from formal exclusion from meaningful political power.

Chartism was born from frustration with the limits of the Reform Act of 1832. The movement challenged the mechanisms that enabled aristocratic control over parliament, with radical reform advocated as the means to empower people with the rights of citizenship. William Lovett, one of Chartism's architects, framed such reforming steps as the foundation stone of a utopian alternative to 'Old Corruption'. The 'People's Charter', Lovett proclaimed in a pamphlet co-written with John Collins, 'is calculated to secure to *all classes of society their just share of political power*, and

[71] For the origins of Chartism, see Malcolm Chase, *Chartism: A New History* (Manchester: Manchester University Press, 2007), pp. 1–19.

[72] Dorothy Thompson, *The Chartists* (London: Temple Smith, 1984), p. 19.

[73] See especially the work of Matthew Roberts: *Democratic Passions: The Politics of Feeling in British Popular Radicalism, 1809–1848* (Manchester: Manchester University Press, 2022), pp. 207–35; *Chartism, Commemoration and the Cult of the Radical Hero* (Abingdon: Routledge, 2020), pp. 178–204; and 'Daniel O'Connell, Repeal and Chartism in the Age of Atlantic Revolutions', *Journal of Modern History*, vol. 90 (2018), pp. 1–39. Also see Christine Kinealy, '"Brethren in bondage": Chartists, O'Connellites, Young Irelanders and the 1848 uprising', in Dónal Ó Drisceoil and Fintan Lane (eds.), *Politics and the Irish Working Class, 1830–1945* (Basingstoke: Palgrave Macmillan, 2005), pp. 87–112.

[offers] one of the most important steps to all social improvement'.[74] Social degradation and destitution were understood by the Chartist strategists such as Lovett not as the consequence of capitalist exploitation, but rather a lack of representative government.[75] Robert Gammage, a Chartist who became the movement's first major historian, emphasised this mentality in his influential study from 1854:

> The masses look on the enfranchised classes, whom they behold reposing on the couch of opulence, and contrast that opulence with the misery of their own condition. Reasoning from effect to cause there is no marvel that they arrive at the conclusion – that *their exclusion from political power is the cause of our social anomalies.*[76]

O'Connellite conceptions of Repeal were grounded in a similar logic. Repealers blamed the lack of manufacture and rise in poverty in Ireland not on global or national economic trends, but on the loss of Irish self-government.[77] For Repealers, the inability to direct legislative and executive power explained Ireland's social problems, chiming with the Chartist analysis of the impact of political exclusion of the unfranchised. In this reading, the Union stripped Ireland of representative government, and socio-economic distress was the result. The Act of Union, affirmed William O'Neill Daunt, a senior O'Connellite figure, 'is the direct source of much of the evil that our country suffers', with the loss of self-government annihilating 'our power of self-protection'.[78] Just as Chartists believed that the realisation of the People's Charter would promote social harmony in Britain through equalising political rights, Daunt believed the restoration of a parliament in Dublin would do the same in Ireland.[79] Both the Repealers and Chartists internalised that the *constitution* was the key to social improvement.

74 William Lovett and John Collins, *Chartism: A New Organization of the People, Embracing a Plan for the Education and Improvement of the People, Politically and Socially* (London: J. Watson, 1840), p. v. Emphasis in original.

75 For this, see Gareth Stedman Jones, 'Rethinking Chartism', *in Jones, Languages of Class: Studies in English Working-Class History, 1832–1982* (Cambridge: Cambridge University Press, 1984), pp. 90–178.

76 R. G. Gammage, *History of the Chartist Movement, 1837–1854* (Newcastle-On-Tyne: Browne & Browne, 1894; first published 1854), p. 9. My emphasis.

77 O'Connell, *Fourth Letter*, p. 34; Ensor, *Anti-Union*, p. 141.

78 W. J. O'Neill Daunt, *Repeal of the Union: A Letter from W. J. O'Neill Daunt, Esq., to the Landlords of Ireland* (Dublin: Loyal National Repeal Association, 1846), p. 2.

79 Ibid., p. 13. For the Chartist interpretation of this theme, see Peter Gurney, *Wanting and Having: Popular Politics and Liberal Consumerism in England, 1830–1870* (Manchester: Manchester University Press, 2015), p. xi.

There are other points of similarity here. While O'Connell's well-known disdain for the Chartists – born from his mistrust of a movement occupying a similar radical political space as the Repealers, and the Chartists' ambivalent attitude to violence – was genuine, the public animosities should not distract us from the intellectual commonalities between the two movements.[80] Both were founded on similar appeals to representative democracy that empowered the 'People', and the transformative promise of inclusion into the political nation. While the campaigns for the Charter and Repeal were grounded in appeals to constitutional traditions (Saxon custom for the Chartists and the more recent constitution of 1782 for the Repealers), both also deployed what one historian of Chartism has labelled a 'democratic idiom'.[81] This was a new departure in British politics. Chartist print culture, most particularly the *Northern Star*, the most prominent newspaper to emerge from the movement, was the site of an explosion of democratic tropes during the 1830s and 1840s. For the most part, appeals to democracy implied ideas of political equality, meaningful representation, and realising the potential of the individual through self-government.[82] For Lovett and Collins, democracy in its modern form was equated with 'popular representation', ensuring that the voices of the hitherto unenfranchised masses were heard.[83]

'Democracy' was as much a rhetorical marker for the O'Connellites as it was for the Chartists, providing a language and method (in terms of mass demonstrations) to lay siege to a political system that formally excluded most people. O'Connell claimed in parliament that the grievances that he personified were legitimate because he was the 'representative of the people'.[84] John O'Connell believed that his father's election as Lord Mayor of Dublin in 1841 would further legitimise the Repeal cause, as the office bestowed 'a legally recognized *lordship* from *the people*'.[85] Repeal dinners, like Chartist social occasions, often heard toasts to 'the People' as the source of political power.[86] In 1834, O'Connell was challenged by Sir

80 Roberts, 'O'Connell, Repeal and Chartism', p. 1.

81 For the appeal to the Saxon constitution, see Epstein, 'Constitutional idiom', p. 564, and Josh Gibson, 'The Chartists and the constitution: revisiting British popular constitutionalism', *Journal of British Studies*, vol. 56, no. 1 (2017), p. 71. For the 'democratic idiom', see Gurney, *Wanting and Having*, pp. 105–43.

82 Joanna Innes, Mark Philp and Robert Saunders, 'The rise of democratic discourse in the Reform era', in Innes and Philp (eds.), *Re-Imagining Democracy*, pp. 122–3.

83 Lovett and Collins, *Chartism*, p. 9.

84 Colantonio, '"Democracy" and the Irish people', p. 164.

85 John O'Connell to Daniel O'Connell, 9 November 1841, in O'Connell, *Correspondence of O'Connell*, vii, p. 125. Emphasis in original.

86 See, for example, *Freeman's Journal*, 25 January 1837, 23 April 1841, 20 July 1844.

Henry Jervis, an officer in the Royal Navy from Wexford, to define the 'People' he (O'Connell) claimed to represent. In response, O'Connell equated the 'People' with the politically voiceless:

> All those not possessed of prerogative or privileged capacities. *Not* the King in his corporate capacity – *not* the peers in their privileged state – but all those who are neither King nor peers. In short, the Commons, for whose benefit the King *ought* to reign; and for whose benefit alone the privileges of the peers *ought* to exist.[87]

But the 'People', in the Repeal imagination, were dually disenfranchised, being excluded from representative government through the formal denial of voting rights (there was one voter per 116 inhabitants in the Irish boroughs *after* the Irish Reform Act of 1832),[88] and by virtue of their Irishness. The *Citizen*, a short-lived non-O'Connellite radical journal, pointedly made the case that all of the offices that governed Ireland were headed by 'foreigners', nullifying any advantages that might flow from the Reform Act.[89] Coupled with the disproportionately low number of Irish MPs, Repeal was presented by *The Citizen* as an alternative to the existing 'virtual exclusion of the people of Ireland from the right of representation'.[90]

Indeed, Repeal sentiment stressed the 'national' question over the franchise as the chief grievance. In 1843, John O'Connell made the case that if the franchise was radically reformed, Irish interests would continue to suffer. 'What real influence over legislation can a people have', O'Connell asked, 'whose representatives are a miserable minority in the legislative body?' Without a change to the weighting of Irish representation and influence over political power, O'Connell lamented that an extension of the suffrage 'is but an extension of a mockery'.[91] Such an outburst encapsulated the ideological battles *within* radicalism over the case of Ireland; for John O'Connell, a self-proclaimed democrat, franchise reform would not in itself address Irish exclusion from political power.

The Repeal agitation escalated during the 1840s, with O'Connell deliberately bringing the 'People' more to the fore in political argument. The most striking example of this was, of course, the 'monster' meetings of

[87] Fitzpatrick, *Correspondence of O'Connell*, i, p. 397.

[88] K. Theodore Hoppen, *Elections, Politics, and Society in Ireland, 1832–1885* (Oxford: Oxford University Press, 1984), p. 2.

[89] 'Result of the election', *Citizen*, vol. 4, no. 23 (1841), p. 109.

[90] Bullen, *Five Reports of the Committee of the Precursor Association*, pp. 5, 10.

[91] John O'Connell, *Letters to Friends in Connaught, Respectfully Addressed to Various Parties in that Province* (Dublin: J. Browne, 1843), p. 33.

1843, dubbed at the time by the O'Connellites as the 'Repeal Year'. These outdoor rallies, attended by hundreds of thousands of people in some cases, have been described as a mode of 'constitutional intimidation' by one historian, and a 'people's festival' by another, both of which illuminate different aspects of the tactic.[92] The monster meetings gave a visible form to the 'People', bolstering the popular legitimacy of the Repeal movement within Ireland. This was, however, a top-down process. Indeed, O'Connell and the Repeal Association were wary of the taint of the 'wild democracy', a frequently used term deployed by hostile observers (such as the young Tory, Isaac Butt) to imply mob rule and anarchy.[93] Repeal wardens were given signs to wear on their hats to transform them into 'O'Connell's Police' at the monster meetings, ensuring that order was maintained within the crowd.[94] Democracy, as preached by the Repealers, was respectable in nature, with the 'People' led by responsible men. Much of O'Connell's disdain for the Chartists stemmed from his belief that the people of England were being mobilised by *irresponsible* men. 'The Chartists are the best allies of the Tories', O'Connell bitterly complained in 1839, because they 'drive from the support of the popular cause all the timid, almost all the wealthy, and very many of the middle classes'. Chartist attempts to organise in Ireland were, in his view, an attempt to contaminate Repeal with criminality and violence.[95] O'Connell's assertion that the agitation for Repeal should be 'peaceable and legal' – 'there should be no threat, no menace' – stood in stark contrast to the Chartist mantra of 'peacefully if we can – forcibly if we must'.[96]

As these differences suggested, the Repeal Association's thinking on the electoral franchise was profoundly shaped by ideas of respectability. The O'Connellites formally favoured a franchise based on household suffrage (thus maintaining a property bar on voting), which brought the movement closer to the middle-class liberals of the Anti-Corn Law League than the Chartists.[97] The Association thus balanced appeals to democratic sentiment

[92] McCaffrey, *O'Connell and the Repeal Year*, p. 51; MacDonagh, *Emancipist*, p. 229.

[93] Isaac Butt, *Repeal of the Union: the Substance of a Speech Delivered in the Corporation of Dublin, on 28th February, 1843, on Mr O'Connell's Motion to Petition for a Repeal of the Legislative Union* (Dublin: William Curry, Jr. and Co., 1843), p. 28.

[94] Loyal National Repeal Association of Ireland scrapbook, Ray papers, Burns Library, MS2007-019, file 1/11.

[95] *Morning Post*, 20 August 1839. For the difficulties that Irish Chartists faced, see Kinealy, 'Brethren in bondage', pp. 91–4.

[96] Daniel O'Connell, *First Series of Reports of the Loyal National Repeal Association of Ireland, with a Dedication to the People of Ireland* (Dublin: J. Browne, 1840), p. vii.

[97] Ibid., p. 5.

with opposition to universal suffrage, with a prominent place given to respectability. An instructional booklet for Repeal wardens (the grassroots organisers of the national campaign across Ireland, tasked with organising the collection of the Repeal Rent) stated that the first qualification for the job was the possession of a 'good moral character', and the second was the necessity of clergy support.[98] The involvement of the clergy in O'Connellite politics was one of its most contentious features – the northern publisher, William McComb, for one, deployed the popular mantra that Repeal was an unscrupulous attempt to create a Catholic ascendancy[99] – but clerical support aided the optics of respectability.

While O'Connell was criticised by opponents for his demagoguery, his leadership was an exercise in tempering the excess of a mass movement that challenged the status quo. Democracy was, in O'Connell's mind, a political arrangement in which a wide franchise was in operation, but the structure of power remained centred on a small number of representatives. A political movement with a strong leader, centralised power, and clergy support was, therefore, entirely consistent with O'Connellite democratic principles. In his insightful study of Ireland from 1838, the French politician and writer Gustave de Beaumont recorded that O'Connell exercised 'a sort of dictatorship' over the Irish people, despite not possessing any state power. An astonished Beaumont wrote that 'I do not know if, in the history of nations, a single example of such a destiny could be found'. The Repeal movement was an 'empire of a single man'.[100] This was the achievement of O'Connell: he became (and self-identified as) the personification of Irish popular sovereignty. Such was O'Connell's grip over the popular mind in Ireland that Beaumont affirmed the revolutionary potential of the Repeal movement. 'The purpose is to prepare a petition to parliament', mused Beaumont, 'but what would be the result if, instead of asking for petitions, the association demanded bayonets?'[101] He did not provide an answer.

For all the revolutionary potential of the crowd in 1843, the rhetoric used by senior figures in the movement channelled the democratic idiom away from expressions of popular sovereignty and towards an ideal of a

[98] *Instructions for the Appointment of Repeal Wardens and Collectors of the Repeal Fund* (Dublin: J. Browne, 1843), p. 5.

[99] William McComb, *The Repealer Repulsed! A Correct Narrative of the Rise and Progress of the Repeal Invasion of Ulster*, ed. Patrick Maume (Dublin: UCD Press, 2003; first published 1841), p. 4.

[100] Gustave de Beaumont, *Ireland: Social, Political and Religious*, ed. W. C. Taylor (Cambridge, MA: Harvard University Press, 2006; first published 1839), pp. 224, 228.

[101] Ibid., p. 220.

meaningful mixed constitution. O'Connell regularly spoke warmly of the institution of the monarchy, and especially the person of Victoria.[102] His *History of Ireland*, published in 1843, was dedicated to 'the Queen of Great Britain and Ireland', and affirmed the determination of the Irish people 'to preserve their allegiance to the Throne', despite continued British misrule.[103] Explicit loyalty to the Crown was also coupled with an appeal to another component of the mixed constitution, namely the aristocratic element. While landlordism in Ireland was equated with conquest, Repealers hoped that the Irish gentry would take their place as natural leaders of the nation within an Irish parliament. O'Neill Daunt argued that the 'national spirit' of the Irish aristocracy had waned because of a lack of a domestic parliament, which had deprived Ireland of powerful and connected political advocates.[104] If the aristocracy aligned themselves with the wider population of Ireland, they could claim a sense of popular legitimacy, offering the potential for more harmonious class-based relationships on the land.[105]

The creation of an Irish mixed constitution was most developed by John O'Connell in a pamphlet from 1844. Irish Repealers desired 'a full and free representation of the people', he asserted, but this was balanced by a devotion to constitutional monarchy and the ideal (if not the current practice) of a paternalistic aristocracy. A restored legislature would provide checks and balances to the different component parts, be it the democracy, lords, or Crown. Indeed, O'Connell posited this vision of Repeal as potentially the only constitutional method that could restrain the political anger of the masses. 'A most certain means of preventing the spread of extreme democracy in Ireland' could only be realised, O'Connell argued,

> By the wealthier and titled classes putting themselves at the head of the popular movement. This once done, and done heartily, they would soon find their legitimate influence far more than sufficient to check the tendencies so dreaded, and to keep the popular mind within limits that the most timid could desire.[106]

[102] For the pro-monarchist sentiment within Repeal politics, see James H. Murphy, *Abject Loyalty: Nationalism and Monarchy in Ireland during the Reign of Queen Victoria* (Cork: Cork University Press, 2001).

[103] Daniel O'Connell, *A Memoir on Ireland: Vol. 1: 1172–1660* (Dublin: Charles Dolman, 1843), p. vi. This was the only volume that was published.

[104] William J. O'Neill Daunt, *Mr Daunt's Speech at the Repeal Association, in Refutation of the Anti-Repeal Fallacies Adopted from Spring Rice and Others by Lord Shrewsbury, also Mr Daunt's Speech at the Meeting Held in Edinburgh for Repeal* (Dublin: J. Browne, 1843), p. 9.

[105] William J. O'Neill Daunt, *Ireland and Her Agitators* (Dublin: John Browne, 1845), p. 140.

[106] John O'Connell, *An Argument for Ireland* (Dublin: John Browne, 1844), p. 27.

The attraction of a mixed constitution for a self-governing Ireland, led by aristocrats and property owners, gave Repeal a civic humanist tinge, more in line with the thought of Polybius, the ancient Greek authority on the Roman constitution, than the radical democratic ideas of Emmanuel Joseph Sieyès (or, indeed, in an Irish context, Theobald Wolfe Tone).[107] The images of O'Connell, Grattan, and Flood on the revived 'Volunteers of 1782' membership certificate were joined by hereditary rulers from the distant past, including the semi-fictitious High King Nath Í mac Fiachrach and the Earl of Tyrone, Hugh O'Neill.[108] The Repeal cause was built on the ideal of democracy but pined for ancient lineages and aristocratic patronage.[109]

## Young and Old Ireland

Daniel O'Connell drew on the language of the 'nation' in asserting the case for the Repeal of the Union. He was fond of repeating Barrington's critique of the Union, which equated self-government with nationhood; anything less rendered a country merely a province.[110] O'Connell, however, had little time for mythic and romantic conceptions of nationhood that were coming increasingly into vogue throughout Europe during the 1830s and 1840s. While the Repeal of the Union was presented as righting a historical wrong – chiefly a centuries-old conquest, which culminated in the extinguishing of national parliament – it is striking how little O'Connell deployed arguments based on the *distinctiveness* of the Irish as a nation. During his four-hour keynote speech on Repeal at the Dublin Corporation in 1843, O'Connell's use of the 'nation' was as a collective term for the 'people'. He drew on a form of ancient constitutionalism, based on English notions of liberty, rather than the notion of timeless nationality to explain the aspiration for Repeal:

> As fast as men congregated under the standard of the English in this country, the privilege of being represented was an essential part of their rights. That was the universal custom that prevailed ... Ireland had a

[107] For Polybius and the idea of a balanced constitution, see Donald Walter Baronowski, *Polybius and Roman Imperialism* (London: Bloomsbury, 2011), pp. 154–5.

[108] Loyal National Repeal Association of Ireland scrapbook, Ray papers, Burns Library, MS2007-019, file 1/4.

[109] So too did elements within Chartism: see Chase, *Chartism*, p. 13.

[110] Daniel O'Connell, *Repeal of the Union: Mr O'Connell's Address to the Jury in the Case of the King vs Barrett, Proprietor of the Pilot; Delivered in the Court of King's Bench. On Tuesday, November 26th, 1833* (Dublin: P. Byrne, 1833), p. 37; *Instructions for the Appointment of Repeal Wardens*, p. 3.

> parliament as old as England; it rose spontaneously from the congregation of freemen ... It had existed, not, as I have said, as a favour, a concession, or a grant, but the inherent right of freedom.[111]

The right to a domestic parliament, therefore, came from Ireland's timeless constitutional inheritance, not its nationality *in of itself.*

A new newspaper associated with the Repeal Association, called the *Nation*, glowingly reported on O'Connell's speech, praising the Repeal chief's detailed case against the Union.[112] The *Nation* was established in 1842 by three youthful members of the Repeal Association: Thomas Davis, an enigmatic Trinity College Dublin educated Protestant; Charles Gavan Duffy, an industrious Catholic newspaper editor; and John Blake Dillon, a recently qualified Catholic lawyer. This was the nucleus of the grouping that became known as 'Young Ireland', which also included talented writers and orators such as John Mitchel and Thomas Francis Meagher.[113] The Young Irelanders used the *Nation* and other publications to glorify Irish nationality, stressing its mythic and historic qualities.[114] This was a rather different interpretation of history from that deployed by O'Connell, one that emphasised the self-contained legitimacy of the ancient Irish nation rather than the existence of English liberties in Ireland.[115] Irish sovereignty radiated naturally from the nation, but the nation demanded training to harness its potential. The Young Irelanders self-consciously aimed to fulfil this role within Irish society. As Duffy recorded with characteristic modesty in his memoir, 'the *Nation* was not a journal designed to chronicle the small beer of current politics, but to teach opinions'.[116]

The main 'opinion' advanced by Duffy and his initial partners in the venture of the *Nation*, Davis and Dillon, was that the Irish were an ancient nation with a historic right to self-government rooted in the distinctiveness of the people. While the campaign to Repeal the Union promised the resumption of a parliament in Dublin, the Young Irelanders were concerned about the capacity of the Irish genius to fulfil its national potential

111 Levy, *Three Days' Discussion in the Dublin Corporation*, p. 21.

112 *Nation*, 4 March 1843.

113 T. F. O'Sullivan, *The Young Irelanders* (Tralee: Kerryman Ltd., 1944) is indispensable for biographical details on individuals associated with the movement.

114 For an excellent overview, see Ann Andrews, *Newspapers and Newsmakers: The Dublin Nationalist Press in the Mid-Nineteenth Century* (Liverpool: Liverpool University Press, 2014), pp. 18–130.

115 James Quinn, *Young Ireland: The Writing of Irish History* (Dublin: University College Dublin Press, 2015). David Dwan, *The Great Community: Culture and Nationalism in Ireland* (Dublin: Field Day, 2008), pp. 32–5.

116 Charles Gavan Duffy, *My Life in Two Hemispheres*, 2 vols. (London: T. Fisher Unwin, 1898), p. 65.

in such a scenario. The first edition of the *Nation* protested a creeping Anglicisation that was eradicating the unique aura of the Irish character, creating a sycophantic national mindset.[117] In this analysis, political self-government was not enough; intellectual self-government was required to truly realise Irish freedom. The Young Ireland mission explicitly connected education to freedom, with the recovery of a national culture critical to Irish political regeneration.[118] For Davis and the Young Irelanders, the nation was the fundamental building block of political and cultural life, an idea that would resonate well beyond the 1840s.[119]

The influential ideas of the Italian nationalist Giuseppe Mazzini – culture as part of the national struggle, the importance of education, the openness to the use of violence – are commonly associated with Young Ireland.[120] Certainly, the Young Irelanders empathised with the Mazzinian impulse to cultivate the national self as a precursor to meaningful government. For Thomas Davis, political freedom meant the development of a distinctive consciousness, underpinned by the revitalisation of the 'native' language, the writing of a lionised history, and the sponsoring of national art and literature. The library was as much a political space to ferment national liberation as the chambers of a parliament. While the Repeal Association was Ireland's primary national movement, Davis believed that it should be sponsoring cultural revitalisation as part of its political mission, setting up reading rooms around the country, and publishing a bilingual newspaper.[121]

The priority that Davis placed on such cultural-based activism has been traditionally interpreted as a manifestation of 'romantic nationalism', but an over-reliance on this concept can obscure the Young Irelanders' understanding of, and contribution to, contemporary political ideas.[122] The Young Ireland-inspired 'cultural turn' in Irish writing was an attempt to assert the sovereignty of the Irish nation within the spiritual realm, a rather different thing from the O'Connellite focus on Ireland's appropriate

[117] *Nation*, 15 October 1842.

[118] Charles Gavan Duffy, *Young Ireland: A Fragment of Irish History, 1840–1845* (London: T. Fisher Unwin, 1896), p. 53.

[119] Christopher Morash, *Young Ireland: A Global Afterlife* (New York: New York University Press, 2023), p. 193.

[120] Michael Huggins, 'The *Nation* and Giuseppe Mazzini', *New Hibernia Review*, vol. 17, no. 3 (2013), pp. 15–33, esp. p. 20.

[121] Thomas Davis, *The Prose Writings of Thomas Davis*, ed. T. W. Rolleston (London: Walter Scott, n. d. [1890]), pp. 208–11.

[122] A point made in David Dwan, 'Romantic nationalism: history and illusion in Ireland', *Modern Intellectual History*, vol. 14, no. 3 (2017), pp. 717–45.

constitutional apparatus, but no less *political*.[123] This body of work was underpinned by certain assumptions concerning the rights of citizens, political economy, and popular sovereignty. Davis should not be viewed only through his dreamy writings on ballads, poems, and songs: he, and other Young Irelanders, wrote hard-headed commentaries on day-to-day political matters that at times clashed with opinion within the wider Repeal movement. The Young Irelanders rebuked O'Connell for his flirtation with federalism.[124] Davis developed a French-inspired form of political economy that prioritised small landholders, rejecting the free-trade doctrines popular within the O'Connellite leadership.[125] There were, then, clear lines of demarcation on key political questions between the Young Irelanders and 'Old Ireland'. The final split that occurred between the Young Irelanders (who regrouped as a formal organisation called the Irish Confederation) and the Repeal Association in 1846 should not be read as the logical outcome of irreconcilable 'romantic' and 'enlightenment' ideologies, but as profoundly *political* disagreements.

Davis, like Mazzini, pushed the idea of 'culture' as a unifying force; like the Italian, he also articulated a form of popular sovereignty that reimagined the relationship between the citizen and the state. Mazzini affirmed in 1832 that the ideal of representative government rested on the 'nation', the 'only sovereign' in a political society. A national government was one that reflected and represented the diversity of the nation itself.[126] The contents of the *Nation* chimed with this sentiment. The first issue rejected all political and religious labels that divided the Irish people. The paper denounced the Irish aristocracy for abusing their position of privilege and creating a 'master and slave' relationship with their tenants, but also echoed O'Connellite hope for the propertied class to align themselves with, rather than against, the nation.[127] The defection of William Smith O'Brien, a Conservative MP for Limerick County and member of one of the most ancient families in Ireland, to the Repeal cause in 1843 was a real coup in this regard. On making the shift, O'Brien lamented that Ireland

123 Partha Chatterjee, *The Nation and Its Fragments: Colonial and Postcolonial Histories* (Princeton, NJ: Princeton University Press, 1993), pp. 6, 9.

124 *Nation*, 2 November 1844.

125 James Stafford, *The Case of Ireland: Commerce, Empire and the European Order, 1750–1848* (Cambridge: Cambridge University Press, 2022), pp. 240–1.

126 Giuseppe Mazzini, 'On the superiority of representative government', in Stefano Recchia and Nadia Urbinati (eds.), *A Cosmopolitanism of Nations: Giuseppe Mazzini's Writings of Democracy, National Building and International Relations* (Princeton, NJ: Princeton University Press, 2009), p. 50.

127 *Nation*, 3 December 1842.

had 'sunk into a feeling of settled despair of obtaining good government for their country through the instrumentality of British legislation', and believed that other members of the aristocracy would follow suit.[128] Davis, however, was more downbeat on the potential for Irish landlords to assume leadership roles, pointing out that a classical republican framework – in which the aristocracy found purpose within 'local institutions' and 'corporate rights' – had little basis in the Irish historical experience.[129]

Despite this, classical republicanism was a critical component of the Young Ireland mentality. In his address to the Historical Society at Trinity College in 1840, Davis made the very Davisian point that students can study 'difficult literature of any foreigners, ancient or ancient', but understanding can only occur through the embrace of 'native literature'. The latter taught students how to 'think and feel'.[130] That said, Davis's writings are replete with flourishes from Aristotle and Cicero, emphasising the need to cultivate civic virtue for the common good of a polity. In the same address at TCD, Davis quoted Cicero in advocating a republican conception of citizenship:

> You must act as citizens, and it is well, 'non nobis solum nati sumus, ortûsque nostra partem patria vindicat' ['we are not born for ourselves alone, but our country claims for itself one part of our birth'].[131] Patriotism once *felt* to be a *duty* becomes so. To act in politics is a matter of duty everywhere; here, of necessity. To make that action honourable to yourselves, and serviceable to your country, is a matter of choice ... You now abound in patriotism, and are sceptical of public corruption ... You will be solicited to become the barking misleaders of a faction ... Be jealous of your honour and your virtue *then*; yield not.[132]

The *Nation* frequently published articles that drew on other classical republican themes, such as the ideal of the armed citizen (the supreme defender of liberty) and the binary condition of the freeman and slave.[133] 'Ireland has been a land of slaves', the *Nation* pronounced in 1843, 'we step within it unfettered, the first generation of partial freemen'.[134] The *Nation's* unwavering support for the right of Irish people to bear arms was not a precursor of Young Ireland militancy, but a manifestation of a

[128] William Smith O'Brien, *Speeches of William Smith O'Brien, Esq., on the Causes of Discontent in Ireland*, 2nd ed. (Dublin: J. Browne, 1843), p. 7.
[129] Davis, *Prose Writings*, p. 280. [130] Ibid., p. 16.
[131] I have taken the translation from Marcus Tullius Cicero, *On Duties*, ed. M. T. Griffin and E. M. Atkins (Cambridge: Cambridge University Press, 1991), 1:22.
[132] Davis, *Prose Writings*, pp. 39–40. Emphases in original.
[133] See, for example, *Nation*, 28 November 1842. [134] *Nation*, 30 September 1843.

republican ideal of liberty. 'To carry arms is the first right of man', Davis wrote, 'for arms are the guardians of property, honour, and life'.[135]

The use of such classical republican tropes was, of course, not new in Ireland, nor was it unique in a contemporaneous global context.[136] There was, however, an obvious difficulty with the practical application of the political ideas associated with ancient city states in the modern world, and, indeed, classical republicanism was superseded by liberalism as the ideological expression of liberty *par excellence* during the nineteenth century.[137] But what made the writings of the Young Irelanders so compelling was the ability of Davis and other writers to blend this political tradition, based on rights and duties, with the ideal of the nation, creating a civic and political form of Irishness. Davis's most famous ballad, 'A Nation Once Again', written in 1844, constructed the national ideal as a renewed expression of classical patriotism:

> When boyhood's fire was in my blood,
> I read of ancient freemen,
> For Greece and Rome who bravely stood,
> Three hundred men and three men.[138]
> And then I prayed I yet might see
> Our fetters rent in twain,
> And Ireland, long a province, be
> A nation once again.[139]

The nation, as an entity constructed on classical republican norms of duty, had little time for religious differences or exclusive claims by any denomination to an Irish identity. Young Ireland's dogged assertion of the need for secular education in Ireland, which ran afoul of the O'Connell-Catholic clergy alliance and caused a major split in the movement in 1845, should also be seen in this republican light.[140]

135 Davis, *Prose Writings*, p. 282; *Nation*, 1 July 1843.

136 For Irish manifestations, see Stephen Small, *Political Thought in Ireland, 1776–1798: Republicanism, Patriotism and Radicalism* (Oxford: Oxford University Press, 2002), pp. 83–112. The classic text charting the spread of classical republicanism is J. G. A. Pocock, *The Machiavellian Moment: Florentine Political Thought and the Atlantic Republican Tradition* (Princeton, NJ: Princeton University Press, 2003; first published 1975).

137 Quentin Skinner, *Liberty before Liberalism* (Cambridge: Cambridge University Press, 1998), pp. 1–2.

138 This refers to the 300 Spartans who fought to the death at the Battle of Thermopylae in 480 BC, and the three Romans who held the Pons Sublicius bridge in 509 BC.

139 Thomas Davis, *The Poems of Thomas Davis: With Notes, Historical Illustrations, etc., and an Introduction by John Mitchel* (New York: P. M. Haverty, 1860), p. 93.

140 Quinn, *Young Ireland*, pp. 87–8.

Davis died at the age of thirty-one in 1845, just as the first ominous signs of the Famine came to light. The project of the *Nation* continued with what Duffy called the 'new men', with Thomas Francis Meagher, Thomas D'Arcy McGee, Thomas Devin Reilly, John Martin, and John Mitchel coming to the fore as journalists and Repeal activists.[141] Mitchel became the *Nation's* chief writer following the death of Davis. He, more than any of his contemporaries, was enraptured by the writings of Thomas Carlyle, which revolted against liberal and Benthamite notions of 'progress'. While Carlyle depicted Irish migrants to British towns in ghastly racist terms, his real target was industrialisation and the ubiquity of Ricardo-inspired laissez-faire doctrines of political economy, both of which he believed debased humanity through the prioritisation of material gain.[142] In this sense, Carlyle was speaking the language of Mitchel and other Young Irelanders, who were also at war with liberal modernity in their pursuit of reinvigorating the Irish national character.[143]

Mitchel, inspired by Carlyle, attacked the economic power of the British as a contributing factor in the degradation of Irish national character. As the world's most successful purveyor of mechanisation and industrial capitalism, Britain was, in Mitchel's reading, a modern Hades, sapping the creativity and dignity of the population.[144] The new 'science' of political economy, according to Mitchel, provided cover for the propagation of opulent materialism, with cheap foreign goods weakening local production and undermining national distinctiveness.[145] While laissez-faire doctrines were very much in vogue with the repeal of the Corn Laws in 1846, the Young Ireland interpretation positioned such a take on political economy as an extension of British control over Ireland. The leading advocate of free trade, David Ricardo, believed that the 'pursuit of individual advantage is

141 Charles Gavan Duffy, *Four Years of Irish History, 1845–1849: A Sequel to 'Young Ireland'* (London: Cassell, Petter, Galpin, and Co., 1883), p. 7.

142 The classic depiction of Carlyle as an anti-Irish racist is L. Perry Curtis, *Apes and Angels: The Irishman in Victorian Caricature*, revised ed. (Washington, DC: Smithsonian Institution Press, 1996; first published 1971). This has been contested by John Morrow, 'Thomas Carlyle, "Young Ireland" and the "condition of Ireland question"', *Historical Journal*, vol. 51, no. 3 (2008), pp. 643–67.

143 R. F. Foster, *Words Alone: Yeats and His Inheritances* (Oxford: Oxford University Press, 2011), p. 49.

144 James Quinn, 'John Mitchel and the rejection of the nineteenth century', *Éire-Ireland*, vol. 38 (2003), p. 92.

145 Michael Huggins, 'A strange case of hero-worship: John Mitchel and Thomas Carlyle', *Studi Irlandesi*, no. 2 (2012), pp. 329–52.

admirably connected with universal good of the whole'.[146] Mitchel, however, rejected such a reading. Chiming with eighteenth-century critics of free trade, he argued that so-called universalist political economic theories hid a power dynamic that merely perpetuated the power of rich countries.[147] Mitchel asserted that political economy, as espoused by Britain, was the language of aggression, and, far from serving 'universal good', it possessed a jingoistic national identity.[148]

The logic of Mitchel's stance was that, if laissez-faire doctrines were 'British', then protectionism was an 'Irish' form of political economy. Indeed, such protectionist logic, associating free trade with British dominance, was a wider European concern. French protectionists infused economic argument with 'Anglophobia', fearing the dominance of Britain in a free-trade era.[149] Mitchel's sentiments also chimed with the German theorist Friedrich List, who made the case that every nation should be allowed to decide the protectionist framework to develop its distinctive productive powers.[150] While there were protectionists within pockets of British and Irish political economic thinking (such as George Poulett Scrope, who argued that Irish agriculture risked annihilation in a free-trade scenario), it was Mitchel who most starkly presented the incompatibility of Britain and Ireland.[151] At the height of the Famine, Mitchel published a short edition of writings by Jonathan Swift and George Berkeley under the sardonic title *Irish Political Economy*. The tone of his preface was bitter: 'Now, as then [the 1720s], if Irishmen are hungry, it is that Englishmen may be filled'. England did not starve, Mitchel asserted, because it was governed by Englishmen. The cause of the Famine, the reason why Ireland's rural population was wretched and destitute, was that the Irish had submitted to be 'ruled by strangers' who imposed foreign

[146] David Ricardo, *The Principles of Political Economy and Taxation* (London: John Murray, 1817), p. 156.

[147] Istvan Hont, *Politics in Commercial Society: Jean-Jacques Rousseau and Adam Smith*, ed. Béla Kapossy and Michael Sonenscher (Cambridge, MA: Harvard University Press, 2015), p. 128.

[148] Thomas A. Boylan and Timothy P. Foley, *Political Economy and Colonial Ireland: The Propagation and Ideological Function of Economic Discourse in the Nineteenth Century* (London: Routledge, 1992), p. 8.

[149] David Todd, *Free Trade and Its Enemies in France, 1814–1851* (Cambridge: Cambridge University Press, 2015), pp. 14–15.

[150] Keith Tribe, *Strategies of Economic Order: German Economic Discourse, 1750–1950* (Cambridge: Cambridge University Press, 1995), p. 55.

[151] George Poulett Scrope, *How is Ireland to be Governed? A Question Addressed to the New Administration of Lord Melbourne in 1834, with a Postscript, in which the same question is addressed to the Administration of Sir Robert Peel in 1846* (London: James Ridgway, 1846), p. 40.

economic ideas on the country.[152] The connection between representative government and political economy was also taken up by Mitchel's Young Ireland colleague Thomas Francis Meagher. In 1846, Meagher claimed that the inability of the Irish to wield political power left the country vulnerable to the toxic influence of 'foreign' economic ideas. This produced a crippling anomaly: 'the Irish belong to Ireland' but 'Ireland does not belong to the Irish'.[153] The lack of representative government was the reason why, in the minds of those behind the *Nation*, Ireland was starving.

Mitchel and Meagher swiftly became the most prominent militant voices within Young Ireland. The tone of the *Nation* became more Anglophobic.[154] Rather than follow O'Connell in making constitutional peace with the British, Mitchel, increasingly radicalised by the dreadful scenes of Famine and the grotesquely inadequate Whig government response from 1846, preached the message of hatred.[155] His contribution to the political discourse was a potent fusion of anti-modern romanticism and intense nationalism driven by a thirst for vengeance.[156] The politicisation of hatred created a space within the imagination of Young Ireland for violence. As early as November 1845, Mitchel advocated destroying railways to hinder the British Army in Ireland and used the word 'ambush' in reference to troops. The following year, Meagher proclaimed that the 'patriot's sword' was a 'sacred weapon' that never should be disowned, a direct refutation of O'Connell's vehement opposition to violence.[157] While Davis was canonised by his Young Ireland peers, including Mitchel, as a prophet of national rejuvenation, his quixotic idealism and classical inflections were largely jettisoned in favour of a more robust and confrontational style.[158] But for all their increasing belligerency, the Young Irelanders largely remained wedded to the ideal of Repeal of the Union as a framework for self-government. In 1846, the *Nation* published an article entitled 'Repeal vs the Repeal Association', which cast those in favour of

152 John Mitchel (ed.), *Irish Political Economy, by Jonathan Swift, Dean of St Patrick's and George Berkeley, Bishop of Cloyne* (Dublin: Irish Confederation, 1847), pp. iv–v.

153 Thomas Francis Meagher, *Speeches on the Legislative Independence of Ireland* (New York: Renfield, 1853), p. 40.

154 Morash, *Young Ireland*, p. 37.

155 Peter Gray, *Famine, Land and Politics: British Government and Irish Society, 1843–1850* (Dublin: Irish Academic Press, 1999) is the most lucid account of the government's response to the Famine.

156 Michael Huggins, 'John Mitchel and his biographers', *Irish Historical Studies*, vol. 38, no. 150 (2012), p. 255.

157 *Nation*, 22 November 1845; ibid., p. 89.

158 See, for example, Mitchel's introduction to Davis, *Poems*, and the celebratory Charles Gavan Duffy, *Thomas Davis: The Memoirs of an Irish Patriot* (London: Kegan Paul, Trench, Trübner, and Co., 1890).

the theoretical right of physical force (i.e. the Young Irelanders) as the true Repealers, with the 'moral force' side (the 'Old Irelanders') dismissed as unpatriotic 'place hunters' who had lost their way by cosying up to the Whig party.[159] As late as September 1847, Thomas D'Arcy McGee delivered a lecture that pressed for a new political dispensation that resembled the classic O'Connellite vision, with the 'restoration' of the Irish constitution and recognising the British monarch as the 'Queen of Ireland'.[160] In a rebuff to the Whig Prime Minister, John, Lord Russell, in 1846, the *Nation* stressed that it did not advocate 'separation [between Ireland and Britain] as its end, but National Independence'.[161] Critically, there was still a distinction between the two, despite the increasing pugnacity of the Mitchelite wing of Young Ireland. Duffy later recorded that, for all the fury of Mitchel in 1847, he was not thinking of 'separation or a republic'.[162] The turn to separatism *as* national independence came only in 1848, as revolution swept across Europe.

While the need for self-government was pressed throughout the Famine years, the design of such a scheme was lost in the noise surrounding the debate over the legitimacy of political violence and the subsequent split within the Repeal movement. With O'Connell's death in 1847 and the seemingly unstoppable spread of hunger and disease in the countryside, the Repeal cause essentially became defunct. O'Connell had supported the Whigs as the surest way to deliver positive changes to Irish policy on their return to power in 1846, but was confronted by the brutal truth of laissez-faire. After John O'Connell spoke of his hope for reconciliation between Young and Old Ireland – on the proviso that the *Nation* renounced the right to resort to violence – Mitchel issued a characteristically barbed response:

> The physical force that won the freedom of France, Greece, and Belgium, in his [John O'Connell] own memory, cost fewer human lives than the Whigs have sacrificed to Political Economy, since the day of the Secession.[163]

The fateful irony was that Young Ireland itself split over the issue of violence at the end of 1847. Mitchel advocated a radical programme of passive resistance and the withdrawal of rents, with the possibility of physical force held in reserve. A vote was taken in the Confederation and Mitchel lost: he was removed from his position of prominence in the

[159] *Nation*, 31 October 1846. [160] *Nation*, 2 October 1847. [161] *Nation*, 27 June 1846.
[162] Duffy, *Four Years*, p. 170. [163] *Nation*, 10 April 1847.

*Nation*. The more moderate Young Irelanders, such as Duffy and Smith O'Brien, were appalled by Mitchel's scheme, worrying that it would provide a green light for a crackdown on their circle. While they could accept the *theoretical* right to use violence in 1846, the turn to *actual* violence was of course more testing, at least at this time.[164]

The revolution in France in February 1848 changed everything. Despite fracturing over the appropriate role of passive resistance and violence only months before, a Young Ireland delegation visited the Second Republic to secure backing for a rebellion. They received the disappointing news that the French were unwilling to engage in an offensive against the United Kingdom.[165] Nonetheless, from April, the *Nation* commenced a regular series of articles called 'The Irish Revolution', which collected news of pike training and drilling from around the country.[166] After his dismissal from the *Nation*, Mitchel founded the *United Irishman* newspaper, which, with its name and political message, cultivated a cult of '1798'. It was in the pages of the *United Irishman* that the uncompromising tone of Mitchel's future works, such as *Jail Journal* (1854) and *The Last Conquest of Ireland (Perhaps)* (1860), was debuted. The *United Irishman* claimed to speak for 'pauper public opinion', and published columns headed 'Our War Department', which gave instructions on drilling and using pikes.[167]

Mitchel's transformation into 'the voice of the poor' may have been in part the influence of a relative newcomer to the Young Ireland circle, James Fintan Lalor. Lalor was the son of a prominent Repealer but rejected his father's faith in O'Connell during the Famine. Lalor articulated an ideal of national independence that fused political self-government *and* popular ownership of the land throughout 1847 and 1848. This was a strikingly original perspective at the time; but Lalor was not, however, a straightforward separatist. While he condemned 'simple Repeal' as constitutionally absurd, as he was certain that two unequal legislatures under the Crown would inevitably reproduce a familiar pattern of dominance and submission, Lalor advocated a federalist scheme based on the US model.[168] So, while he emotively suggested that 'Tone and Lord Edward [Fitzgerald]

164 Andrews, *Newspapers*, p. 114.

165 Christine Kinealy, *Repeal and Revolution: 1848 in Ireland* (Manchester: Manchester University Press, 2009), p. 146.

166 *Nation*, 1, 15, 29 April, 6 May 1848.

167 *United Irishman*, 15 April 1848.

168 James P. Bruce, *Ireland's Hope: The 'Peculiar Theories' of James Fintan Lalor* (Wilmington, DE: Vernon Press, 2020), p. 23.

died' to destroy the tie between Ireland and Britain, Lalor was not, like his heroes from 1798, calling for an Irish republic.[169]

Lalor was in fact closer to the agrarian reformer, William Connor, than Theobald Wolfe Tone. Connor published *The True Political Economy of Ireland*, a radical call for legislative intervention to abolish 'rank-rent', 'the great master evil in Ireland', in 1835.[170] Both Connor and Lalor used the eighteenth-century authority on English common law, William Blackstone, for radical means, detaching his mantra that the earth was 'the general property of all mankind' from his later (conservative) assumption that the first occupier was the legitimate owner of the land.[171] Connor reasoned that the 'industrious man' was the legitimate occupier of the soil, not the 'indolent' aristocrat; Lalor went further, rejecting the premise that the first occupier could be defined.[172] What was left in this critique of Blackstone was a model of land ownership constructed on natural rights and justice. But what made Lalor's writings unique was their coupling of popular ownership of the land and self-government, a vision of national independence that fused the political and the social. Through a series of articles, first in the *Nation*, and then in the provocatively named *Irish Felon*, Lalor robustly asserted that the Repeal of the Union was meaningless unless the 'conquest' was also repealed.[173] Such a seismic change could only be secured through arms, but Lalor legitimised the use of revolutionary violence as the pathway to the creation of a land tenure system based on consent rather than conquest. As it was the right of man to possess land, which was God's creation, reasoned Lalor, man had the duty to resist the breach of this natural law.[174]

In his detailed account of these years, Duffy claimed that Mitchel was 'fascinated' by the radical ideas of Lalor.[175] Mitchel's overt appeals to the rural peasant in the *United Irishman* to reclaim 'Ireland for the Irish' certainly had echoes of Lalor's combativeness, while also revealing that Mitchel had overcome a Carlylean (and wider Young Irelander, it should be said) appeal for the aristocracy to assume their natural position as the

[169] *Irish Felon*, 1 July 1848; reprinted in L. Fogarty (ed.), *James Fintan Lalor, Patriot and Political Essayist, 1807–1849* (Dublin: Talbot Press, 1918), pp. 78–80.

[170] William Connor, *The True Political Economy of Ireland: or, Rank-Rent the One Great Cause of all her Evils: with its Remedy* (Dublin: W. F. Wakeman, 1835), p. xii. For Lalor's connection to Connor, see Marta Rámon's excellent introduction to James Fintan Lalor, *'Faith of a Felon' and Other Writings*, ed. Marta Rámon (Dublin: UCD Press, 2012), pp. 8–11.

[171] William Blackstone, *Commentaries on the Laws of England* (Oxford: Oxford University Press, 1765; first published 1763), ii, p. 2.

[172] Connor, *True Political Economy*, p. 12; Lalor, *'Faith of a Felon'*, p. 137.

[173] Lalor, *'Faith of a Felon'*, p. 102. [174] Ibid., pp. 100–1. [175] Duffy, *Four Years*, p. 476.

leaders of the people.[176] Duffy, who loathed Mitchel, mocked the idea that starving Irish peasants could be transformed into a revolutionary army.[177] Lalor, for his part, penned a lengthy think piece in the *Irish Felon* on 1 July, which suggested that the only alternative to armed resistance was the obliteration of the peasant. The Famine had started a revolution on the land, Lalor warned, but it threatened to 'leave Ireland *without a people*, unless it be met and conquered by a revolution which will leave it without landlords'.[178]

The irony was that when the rising in the countryside came in late July 1848, it was led not by Mitchel (whose writings saw him convicted of treason-felony two months previously), nor Lalor (who was arrested days before), but Duffy's faction of Young Ireland, under the 'military' leadership of William Smith O'Brien. O'Brien issued a proclamation on behalf of the Confederation in May that asserted the right to arm to protect Ireland 'from all foes'.[179] In July, Russell's government cracked down on perceived seditious movements in Ireland, authorising the raid of the office of the *Nation*, the suppression of various Irish radical newspapers, and the arrest of prominent Young Irelanders, including Duffy. Habeas corpus was suspended on 25 July. The remaining Young Irelanders scattered, regrouping in the south to prepare for a rising. The first (and final) shots of rebellion occurred at the end of July, when O'Brien marched to Ballingarry, County Tipperary, with some 1,500 men; after a skirmish with the Royal Irish Constabulary (RIC), the rebels fled.[180] Thus ended Ireland's '1848'. In retrospective accounts, O'Brien and another prominent Young Irelander, Michael Doheny, blamed the Catholic clergy in the south and west for undermining the rebellion by urging the peasantry not to get involved.[181] The lesson that Doheny took from the experience was that revolutionary success required 'preparation under cover of secrecy', which became a defining aspect of the Fenian movement that he went on to co-found in the following decade.[182]

176 *United Irishman*, 29 April 1848; Thomas Carlyle, *Past and Present* (London: Chapman & Hall, 1843), p. 289.
177 Duffy, *Four Years*, p. 477.
178 *Irish Felon*, 1 July 1848; reprinted in Fogarty, *James Fintan Lalor*, p. 81. Emphasis in original.
179 *Nation*, 6 May 1848.
180 There is an excellent overview of the rising in Kinealy, *Repeal and Revolution*, pp. 183–210.
181 John Mitchel, *Jail Journal: or, Five years in British Prisons* (New York: *The Citizen*, 1854), p. 277. Michael Doheny, *The Felon's Track: or, A History of the Late Attempted Outbreak in Ireland* (New York: H. Holbrooke, 1849), p. 92.
182 Doheny, *Felon's Track*, p. 167.

The oddity of the rebellion was not the incompetence of the leaders, nor the lack of a popular uprising, but how *inarticulate* Ireland's '1848' was. The politics of Young Ireland fermented in newspapers, ballads, and essays, to the extent that the term 'literary rebellion' has been used to describe the events of 1848.[183] But despite the presence of some of the most gifted writers in Ireland, there was no textual proclamation of the Irish Republic as there had been in 1803 (and, more obviously, as there was in the rebellions of 1867 and 1916). Indeed, it was not clear what the rebels wanted: the leaders felt they had no choice in the face of the suspension of habeas corpus, but this does not mean there was a coherent vision for a revolutionary state. Inspired by the French Revolution earlier that year, the use of the term 'Irish Republic' became more prominent in the public utterances of the Young Irelanders in 1848. At a rally in Clonmel, Co. Tipperary, in April, Smith O'Brien announced to a cheering crowd that

> he only had to state at present, so far as his own personal opinion was of weight, he was in favour of Ireland being governed by the Queen, Lords, and Commons of Ireland. If that was not conceded, his alternative was – an Irish Republic.[184]

This was hardly an ideological preference for a republican form of government. The constitutional vision for a future self-governing Irish polity remained fluid within the Young Ireland mind and continued to follow British constitutional norms.

That said, O'Brien's separatism provides an arresting insight into the radicalisation of Irish opinion that occurred during the Famine. At a meeting of the Irish Confederation the previous month, Duffy warned that this was the last chance for the British government to concede Repeal: withholding self-government was inflaming opinion in Ireland, and 'men will not spill their blood to cement the connexion with England, but to lie like a dead sea between us forever'.[185] Despite this threatening rhetoric, Duffy, like O'Brien, would have been content with 'simple Repeal', with Ireland gaining the same constitutional institutions as Britain. The 'Irish Republic' became a trope deployed by an increasingly volatile separatist impulse within Young Ireland at the height of the tragedy of the Famine. The shape of that Republic, however, remained undefined in the minds of its protagonists.

183 Richard Davis, *The Young Ireland Movement* (Dublin: Gill & Macmillan, 1988), p. 164.
184 *Nation*, 15 April 1848. 185 *Nation*, 25 March 1848.

## The Persistence of Traditions

In 1846, Robert Holmes published a popular pamphlet with the provocative title, *The Case of Ireland Stated*, a deliberate homage to William Molyneux's famous tract from 1698. The title page was prefaced by a quote from the *Second Treatise of Government* by John Locke that suggested that the 'liberty of man' could only be curtailed by a 'legislative power' that is 'established by consent in the commonwealth'.[186] Holmes married into the Emmet family (he appeared to have no knowledge of the 1803 rebellion, although was arrested on its eve) and became a prominent figure at the Irish Bar, defending a number of Irish political prisoners, including John Mitchel in May 1848.

During Mitchel's trial, Holmes articulated a Lockean contractual theory of the Union to justify his defendant's alleged seditious words. 'Ireland is an enslaved country', Holmes told the jury. He carried on:

> A great mistake, in my opinion, is entertained by persons that there cannot be slavery, that no man can be a slave, except he is actually in chains, or is subject to the lash of the planter who flogs the negro . . . Slavery, gentlemen, the slavery of a people consists in this – that they do not make the laws themselves by which they are governed, but those laws are made for them either by another nation or another individual.

As Holmes conceded, the term 'slavery' had obvious parallels with the worst excesses of the American republic, but he was eager to reclaim the term with its classical humanist connotations.[187] This enabled Holmes to bolster Mitchel's defence with an appeal to natural rights: 'an enslaved people, enslaved contrary to the laws of Providence, has a right, if necessary, by force of arms to obtain liberty even at the hazard of life itself'.[188] This echoed Locke's *Second Treatise*, which colourfully asserted that 'he who makes an attempt to enslave me thereby puts himself into a state of war with me'.[189] Physical force in this instance was a Lockean imperative to combat the unnatural state of political slavery.

Holmes's intervention serves as a useful reminder that Irish political language during the era of the Famine was multifaceted and borrowed

[186] Robert Holmes, *The Case of Ireland Stated*, 5th ed. (Dublin: James McGlashan, 1847), title page.
[187] The irony of deploying such a rhetorical trope in defending Mitchel cannot, however, go without comment.
[188] John George Hodges, *Report of the Trial of John Mitchel for Felony* (Dublin: Alexander Thom, 1848), pp. 42, 45.
[189] John Locke, *Political Writings*, ed. David Wootton (Indianapolis, IN: Hackett Publishing Co., 2003), p. 269.

from a number of traditions. Holmes was not an outlier in his embrace of Locke, as O'Connell was fond of quoting from the *Two Treatises* to 'prove' the illegitimacy of the Union. The persistence of such Lockean themes is a reminder that the vocabulary of politics in Ireland during the era of the Famine cannot simply be boiled down into a 'unionist' and 'nationalist' binary. The fact that Holmes deployed ideas from the pages of the *Two Treatises* to defend the violent anti-Englishness of John Mitchel in a court of law speaks volumes for the diversity of Irish political thought. But this should not mask the centrality of one vital assumption within the Irish political mind in the age of O'Connell, shared by all advocates of Repeal. Holmes powerfully concluded his *The Case of Ireland Stated* with a forceful expression of this premise:

> Famine is a scourge which visits nations rarely, and but for a season. The scourge of misgovernment is more frequent, more general, more lasting, and more fatal to the happiness of man.[190]

Many enemies of Repeal, as we shall see, also agreed.

[190] Holmes, *Case of Ireland Stated*, p. 101.

CHAPTER 4

# *Irish Conservatives, Conditional Unionism, and Contractarian Thought*

> Repeal can never take place until the Protestants of Ireland are disgusted by, and alienated from, the English Government.[1]
>
> Samuel Ferguson (1833)

> The policy of the government seems to be, not to govern with a liberal and impartial spirit, but to be facetious and exclusive – servile to the priest, and revolutionary radical – hostile to the Protestant loyalist and his church.[2]
>
> Anthony Meyler (1838)

At a meeting of the Protestant Conservative Society in June 1832, Rev. John B. McCrea alerted the membership that he was aware of an instance in which Protestant orphans were kidnapped, sealed into a barrel, and taken to 'a Popish house'. Once released, 'they were kept until fully initiated into all the mysteries of the Roman Catholic system'. Such a plot was testament, McCrea believed, to the 'ingenuity and perseverance in which Roman Catholics applied themselves to the seduction of the children of Protestants'.[3] McCrea was one of the prominent figures within Tory society in Dublin during the late 1820s and early 1830s, a time when Catholic Emancipation and parliamentary reform drastically altered Irish political life. Despite his status as a dissenting minister within a wider Protestant political world dominated by Anglicans, McCrea was a senior figure in the Orange Order's chaplaincy and was awarded the freedom of Dublin in 1829 for his anti-Emancipation activism.[4] He embraced the label 'Tory Dissenter', which he believed was 'equivalent with inexorable

1 *Dublin University Magazine*, November 1833, p. 588.
2 Anthony Meyler, *Irish Tranquillity Under Mr O'Connell, my Lord Mulgrave, and the Romish Priesthood* (Dublin: Wm. Carson, 1838), p. 20.
3 *Belfast Newsletter*, 12 June 1832.
4 Jacqueline Hill, *From Patriots to Unionists: Dublin Civic Politics and Irish Protestant Patriotism, 1660–1840* (Oxford: Oxford University Press, 1997), p. 339; David Fitzpatrick, *Descendancy: Irish Protestant Histories since 1795* (Cambridge: Cambridge University Press, 2014), p. 86.

hostility to everything, whether called political or religious, that would give to the man of sin an iota's advantage of the Spirit's jurisdiction'. The chief 'man of sin' was he who spread Catholic doctrine. 'God-insulting popery, [which] is the climax of Satan's policy', McCrea affirmed, was 'the grand engine of all confederated wickedness'.[5] The lingering penal laws and the mobilisation of the Catholic Association ensured that religious identity moulded the shape of political rights and obligations, perpetuating the Protestant-Catholic divide in Ireland. With the emergence of the 'priest' as a political figure in Ireland, Protestants such as McCrea reasoned that such a dangerous foe demanded to be confronted in the spiritual and earthly realms.

The Protestant orphans that McCrea alleged were seized by Catholics were thus proselytised into a false faith *and* political degeneracy. The outlandish scheme was internalised as another skirmish in 'the systematic warfare against Protestant principles and Protestant institutions' waged by Irish Catholics.[6] In a lecture to the Orange Institution of Dublin in 1835, later published as a pamphlet, McCrea connected 'Christian liberty' to the 'social state of man'. He cited wisdom, justice, and charity as the hallmarks of Protestantism; and as the boundaries of the political sphere were fixed by the moral virtues that emanate from a society, Protestant teaching was fundamental to enlightened political action. Catholicism, as the antithesis of Protestantism, was, in McCrea's reading, corrosive of political virtue. In this sense, Catholic Emancipation had been a regressive political step:

> There can be no such thing as equal rights, in the proper sense, until men are brought under the influence of those principles whereby everyone looks not at his own good alone, but also to the good of others. Take, for example, a nation or a section of a nation where infidelity or superstition prevails. In the absence of that revelation the entrance of which giveth sight to the blind and understanding to the simple, what do we see but intolerance, anarchy, and every evil work?[7]

A fear of a politically active and enfranchised Catholic majority permeated McCrea's words. The accession of William III confirmed Protestantism's place as 'the constitutional religion of these realms',[8] but the rise of a

[5] J. B. McCrea, *The Cause of Irish Protestant Orphans: The Cause of Godliness and Loyalty* (Dublin: Richard Moore, [1833]), p. 9.

[6] Ibid., p. 18.

[7] J. B. McCrea, *The Lord's Spirit the Spirit of Liberty: A Discourse to the Orange Institution of Dublin, on the Twelfth of July, to Commemorate the Revolution by William the Third* (Dublin: William Warren, 1835), p. 24.

[8] Ibid., pp. 25–6.

politicised Catholicism in Ireland threatened this status quo. McCrea spoke of the need to maintain 'our yet Protestant empire', projecting the shifting Irish political dynamics onto an imperial stage: if Ireland fell, the empire would surely follow.[9]

McCrea voiced many of the fears of Irish Toryism during the 1830s and 1840s. The Tory platform in Ireland was deeply traumatised by Catholic Emancipation, the Reform Act, and the subsequent rise of the Repeal of the Union agitation. This brand of Toryism was underpinned by a distinct yearning for the days of the Protestant Ascendancy, although some of its more thoughtful adherents realised that those days were over and an accommodation with the new forces in Irish and British life was required. The political makeup of Toryism in Ireland was distinctly Protestant, reflecting the divisions within the wider body politic that crystallised during the first few decades after the Acts of Union.[10] Sectarianism was an important political factor in Ireland, but there was more to Toryism than reactionary bigotry. Religion was, of course, a key plank of post-French Revolution European conservatism, with conservatives across the continent defending established church structures as promoters of social order.[11] The dynamics of Irish Toryism were not, from a European perspective, that unusual.

For McCrea, religion was 'the foundation of patriotism'.[12] In this spirit, Tories in Ireland positioned themselves as the chief protectors of the Protestant constitution, which emphasised the idea of mixed government and Protestant succession to the throne.[13] The Irish Protestant was imagined as the last bastion in a global struggle against popery. Religion and conservative politics became intermeshed because Protestantism and the constitution itself were threatened by the growing political assertiveness of Catholics in Ireland. It was no coincidence that many senior figures associated with Irish Toryism – McCrea, Henry Cooke, T. D. Gregg, and Mortimer O'Sullivan – were evangelical clergymen, increasingly drawn from across the Protestant denominations.[14]

[9] J. B. McCrea, *Education Board of Ireland*, 2nd ed. (Dublin: J. Hoare, 1833), p. 4.

[10] K. Theodore Hoppen, *Elections, Politics, and Society in Ireland, 1832–1885* (Oxford: Oxford University Press, 1984), p. 279.

[11] Edmund Fawcett, *Conservatism: The Fight for a Tradition* (Princeton, NJ: Princeton University Press, 2020), p. 6.

[12] McCrea, *Lord's Spirit*, p. 29.

[13] Allan Blackstock, *Loyalism in Ireland, 1789–1829* (Woodbridge: Boydell Press, 2007), p. 2; J. C. D. Clark, *English Society, 1688–1832: Ideology, Social Structure and Political Practice during the Ancien Régime* (Cambridge: Cambridge University Press, 1985), pp. 396–7.

[14] Alvin Jackson, *The Two Unions: Ireland, Scotland, and the Survival of the United Kingdom, 1707–2007* (Oxford: Oxford University Press, 2012), pp. 286–7; Andrew R. Holmes, *The Irish*

The challenge of the post-Emancipation period was the need to reorient Irish Protestantism to meet the new threats of political Catholicism and democratic ideas. This was, however, far from straightforward. The Acts of Union promised incorporation into a larger Protestant polity, transforming the Irish minority into a British majority. But this apparent safety blanket for Irish Protestants was threatened by the ruptures of the late 1820s and early 1830s. One pamphleteer interpreted Catholic Emancipation and the onset of the Repeal campaign as dangerous shifts towards popular sovereignty, with an agitated public opinion in Ireland seemingly taking precedence over parliamentary deliberation. It was necessary, the writer argued, for 'those who possess property and influence' to organise to block the erection of 'a democracy upon the ruins of our constitution'.[15] This call to arms underpinned much Irish Tory activism during the 1830s, which centred increasingly on ideas of self-reliance, driven by a distrust of the machinations of the Westminster political bubble. There was also much public soul-searching among Irish Tories concerning the status of the Union itself. Tories in Ireland interpreted the Acts of Union as a contract between two kingdoms – a 'solemn treaty' between Ireland and Britain, in the words of one pamphleteer – with rights, duties, and obligations for each side to uphold.[16] But as Ireland entered the devastation of the Famine years in the 1840s, some Irish Tories publicly questioned whether British misgovernance rendered the contract void.

## Tories and Conservatives

An argument made by some English Tory opponents of the Reform Act of 1832 was that it was not parliament that was corrupt, but the people: an extension to the franchise would merely 'multiply the number of greedy patronage-seekers within the electorate'.[17] In Ireland, this sentiment was intensified by demographic realities. A number of anti-O'Connellite pamphleteers in the early 1830s voiced their fears of a new Catholic ascendancy created through the toxic mix of parliamentary reform and Repeal: the spectre of an empowered and vengeful O'Connell, harnessing

*Presbyterian Mind: Conservative Theology, Evangelical Experience, and Modern Criticism, 1830–1930* (Oxford: Oxford University Press, 2018), p. 15.

15 'A Protestant of the Established Church', *The Repeal of the Union Considered* (Dublin: Richard Milliken and Son, 1831), pp. 3, 5, 35.

16 Ibid., p. 35.

17 Philip Harling, 'Parliament the state, and "Old Corruption": conceptualizing reform, *c.*1790–1832', in Arthur Burns and Joanna Innes (eds.), *Rethinking the Age of Reform: Britain 1780–1850* (Cambridge: Cambridge University Press, 2003), p. 108.

an increasingly bitter sectarian body politic, threatened the Irish Protestant minority and, indeed, Ireland's entire constitutional connection with Britain.[18] The Rev. Tresham Dames Gregg, a Dublin-born clergyman who served in several Anglican churches in Yorkshire during the 1830s, condemned the willingness of 'our governors to disregard the opinions of the Protestants of Ireland', as parliamentary reform 'will throw the representation of that country into the hands of the papists'.[19] John Wilson Croker, a pivotal Irish Tory figure and opponent of reform, feared that the masses would become omnipotent in the new dispensation, fatally damaging the existing constitution. In an article published in 1831, Croker registered a Burkean belief that governments 'were originally constituted for the express purpose of presenting and resisting change', and should have a 'strong tenacity to things *as they are*'.[20] Croker was not a wholly reactionary opponent of parliamentary reform: he favoured incorporating 'matured' public opinion into political deliberation, but feared the impact of sudden and violent manifestations of popular mood.[21] Croker was instrumental in modernising British Toryism during the 1830s, providing the intellectual context through his periodical writings for Robert Peel's shift to 'Conservatism' – a term, in fact, invented by Croker.[22]

Peel's 'Tamworth Manifesto' of 1834 is typically viewed as a founding document of modern conservatism.[23] The 'manifesto', which was a widely circulated address to Peel's constituency electorate, was indeed a watershed moment; as one later commentator put it, the proclamation 'gave some offence and caused some alarm to old-fashioned Tories at the time of its appearance', because of its acceptance of the principle of parliamentary reform and the desire to win over public opinion.[24] Peel was reinventing the traditional Tory respect for institutions of authority for the post-reform

[18] For this line of argument, see 'H. N.', *An Address to the People of Ireland on the Repeal of the Legislative Union Between Great Britain and Ireland* (Dublin: Richard Milliken and Son, 1831), pp. 12–13; Anon., *Repeal or No Repeal: Repeal of the Union Considered in its Practical Bearings* (London: James Ridgway and Sons, 1833), pp. 13–14; Anon., *Ireland. Ignorance. 'Repeal'* (London: James Ridgway, 1833), pp. 11–12.

[19] 'M. S. G.' [T. D. Gregg], *Letters to J. E. Gordon, Esq., MP* (London: L. B. Seeley and Son, 1832), pp. 51–2.

[20] [John Wilson Croker], 'Friendly advice to the Lords on the Reform Bill', *Quarterly Review* (July 1831), pp. 507, 539. My emphasis.

[21] Ibid., p. 518.

[22] Robert Portsmouth, *John Wilson Croker: Irish Ideas and the Invention of Modern Conservatism* (Dublin: Irish Academic Press, 2010), pp. 134–5.

[23] R. J. White, *The Conservative Tradition*, 2nd ed. (London: Adam & Charles Black, 1964), pp. 10–11.

[24] J. R. Thursfield, *Peel* (London: Macmillan and Co., 1891), p. 136.

age, fusing the imperative to 'conserve' with more popular interests. Peelite Conservatives adopted what Emily Jones has described as a Burkean 'active conception of maintenance': change must be allowed to occur – naturally and organically – to preserve and, indeed, improve on what was fundamentally good in a society.[25] Croker was a forthright champion of such Burkean thinking, believing that it represented a middle way between the extremes of reactionary Toryism and radical Whiggism. Through the pages of the *Quarterly Review* through the early 1830s, he propagated the cause of what he called 'the conservative party', which should be founded on the principles of 'enlightened Toryism' and ready to engage with an expanded electorate.[26] Croker's brand of Conservatism also recognised the need for change to defuse crisis moments. While many Tories rejected the premise of Catholic Emancipation out of hand, Croker, for example, supported the measure, fearing that the continuing refusal to incorporate Catholics into the constitution would trigger 'an Irish rebellion, and perhaps a Reform ferment in England also'.[27] The problem, as he saw it at the time, was that Emancipation risked coming too late to truly resemble a heartfelt attempt at reconciliation between the British political classes and Irish majority opinion. Croker was also aware that the sudden shift away from the 'ultra-Tory' platform of anti-Catholicism also threatened to alienate Protestants in Ireland.[28]

Croker was accurate in his assessment about the likely consequences of Catholic Emancipation in Ireland. The rapidity of the rise of the Repeal of the Union platform, which was constructed on the foundations of the Catholic Association, disaffected those who viewed the Emancipation settlement as the final act in recalibrating Ireland's constitutional relationship with Britain. Liberal Presbyterians such as Sir James Emerson Tennent, who was elected MP for Belfast in 1832, supported Catholic Emancipation as a form of political justice, but were exasperated at O'Connell raising the Repeal flag. 'If I am less liberal in my opinion', Emerson told the House of Commons in 1834, 'I owe my conversion to O'Connell'.[29] Indeed, other liberal reformers in Belfast became more

[25] Emily Jones, *Edmund Burke and the Invention of Modern Conservatism, 1830–1914* (Oxford: Oxford University Press, 2017), p. 179.

[26] Portsmouth, *Croker*, pp. 137–8.

[27] Croker to Lord Hertford, 21 February 1832, in Louis J. Jennings (ed.), *The Croker Papers: The Correspondence and Diaries of the Late Right Honourable John Wilson Croker*, 2 vols. (New York: Charles Scribner's Sons, 1884), i, p. 541.

[28] Portsmouth, *Croker*, p. 110.

[29] Quoted in John Bew, *The Glory of Being Britons: Civic Unionism in Nineteenth-Century Belfast* (Dublin: Irish Academic Press, 2009), p. 135.

overtly unionist following the launch of the Repeal campaign in 1830.[30] Emerson broke from the Whigs in 1834 and eventually drifted towards the Conservatives. Such was his fear of the Repeal agitation that he predicted that every Irish Protestant would 'become in his own defence a conservative'.[31] This *defensive* posture taken by Emerson is worthy of note, as it became a staple of Irish Toryism in the age of O'Connell.

O'Connell was not, of course, a doctrinaire separatist, but from an Irish Protestant perspective, Repeal threatened Ireland's British connection. In the post-Emancipation political landscape, Irish Tories increasingly saw themselves as the final bulwark of the Union in Ireland, the chief upholders of Protestant values and loyalty to the Crown and constitution.[32] The O'Connellites, on the other hand, according to Tory pamphleteers, contained 'not one man of rank'[33] (a point that was clearly untrue, as the background of Thomas Wyse demonstrates) and were intent on fostering 'treason and rebellion'.[34] The spectre that haunted the Irish Tory mind was another '1641', a reference to the alleged massacre of Protestant planters in Ulster by dispossessed Catholics during the Wars of the Three Kingdoms. The grisly atrocities of 1641 were grossly exaggerated by Sir John Temple in his notorious book *The Irish Rebellion* (1646), which remained in print during the eighteenth and early nineteenth centuries.[35] Temple's work did much to entrench the idea of a premeditated attempt to exterminate the Protestants in Ireland; the frontispiece of the final edition in 1812 warned Protestants to keep on 'their Guard against the Encroachment of Popery'.[36] In addition, annual sermons were held on 23 October, the anniversary of the outbreak of the rebellion, which reinforced Irish Protestants' sense of dread of the intentions of their Catholic neighbours.[37] The shedding of Catholic deference in the aftermath of the Union was deeply troubling for Irish Protestants, and the threat of another '1641'

30 Jonathan Jeffrey Wright, *The 'Natural Leaders' and Their World: Politics, Culture and Society in Belfast, c.1801–1832* (Liverpool: Liverpool University Press, 2012), p. 134.

31 Ibid.

32 Andrew Shields, *The Irish Conservative Party, 1852–1868: Land, Politics and Religion* (Dublin: Irish Academic Press, 2007), p. xiii.

33 Anon., *Cursory Observations on the State of Ireland* (Dublin: printed for the author, 1831), p. 16.

34 'Civis', *Thoughts on the Repeal of the Union* (Dublin: Richard Moore, 1831), p. 5.

35 T. C. Barnard, *Irish Protestants Ascents and Descents, 1641–1770* (Dublin: Four Courts Press, 2004), p. 9.

36 John Temple, *The Irish Rebellion: or a History of the Attempts of the Irish Papists to Extirpate the Protestants in the Kingdom of Ireland, Together with the Barbarous Cruelties, and Bloody Massacres which Ensued Thereupon* (London: White, Cochrane and Co., 1812; first published 1646).

37 T. C. Barnard, 'The uses of 23 October 1641 and Irish Protestant celebrations', *English Historical Review*, vol. 106, no. 421 (1991), pp. 889–920.

was invoked frequently in political speeches and writings within the polarising sectarian climate of the 1820s and 1830s.[38] That politicised Catholicism was being aided and abetted by successive Tory *and* Whig administrations – Wellington's government piloted through the Catholic Relief Act in 1829, while the Whigs and O'Connellites struck up an informal partnership in 1835 – contributed to the renewed fears of Irish Protestantism.

The breaking of the Protestant constitution with the coming of Emancipation pushed Irish Tories into new modes of thought and organisation, predating Peel's plea for a modern conservatism to meet the demands of the age. If the mission of the Reform Act was to expand the aristocratic constitution to encompass the interests of the growing middle classes, Toryism attempted something similar in Ireland.[39] The Irish Protestant Conservative Society was established in 1831, representing the first practical reaction to the post-Emancipation dispensation.[40] Led by Rev. Charles Boyton, a Fellow of Trinity College Dublin (TCD) and key personality within Dublin Toryism in the early 1830s, the Society responded to O'Connellism by mimicking its populism. One of the aims of the Society was the establishment of a Protestant version of the 'Catholic Rent', the chief fundraising mechanism that powered the Catholic Association during the 1820s.[41] Like the Catholic Association, the Irish Protestant Conservative Society envisaged the rent not only as a source of income, but as a means to construct a political community that spanned the length of the island.[42] 'The poor man who pays his 6d.', affirmed one advocate, 'is sure to feel as much interest as he who pays pounds'.[43] Like the contributors to the Catholic Rent, those who paid the 'Protestant Rent' were in a sense mobilised, publicly highlighting the strength of feeling relating to the cause.[44] The Society was eager to mobilise Protestants of all classes and denominations to broaden the Conservative platform, with the intention of uniting traditional Tories from the landed

38 John Gibney, *The Shadow of a Year: The 1641 Rebellion in Irish History and Memory* (Madison: University of Wisconsin Press, 2013), pp. 62–3.

39 Norman Gash, *Politics in the Age of Peel: A Study in the Technique of Parliamentary Representation, 1830–1850* (London: Longmans, 1966; first published 1953), p. 17.

40 Hoppen, *Elections, Politics, and Society*, p. 280.

41 Michael Keyes, *Funding the Nation: Money and Nationalist Politics in Nineteenth-Century Ireland* (Dublin: Gill & Macmillan, 2009), pp. 9–42.

42 *Speech Delivered by the Rev. C. Boyton, FTCD, at a Meeting of the Protestant Conservative Society, on Tuesday, the 10th July, 1832* (Dublin: J. Hoare, 1832), pp. 9–10.

43 Anon., *Plain and Practical Hints, for the Serious Consideration of all Protestants, and Particularly of Conservatives, by a Member of that Society* (Dublin: Richard M. Tims, 1833), p. 7.

44 *Belfast Newsletter*, 17 July 1832.

class with the 'lower orders' behind one banner.[45] This marked a dramatic shift in Irish Tory thought. In emphasising the need for pan-Protestant unity, Boyton suggested to the Society in 1832 that Irish Toryism had hitherto been incapacitated by complacency:

> Sir, our past misfortunes can be traced to our own faults. For years, when the Protestants of the country were assailed, the practice was to repose and to throw ourselves back upon the existing government for safety – (hear) – and while a powerful party [the Catholic Association] was formed, concentrated, and brought to formidable maturity by our opponents, we still postponed to meet it by similar means; we clung around the neck of the existing government until our helpless imbecility became a burden upon them too heavy to be sustained (hear, hear).[46]

It was a revealing admission: Catholic Emancipation occurred partly because Toryism was ill equipped to meet the challenges of a popular political campaign, and London could not be trusted to provide unconditional support for the Protestant minority in Ireland. The Irish Tory ambition to construct a national organisation that mobilised Protestant opinion echoed the Peelite 'Conservative' initiatives in the immediate post-reform period; but for the former, redesigning the mode of political action was an existential imperative.

The Irish Protestant Conservative Society was dissolved in 1834, as its organisers feared breaching the Coercion Act introduced by the Whigs. In an unexpected move, Boyton, alienated by the Reform Act and the heavy-handed security legislation directed at Ireland, opened a dialogue with O'Connell with the view to building a potential anti-Whig coalition. O'Connell eagerly encouraged an alliance between Tories and Repealers, although he was aware of the pitfalls. 'It is true it may lead to nothing', he confided in his lieutenant, P. V. Fitzpatrick.

> It may be an ebullition of disappointed *expectation* on his part but I hope it is rather a symptom of his really entertaining those sentiments of honest Irishism which I often and with pleasure perceive to mix with his party politics. He [Boyton] is at all events right in his conjecture that the policy of this Administration is purely *English domination* over the Irish of all parties.[47]

O'Connell was correct with his initial thought: the talks did not result in any new political departure based on an anti-Whig alliance. Boyton

[45] *Speech Delivered by Boyton … Meeting of the Protestant Conservative Society*, pp. 3–4.

[46] Ibid., p. 13.

[47] Daniel O'Connell to P. V. Fitzpatrick, 21 February 1833, in Maurice R. O'Connell (ed.), *The Correspondence of Daniel O'Connell*, 8 vols. (Dublin: Irish Manuscripts Commission, 1977), v, p. 10. Emphases in original.

apparently listened carefully to the proposals of O'Connell, which played down notions of a post-Repeal social revolution, stressing the sanctity of property rights and religious freedom in a self-governing Ireland, but he could not formally commit Irish Toryism to such a radical step. As Fitzpatrick recorded, Boyton lamented that 'his party' was animated 'by an abstract detestation of Popery which seems to forbid all hope of coalition'.[48] Not for the first time nor the last in Ireland, the toxicity of sectarianism was impossible to overcome; but the warmness between Boyton and O'Connell should not obscure the fact that they envisaged Repeal as performing very different tasks. For O'Connellite Repealers, the end of the Union was equated with the final destruction of Protestant privilege in Ireland; for Tory Repealers, the restoration of the Irish parliament represented the means to protect the Protestant interest.

Still, this episode does much to illuminate the fluidity of Irish political thought during the early 1830s. Part of O'Connell's proposal to Boyton was the retention of the 105 Irish MPs in Westminster following the restoration of the Irish parliament.[49] This represented a move away from the literal definition of 'Repeal', as the Union would be dramatically reformed, not terminated.[50] This concession from O'Connell was made to appeal to the unionism of the Irish Tory position, which he did not view as incompatible with the return of a parliament in Dublin. From Boyton's perspective, Irish Tories needed to show more self-reliance, particularly in electoral politics. As well as articulating the need for an organisation that spanned Ireland, he made the case that 'good government' relied on getting 'good members at the elections'.[51] The protection of the Church of Ireland, the rights of property, and the 'lawful privileges' that came from being part of the United Kingdom thus rested on the return of high-calibre Irish Tories to Westminster; it could not be taken for granted, as Boyton alluded, that the government had Irish Toryism's best interests at heart. The return of an Irish parliament and the likelihood of a strong Tory presence therein (especially if the franchise was connected to a high property bar) was, therefore, not a wholly unattractive option. Indeed, Repeal gained some traction among the Protestant members of several

[48] W. J. Fitzpatrick, *Correspondence of Daniel O'Connell: the Liberator*, 2 vols. (New York: Longmans, Green, and Co., 1888), i, p. 327.

[49] O'Connell to Fitzpatrick, [*c.* 22 March 1833], in O'Connell, *Correspondence of O'Connell*, v, p. 21.

[50] O'Connell's proposal resembles the definition of Home Rule in the bills of 1893 and 1912, in which an Irish presence in Westminster would be retained after the creation of a parliament in Dublin.

[51] *Speech Delivered by Boyton ... Meeting of the Protestant Conservative Society*, p. 11.

Dublin city guilds in 1832 as a method (as the city commons put it) 'to recover the advantages we have lost'.[52] Boyton personified a form of 'conditional unionism', which constantly measured the value of the Union by the government's ability to protect the Protestants of Ireland and the Anglican Church. The concession of Catholic Emancipation, and the subsequent emergence of a Whig programme with little sympathy for Irish Toryism, undermined his trust in the Union. While Irish Tories upheld the Crown, Protestantism, and empire as the common symbols of a British national identity that bound together the component countries of the United Kingdom, the preferred structure of *government* was less certain.

Boyton resigned his TCD Fellowship in 1833, and thereafter took little part in active politics. His influence in shaping the immediate future of Irish Toryism was, however, immense. He was instrumental in the attempt to build a distinctly *Irish* Tory movement, recognising the need to construct an organisational infrastructure to mirror the post-reform times. Boyton may have voiced his fears of 'spirit of popularism' and denounced democracy as the 'master-poison of the age',[53] but he was attuned to the need to broaden the appeal of the Irish Tory platform. 'If a revolution is to ensue', he told a meeting in 1834, it is a wiser choice to be its 'leaders [rather] than its victims'.[54] Mobilisation, public meetings, and publishing pamphlets was, Boyton believed, critical to renewing the leadership credentials of Tory Ireland. While the Irish Protestant Conservative Society disbanded in 1834, other organisations, imbued with similar aims, swiftly followed in its wake. Boyton wished to construct a strongly patriotic Irish conservative movement that avoided the reactionary Toryism which celebrated the worst excesses of the penal laws. He also despised absentee landlords, so often identified as part of the Irish Tory tribe, for their failure to take leadership positions, both on their estates and nationally.[55] What O'Connell referred to as Boyton's 'honest Irishism' was at the heart of his conditional unionism: the Irish Tory dilemma concerned the competing pulls of what was in Ireland's best interests and those of the wider United Kingdom. From the perspective of Tories such as Boyton during the 1830s and 1840s, these two interests appeared only rarely to align.

52 Hill, *From Patriots to Unionists*, p. 350.
53 Charles Boyton, *Observations on the Church; its Relation to the State; the Authority of its Governors; and the Duties and Obligations of its Ministers* (Dublin: Milliken and Son, 1838), p. 25.
54 *DUM*, September 1834, p. 343.
55 *Speech Delivered by Boyton … Meeting of the Protestant Conservative Society*, p. 18.

## Defining Irish Conservatism: Politics and the *Dublin University Magazine*

Alongside the imperative to organise and mobilise the Irish Tory interest, Boyton also played a role in nurturing a new generation of thinkers and activists through his connection to TCD. Boyton was a tutor to a young Isaac Butt, the latter of whom entered TCD as a precocious fifteen-year-old in 1828, and imbibed much of his mentor's instinctive political mindset that blended an uncompromising commitment to Protestantism with sympathy for Ireland's nationality. Butt, along with other 'Tory juveniles' (to use Malcolm Brown's impish phrase)[56] such as the brothers, Samuel and Mortimer O'Sullivan, Charles Stuart Stanford, and John Anster, set up the *Dublin University Magazine* (*DUM*) in 1833, which became the periodical *par excellence* for Boytonist conservative thought. Other notable literary figures, such as Samuel Ferguson, Charles Lever, and Sheridan Le Fanu, contributed to the *DUM* after its establishment.[57] The tone of the *DUM* was relentlessly Protestant – a trait that can be traced to the O'Sullivan brothers as the outlet's early ideological patrons – but its pages often drew attention to political anxiety with the constitutional status quo.[58] During Butt's editorship (1834–8), the *DUM* positioned itself as a champion of the new conservatism. 'The Tory of old was often the misguided defender of preposterous theories of the sacredness of all authority', the *DUM* reflected in 1837; 'the Conservative of modern times', on the other hand, 'is the rational defender of tried and established institutions that have vindicated their propriety by their permanence, against the idle and mischievous spirit of change'.[59]

Despite the decidedly 'modern' take on political ideology, the *Magazine's* overt and uncompromising Protestantism chimed more with an older Toryism. The tone was set by Samuel and Mortimer O'Sullivan, Catholic converts to Protestantism who embraced their new calling with fanaticism. Both brothers became clergymen, skilled writers, and well-known controversialists.[60] William Carleton, another significant literary

[56] Malcolm Brown, *The Politics of Irish Literature: From Thomas Davis to W. B. Yeats* (Seattle: University of Washington Press, 1972), p. 59.

[57] Indeed, Le Fanu bought the *DUM* in 1861: see W. J. McCormack, *Sheridan Le Fanu*, 3rd ed. (Stroud: Sutton Publishing Ltd., 1997), p. 138.

[58] Wayne E. Hall, *Dialogues in the Margin: A Study of the Dublin University Magazine* (Gerrards Cross: Colin Smythe Ltd., 2000), p. 39.

[59] *DUM*, February 1837, p. 180.

[60] Desmond Bowen, *The Protestant Crusade in Ireland, 1800–1870* (Dublin: Gill & Macmillan, 1978), p. 117.

talent who contributed to the *DUM*, admired the 'eloquence' of the O'Sullivans, especially Mortimer.[61] Mortimer's politics were determined by his unbending evangelicalism, at the heart of which was a profound anti-Catholicism. He described the Catholic Church as a Satanic institution, as it professed to be holy while 'prohibit[ing] men from learning what God had taught' through the denial of private Bible study. Catholicism's authoritarian nature, symbolised by the infallibility of its teachings, O'Sullivan warned, characterised the chief threat to religious and humanist liberty. 'Such is the Church of Rome', O'Sullivan opined in 1833, 'a monstrous nightmare, without form or consistence, whose power is in the stagnation of abused human faculties, not in its own strength or subtlety'.[62]

Given the minority status of Protestants in Ireland, O'Sullivan was at pains to stress the need for unity and – like Boyton – self-reliance in the face of an indifferent government. The need for organisations to protect Protestantism in Ireland, such as the Orange Order, was a manifestation of a social contract that was badly frayed by a legislative programme that seemingly strengthened Catholicism. O'Sullivan argued that a 'well-ordered government' was one that 'affords protection to the subject'; if this protection was not forthcoming, the subject could legitimately establish extra-parliamentary societies to fulfil this need. The 'inadequacy of law', O'Sullivan declared, 'must be compensated by private endeavour'.[63] O'Sullivan made these observations against the backdrop of the 'Tithe War', a mass form of civil disobedience aimed to disrupt the collection of the tithe which paid for the upkeep of the Church of Ireland. The 'War' descended into violence in various parts of Ireland, at times directed explicitly against Protestants.[64] While some observers, such as the Frenchman Gustave de Beaumont, who visited Ireland with Alexis de Tocqueville in 1835, believed that the abolition of the tithe was a mandatory step towards the imperative of equality between the status of Protestantism and Catholicism,[65] O'Sullivan and like-minded Protestants

61 David O'Donoghue (ed.), *The Life of William Carleton*, 2 vols. (London: Downey & Co., 1896), i, p. 231.

62 Mortimer O'Sullivan, *A Guide to an Irish Gentleman in his Search for a Religion* (Dublin: William Curry, Jr. and Co., 1833), pp. 321, 335.

63 Mortimer O'Sullivan, *Case of the Protestants of Ireland, Stated in Addresses Delivered at Meetings in Dublin, Liverpool, Bristol, and Bath, in the Year 1834* (London: John Hatchard & Son, 1836), pp. 44–5.

64 Richard McMahon, *Homicide in Pre-Famine and Famine Ireland* (Liverpool: Liverpool University Press, 2013), p. 134.

65 Gustave de Beaumont, *Ireland: Social, Political and Religious*, ed. W. C. Taylor (Cambridge, MA: Harvard University Press, 2006; first published 1839), pp. 329–30.

tended to interpret such a move in a more zero-sum manner. The anti-tithe campaign was connected to the O'Connellite movement; O'Sullivan warned that the Repeal platform was little more than a cover to 'extirpate Protestantism and effect a separation from England'.[66] The Church of Ireland and the Union were 'hated' by Irish Catholics because they were the chief obstacles to the 'establishment of Romish ascendancy'.[67] He believed that the government was attempting to reconcile the 'enemies of the British connexion'; but the surrender of the Church of Ireland's establishment status, as a concession to the O'Connellites, would mark the first step towards the 'dismemberment of the empire'.[68]

From an Irish Tory perspective, then, the stakes were high. Politics and religion were intimately linked in the thought of Mortimer O'Sullivan, as they were existential concerns. This worldview was often found in the pages of the *DUM*, which also tended to read political matters through the lens of religion. The *DUM* should be understood as part of the wider project to mobilise and disseminate Irish Toryism in the aftermath of Emancipation and parliamentary reform. The self-reliance ethos was again to the fore in the *DUM*: apathy among Irish Protestants was frequently cited as a danger equal to the O'Connellites or English Whigs.[69] The sectarianism of the *DUM* was justified by referring to the Catholic Church as a foreign power, seeking to disrupt the harmony of the Protestant United Kingdom. In his first editorial, Butt asserted that, given that the United Kingdom is 'a Protestant State', and once it ceases to be Protestant, 'her government is at an end'. To preserve the state, reasoned Butt, 'every means' should be used 'to destroy and exterminate Popery in Ireland'. Butt was eager to temper his acerbic words with a declaration of 'love' for Ireland and 'our Roman Catholic brethren', making a profound distinction between 'Catholicism' and 'Popery'; the former was superstition masquerading as religion, the latter was a political project dedicated to the fall of global Protestantism.[70] Parliamentary reform was condemned as a conspiracy against the mixed and balanced constitution, with the effect of rendering one part – the House of Commons – omnipotent.[71] This was a worrying development for Irish Tories, as there was a more visible O'Connellite presence in the Commons after 1833. After the 'Lichfield Compact' of 1835, which created a working relationship between the Whigs and the Repealers, these concerns ratcheted up. An article in the

[66] O'Sullivan, *Case of the Protestants of Ireland*, p. 47. [67] Ibid., p. 126. [68] Ibid., pp. 103–4.
[69] Hall, *Dialogues in the Margin*, p. 57. [70] *DUM*, August 1834, pp. 121, 128.
[71] *DUM*, February 1835, p. 117.

*DUM* on Orangeism in 1835 emphasised the Irish Tory cry for 'defensive associations' in Ireland to uphold Protestantism in the face of governmental pandering to O'Connellism.[72] There would be no need for the Orange Order if Irish Protestants were 'satisfied that they are secure', but this was an impossibility in the age of menacing 'popish agitation'.[73]

The *DUM* was, however, more than a mouthpiece of Orangeism. While positioning Ireland as a citadel of a global Protestantism, the journal provided an outlet for the descendants of the Protestant Ascendancy to make sense of their Irishness within the framework of the Union.[74] In the words of Joseph Spence, the centrepiece of the Irish Tory philosophy that informed the *DUM* was a refusal to accept that unionism was a barrier to promoting 'the cause of Irish nationality as ardently as those who professed "nationalism" as a political creed'.[75] To this end, the periodical published a wide range of historical, antiquarian, and literary-inflected articles that connected contemporary Irish Toryism to Ireland's past glories, especially the eighteenth-century Patriot tradition.[76] The Union was framed as a partnership of equals; Ireland's rich historical and literary traditions gave no pause to notions of Irish inferiority within the United Kingdom. Responding to O'Connell's argument that the Union slashed the political status of Irishmen through the destruction of self-government, the *DUM* cited Hugo Grotius to insist that nations did not lose privileges on joining a confederacy. The Union, in fact, politically enhanced the rights of the Irish: 'in addition to being an Irishman', the *DUM* celebrated, 'he is likewise a citizen of the most enlightened and commanding nation in modern times'.[77]

The reality of the Union was, however, decidedly more mosaic. The political mood of the *DUM* oscillated intensely between hope and despair, often in the same article. The most striking early example of this can be found in a celebrated article by Sir Samuel Ferguson, the northern poet and antiquarian. Ferguson was uncomfortable with the levels of anti-

[72] *DUM*, April 1835, p. 490. [73] Ibid., p. 485.

[74] Colin W. Reid, 'Citizens of nowhere: longing, belonging and exile among Irish Protestant writers in Britain, c.1830–1970', *Irish Studies Review*, vol. 24, no. 3 (2016), p. 260.

[75] Joseph Spence, 'The philosophy of Irish Toryism, 1833–1852: a study of the reactions to liberal reformism in Ireland in the generation between the first Reform Act and the Famine, with especial reference to expressions of national feelings among the Protestant Ascendancy' (University of London PhD thesis, 1991), p. 10.

[76] As Roy Foster notes, this idea was also articulated by the writers of the *Nation* a decade later, one of many intellectual references shared by the two publications. R. F. Foster, *Words Alone: Yeats and His Inheritances* (Oxford: Oxford University Press, 2011), p. 53.

[77] *DUM*, June 1834, p. 721.

Catholic venom that Butt injected into the *DUM*, which he believed were goaded on by the O'Sullivan brothers on the editorial board.[78] Nevertheless, Ferguson was not immune from interpreting the political world through the prism of religious fear. 'A dialogue between the head of heart of an Irish Protestant' was published anonymously in the *DUM* in November 1833, and remains one of the most profound insights into the alienation of post-reform Irish Toryism.[79] Written in the context of disillusion with the Whig government's Irish policy – chiefly the excesses of reform and coercion – Ferguson voiced his frustration at Protestants personifying the 'safeguards of [the] British connection' in Ireland, while being 'deceived, insulted, spoiled, and set at defiance' by the state. Ferguson was conflicted in expressing his sympathy for the downtrodden Catholics of Ireland because of a fear of their revolutionary potential. Repeal was the 'stalking horse' for a new Catholic ascendancy, which might result in the 'enforcement of those laws entrusted to the pikes of the sans-culottes'.[80] Despite his discontent with the direction of travel within the Union, Ferguson feared that Repeal would inevitably lead to separation, with a barbaric religious war in Ireland to follow. The 'heart' of the article's title recognised the historic suffering of the Catholic priesthood in Ireland and admitted their devotion to the poor; but the 'head' saw the fermenting of 'another rebellion of 1641'.[81] Irish Protestants were loyal to the British constitution, but that constitution was not loyal to them; they styled themselves as the natural leaders of a country that rejected their leadership. Ferguson lamented the precariousness of the Irish Protestant position in a biting passage:

> I am tormented and enraged by the condition to which our loyalty has brought us. Deserted by the Tories, insulted by the Whigs, threatened by the Radicals, hated by the Papists, and envied by the Dissenters, plundered in our country-seats, robbed in our own town houses, driven abroad by violence, called back by humanity, and, after all, told that we are neither English nor Irish, fish nor flesh, but a peddling colony, a forlorn advanced guard that must conform to every mutinous movement of the pretorian rabble – all this, too, while we are the acknowledged possessors of nine tenths of the property of a great country, and wielders of the preponderating influence between two parties; on whose relative position depend the

78 Eve Patten, *Samuel Ferguson and the Culture of Nineteenth-Century Ireland* (Dublin: Four Courts Press, 2004), p. 61.

79 While the 'Dialogue' was published anonymously, it is included in a bibliography of Ferguson's work in his wife's detailed biography. Mary Catherine Ferguson, *Sir Samuel Ferguson in the Ireland of his Day*, 2 vols. (Edinburgh: William Blackwood and Sons, 1896), ii, p. 369.

80 *DUM*, November 1833, p. 588. 81 Ibid., p. 590.

> greatest interests in the empire. I love this land better than any other. I cannot believe it is a hostile country. I love the people of it, in spite of themselves, and cannot feel towards them as enemies.[82]

This extraordinary outburst was the most lucid articulation of the political and social isolation felt by Irish Protestantism in the age of O'Connell.

The *DUM* offers a vivid insight into the mentalities of Dublin Tories in the aftermath of reform. Its pages were permeated with questions of national authenticity, as Ferguson's 'Dialogue' showcased: with a perception of being 'neither English nor Irish' (to use Ferguson's repine), Tories such as Ferguson struggled to define their position within the United Kingdom and Ireland. As a result, the *DUM* veered quite dramatically between different ideological positions. Articles voiced full-throated denunciations of O'Connellism as a Popish conspiracy before expressing a love for O'Connell's misguided followers. Ireland was presented as both a kingdom with a proud historical record of political independence from Britain and a semi-colonial entity in which Irish Protestants were merely a British garrison. As Ferguson's disdain of the 'peddling colony' charge demonstrated, the perceived colonial dimensions of the Ireland of their time unsettled some of the young Turks in the *DUM* ranks. Another famed article, 'English theories and Irish facts' (1835), often cited due to the provocative dichotomy of its title, expressed regret that a more robust colonial form of government was not adopted in Ireland to foster 'a complete conformity to English habits and laws': the 'native Irish', the article professed, enjoyed the rights of British citizenship, but lacked understanding of the reciprocal duties.[83] But while some *DUM* writers believed that Irish Protestants were the descendants of the leaders of the ancient kingdom of Ireland, others interpreted Protestantism as the offspring of colonialism. 'There is no use hiding the broad through unpalatable fact', one author conceded in 1833, 'that the Protestant population are an English garrison which is holding this island in its allegiance to England'. As 'a garrison in a half-conquered and half-resisting country', the implications were stark:

> if it [Irish Protestants] be once withdrawn, or if it deserts its banners, or if it emigrate, there will be neither safety for the property, nor security for the allegiance of this island, and the ascendency of England is shivered to atoms![84]

In other words, the Protestants of Ireland were *the* personification of the Act of Union, a legislative vision made flesh and blood. Without them, the

[82] Ibid., p. 591. [83] *DUM*, December 1835, pp. 682–4. [84] *DUM*, May 1833, p. 472.

British connection would wither and die. This sentiment animated several organisations, such as the Protestant Colonisation Society of Ireland, which attempted to reclaim Irish wasteland to rehome potential emigrants.[85] The defensiveness of Irish Protestantism was not simply an outward projection of a sense of siege mentality, but a reflection on the structural problems in fully assimilating Ireland into the wider United Kingdom. If O'Connell is more loved by the bulk of the Irish people than the queen, the *DUM* surmised, the British connection was gravely threatened.[86]

While issues pertaining to nationality in the *DUM* have captured the attention of scholars,[87] the periodical was partly, we should not forget, a political organ, and acted as a guide to the constitutional ideas of Irish Toryism. In drawing his 'Dialogue between the head and heart' to a close, Ferguson asserted that the reason why the political mood in Ireland appeared so embittered was because of 'English *misgovernment*', not the shackles of ancient hatreds.[88] The theme of how Ireland is governed, and how it ought to be governed, was a prominent motif of the *DUM*. This is not to say that a consistent line was presented. Ferguson's fulmination that Irish Tories were neither 'fish nor flesh' encapsulated a fluidity in how the writers for the *DUM* understood Ireland's relationship with Britain. The *Magazine*, for example, veered dramatically between denouncing the Act of Union as a wrecking ball to a distinctive Irish constitutional tradition and hailing the British connection as Ireland's only salvation.[89]

Some things were, however, more consistently articulated. The *DUM* stoutly defended the Church of Ireland from the gaze of successive reforming governments during the 1830s, interpreting any serious legislative alteration in Church practice as an attack on Protestantism itself. A Whig proposal to commandeer surplus Irish Anglican income in 1835 was fiercely denounced by the *DUM*: if Church property was confiscated by the state for secular purposes, the Union, which fused the Irish parliament *and* Church to its British counterparts, was a mockery.[90] A morbid declinism was often present in the pages of the *DUM*, studded by a belief that the Repeal of the Union was an inevitability, a process

[85] *Transactions of the Protestant Colonisation Society of Ireland, Reported at a Public Meeting of Subscribers, in the Dublin Institution, on Thursday, May 24, 1832* (Dublin: J. Hoare, 1832), p. 29.
[86] *DUM*, October 1844, p. 447.
[87] Most notably Spence's sparkling thesis, 'The philosophy of Irish Toryism'.
[88] *DUM*, November 1833, p. 592. Emphasis in original.
[89] Contrast, for example, *DUM*, August 1834, p. 132, and July 1843, p. 109.
[90] *DUM*, August 1835, p. 134.

accelerated by an aloof government oblivious to the perils posed to Irish Protestantism by the O'Connellite political ascendancy.[91] The global implications of the undermining of the Irish Tory platform were continually emphasised, with the condition of Ireland taken as a microcosm of the wellbeing of the Empire.[92]

A potent anti-democratic aesthetic was also an obvious feature of the *DUM's* political writings. In 1838, the *Magazine* queried whether the government had fallen under the 'cloven foot of democracy' in its dalliances with O'Connellism.[93] The notion of universal suffrage was condemned on the perceived absurdity of '*counting* suffrages instead of *weighing* them': any newly enfranchised masses threatened the representation of sound 'interests', risking a fall into a Tocquevillian tyranny of the majority.[94] The Irish context, in which Toryism represented a minority political perspective, was rarely missing in *DUM* analyses of such radical reforming concepts. If the 'will of the majority' was the arbiter of political decisions, the Church establishment in Ireland would fall, replaced by a new Catholic ascendancy. A lack of political education and the predominance of Anglophobia among the bulk of the population, the *DUM* claimed, ensured that a democratic franchise would be a dangerous weapon in Ireland. In a critical review of Beaumont's piercing study, *L'Irlande: Sociale, Politique et Religieuse*, in 1839, the *DUM* asserted that the majority of the Irish population did not tolerate 'any difference of opinion' and had slavish tendencies to follow despotic leaders. The 'liberty which they seek', pronounced the *DUM*, 'is that which is most favourable to the views of the demagogue, who demands power for the masses rather than freedom for individuals'.[95] The following year, the *DUM* reviewed the second volume of *Democracy in America*, by Beaumont's great friend, Tocqueville. 'Democracy', as it appeared in the pages of Tocqueville, surmised the *DUM*, did not equate to 'freedom', but to 'equality', meaning 'the absence of privilege'.[96] It went unspoken in the review, but this analysis was coloured by the Irish Tory context, which stressed that the 'privileges' held by Protestantism were the last remaining bulwarks against the rise of a democratic Catholic nationalism driven by vengeance. 'Equality' was thus an existential threat.

Universal suffrage also risked tipping the balance of power in the mixed constitution which defined British governance. The *DUM* imagined a

[91] *DUM*, July 1836, pp. 6–7. [92] *DUM*, November 1837, p. 520.
[93] *DUM*, March 1837, p. 353. [94] *DUM*, February 1837, pp. 183–4.
[95] *DUM*, July 1839, p. 112. [96] *DUM*, November 1840, pp. 546–7.

popular assembly inevitably asserting its power over the Crown and peers, ultimately dismantling the constitutional norms of careful deliberation and a pluralistic decision-making process, which had hitherto promoted stability through reconciling a 'variety of classes'. Supreme power should continue to reside in a mixed constitution, which provided a framework for careful deliberation and the articulation of a range of interests, achieving stability through reconciling a 'variety of classes'. The *DUM* presented the British mixed constitution as the pinnacle of how the exercise of power should be structured in a modern state. That constitution was, of course, distinguished by the interconnectedness of the Crown, Lords, and Commons, but the *DUM* also believed that a fourth constituent element was virtually represented, namely 'the democracy excluded from electoral privileges'. Given this array of interests, there was simply no need to radically alter this constitutional setup through an increase in suffrage. The constitution should decide the political direction of the state, not the 'people'.[97] The concept of 'representative government' was also belittled as an attempt to assert the sovereignty of the people in an indirect manner. Such a system gave the voters too much control over their representatives, creating a perverted parliamentary class of 'pledged partizans' rather than the dignified ideal of the 'deliberative councillor'.[98]

This is not to say that the *DUM* believed that the practice of the British constitution mirrored the theory. The *Magazine* condemned the enfranchisement of the £10 freeholder in Ireland in 1829, which in effect granted more political power to the Catholic clergy in Ireland. The impoverished fate of the £10 freeholder in Ireland rendered him very different to his socially aspirational English equivalent. 'Popular power', lamented the *DUM*, 'is one thing in a country where the people are far advanced in knowledge and civilisation', but quite another in 'a country where the mass of the population are sunk low in ignorance and its consequent degradation'.[99] The Irish £10 freeholder was estranged from landlordism and socially distant from the wider population: he was the tool of the priesthood *par excellence*, the foot soldier of O'Connell's demagogy. This was one of the most notable cases wearily identified by the *DUM* as a misguided effort to employ an 'English theory' (that the £10 freeholder should enjoy the suffrage) to incongruous 'Irish facts' (the £10 freeholder in Ireland was the slave of Popish superstition). The anatomy of Irish suffrage became a more pressing political point after the Whigs' so-called

97 *DUM*, May 1838, pp. 643–5.
98 *DUM*, February 1837, pp. 185–7.
99 *DUM*, April 1835, p. 376.

Lichfield House agreement with O'Connell in 1835, which resulted in the programme of 'justice to Ireland' through additional reforms.[100] Given that the *DUM* asserted that the parliamentary might of O'Connellism was concocted from a toxic mix of the ignorant yet enfranchised masses and the Catholic clergy, the Lichfield House development was deeply troubling. After 1835, the *DUM* equated 'misgovernment' with the O'Connellite influence over the Whigs.[101] The Irish Lord Lieutenant, Lord Mulgrave, was castigated as a 'despot', with O'Connell as 'a viceroy over him' – an arrangement sanctioned by the government itself.[102]

As this analysis revealed, the Whigs' pivot towards the O'Connellite movement was interpreted by the *DUM* as constituting a form of tyrannical rule. The government was acting at the behest of a 'factional' interest in Ireland: the logical direction of travel, a dismayed *DUM* concluded, was a British embrace of Repeal.[103] The *DUM* used the creation of a Whig-O'Connellite nexus to agitate for the creation of a new conservative party in Ireland to challenge the narrative that the Repealers spoke for the country. Conservatives should avoid allowing 'their enemies' to assume the 'imposing appearance of being the popular party' and assert the Tory claim to 'the national cause'.[104] Drawing on the Peelite idiom, the *DUM* pleaded to 'our Tory friends' to 'convert their passive, defensive Toryism' into 'an active energetic spirit of Conservatism'. The alternative for Tories was inevitable 'anarchy and ruin', imaginatively conjured up as 'ebbing and glowing from the democracy of the "Poissardes" to the despotism of a Robespierre'.[105] If the political clout of the Repealers lay in organisation and mobilisation, the *DUM* pushed Irish conservatives to follow this example with grave urgency.

## Defenders of the Faith

The Irish Metropolitan Conservative Society (IMCS) was established in November 1836, with Francis Hodgkinson, the Vice Provost of TCD, as its president. Tellingly, a letter of support from a sitting Tory MP, as well as Rev. Mortimer O'Sullivan, referred to the new organisation as the

100 Jay R. Roszman, '"Ireland as a weapon of warfare": Whigs, Tories, and the problem of Irish outrages, 1835 to 1839', *Historical Journal*, vol. 60, no. 4 (2017), p. 975.

101 For example, see *DUM*, April 1838, p. 530.

102 *DUM*, December 1837, p. 703.

103 *DUM*, July 1836, p. 7.

104 Ibid., p. 9.

105 *DUM*, September 1836, p. 297. The Poissardes were the market women who marched to Versailles in October 1789.

'Metropolitan Protestant Association'.[106] The stated mission of the new Society was threefold: uniting the Protestants of Ireland behind one political body; the promotion of registration of Protestant voters; and the establishment of loan funds to assist 'the humbler classes of Protestants'.[107] These latter two aims highlighted the Tory adaption to the new era of post-reform politics, with the Protestant interest being defined by a preparedness to engage in electioneering and a pan-class appeal to denominational unity.

The list of supporters that was printed following the first public meeting of the Society revealed a largely urban body, with numerous professional men in its ranks. There was a distinct lack of aristocratic and gentry figures, further anticipating the shedding of the old Tory skin. Indeed, while the Society upheld the rights of property as an abstract political imperative, the *wrongs* of Irish property in practice were not evaded. A report commissioned by the Society condemned the practice of landlordism in Ireland, pinning much of the blame for the social and religious backwardness of the Irish peasant on the gentry:

> Your Committee would respectfully state their conviction, that the extreme dangers to which you are now exposed are in a great degree, if not entirely attributable to the fact, that the Protestants of this country contented themselves for ages past with preserving the constitution, enforcing the laws, and maintaining a connexion with England. They omitted to improve their estates and disregarded the spiritual welfare of those who dwelt on them; they affected to think themselves English instead of raising their native country to a moral rank, in which they might be proud to own themselves her sons.[108]

In other words, the paternal link between landlord and tenant had been broken. The 'metropolitan' Tories now seized the leadership of Irish conservatism.

The IMCS was founded in the same year as the Orange Order was formally (if only symbolically) dissolved, in the face of an impending government ban on the latter organisation. Orangemen had become a notable presence during the election in 1835, dominating the streets of Belfast and engaging in sectarian rioting in Armagh.[109] The *DUM*,

[106] *Morning Post*, 18 November 1836. [107] Ibid.

[108] *Report of the Proceedings at the First Public Meeting of the Irish Metropolitan Conservative Society, Held at their House, 19 Dawson Street, on the 16th of November, 1836* (Dublin: Irish Metropolitan Conservative Society, 1836), p. 5.

[109] Hoppen, *Elections, Politics, and Society*, p. 320.

however, stressed the Order's place as a form of 'self-preservation' for Protestants.[110] This trope was common in pro-Orangeism pamphlets in the few years following reform, with Protestant commentators expressing grave concern about the Whig administration empowering the O'Connellite movement through an assault on the pillars of Protestantism in Ireland.[111] At the first meeting of the IMCS, Robert Plunkett announced that the new society was not intended to act as 'a substitute for Orangeism', but to urge Protestants to recognise that politics in the aftermath of reform had radically changed. The extension of the franchise demanded the modernisation of political organisation. 'We are', Plunkett declared, 'essentially a body associated for the purpose of Conservative registration'.[112] John West, the MP for Dublin City, followed Plunkett in proclaiming that 'the battle of the Constitution must be fought at the registries'.[113]

Voters were thus replacing 'interests' as the primary mechanism of securing political representation, a trend that Irish Tories grasped by the mid 1830s. Like the writings exhibited in the *DUM*, the IMCS was a manifestation of an Irish Protestant belief that inaction was simply not an option in the face of the ebullience of O'Connellism; those who wished to maintain the British constitution in Ireland were forced to meet the Repealers on their own terms. The mobilisation of Tory voters was more important than the old aristocratic networks in this new age. In its report of the founding of the IMCS, the *DUM* optimistically hoped that the stimulus was now in place to encourage the creation of local associations throughout Ireland, 'to secure a fair representation for the sentiments and feelings of the really qualified voters of the constituencies of the country'.[114]

Despite the emphasis on grassroots mobilisation to amplify Irish Conservatism, the IMCS was resolutely opposed to any further democratisation of the franchise, which, it was feared, would disproportionately increase the number of Catholic voters. The wider political vision of the IMCS was profoundly shaped by virulent anti-Catholicism, which perpetuated the idea that the Catholic Church was undermining Protestantism on a global scale. The first 'special report' published by the IMCS centred on the Catholic Church and its 'organised conspiracy' to undermine the Protestant constitution of the British state through a

[110] *DUM*, April 1836, p. 408.

[111] 'A Voice from the North', *To the Orangemen of Ireland* (Belfast: Stuart & Gregg, 1835); O'Sullivan, *Case of the Protestants of Ireland*, p. 19.

[112] *Report ... First Public Meeting of the Irish Metropolitan Conservative Society*, pp. 14, 17.

[113] Ibid., p. 22.

[114] *DUM*, January 1837, pp. 11–12.

sustained assault on the Church of Ireland.[115] On the face of it, the enduring presence of such anti-Catholicism within the IMCS platform suggests that underneath the veneer of modern, Peelite-esque conservatism in Ireland, the animating impulse remained reactionary bigotry. But such a judgement overlooks a fundamental component of Irish conservatism in Ireland: the Catholic Church was feared as a *political* threat to the Protestant conceptions of liberty. Faced with an ascendant Repeal movement, which crystallised Catholic indifference to the fate of the Act of Union, and a Whig reliance on the O'Connellites for parliamentary arithmetic, the IMCS positioned itself as the defender of the Protestant constitution and the true voice of Irish patriotism.

The writings of Dr Anthony Meyler, a founding member of the IMCS, showcased this sentiment. Meyler was a medical doctor and well-known lecturer within the Dublin circuit, who campaigned for better ventilation in public buildings to improve respiratory health.[116] He was also a Catholic convert to Protestantism. In 1838, he published a blistering attack on O'Connellism and the Whig government for enabling the 'Popish clergy' to stoke 'the rebellious and lawless feelings now so prevalent'. Meyler's conception of the future was shaded with dystopian colours, fearful of the political clout of Irish Catholicism. With the 'unholy compact' between the Whigs and O'Connellites, he affirmed that 'Ireland is now governed by the agency of a Popish faction'. 'A tremendous crisis is approaching', he speculated,

> and we are on the eve of a struggle between the peasantry, goaded on by their priests, and the Protestant Church and its members. Ireland is the field where the battle of religious freedom and the constitution may again be fought; and unless the Protestants awake to a sense of their danger, and take the necessary measures of security, the priests will be the rulers of the country.[117]

Ireland as the battlefield of the constitution, the site of a confrontation between Protestant liberty and Catholic tyranny, was a chief animating impulse within Irish Toryism in the age of O'Connell.

[115] *Authentic Reports of Special Meetings of the Irish Metropolitan Conservative Society: on the Policy of the Church of Rome in this Country in her Advocacy of the Voluntary System: a Lecture Delivered by Rev. J. C. Martin* (Dublin: IMCS, 1837), pp. 8–9.

[116] Anthony Meyler, *Observations on Ventilation, and on the Dependence of Health on the Purity of the Air which we Respire* (London: Longman, Hurst, Rees, Orme, and Brown, 1818). For Meyler's lecturing interests, see Enda Leaney, 'Provincial science lectures in nineteenth-century Ireland', *Irish Historical Studies*, vol. 34, no. 135 (2005), p. 269.

[117] Meyler, *Irish Tranquillity*, pp. iii, iv–v.

Meyler's words have a reactionary ring to them, but his stance was more nuanced than his rhetoric suggested. While much of his argument revolved around the rejection of Catholicism as a form of enlightened Christianity – 'I loathed the dark bondage of that superstition in which their minds were held captive'[118] – he acclaimed the redemptive potential of responsible political rights to temper Irish unrest. Meyler supported Catholic Emancipation, believing that the restoration of the privileges of citizenship to the Irish majority would foster a more critical mind, eventually overthrowing the influence of the dominating priest.[119] The experience of the immediate post-Emancipation age, however, shattered his hopes. While the Catholic Relief Act created theoretical political equality among the Catholics and Protestants of Ireland, Meyler criticised the 'injudicious extension of the elective franchise' in 1832 for ushering in a new religiously based ascendancy led by O'Connell.[120] In Meyler's reading, the political equilibrium created in 1829 was destroyed only three years later by the earthquake of parliamentary reform. It was the extension of the franchise, not Catholic Emancipation, that empowered the Irish priests. The newly enfranchised Catholic voters had become the foot soldiers of O'Connellism, a terrifying political machine lubricated by rampant anti-Protestantism.

The alliance between the O'Connellite MPs and the Whigs was, therefore, according to Meyler, one of the most debilitating aftershocks of parliamentary reform. Indeed, he framed this arrangement as a crisis of political power, as the constitutional norms that underpinned legitimate governance in the United Kingdom were overthrown; the government was now in the hands of a pernicious faction. He argued that 'the authority of government should be based on the property, the morality and the intelligence of the country', established political norms that had been overturned in the years since parliamentary reform. 'The Roman Catholic tenant should not legislate for his Protestant landlord – the Romish priest should not legislate, as he does, for the Protestant Church'.[121] Particular ire was directed at Lord Mulgrave, the Whig Lord Lieutenant for Ireland, who, in an attempt to court popularity in Dublin, failed to comprehend the true character of Irish political factions.[122] Mulgrave had, Meyler insisted, 'mistook the noisy uproar of a violent, though insignificant party, for the sober and deliberate voice of the nation'.[123] With this 'violent' faction

[118] Ibid., p. vi. [119] Ibid., p. vii. [120] Ibid., p. 2. [121] Ibid., p. ix.

[122] K. Theodore Hoppen, *Governing Hibernia: British Politicians and Ireland, 1801–1921* (Oxford: Oxford University Press, 2016), pp. 77–8.

[123] Meyler, *Irish Tranquillity*, pp. 31–2.

apparently influencing government policy, the fabric of political authority was coming undone. Meyler rejected a Rousseauean interpretation of government as 'an imaginary compact', 'a mutual surrender of certain natural rights for a common object', stressing instead that political authority is invested with legitimacy only because of an ability to provide security of life and property. He mounted a classical conservative argument that political power should be retained only by those who demonstrated 'wisdom', 'knowledge', 'experience', and 'intelligence'. Society was on a path of certain destruction if 'a lawless and ignorant populace' was invested with authority.[124]

Meyler may have rejected contractarian theories of government based on the surrender of natural rights, but he, like other Irish Tories, framed the Acts of Union as a contract between two historic nations. In operating in an alliance with the political representatives of the Catholic clergy, the Whig administration threatened to renege this contract; Meyler appealed for British parties to adopt a more holistic approach to Ireland to reset the political clock. It was for those in power in Britain to 'consolidate the union' as a reparation for 'centuries of misrule'.[125] Ireland was part of a Protestant kingdom, and the only sustainable path maintaining this status was the 'education of the people in the religion of the gospel'.[126] Given the winds of political change, Meyler was, however, pessimistic. While some Tories such as Emerson Tennent threw cold water on the robustness of the Whig-Radical nexus,[127] Meyler feared that the United Kingdom was sleepwalking into a revolutionary situation. Reform and the ascent of political radicalism threatened the traditional institutions of the British state, such as the Church of England and the House of Lords; in Ireland, the Catholic priesthood was empowered via the 'agency of the peasantry'.[128] Fear for the future of Ireland and the Union propelled Meyler into action with the IMCS.

The contractarian interpretation of the Acts of Union implied equal partnership of the United Kingdom. As such, Irish unionists could, in theory, withdraw their consent to the settlement of 1800, if British actions were deemed to render the connection void. The practical consequences of this stance were, however, difficult for Irish conservatives to articulate. The IMCS published a speech by Meyler in 1840 centring on the destabilising

[124] Ibid., pp. x–xi. [125] Ibid., p. 109. [126] Ibid., p. 119.

[127] *Report of the Speeches and Proceedings at the Belfast Society's Fourth Anniversary Dinner, Held on Tuesday, December 20, 1836, in the Conservative Hall, Belfast*, 2nd ed. (Belfast: G. Phillips, 1837), p. 15.

[128] Meyler, *Irish Tranquillity*, p. 117.

character of politics since the passage of Catholic Emancipation. A number of key Irish conservative assumptions were articulated: the extension of the vote corrupted the Catholic peasant, rendering him a tool of the priest; the phrase 'justice for Ireland' was a cover for the creation of a Catholic ascendancy; and rebellion threatened to overwhelm the defenders of the Protestant faith and the Union.[129] Meyler dwelt on the lost cause of post-Emancipation political harmony in Ireland, accusing the Whigs of merely emboldening the O'Connellites. The object of Emancipation, for Meyler, was to increase conformity to the laws from the hitherto excluded Catholics. There was potential to unite 'the gentry of both persuasions in the bonds of amity', but sectarian differences had been stoked by O'Connell, forcing Catholic landlords to relinquish 'their legitimate influence' as political leaders and fall into the 'degrading bondage' of 'priestly and peasant despotism'.[130]

Meyler's belief in the potential of Emancipation to strengthen conservative social norms of hierarchy and diffidence across Ireland offers an insight into a particular Irish Tory body of ideas. Emancipation was a lost opportunity to expand political liberty throughout Ireland: the creation of a more inclusive form of Irish citizenship should have challenged the clerical grip over the Catholic population. In this sense, Emancipation was a theoretically stronger method to tackle 'superstition' and priestly domination than the penal laws themselves. In a series of public letters to Lord Stanley, who served in Peel's administration in 1841, Meyler conceded that the penal laws 'passed the legitimate boundaries of legislation' because they victimised the laity as much as the Catholic clergy. Meyler was comfortable with 'restrictive laws' directed at the latter group, but in making the Irish majority suffer a loss of political rights, alienation festered in the place of loyalty. The exclusion of Catholics from the legislature was a hammer blow to reconciliation.[131] Coupled with the expansion of the franchise, the landed interest in Ireland had been diminished beyond repair. Meyler recorded that the age of 'high ascendancy and exclusive Toryism in Ireland has passed away' and was not likely to return. Instead, conservatives needed to find a compromise with what he termed 'a new element' within Irish political thought called 'liberty', lest it become monopolised by the 'Popish priesthood'.[132]

[129] *The Address of the Metropolitan Conservative Society of Ireland to the Protestants of Great Britain, Along with a Speech Delivered by Doctor Meyler* (Dublin: W. Warren, 1840), pp. 4, 10, 14, 16.

[130] Ibid., pp. 36–7.

[131] Anthony Meyler, *Six Letters Addressed to Lord Stanley, on the Political and Religious Condition of Ireland* (Dublin: William Carson, 1841), pp. 6–7.

[132] Ibid., p. 13.

Meyler defined 'liberty' as freedom to constitutional rights. As such, liberty was not an abstraction in his imagination, but a political concept that derived its features from 'character of the people with whose government it is blended'.[133] The problem in penal law-era Ireland was that the majority of the people and the government endured an antagonistic relationship, allowing the Catholic Church to assume the status of a distinctive political authority working in opposition to the state. 'Liberty' within Catholic Ireland, therefore, implied a rather different thing than in Protestant Ireland. Meyler regretted the Irish Tory acquiescence in this state of affairs, which contributed to the sectarian nature of political life in Ireland. As the natural figures of authority in a largely feudal society, Meyler lamented the inability of Irish Tories in providing leadership to a wider political community than Protestants. This was compounded by a failure of government since the Union, which 'neglected to educate the people out of the superstition in which they were immersed'.[134] These factors had potentially lethal consequences, which Meyler spelled out with apocalyptic gloom. 'The Protestants of Ireland now stand on a volcano, unknowing how soon it may explode, or when the massacre of 1641 may be repeated'.[135] The only hope for political stability in Ireland was, according to Meyler, the Emancipation of the Catholic people from their priesthood; in other words, nothing short of a second Reformation.[136]

The unspoken consensus within Irish conservatism was, however, that such a radical solution was impossible. Meyler uncompromisingly claimed that Ireland was 'rotten to the very core', destroyed by the unchecked influence of 'Popery', aided and abetted by British indifference and inaction.[137] Hopelessness was a recurring theme within Irish conservative writing during the high age of O'Connell and the Repeal movement. Policies relating to religious practice emanating from London were widely criticised for empowering O'Connellism. For Meyler, the British grant to the Catholic seminary in Maynooth was, in essence, a state-sanctioned sponsorship of treason, given the production of a priesthood 'eminently turbulent and disloyal'.[138] Other Tories followed suit. In judging the 'usefulness' of the Church of Ireland, John Campbell Colquhoun, a Scottish conservative, condemned the failure to teach 'the people the Gospel in their own language', ensuring that Anglicanism remained a

[133] Ibid., p. 19. [134] Ibid., p. 74. [135] Ibid., p. 23. [136] Ibid., p. 24. [137] Ibid., p. 72.

[138] *A Speech, Delivered by Doctor Meyler, at the Great Meeting of the Irish Metropolitan Conservative Society, on a Petition to the House of Commons, Praying that the Annual Grant Hitherto Voted to the Roman Catholic College at Maynooth may be Discontinued* (Dublin: Joshua Porter, 1839), p. 14.

minority denomination despite its official status in Ireland. In explaining Irish unrest, Colquhoun blamed the state for maintaining a distant and hostile relationship with the Catholic population.[139]

A more forthright argument was made by Rev. Tresham Dames Gregg, one of the staunchest opponents of Catholicism in Ireland. In 1840, Gregg published the uncompromisingly titled *Protestant Ascendancy Vindicated*, which was a hostile response to the reform of the Dublin Corporation. The Dublin Corporation was a bastion of Protestantism within Irish civic society, but it fell victim to the wider pattern of municipal reform implemented by the Whigs after 1835.[140] In Ireland, this took the form of the destruction of the Protestant privileges within local government. By November 1841, the grim reality of this reform for Irish conservatives was clear: Daniel O'Connell became the Lord Mayor of Dublin. Gregg began *Protestant Ascendancy Vindicated* with the bleak declaration that Ireland is 'the most miserable country in the world', a condition fostered solely by 'Popery'. Given this, he saw salvation for Ireland only in a restored Protestant Ascendancy. Gregg framed this argument expansively, expressing a desire to reclaim Protestant rights beyond those threatened to be lost at the Dublin Corporation. 'Protestant Corporations', he affirmed, 'are only consistent with a Protestant constitution'. The logic of this stance was that opposing the reform of corporations was not enough if the 'great Protestant system' – the wider constitution – was dismantled as a sop to Irish Catholics and O'Connellite radicals.[141] Gregg defined 'freedom' as the birthright of Protestants, contrasting this virtue with the 'slavery' imposed by the Catholic Church on its adherents. It followed, then, that a 'Protestant constitution' represented the apex of political achievement. This logic pushed Gregg to assert that there was little point in defending the Protestant privileges of one part of the constitution – the corporations – while the remainder was smashed by a factionalist government: 'Let us seek to retain our Protestant Corporations not as anomalous institutions, exclusively Protestant, when everything else has been Papalised'.[142] The revitalisation of the 'Protestant Ascendency' in Gregg's imagination rested on two pillars: the maintenance of the Church of Ireland, supported 'by a

[139] J. C. Colquhoun, *The Uses of the Established Church to the Protestantism and Civilization of Ireland*, 2nd ed. (London: Hatchards, 1839), p. 12.

[140] Hill, *From Patriots to Unionists*, p. 365.

[141] T. D. Gregg, *Protestant Ascendancy Vindicated, and National Regeneration, Through the Instrumentality of National Religion, Urged; in a Series of Letters to the Corporation of Dublin* (Dublin: D. R. Bleakley, 1840), p. 6.

[142] Ibid., p. 121.

provision from every member of the community' (a euphemism for the old tithe system); and the government of the country 'exclusively in the hands of Protestant Christians'.[143] While Gregg warned against interfering in the religious practices of individual Catholics, and condemned the old penal laws for doing so, he demanded at the same time the expulsion of Catholic MPs from Westminster to ensure 'Scriptural policy' can be enacted without opposition.[144]

Gregg's stance was extreme, but it was representative of the broad currents of Irish conservative thought in the era of O'Connell. At the heart of his position was that politics and religion were – and should be – intimately intertwined. 'The man who says that religion has nothing to do with politics', Gregg wrote in 1847, 'aims a mortal blow at all establishments for religion'.[145] The defence of 'Protestant' political institutions was more than religious zealotry: Gregg believed that the constitutional privileges afforded to Ireland stemmed from Protestantism.[146] 'Britain is free, because she is Protestant', Gregg recorded in 1840.[147] Ireland stood, in stark contrast, as an 'enslaved country', where neither Catholics nor Protestants were free, because of 'Romanism' and the constitutional dilution of Protestantism.[148] This echoed the *DUM*'s assertion that Ireland was, in essence, a 'medieval society' in which priestly domination underpinned 'political superstition' and religious fanaticism. The Union was presented as the light of modernity, as Ireland gained 'the advantages of institutions centuries in advance of her state of civilisation'.[149] But these 'institutions' were being chipped away by British neglect of the Protestant ethos of the Union. Gregg strongly endorsed the self-reliance motif that was frequently articulated by Irish conservatives during the 1830s and 1840s, calling for men of talent to actively represent Ireland at Westminster. If the course of history since 1801 was a guide, passive reliance on British statesmen would prove fatal for Ireland and the wider imperial world. If political liberty was connected to Protestant values, then Irish Protestantism stood as a guardian of freedom. 'Nothing but the spread of truth', Gregg reasoned, 'can recover Great Britain, regenerate Ireland, and save the empire from ruin'.[150] This was the crux of the matter. The unionism of many Irish conservatives in the era of O'Connell was

[143] Ibid., p. 64. [144] Ibid., pp. 83, 98.
[145] T. D. Gregg, *Free Thoughts on Protestant Matters*, 2nd ed. (Dublin: W. Curry, Jr. & Co., 1847), p. 44.
[146] Ibid., pp. 77–8. [147] Gregg, *Protestant Ascendancy Vindicated*, p. 11.
[148] Gregg, *Free Thoughts*, p. 121. [149] *DUM*, October 1844, pp. 442, 448.
[150] Gregg, *Free Thoughts*, p. 399.

nourished not by a shared national identity with the British, but a belief that Protestantism and political freedom remained intertwined.

## The Union on Trial

In 1848, Daniel Owen Madden, a literary associate of Young Ireland, extolled the virtues of the Irish bar. From the mid eighteenth century, Madden asserted, the Irish bar has 'produced more orators than the English body of lawyers'. The English law profession may have been 'endowed with unconquerable industry and solid talent', but their Irish counterparts dazzled with their 'eloquence, enthusiasm, and the fire of genius'.[151] This perception was shared by a number of nineteenth-century contemporaries, who stressed that the courtroom was the professional environment for several of the most talented men in Ireland.[152] In high-profile cases during the nineteenth century, lawyers became notable public figures, and there was a huge appetite for legal news and an appreciation for eloquent court speeches. The trials of the Young Irelanders in 1848 offer a dramatic snapshot of this phenomenon. Several prominent Irish conservatives served as defence lawyers for the likes of John Mitchel and William Smith O'Brien before and after the 1848 rebellion; their legal arguments placed the Union on trial as much as the men charged with sedition and high treason.

The courtroom has been recognised as a performative – and deeply political – space for legal teams, defendants, juries, and onlookers.[153] The nineteenth-century courtroom was used by Irish separatists to legitimate acts of high treason against the British Crown, and to denounce the very essence of British law in Ireland. From Robert Emmet's prized oratory from the dock in 1803 through to Roger Casement's famous speech during his trial in 1916, the courtroom was not simply a site of deliberation and justice; it was also a space to advocate separatism through oratory.

151 Daniel Owen Madden, *Revelations of Ireland in the Past Generation* (Dublin: James McGlashan, 1848), p. 2.

152 See, for example, Richard Lalor Sheil, *Sketches of the Irish Bar*, 2 vols. (New York: Redfield, 1854). J. Roderick O'Flanagan, *The Irish Bar: Comprising Anecdotes, Bon-Mots, and Biographical Sketches of the Bench and Bar of Ireland* (London: S. Low, Marston, Searle, and Rivington, 1879); 'Report of the recent state trials', *Dublin Review*, vol. 16, no. 32 (June 1844), p. 378.

153 Katie Barclay, *Men on Trial: Performing Emotion, Embodiment and Identity in Ireland, 1800–45* (Manchester: Manchester University Press, 2019), p. 5; Myles Dungan, *Conspiracy: Irish Political Trials* (Dublin: Prism, 2009), p. xv; Michael T. Davis, Emma Macleod and Gordon Pentland (eds.), *Political Trials in an Age of Revolutions: Britain and the North Atlantic, 1793–1848* (London: Palgrave Macmillan, 2019), p. 6.

A distinctive literary culture developed around seditious 'speeches from the dock', which emphasised the patriotic virtues of generations of rebels against the British connection in Ireland.[154] Political trials were, however, not monologues: it was often the lawyers who were the dramatic stars of the show. This was the case for several of the trials in 1848, particularly those featuring Isaac Butt as the defence counsel. For Butt, the trials of 1848 became an occasion to publicly critique the structure of government in Ireland that had resulted in the devastation of the Famine, which fuelled the desperate attempt by Irish patriots to wage war on the Crown. The Young Ireland rebels may have been misguided in their attempt to wage war against the Crown, but the attempt at insurrection raised a troubling question for Irish Tories as the Famine disseminated the Irish countryside. What if the Young Irelanders were fundamentally correct in their analysis of the Union?

Indeed, elements within Young Ireland and Tory Ireland converged during the 1840s, even before the onset of the Famine. Irish conservatives looked to Britain's constitution as a great charter of freedom, upholding a liberty that was rooted in, and intertwined with, the principles of Protestantism. The prevailing sense among conservatives such as O'Sullivan, Meyler, and Gregg was that successive governments had, since 1829, eroded the social contract that underpinned the legislative Union. But such an interpretation struggled to articulate a political alternative, given that the idea of the Repeal of the Union was intimately bound up with the assertive Catholicism of O'Connell. With the founding of the *Nation* in 1842, however, a less Catholic-centred interpretation of self-government found a platform, which attracted several Irish Tories. Established writers, such as William Carleton and James Clarence Mangan, appeared in both the *DUM* and the *Nation*, encapsulating the shared sense of pride in Irish history, antiquities, and folklore within the two publications, which transcended political divisions.[155] But there were other notable intersections between the Tory and Repeal worlds beyond the pages of the *Nation*, with the courtroom emerging as a pivotal space to explore the potential for a meaningful political synthesis. Suggestive glimpses of a possible Irish Tory-Young Ireland consensus appeared during James Whiteside's defences of Daniel O'Connell and Charles Gavan Duffy against charges of sedition in 1843 and 1844.

[154] The most striking example was A. M. Sullivan and T. D. Sullivan, *Guilty or Not Guilty? Speeches from the Dock, or Protests of Irish Patriotism* (Dublin: no publishing house, 1867). See Chapter 5, p. 211, for a more detailed discussion.

[155] Foster, *Words Alone*, pp. 52–4.

James Whiteside was, by the 1840s, a major presence within the Irish bar. His political thought was framed, like his Irish conservative contemporaries, by the connections between Protestant liberty and responsible government.[156] Whiteside was particularly regarded for his eloquence, and his defence of Duffy in 1844 was widely praised as a master class of courtroom rhetoric. The *DUM* recorded that Whiteside's address was 'almost unrivalled in the annals of oratory'.[157] His performance was apparently so powerful that it moved many in the courtroom to tears.[158] Whiteside's argument was constructed around a critique of the Union which appealed not to abstract national sentiment but to a materialist interpretation of the shortcomings of constitutional centralisation. The *DUM's* praise for Whiteside's approach spoke volumes about the conditionality of unionism within the ranks of Irish conservatism, even before the horrors of the Famine began to devastate the potato crop. Indeed, following Whiteside's spirited defence of Duffy, Young Ireland voiced their hopes of further collaborations with Irish conservatives: the *Nation* pinned its hopes on 'a rising race of Irish lawyers', a number of whom were associated with the *DUM*, to transform the Irish bar into a nationally minded institution.[159]

While this burden of expectation initially rested on Whiteside, it was the younger *DUM*-affiliated lawyers, Isaac Butt and Samuel Ferguson, who publicly gravitated towards Young Ireland after the aftermath of the state trials of 1844.[160] Butt was one of the most gifted young Tories of his day, a man who combined intellectual vigour, an affable character, and a classical style of oratory. He had been, as we saw earlier, an editor of the *DUM* during the 1830s; in addition, he was elected to the Whateley Professorship in Political Economy at TCD in 1836, a position he held until 1841.[161] It was the great Repeal debate at Dublin Corporation in

156 Patrick Maume, 'Unionists and patriots: James Whiteside, the Irish bar and the dilemmas of the Protestant nation in Victorian Ireland', in Allan Blackstock and Frank O'Gorman (eds.), *Loyalism and the Formation of the British World, 1775–1914* (Woodbridge: Boydell Press, 2014), pp. 145–62.

157 *DUM*, March 1849, p. 333.

158 Charles Read and T. P. O'Connor (eds.), *The Cabinet of Irish Literature: Selections from the Works of the Chief Poets, Orators, and Prose Writers of Ireland*, 4 vols. (London: Blackie and Son, 1880), iv, p. 65.

159 *Nation*, 23 March 1844.

160 It should be noted that Whiteside was abroad for much of 1845–7; his *Italy in the Nineteenth Century*, 3 vols. (London: Richard Bentley, 1848) was based on his Italian travels during this time.

161 For Butt's tenure as Whateley Professor, see Alan O'Day, 'Isaac Butt and neglected political economists', in Noel Thompson and Nigel Allington (eds.), *English, Irish and Subversives among the Dismal Scientists* (Bingley: Emerald, 2010), pp. 375–401, and Colin W. Reid, '"A voice for Ireland": Isaac Butt, environmental justice, and the dilemmas of the Irish land question', in Matthew Kelly (ed.), *Nature and the Environment in Nineteenth-Century Ireland* (Liverpool: Liverpool University Press, 2019), pp. 55–74.

1843, however, that catapulted Butt into national prominence. As a young alderman at the Corporation, Butt was chosen to counter Daniel O'Connell's motion to petition parliament in favour of the Repeal of the Union. O'Connell spoke for over four hours, focusing on the extreme poverty that blighted many parts of Ireland, which he connected to a lack of self-government. Butt's reply emphasised the exalted status that the Union had granted Ireland and the Irish. 'I am satisfied', Butt told the Corporation, 'that we have all a much greater stake in the strength and in the prosperity of the empire at large, than we can have in any petty and separate interest of any of its component parts'.[162] Indeed, Butt argued that the Union was a more logical framework of governance than a return of a parliament in Dublin, as the Irish understanding of political liberty was rooted in 'Anglo-Saxon rights'. 'The liberties of our country', Butt declared, can be traced 'no higher than the English conquest'.[163] Butt was critical about how O'Connell had weaponised the concept of Repeal, which he believed had inflamed the political mood of the country. Despite this, Butt conceded that the emotional appeal of a restoration of a parliament in Dublin was potent.[164] Nevertheless, he hoped that his vision of a harmonious Union, with Ireland enjoying a privileged role within a greater kingdom and empire, would trump the lure of O'Connellite sentiment. But as Ireland moved into the era of the Famine, the conditionality of Butt's unionism came increasingly to the fore.

Irish Toryism hit a crisis point with the onset of the Famine; the perception that the Union state was unable – or even unwilling – to alleviate the devastation of the blight led some unionists to question Ireland's constitutional status. Butt's vision of the United Kingdom as a multinational melting pot, imbued with a shared imperial purpose and common interests, was fractured by the Famine. In 1847, he published *A Voice for Ireland*, a blistering attack on the nature of Irish governance:

> Irishmen were told that in consenting to a Union which would make them partners with a great and opulent nation, like England, they would have all the advantages that might be expected to flow from such a nation. How are these expectations to be realised, how are these pledges to be fulfilled, if the partnership is only to be one of loss, and never of profit to us?[165]

[162] Isaac Butt, *Repeal of the Union: the Substance of a Speech Delivered in the Corporation of Dublin, on 28th February, 1843, on Mr O'Connell's Motion to Petition for a Repeal of the Legislative Union* (Dublin: William Curry, Jr. and Co., 1843), p. 6.

[163] Ibid., p. 9. [164] Ibid., pp. 62–5.

[165] Isaac Butt, *A Voice for Ireland, the Famine in the Land: What Has Been Done and What is to be Done* (Dublin: J. McGlashan, 1847), p. 22.

Butt was moving closer politically to his Repealer contemporaries. 'Can we wonder if the Irish people believe', Butt fumed, '*and believe it they do* – that the lives of those who have perished, and who will perish, have been sacrificed by a deliberate compact to the gains of English merchants'. The humanitarian failure of theories of free market political economy had, Butt asserted, 'created among all classes a feeling of deep dissatisfaction, not only with the ministry but with English rule'.[166] The Famine, in other words, grimly brought to the surface the tensions inherent within the Union itself.

At the beginning of 1848, the *DUM* published an anxious article outlining the dangers and duties of Irish conservatives and the landed interest during the humanitarian crisis that was unfolding in the countryside. A stark warning leapt out of the pages: either the government intervened in a meaningful way in Ireland – the expansion of tenant rights was the most significant idea floated in the *DUM* – or the Union would perish from neglect. 'Conservatives in Ireland', the *DUM* counselled, 'should prepare for that which is most to be dreaded'.[167] Some conservatives were, however, more advanced than the *DUM's* position, and came to advocate – with a reluctant inflection – the Repeal of the Union. In April 1848, the *Morning Chronicle* reported that Butt, 'heretofore a prominent Conservative of the Orange school', was preparing to be 'the great gun' of the newly established Protestant Repeal Association.[168] This organisation was founded by Samuel Ferguson, with the aim of giving voice to the exasperation and disenchantment felt by Protestants at how unresponsive the Union government was to Ireland's plight. While this body shared the common goal of repealing the Union with the more classical republican-inspired Young Irelanders, their respective emphases were very different. Young Ireland articulated the claims for independent nationhood; the Protestant Repeal Association emphasised that a constitutional breach had occurred and required correction.[169] The Acts of Union were, therefore, viewed very differently by the two camps. The Irish conservatives who formed the Protestant Repeal Association believed that the Union was, in essence, a contract between two nations, but one of these partners – England – had not lived up to its obligations; Young Ireland, on the other hand, increasingly rejected the Union as a blight on Irish nationhood.

These differences in viewpoint were evident at the first meeting of the Association in Dublin in May, at which Ferguson read a resolution that

[166] Ibid., p. 10. [167] *DUM*, January 1848, pp. 150, 154–5.
[168] *Morning Chronicle*, 26 April 1848. [169] Patten, *Samuel Ferguson*, p. 117.

stressed the Association's rather negative rationale to terminate the Union: 'Resolved – That national prosperity is based on social confidence, and that social confidence in Ireland cannot be expected to exist while the Government is conducted, and the laws are made, by strangers to the Irish people.'[170] Butt was absent from this meeting, but the *Morning Chronicle* carried intelligence a few days later of his apparent intentions: 'It is asserted that Mr Butt, Q.C., who is to defend Mr Meagher next week, is to declare himself a Repealer on the occasion of his address to the jury.'[171]

Butt's performance as defence counsel for Meagher and O'Brien in their trials for sedition in May 1848 was thus sharpened by his rising sense of disillusion with the British constitution as it operated in Ireland. Meagher, himself an able rhetorician, as underlined by his infamous 'Sword' speech refuting non-violent O'Connellism from 1846 – 'Be it for the defence, or be it for the assertion of a nation's liberty, I look upon the sword as a sacred weapon'[172] – found his defence counsel adopting a strategy that justified the use of such language. Butt's case pivoted on the idea that Young Ireland's politics were motivated by an anti-unionist rather than anti-monarchy sentiment, a distinction that rebuffed the charge of sedition against the Queen. The evocative defence rested on constitutional rather than personal matters, as Butt denounced the failure to enact the constitution of 1688 in Ireland, ensuring that the Irish did not enjoy the same political and legal liberties as the English, the latter of whom were 'governed by the opinions of a free people'. The very fact that Young Ireland leaders were accused of sedition for proclaiming Ireland's right to freedom, Butt contended, demonstrated the legal discrepancies between the two islands. He concluded in a Lockean vein: as the *Times* reported, Butt 'proceeded to defend the sacred right of resistance, by which the liberties of the people should be maintained against aggression'.[173] While the conclusion of Butt's robust address brought prolonged bouts of applause, including from other lawyers, he did not make, despite the *Morning Chronicle's* report the week before, a formal declaration for Repeal.[174] This was indicative of Butt's political dilemma: while his legal and polemic language was permeated with critiques of how the centralised Union state operated in Ireland, this was combined with an inherent

[170] *Morning Chronicle*, 11 May 1848. Also see Ferguson, *Sir Samuel Ferguson*, i, p. 248.
[171] *Morning Chronicle*, 13 May 1848.
[172] Arthur Griffith, *Meagher of the Sword: Speeches of Thomas Francis Meagher in Ireland, 1846–1848* (Dublin: M. H. Gill & Son, Ltd., 1916), p. 36.
[173] *Times*, 18 May 1848.
[174] Terence de Vere White, *The Road of Excess* (Dublin: Browne and Nolan Ltd., 1946), pp. 120–1.

loyalism to the British Crown. The dynamics of this tension, and the ambiguous political space in which Butt found himself inhabiting during the Famine, studded his defence of William Smith O'Brien against the charge of sedition.

Like Meagher's defence, Butt cast O'Brien's case in broad national terms rather than a narrow personal interpretation. Butt emphasised his client's aristocratic respectability, asserting that political culture in Ireland had become corrupted when such a man could be pronounced guilty of treasonous behaviour. O'Brien's agitation was not against the Crown, Butt reasoned, but against the Acts of Union. In exhorting the Irish population to arm themselves, O'Brien had highlighted the constitutional gap between Ireland and Britain, as '[e]very man in a free country had the right to carry arms'. Butt's oratory again embraced Lockean language denoting the relationship between the citizen and sovereign – his use of the rhetorical trope 'slave' to describe the political status of the Irish under the Union explicitly drew on Locke's dictum of resisting an arbitrary power that inflicted slavery[175] – and attempted to further politicise O'Brien's case. This politically charged legal argument was similar in rhetorical nature to Robert Holmes's defence of John Mitchel in May 1848, which stressed Ireland's constitutional subordination under the Union.[176] Butt's extraordinary appeal at the conclusion of the speech made a virtue of O'Brien's actions, emphasising the ethos of his client through a plea saturated in political pathos:

> I ask you to decide this case as you ought by law to decide it, in judging of Mr Smith O'Brien's intentions, upon the supposition that Repeal is desirable for the country, and that the taking away of our native parliament was a grievous wrong. If you deal with the question in that way, how can you find a verdict of guilty? If you find a verdict of guilty, it must be upon your preconceived political opinions. But again I say, and I announce it fearlessly, that you must decide the case as if Repeal was desirable for the country.[177]

It was a master class in rhetorical practice. What made Butt's address so compelling was that the words were grounded within his own character: his stringent defence of O'Brien was informed by his own personal dilemma over the future of Irish governance. Butt's oratory was a

[175] John Locke, *Two Treatises of Government*, ed. Peter Laslett (Cambridge: Cambridge University Press, 1988), p. 412.

[176] *The Queen against John Mitchel* (1848), 6 St Tr NS 599, p. 660.

[177] *The Queen against O'Brien, and the Queen against Meagher* (1848), 6 St Tr NS 571, p. 591.

principled critique of the Union that was at once heartfelt and intellectually devastating. His decision not to pursue a more formal forensic style was vindicated: like the Meagher trial, the jury failed to convict, and O'Brien walked away from court a free man. Immediately after the collapse of the trial, O'Brien addressed supporters, praising the 'patriotic sentiments' of Butt, 'and expressed his belief that it was the dawn of a new nationality for Ireland'.[178]

The aftermath of the attempt at armed insurrection in July 1848, however, highlighted the limitations of this 'new nationality'. Following the Young Ireland revolt at Ballingarry, south Tipperary, the language of the Irish conservative lawyers dramatically shifted away from abstract justifications of resistance. In September, William Smith O'Brien, and other leading Young Irelanders, found themselves back in the courtroom facing charges of treason-felony. One month before the keynote trials, Butt defended Kevin O'Doherty, with his address once again emphasising the denial of liberty to Ireland under the British constitution in its current form. There was, however, a marked difference in tone from the May speeches: after the July rebellion by the Young Irelanders, Butt avoided overt avocation of rebellion. His defence of O'Doherty's 'intention of familiarising the Irish people to the use of arms and to war', chiefly through articles which appeared in the *United Irishman*, was couched in the rhetoric of the right to bear arms, the highest distinction of a free country. Yet this defence was prefaced by a revealing line:

> At another time, *if this country were peaceable*, and if the divisions which now distract the country were removed, I would say the man who taught the country the dignity of an armed nation, was doing them a noble service.[179]

Theoretical appeals to resist an unjust government were punctured by the actualities of Young Ireland violence. The jury failed to agree on O'Doherty's fate during the first two trials, but he was convicted and exiled during the third trial. Facing Butt across the courtroom was James Whiteside, the defender of Gavan Duffy just a few years before, but now part of the counsel for the Crown. Whiteside gained a renewed prominence in October when he accepted O'Brien's brief in the highest profile Young Ireland trial following the attempted rebellion.

While Whiteside lacked connections with the young Protestant intellectuals associated with the *DUM*, such as Butt, Ferguson, and Charles

[178] *Nation*, 20 May 1848.
[179] *The Queen against O'Doherty* (1848), 6 St Tr NS 831, p. 864. My emphasis.

Lever, he shared many of their political tastes and assumptions. Like Butt, for example, he wrestled with how best to reconcile the eighteenth-century Patriot legacy of enlightened Protestant leadership, national virtue, and rhetorical eloquence with nineteenth-century realities of centralised Union, Catholic Emancipation, and the seemingly irresistible march of democracy. While Butt ultimately failed to resolve these tensions within the framework of the Union, pushing him towards an advocacy of federalism in 1870, Whiteside was able to square Protestant Patriotism with his unionism. He was aware of Protestant sentimental attachment to College Green, the site of the 'old' Irish parliament, which stood as a monument to an age of national leadership and men who held a mythic status. When reflecting on the Union debates in the Dublin parliament, for instance, Whiteside questioned which side he would have followed. Given the rhetorical power of the anti-unionist case, he imagined finding himself spellbound by 'the gravity of Saurin's argument – enchanted by the eloquence of Bushe – convinced by Plunket – inflamed by Grattan'.[180] But this, he recognised, would have been a mistake. For all the eloquence contained within the walls of College Green, for all the passionate articulation of national indignation of the late 1790s, the theory of Union was much more attractive than the colonial subordination that hitherto existed. In Whiteside's view, an informed Irish citizenry, part of a greater imperial polity, was a greater beacon of the liberties enshrined in the British constitution than an outdated provincial parliament.[181]

As his celebrated performance as defence counsel for Duffy demonstrated, Whiteside's unionism was intellectually broad enough to conceptualise resistance against British rule in Ireland as a crisis of government rather than doctrinal separatism. While his defence of William Smith O'Brien in 1848 should be viewed against this backdrop, the Young Ireland resort to *literal* rather than theoretical violence ensured that Whiteside was forced to adopt a rather different approach to his legal colleagues the previous May. Amidst much press attention (including special supplements in newspapers),[182] the Special Commission that presided over the Young Irelanders' trials for high treason sat in September and October. Such was the perceived power of Whiteside's defence of O'Brien that it was afterwards published in pamphlet form and as part of

[180] James Whiteside, *The Life and Death of the Irish Parliament: A Lecture* (Dublin: Hodges, Smith and Co., 1864), p. 196. Also see Maume, 'Unionists and patriots', pp. 145–6.

[181] Whiteside, *Life and Death*, pp. 104, 202. [182] *Belfast Newsletter*, 6 October 1848.

William C. Townsend's *Modern State Trials*, a volume of recent legal history issued by a major London publisher.[183]

Given the nature of the charge and O'Brien's unquestionable role in the rebellion, success for the defence team appeared highly unlikely. Nevertheless, Whiteside's much-praised address to the court was infused with aspects of the eighteenth-century Patriot tradition. In constructing the case for O'Brien's defence, Whiteside downplayed O'Brien's revolutionary intent, not only by emphasising his aristocratic pedigree but also by forensically deconstructing the notion that 'treason' described what happened in Ballingarry. Whiteside rejected the idea that O'Brien wished to wage war to threaten the Queen's life: he insisted instead that the Young Irelander's motives were much more circumspect. Whiteside cited the monarchist and imperial dimensions of O'Brien's Repeal rhetoric during the 1840s, which stressed the compatibility of Irish legislative independence with the Crown and wider empire. The Crown prosecution relayed a speech by O'Brien in which the Young Irelander desired to see 'the formation of a National Guard – an army of volunteers of 1848' as evidence of treasonous intent; but Whiteside coolly affirmed that this alluded 'to a reconstitution of the volunteers of 1782, who were the instruments of such blessings to their country'.[184] The rising of a citizen militia was presented as a praiseworthy exercise in political virtue, not a crude form of treason. That the Young Ireland 'army' which took to the field in 1848 was far from a military force was used by Whiteside for effect: 'Did you ever hear of a body of men with stones going to demolish the monarchy of England?'[185] The speech was in many ways similar to Butt's defence of O'Brien in May: the aristocratic O'Brien was presented as a virtuous, if naïve, political figure guided only by patriotism and a desire to see his country governed well. That he believed this could not be achieved through the British constitution as it stood in Ireland did not make him a revolutionary; if anything, both Whiteside and Butt implied that O'Brien's moral stand to radically change the nature of Ireland's relationship with Britain was noble and courageous. Unlike Butt, however, Whiteside was forced to deal with the actuality of violence in 1848, a very different thing from the classical idealism of citizen armies. Here, Whiteside relied on

[183] James Whiteside, *Whiteside's Defence of Wm. S. O'Brien, Esq., MP: On His Trial for High Treason at Clonmel, on Thursday and Friday, 5th and 6th October, 1848* (Dublin: no publisher details, [1848]).William C. Townsend, *Modern State Trials: With Essays and Notes*, 2 vols. (London: Longman, Brown, Green, and Longmans, 1850).

[184] *The Queen against Smith O'Brien* (1848), 7 St Tr NS 1, p. 225.

[185] *The Queen against Smith O'Brien*, p. 239.

more logos than pathos in explaining O'Brien's behaviour at Ballingarry. O'Brien was not attempting to stoke rebellion in Tipperary, argued the defence; rather his intention was to 'escape and prevent arrest'.[186] The very ineptitude of the escapade was cited as evidence against the idea of revolutionary intent by Whiteside. Barricades were raised not to levy war, but to resist arrest; gunpowder was not seized because there was no plan to 'make war on the Queen'. The reality was, of course, rather different: the failures of the rebellion were more down to O'Brien's profound miscalculations concerning the militancy of the peasantry and the support of the clergy than a lack of revolutionary commitment from the Young Ireland leader.[187] O'Brien came to retrospectively resent the defence's argument, which accentuated the bungling aspects of the Ballingarry disturbance and downplayed the Young Irelanders' desire for national liberation. But given that any declaration of revolutionary intent would have implicated a number of Young Irelanders, O'Brien acquiesced in passive acceptance of his lawyer's counsel.[188]

Whiteside concluded his address, like Butt before him, with an appeal to the jury to question the nature of the Irish body politic under the Union. That O'Brien, an aristocrat from an ancient and respected family, had become radicalised into rebellion was a consequence of the inadequacies that marred the British-Irish connection. Whiteside was careful, however, not to provide as full a critique of the Union as Butt had made in May. The focus was instead resolutely on O'Brien's sense of patriotism. Indeed, the defence counsel's aim was to direct attention away from the affray in Ballingarry and emphasise O'Brien's noble character to win over public opinion; the hope was to ensure the state would find it difficult to impose an overly harsh sentence on a popular patriot.[189] In the end, though, Whiteside's meticulously constructed defence was undone when the prosecution produced a letter from O'Brien to the directors of the Mining Company, dated 29 July, in which the Young Ireland leader proclaimed 'in case the Irish revolution should succeed, the property of the Mining Company will be confiscated as national property'.[190] O'Brien was found guilty by the jury and sentenced to be hanged, drawn, and

186 *The Queen against Smith O'Brien*, p. 240.
187 Richard Davis, *The Young Ireland Movement* (Dublin: Gill & Macmillan, 1988), p. 163.
188 Robert Sloan, *William Smith O'Brien and the Young Ireland Rebellion of 1848* (Dublin: Four Courts Press, 2000), p. 293.
189 John Monsell to William Smith O'Brien, 23 August [1848], William Smith O'Brien Papers, National Library of Ireland (NLI), MS 442/2497.
190 *The Queen against Smith O'Brien*, p. 318.

quartered, although this was later commuted to deportation to Van Diemen's Land.

The courtroom rhetoric adopted by Whiteside in O'Brien's trial had several similarities to Butt's passionate defence of the Young Irelander in May, but was substantially handicapped by the actuality of violence in the summer of 1848. Nevertheless, Whiteside's conclusions emphasised the virtues of patriotism and self-reliance at the height of the Famine, prominent themes which had animated Irish conservative thought since the passing of the Catholic Relief Act. The arguments that Whiteside, along with other conservative lawyers such as Butt, deployed in the courtroom mirrored their growing ambivalence towards the Union, which appeared to provide intellectual support for the growth of a Repeal sentiment within the Irish conservative platform in early 1848. The affray in Ballingarry, however, shattered the apparent rapprochement of Irish conservatism and Young Ireland. Shortly before the rebellion, a conservative pamphleteer sketched out the dangers in importing French revolutionary ideas into Ireland, as any insurrection risked sectarian civil war.[191] And, indeed, once Repeal became stained with the Young Ireland rebellion, conservatives swiftly backed away. Regardless of what occurred in Ballingarry, the emergence of the Protestant Repeal Association was a striking episode within Irish conservative thought. The Association was, however, a minority pastime, even before the rebellion: while Butt placed the Union on trial in his high-profile courtroom appearances in 1848, it is striking that he apparently did not join the Association. The dilemmas of unionism were not resolved in 1848, but quietly faded from public view following the rebellion. The conditionality of the Union within the conservative mindset did, however, receive one more dramatic airing, under the leadership of Isaac Butt in the early 1870s.

## The Union Trap

For Irish conservatives of all stripes in the period between the passage of Catholic Emancipation and the Famine, the British constitution remained the framework to provide political liberty. The Protestant state was a beacon of enlightenment and rationality, in stark contrast to the 'popery' and 'superstition' of the Catholic people of Ireland. Yet, the direction of travel from the early 1830s, when reform dominated the political agenda of

[191] 'An Irishman', *The French Revolution and the Repeal of the Union: an Address to the People of Ireland* (Dublin: Mullen, Corbet, and Co., 1848), p. 6.

the United Kingdom, to the humanitarian disaster of the Famine, via bouts of O'Connellite influence over successive governments, alienated and discombobulated Irish conservatives.

As post-reform governance evolved during this period, a perception grew that the United Kingdom was less a meaningful union of nations and more a quasi-English empire. The Famine, and the painfully inadequate governmental response – and, more to the point perhaps, the infamous Whig maxim of 'Irish property should support Irish poverty'[192] – crystallised Irish conservative doubts about the Union as Ireland's ideal constitutional framework. As the defence lawyer of the radical Young Irelander, Richard D'Alton Williams, in 1848, Samuel Ferguson declared in court that one part of the United Kingdom had no right to assert authority over another. 'We are part and parcel with them of one Imperial body', Ferguson asserted,

> their friends and fellow-labourers for the general good; assuming no jurisdiction over them, suffering no assumption of jurisdiction by them over us, their equals in the eye of the law, members with them while the Union lasts of one United Kingdom; but their slaves never![193]

The government's response to the Famine was so traumatic for Irish conservatives because it shattered the illusion of constitutional equality.

For Irish Tories such as Ferguson, the Union became a trap. Loyalty to the imperial parliament left Tories impotent in Irish affairs, while their insistence on 'Protestant liberty' was weakened by an increasingly tolerant state. For its adherents, unionism stood for an embrace of Protestant cosmopolitanism and imperial greatness, an escape from the unnerving rise of a Catholic majority articulating the language of O'Connellite democracy. The brief Irish Tory flirtation with the restoration of an Irish parliament during the 1840s was a revealing moment. As one pamphleteer put it, England and Ireland were not 'considered one and the same country', what was, from an Irish perspective, the purpose of the Union?[194]

192 David P. Nally, *Human Encumbrances: Political Violence and the Great Irish Famine* (Notre Dame, IN: University of Notre Dame Press, 2011), p. 138.

193 Ferguson, *Sir Samuel Ferguson*, i, p. 208.

194 Sandham Elly, *Potatoes, Pigs and Politics, the Curse of Ireland, and the Cause of England's Embarrassments* (London: Kent and Richards, 1848), p. 34.

CHAPTER 5

# *The Sovereign People*

## *Republicanism and Popular Sovereignty after the Famine*

> For Republicanism, or Monarchism, in the abstract, is nothing – a government is a thing that governs concrete living men under absolute extant circumstances.[1]
>
> John Mitchel (1854)

> If Irishmen want to be citizen soldiers – if they wish for an impartial administration of justice – it appears to us they must look to themselves, and not to English rulers, for these great privileges![2]
>
> *Irish People* (1865)

Ireland after the Famine was a different place. The appalling tragedy resulted in a mass depopulation, as around two million people either died from disease, hunger, or emigrated. The Repeal of the Union campaign, which was paralysed by O'Connell's death in 1847, was terminated by the Famine. Young Ireland was broken and scattered across the world.[3] The Famine shone a chilling light onto the injustices of the tenure system in Ireland, bringing land to the political fore as an issue that tested the legitimacy of parliamentary governance.[4] In 1849, the relaunched *Nation* newspaper wearily captured the contemporaneous political mindset, which had little bandwidth for reimagining the shape of governance in Ireland. Depicting Ireland as 'a sick and disabled man', the *Nation* called for achieving 'preliminary successes' before the 'last and most precious right' – political independence – was won.[5] Given the failure of the 1848 rebellion, the clear lack of appetite for insurrection within the Irish countryside, and

[1] John Mitchel, *Jail Journal: or, Five years in British Prisons* (New York: *The Citizen*, 1854), p. 100.
[2] *Irish People*, 16 September 1865.
[3] Christopher Morash, *Young Ireland: A Global Afterlife* (New York: New York University Press, 2023).
[4] David P. Nally, *Human Encumbrances: Political Violence and the Great Irish Famine* (Notre Dame, IN: University of Notre Dame Press, 2011), p. 215.
[5] *Nation*, 1 September 1849.

the destruction of the Repeal platform, Charles Gavan Duffy, the author of the editorial, believed that new thinking was necessary to stabilise Ireland.

Political innovations did indeed follow the Famine. Duffy was instrumental in founding the Tenant League in 1850, which protested the strengthening of landlord rights enshrined in the Encumbered Estates Act of the previous year. While the League quickly faded away, its establishment marked a watershed in Irish politics: reforms to materially aid farmers and questions over landed rights became dominant aspects within political culture in the decades that followed. Duffy was adamant in later writings that it was correct for the '48-generation to move away from the O'Connellite-Young Irelander prism of national politics that centred on visions of Irish governance and agitate instead for more piecemeal reform. Writing in 1886 on the origins of the Tenant League, he lamented that 'in politics you have to choose not what you would prefer but what you can accomplish'.[6] Yet Duffy was careful at the time not to lose sight of the fundamental reason why such grievances arose in the first place. 'Independence is no longer the first achievement', he recorded in the *Nation* in 1849, 'but the end result of many previous victories'.[7]

While the Tenant League was a decidedly non-revolutionary body, its ethos was intensely radical. Strengthening the legal rights of tenants inevitably implied the weakening of the landlords' absolute grip over land ownership. Duffy, traditionally seen as a conservative figure within the Young Ireland milieu, may have been influenced in his shift to agrarianism by the writings of James Fintan Lalor, who died in 1849.[8] Duffy and Lalor met in prison in 1848, with the two men striking a friendship based on a shared loathing of John Mitchel.[9] But while Lalor advocated the fusion of political independence and the destruction of landlordism, Duffy separated the two issues, relegating the political immediacy of Ireland's constitutional status in favour of addressing agrarian grievances.[10] This philosophy, which was coupled with Duffy's advocacy of parliamentary politics (the Tenant League programme was taken up by the short-lived and clerically

[6] Charles Gavan Duffy, *The League of North and South: An Episode in Irish History, 1850–1854* (London: Chapman & Hall, 1886), p. 30.

[7] *Nation*, 1 September 1849.

[8] Kerron Ó Luain, '"Craven subserviency had vanished. Bitter hostility had arrived": agrarian violence and the Tenant League on the Ulster borderlands, 1849–1851', *Irish Historical Studies*, vol. 43, no. 163 (2019), p. 45.

[9] Charles Gavan Duffy, *My Life in Two Hemispheres*, 2 vols. (London: T. Fisher Unwin, 1898), i, pp. 314–15.

[10] Kevin B. Nowlan, *The Politics of Repeal: A Study in the Relations between Great Britain and Ireland, 1841–1850* (London: Routledge & Kegan Paul, 1965), p. 230.

supported Independent Irish Party at Westminster), alienated Lalorite radicals.[11]

While Duffy was pursuing an agrarian agenda from the early 1850s, his erstwhile political opponents within Young Ireland presented an alternative programme. What remained of the Irish Confederacy following the state trials of 1848 gathered in a new organisation called the Irish Democratic Association.[12] The Association attracted the patronage of the Chartist and former Repeal MP, Feargus O'Connor, and held a number of public meetings throughout 1850 and 1851. While the organisation's emphasis remained national independence, its mission statement mimicked some of the values of Chartism and the wider European turn to socialism. Richard Pigott, the noted Irish journalist and later forger of the Parnell letters, began his career with the Association's newspaper, the *Irishman*: he recorded later that the movement's aims were 'entirely socialistic and revolutionary', with a focus on the creation of a peasant proprietary system.[13] But the Irish Democratic Association was not confined to a radical vision of rural Ireland: its first programme also appealed to the 'rights of labour', the 'working class', and the 'artizan'. The desire of the Association was to 'train the democracy of this country into full and complete knowledge of their power'. Such a Chartist-esque mission had become imperative because 'the rights and interests of the people have been totally neglected by our representatives'.[14] While the Irish Reform Act of 1850 lowered the property-value threshold for voters, thereby tripling the number of rural voters, this was far from enfranchising the Irish 'democracy'. Nevertheless, the Irish Democratic Association petered out by the end of the year.

The Tenant League, Independent Irish Party, and the Irish Democratic Association were all short-lived ventures, but taken together offer a snapshot into the fluidity of the political landscape in Ireland in the immediate aftermath of the Famine. Despite the collapse of these organisations, the critical issues with which they grappled – the nature of land reform, the tug of war between non-sectarian and clerical politics, and the tension between

[11] The classic account remains J. H. Whyte, *The Independent Irish Party, 1850–1859* (Oxford: Oxford University Press, 1958).

[12] Vincent Geoghegan, 'The emergence and submergence of Irish socialism, 1821–1851', in D. George Boyce, Robert Eccleshall and Vincent Geoghegan (eds.), *Political Thought in Ireland since the Seventeenth Century* (London: Routledge, 1993), p. 113.

[13] Richard Pigott, *Personal Recollections of an Irish National Journalist*, 2nd ed. (Dublin: Hodges, Figgis & Co., 1883), p. 31.

[14] *Freeman's Journal*, 6 March 1850.

parliamentary and popular sovereignty – animated Irish thought over the subsequent decades. Radical new ideas of agrarianism, democratic legitimacy, and, most subversively, an underground Irish state flourished in the wake of the Famine, challenging the efficacy of the existing structures of parliamentary government. The most notable manifestation of this radicalism was the formation of a secret society, which included former Young Irelanders, boldly proclaiming the virtues of an Irish Republic achieved through revolutionary means.

## Pikes, Not Pamphlets: Interpreting Fenian Political Thought

The Irish Republican Brotherhood (IRB) was founded by James Stephens in Dublin on St Patrick's Day, 1858. The IRB recruited heavily from small, post-Famine separatist networks, such as the Phoenix National and Literary Society in Co. Cork, and quickly built up a presence throughout the country. The label 'IRB' was not initially in common parlance; early members referred to 'the brotherhood', 'our body', or 'the organisation'.[15] Almost simultaneously, the Fenian Brotherhood was established in the United States by two Irish exiles, John O'Mahony and Michael Doheny. Linking Stephens, O'Mahony, and Doheny was a connection to rebellion in Ireland, as all of them took part in the uprising of 1848. That shattering defeat left an indelible mark on the three men. The grim but essential lesson was that for a rebellion to become the stepping stone towards national revolution, organisation, discipline, and, above all, secrecy, were necessary.

Stephens and O'Mahony relocated to Paris in the aftermath of the Ballingarry debacle, and there they observed the workings of various revolutionary societies, such as the followers of Blanquism.[16] The Parisian interlude may have been crucial in pushing the two Irishmen to reflect on the problems that beset the Irish revolutionary moment of 1848, chiefly the relative conservatism of Young Ireland in the absence of Mitchel and Lalor (William Smith O'Brien apparently pleaded with his peasant army not to violate the sanctity of private property at the height of the rebellion),[17] and the folly of open insurrection. A subversive interpretation

[15] John O'Leary, *Recollections of Fenians and Fenianism*, 2 vols. (London: Downey & Co., Ltd., 1896), i, p. 123.

[16] Niall Whelehan, *The Dynamiters: Irish Nationalism and Political Violence in the Wider World, 1867–1900* (Cambridge: Cambridge University Press, 2012), pp. 43–4.

[17] Malcolm Brown, *The Politics of Irish Literature: From Thomas Davis to W. B. Yeats* (Seattle: University of Washington Press, 1972), p. 113.

of popular sovereignty that manifested itself in separatism, delivered through conspiracy and clandestine organisation, became the raison d'être of the Irish Republican Brotherhood.

While the IRB was not the first Irish separatist group intent on winning political independence through revolutionary means, it was the first that articulated that goal from its inception. Both its revolutionary predecessors, the United Irish and Young Ireland movements, embarked on rebellion as a last resort: they had been open societies, but were radicalised through external events (the French Revolution and the Irish Famine respectively) and government suppression. In opting for a conspiratorial approach with violent insurrection at its heart from the off, the IRB represented a genuinely new departure. It adopted a cell-like structure, with the ideal of 800 active members organised into 'circles', each reporting to an officer. The intention was that individual members should only know the men in their own circle, lessening the disruption of spies and informers.[18] Stephens rather grandly stood at the top of the organisation as the 'Provisional Dictator' or 'Head Centre', the despotic president of the underground Irish Republic.[19]

The IRB's relationship with the Fenian Brotherhood and its successor organisation, Clan na Gael (established in 1867), was testy. The Fenian Brotherhood and the Clan were reminders of the mass migration that had radically altered Ireland since the Famine. Given that more than three million Irish people lived outside Ireland by the end of the nineteenth century, transnational and transatlantic exchanges became an increasingly visible dynamic within political culture.[20] Fenianism was the most powerful political manifestation of the mass migration of the Famine era, providing the diaspora with a direct connection to Irish agitation and fraternal association within their new home.[21] The experience of exile also radicalised conceptions of sovereignty, democracy, and resistance, as evident within aspects of the Irish-American press.[22]

[18] John Newsinger, *Fenianism in Mid-Victorian Britain* (London: Pluto Press, 1994), p. 25.

[19] For Stephens, see Marta Ramón, *A Provisional Dictator: James Stephens and the Fenian Movement* (Dublin: UCD Press, 2007).

[20] David Fitzpatrick, *Irish Migration, 1801–1921* (Dundalk: Dundalgan Press, 1984), p. 5. For examples, see Ely M. Janis, *A Greater Ireland: The Land League and Transatlantic Nationalism in Gilded Age America* (Madison: University of Wisconsin Press, 2015), and Niall Whelehan, *Diaspora Activism and the Irish Land War* (New York: New York University Press, 2021).

[21] Kerby Miller, *Emigrants and Exiles: Ireland and the Irish Exodus to North America* (Oxford: Oxford University Press, 1985), p. 336.

[22] Matthew Knight, 'The *Irish Republic*: reconstructing liberty, right principles and the Fenian Brotherhood', *Éire-Ireland*, vol. 52, nos. 3–4 (2017), pp. 252–71.

The Brotherhood in the US was, in theory, the junior partner to the IRB, an auxiliary network to support the revolution in Ireland. They did not, however, accept a passive role: the American contribution to Irish revolutionary separatism was vast in terms of resources, propaganda, and (significantly) activists, a number of whom were battle-hardened from the Civil War in the US during the 1860s.[23] At times, the initiative for revolutionary action came directly from the US. During the 1880s, two separate factions from the American-based Fenians – the United Irishmen, fronted by the mercurial Jeremiah O'Donovan Rossa, and Clan na Gael – launched deadly dynamite attacks in Britain, independently from the IRB.[24]

While the IRB was formally a separate entity from its US-based sister organisation, the terms 'Fenian' and 'Fenianism' quickly became synonymous with the Irish secret society. The Fenian label was originally coined by O'Mahony, a noted Gaelic scholar, as a homage to the legendary ancient warriors, the Fianna. It was not an unproblematic name for the movement. John Boyle O'Reilly, a member of the IRB who later became the editor of the *Boston Pilot*, a major American Catholic newspaper, believed that the Fenian brand was harmful to the cause. 'Had we been called Republicans or United Irishmen or aught else', he complained to John Devoy in 1871, 'we would have retained respectability – but that meanly-sounding word, with its associations of defeat, dissension, and trickery has been a millstone on the neck of our Nationality for years past'.[25] Non-Irish sympathisers, such as the editor of the *English Republic* magazine, W. J. Linton, were similarly critical, arguing that the 'Fenian' name implied a narrowly defined nationalist conspiracy, detached from the republican international fraternity.[26] Indeed, there are some telling confusions within the semantics of Fenianism. John O'Leary recalled that Stephens used the label 'Irish Republican Brotherhood' as the name of the movement, while Thomas Clarke Luby 'now and then' called the organisation the 'Irish Revolutionary Brotherhood'. O'Leary, for his part, could not recall the use of 'the magic letters' of the 'IRB' before his release

[23] David Brundage, *Irish Nationalists in America: The Politics of Exile, 1798–1998* (Oxford: Oxford University Press, 2016), p. 89.

[24] For these bombing campaigns, see Shane Kenna, *War in the Shadows: The Irish-Americans Fenians Who Bombed Victorian Britain* (Dublin: Irish Academic Press, 2014), and Whelehan, *Dynamiters.*

[25] John Boyle O'Reilly to John Devoy, 28 January 1871, in William O'Brien and Desmond Ryan (eds.), *Devoy's Postbag, 1871–1928*, 2 vols. (Dublin: C. J. Fallon, 1948), i, p. 13.

[26] W. J. Linton, *Ireland for the Irish: Rhymes and Reasons against Landlordism* (New York: American News Company, 1867), p. 16.

from prison in 1871.[27] Rossa used the term 'Irish Revolutionary Brotherhood' exclusively throughout his autobiography.[28] Joseph Denieffe called his memoir *A Personal Narrative of the Irish Revolutionary Brotherhood*, but used 'Irish Republican Brotherhood' several times in the text.[29]

There was, therefore, ambiguity within the letters 'IRB'. On one hand, active members of the IRB would hardly shy away from the revolutionary tag; on the other, not all in the movement were necessarily 'republican' in outlook. John Rutherford, who published a hostile 'secret history' of Fenianism in 1877, declared that the 'great majority' of IRB men were 'Republican only in opposition to English rule', and would have 'any leading man of Irish descent [as] their king, and give him despotic power, on condition that his kingdom should be strictly and exclusively Irish'.[30] Stephens's 'provisional dictatorship' of the movement actively mimicked such a model, and there were, curiously, monarchists, such as O'Leary, within the ranks.[31] While the secretive oath taken by members of the IRB swore allegiance to an Irish Republic, 'now virtually established', the constitutional blueprint of this polity was not sketched out by the movement.[32] This might have been a reflection of the diversity of political opinion within the IRB beyond separatism,[33] but there is another explanation more in keeping with the organisation's image of itself as the embodiment of the Irish people. The revolution was today's glorious purpose; the granular detail of constitution-making was the work of tomorrow.

To take Rutherford's claim as it was intended – that the membership of the IRB was insincere in their republicanism – therefore misses the point. The Brotherhood styled itself as a vanguard liberation movement, tasked with kindling what O'Leary described as a 'Fenian spirit' that 'is ever present' in Ireland.[34] It presented itself as the manifestation of popular sovereignty in Ireland, representing the will of the Irish nation to be free

[27] O'Leary, *Recollections*, i, pp. 123–4.

[28] Jeremiah O'Donovan Rossa, *Rossa's Recollections, 1838 to 1898* (New York: Mariners Harbor, 1898), p. 187.

[29] Joseph Denieffe, *A Personal Narrative of the Irish Revolutionary Brotherhood* (New York: Gael Publishing Co., 1906), pp. 93, 102, and 188.

[30] John Rutherford, *The Secret History of the Fenian Conspiracy: its Origin, Objects, and Ramifications*, 2 vols. (London: C. Kegan Paul & Co., 1877), i, p. 130.

[31] Marcus Bourke, *John O'Leary: A Study of Irish Separatism* (Tralee: Anvil Books, 1967), p. 37.

[32] Denieffe, *Personal Narrative*, p. 25.

[33] This is the argument of Owen McGee, *The IRB: The Irish Republican Brotherhood from the Land League to Sinn Féin* (Dublin: Four Courts Press, 2005), p. 12.

[34] O'Leary, *Recollections*, ii, p. 10.

from British rule, and its right to determine its own structure of government. This was a radical challenge to the parliamentary tradition in Ireland: the IRB bypassed parliamentarianism to offer an alternative path to political change. The people, and not corrupt parliaments, were sovereign within the political thought of this new separatist society: Fenianism was the manifestation of the Irish general will.

This was a subversive new departure in Irish political life. The traditional view of the IRB as representing merely a 'physical force' expression of nationalism does not adequately capture the idea of 'the Republic' as an assertion of popular sovereignty. The ideological trappings of the IRB chimed with – and perfected – the 'anti-parliament' sentiment that first appeared within the extreme fringes of radical politics during the 1770s. The 'anti-parliament' was heralded by radicals who claimed the allegiance of the sovereign people in a clash with the corrupt and unreformed parliament at Westminster.[35] The concept of 'anti-parliament' was conceptualised primarily as an alternative authority, one that claimed popular legitimacy in the face of an oppressive and unrepresentative legal power. In establishing a metaphysical Irish Republic, in proclaiming themselves (as they did from the mid 1860s) the provisional government of that entity, the IRB leadership tapped into an older radical tradition that harnessed popular sovereignty to contest the moral jurisdiction of the state. The Brotherhood positioned itself not as physical force nationalism, but as the legitimate expression of the Irish people to wage war against 'English government in Ireland' and to secure an independent state.[36] The IRB was, in the minds of its adherents, nothing less than the true constituent power in Ireland.

While championing its inherent legitimacy as the expression of a sovereign power, the flagrantly illegal nature of the IRB impacted its ability to partake in political debate. The conspiratorial nature of the IRB and its rejection of 'constitutional' norms also account for the dearth of political tracts in support of Fenianism. Indeed, the *Irish People* newspaper, the closest thing to an official declaration of IRB doctrine, suggested that a hundred pikes were preferable to a thousand pamphlets: words were meaningless without action.[37] But resistance to pamphleteering does not imply that Fenians did not 'think' politically: the very existence of an IRB-sponsored newspaper tells its own story.

[35] T. M. Parssinen, 'Association, convention and anti-parliament in British radical politics, 1771–1848', *English Historical Review*, vol. 88, no. 348 (1973), p. 506.

[36] Rossa, *Rossa's Recollections*, p. 354.

[37] *Irish People*, 19 November 1864; McGee, *The IRB*, pp. 29–30.

The *Irish People* was the brainchild of James Stephens. Stephens envisaged a newspaper as an important outlet to spread Fenian ideas (and raise money) in the aftermath of the mass expansion of the movement following the well-documented funeral of Terence Bellew MacManus in 1861.[38] The *People* also appeared – not coincidentally – at a time when the Dublin press was largely monopolised by a pro-clerical and moderate pro-reform political tone, which was fiercely critical of the IRB's secretive, subversive nature. The *People* was designed to combat this consensus. While the *People* was hardly a commercial success, it marked a definite development in separatist politics in Ireland.[39] The language of separatism was crystallised through the newspaper, as the IRB was forced to articulate its political objectives. This was the revolutionary vanguard attempting to radicalise public opinion not through the propaganda of the deed, but through words, interpretation, and polemic argument.

Some Fenian sympathisers considered it unwise for the IRB to found its own newspaper. Michael Davitt, who joined the IRB in 1865, recorded tongue-in-cheek that Stephens 'did what an Irish conspirator would alone be likely to think of doing – he founded a newspaper to be a mouth-piece for a secret organisation'. There was a serious point here: Davitt believed publishing the *People* was a mistake, as it directly led to the arrest of Stephens and most of the upper tier of the IRB.[40] John Devoy, a talented IRB man who, following his release from prison in 1871, became an integral part of Clan na Gael in the US, disagreed, believing that 'the services of the paper to the Cause ... far outweighed the damage'. Devoy believed that any rebellion against British rule needed to be a popular uprising; and while secrecy was 'essential' to develop a revolutionary plan, 'the people had to be converted to its views and committed to its objects, and that could not be done by a whispering campaign'.[41]

Indeed, by the time that the *Irish People* was founded, newspapers had long been a ubiquitous presence within radical politics. Much has been written about the abolition of the stamp tax and the boom in the

38 R. V. Comerford, *The Fenians in Context: Irish Politics and Society, 1848–1882* (Dublin: Wolfhound Press, 1998; first published 1985), p. 78.

39 For an overview of the *Irish People*, see Ann Andrews, *Newspapers and Newsmakers: The Dublin Nationalist Press in the Mid-Nineteenth Century* (Liverpool: Liverpool University Press, 2014), pp. 188–91; Matthew Kelly, 'The *Irish People* and the disciplining of dissent', in Fearghal McGarry and James McConnel (eds.), *The Black Hand of Republicanism: Fenianism in Modern Ireland* (Dublin: Irish Academic Press, 2009), pp. 34–54; Ramón, *Provisional Dictator*, pp. 135–59.

40 Michael Davitt, *The Fall of Feudalism in Ireland: Or the Story of the Land League Revolution* (London: Harper & Brothers, 1904), pp. 75–6.

41 John Devoy, *Recollections of an Irish Rebel* (New York: Chase D. Young Co., 1929), p. 41.

newspaper business during the nineteenth century, but rather less on newspapers as a status symbol of sorts for a political movement.[42] Publishing a newspaper was a marker of seriousness and intent, especially for a movement or cause that might otherwise be considered 'fringe'. In the Irish context, the success of the *Nation* during the 1840s unquestionably altered the boundaries of political expression and popularised the ideas of Young Ireland. It was no coincidence that the primary figures behind much of the editorial content of the *Irish People* – John O'Leary, Thomas Clarke Luby, and Charles Kickham – cut their teeth within the Young Ireland movement during the late 1840s.[43] The most notorious figure associated with the *Nation*, John Mitchel, believed words as important as action in creating favourable conditions for revolt. In *Jail Journal* (1854), Mitchel recorded his belief that the 'most dangerous enemy' of the government was 'an honest man, armed with a newspaper'.[44] The ranks of Ireland's army, it appeared, would be filled by enthusiastic readers.

The first edition of the *Irish People* appeared in November 1863, and it ran weekly without interruption until the government suppressed the paper in September 1865. In an anti-parliament tradition, the title of the paper was an assertion of popular sovereignty. The central messages preached by the *People* were militant separatism, the bankruptcy of 'constitutional' agitation, the need to untangle the clergy from politics, and the desirability of land reform. An additional central thread running through the paper was the urgency of moral reform in Ireland to enable the country to fulfil its potential as an independent republic. The editorial content of the *People* typically showcased great literary skill, while the paper often carried thoughtful book reviews and occasional flashes of brilliance in its regular poetry column. These literary endeavours provided spaces for women within Fenian politics, most prominently John O'Leary's sister, Ellen, who was a noted poet.[45] The containment of women within the literary pages reveals that, while the IRB believed in a 'sovereign people', women such as Ellen O'Leary were muses rather than citizens.

Still, the *Irish People* was a formidable operation, put together by talented people. While the paper did not have a wide paying audience (many issues were given away for free), its subscription list included several

42 Susie L. Steinbach, *Understanding the Victorians: Politics, Culture and Society in Nineteenth-Century Britain*, 2nd ed. (Abingdon: Routledge, 2017), p. 227.

43 James Quinn, *Young Ireland and the Writing of Irish History* (Dublin: UCD Press, 2016), p. 111; Comerford, *Fenians in Context*, p. 37; Bourke, *O'Leary*, p. 15.

44 Mitchel, *Jail Journal*, p. 192.

45 Rose Novak, 'Ellen O'Leary: a bold Fenian poet', *Éire-Ireland*, vol. 43, nos. 3–4 (2008), pp. 58–84.

notable personalities from outside the realm of Fenianism, such as Isaac Butt and Delia Tudor Parnell, mother of Charles Stewart and the later leaders of the Ladies' Land League, Anna and Fanny.[46] Part of the appeal of the newspaper was its freshness: the *Irish People* pioneered a form of literary separatism in Ireland hitherto absent since the fleeting days of the *United Irishman* and the *Irish Felon* in 1848.

The *People* undoubtedly benefited from the contemporary popularity and influence of John Mitchel's works. Mitchel's most famous book, *Jail Journal*, was published in 1854, and *The Last Conquest of Ireland (Perhaps)* followed in 1860, both of which did much to legitimise anger and hate as valid political emotions.[47] Indeed, the uncompromising content, vigorous style, and scurrilous tone of the *Irish People* closely resembled Mitchel. While Stephens had little time for Mitchel, the *People's* core trio of Luby, Kickham, and O'Leary fell under the Young Irelander's literary spell. O'Leary recalled in his memoir that during the high point of the *Nation* newspaper in the 1840s, 'many, if not most, of the younger amongst us were Mitchelites before Mitchel, or rather before Mitchel had put forth his programme'.[48] Mitchel endured an uneasy relationship with Fenianism, but did much to shape its ideological blueprint.[49] His oeuvre articulated, in vivid Carlylean terms, virtuous hatred of the British Empire (with imperialism condemned as a vehicle for the expansion of soulless laissez-faire), the emasculation of constitutional political struggle, and the nobility of warfare against the oppressor. These were issues that were taken up with zeal by the *Irish People*.

Mitchel's identification of the British Empire as Ireland's enemy, rather than the more traditional 'England', marked a major development in Irish separatist language, and one periodically repeated in the pages of the *People*.[50] In 1860, Mitchel published the ironic *An Apology for the British Government in Ireland*, which argued that the might of British imperialism rested on the exploitation of the other nations, a process that would only end with the 'dismemberment of that Empire'.[51] Mitchel believed that

[46] Devoy, *Recollections*, p. 43.

[47] Paul Bew, *Ancestral Voices in Irish Politics: Judging Dillon and Parnell* (Oxford: Oxford University Press, 2023), p. 47.

[48] O'Leary, *Recollections*, i, p. 4.

[49] Bryan P. McGovern, *John Mitchel: Irish Nationalist, Southern Secessionist* (Knoxville: University of Tennessee Press, 2009), pp. 187–207.

[50] For this, see Niamh Lynch, 'Defining Irish nationalist anti-imperialism: Thomas Davis and John Mitchel', *Éire-Ireland*, vol. 42, nos. 1–2 (2007), pp. 94–103.

[51] John Mitchel, *An Apology for the British Government in Ireland* (Dublin: O'Donoghue and Co., 1905; first published 1860), p. vi.

underneath the veneer of a liberal civilising mission, the structure of power at the heart of the British Empire was unfeelingly bureaucratic, motivated by the dynamics of liberal political economy and capitalist greed. The fruits of the imperial system were 'torture in India, opium in China, famine in Ireland, pauperism in England, disturbance and disorder in Europe, and robbery everywhere'.[52] The British Empire was, as he put it with Carlyle-esque force in *Jail Journal*, the 'Empire of Hell'.[53]

While British imperialism was Ireland's primary enemy, Mitchel was as forcibly hostile to what he saw as a domestic evil: the lure of constitutional politics. Much of Mitchel's post-Famine writings denounced the peaceful political path taken by Daniel O'Connell. Mitchel was at his most unrestrained in *The Last Conquest*. O'Connell had, in Mitchel's estimation,

> used all his art and eloquence to emasculate a bold and chivalrous nation; and the very gratitude, love, and admiration which his early services had won, enabled him so to pervert the ideas of right and wrong in Ireland, that they believed him when he told them that Constitutional 'Agitation' was Moral Force – that bloodshed was immoral ... To him and to his teaching, then, without scruple, I ascribe our utter failure to make, I do not say a revolution, but so much as an insurrection ... when all the nations were in revolt [in 1848].

Mitchel believed that, had O'Connell given the word, the Irish would have mobilised for an epoch-defining revolt during the 1840s. O'Connell, of course, did not advocate rebellion, and this made the 'Liberator', according to Mitchel, 'next to the British Government, the worst enemy that Ireland ever had'.[54] Such an analysis of O'Connellism and the related folly of constitutional politics were explored further in the pages of the *People*.

While Mitchel was suspicious of the IRB, disliking the secretive nature of the organisation, the Fenians gave form to his long-stated desire for the Irish to take up arms and overthrow their British oppressors. In articulating a disdain for constitutional politics and a hatred of British domination of Ireland, Mitchel provided an intellectual framework for violent separatism. The *Irish People* developed many of his themes to legitimise the idea of armed struggle. In a discussion of the Ballingarry 'failure' of 1848 in *Jail Journal*, Mitchel set out a blueprint for a successful revolt in Ireland, which anticipated the rationale of the *Irish People*:

[52] Ibid., p. 3. [53] Mitchel, *Jail Journal*, p. 171.
[54] John Mitchel, *The Last Conquest of Ireland (Perhaps)* (Glasgow: Cameron & Ferguson, 1861), p. 136.

> Before there can be any general arming, or aptitude to insurrection, there must first be sound manly doctrine preached and embraced. And next, there must be many desultory collisions with British troops, both in town and country, and the sight of clear steel, and of blood smoking hot, must become familiar to the eyes of men, of boys, and of women.[55]

Mitchel's rage stemmed from the Famine, which he infamously positioned as a deliberate act of attempted genocide by the British state, driven by Malthusian conceptions of the burden of an 'excessive' population. He argued that the experiences of the Irish during the 1840s legitimised violent insurrection: the horrors of war 'were by no means so terrible as the horrors of peace which their own eyes had seen'. Mitchel believed that the survivors of the trauma were 'ashamed to see their kinsmen patiently submitting to be starved to death, and longed to see blood flow, if it were only to show that blood still flowed in Irish veins'.[56] He framed rebellion as the only method to free the Irish from the clutches of British imperialism and constitutional slavery. The *Irish People* took up this argument with considerable aplomb.

While the *People* ran for only twenty-two months, its ninety-five issues offered a sustained engagement with the idea of shattering the Union. This was positioned as the first stage of the positive transformation of Irish society and, indeed, the wider world order. In a dramatic editorial, written against the backdrop of Britain being dragged into the Second Schleswig War in early 1864, the *People* propounded the possibility of the 'Irish Revolution' becoming one of 'the grandest events in all history'. A small country overthrowing the yoke of the most powerful imperial power of the nineteenth century would 'electrify the world', turning the course of history on its head. 'On that day', declared the editorial,

> prayers of gratitude and blessings shall mount to heaven from trampled regions in every corner of the globe, and Irishmen shall be hailed by the world, not merely as the deliverers of the sacred Isle, but as the redeemers of enthralled mankind![57]

The *People* frequently praised resistance to imperial rule in the colonies, such as the Māori in New Zealand during the Second Taranaki War.[58] But the editorials of the *People* rejected the notion that Ireland should be viewed in the same manner as the 'remote British colonies'; the *People* recognised that the Union, which forced the Irish to be 'politically

[55] Mitchel, *Jail Journal*, p. 147.
[56] Mitchel, *Last Conquest*, p. 154. For the Famine-as-genocide thesis, see p. 219.
[57] *Irish People*, 13 February 1864. [58] *Irish People*, 22 October 1864.

identified with Great Britain', left Ireland a constitutional peculiarity within the Empire.[59] The *People's* identification with the colonised was based on a shared hostility to the British state, and not on the basis that Ireland was a colony. The image of the downfall of the British Empire was conjured first and foremost because such a historic event would mark the end of Britain's domination over Ireland.

There was no question within the Fenian mindset that revolutionary means were the only legitimate method to end British rule in Ireland. The centrality of violence in this process was embraced and heartily repeated throughout the *People's* print run: the accepted logic was that 'no conquered ever regained its independence peacefully'.[60] The 'sword' was praised as the only true way to secure national independence. Constitutional agitation worked only for political and social elites, asserted the *People*, as the 'achievements' of the independent legislature in 1782 and Catholic Emancipation in 1829 demonstrated.[61] In contrast, the overthrow of tyranny during the revolutions in France and America was 'the work of the people', willing to shed blood for freedom.[62] Those who proclaimed to be patriots but affirmed only to a constitutional code were merely willing abetters of British dominance in Ireland. What was needed was not eye-catching political gatherings or the return of MPs to parliament, but the 'silent work' of organising a conspiracy. 'Patriotism, not militarily organised, is worth nothing'.[63] Mass rallies akin to the O'Connellite 'monster meetings' of 1843 were dismissed as 'a mere waste of popular strength', when a policy of 'no-action' prevailed among the leaders. Such examples from Ireland's recent history served to discredit the notion that constitutional struggle could deliver meaningful change.[64] The IRB was never mentioned by name in the *People*, but referenced euphemistically as Ireland's great hope of realising a national rejuvenation through the achievement of separation from Britain. The people 'lost all faith in political action' following the disappointments of elected politicians, but in 1858, the year of the IRB's founding, 'earnest political teachers' once again resurfaced in Ireland.[65]

The *People* denounced a 'slave' mentality that permeated Irish society, ensuring that the national potential could never be realised. The chief cause of this condition was, of course, British domination over Ireland, 'the root of our country's wrongs'.[66] 'A people subject to bad laws are

[59] *Irish People*, 10 September 1864. [60] Ibid. [61] *Irish People*, 28 November 1863.
[62] *Irish People*, 18 June 1864. [63] *Irish People*, 6 February 1864.
[64] *Irish People*, 30 April 1864. [65] *Irish People*, 19 March 1864.
[66] *Irish People*, 3 September 1864.

necessarily slaves', proclaimed an editorial in January 1865. The worst of the 'bad laws' concerned restrictions on gun ownership, which were particularly loathed by the *People*. The right of subjects to arms for self-defence was enshrined in the English Bill of Rights of 1688, but this was, of course, never extended to Ireland. This had been reaffirmed by an updated Arms Act in 1843 and the Crime and Outrage Act of 1847, which placed extremely prohibitive restrictions on the sale of guns in Ireland.[67] The *People* interpreted this as a deliberate ploy to oppress the Irish, as a 'disarmed people' was equated with 'an enslaved people'. The Irish were thus denied the ability to lawfully resist tyranny through arms, which was, technically at least, a right in England.[68] As such, the *People* reasoned that the denial of the right to possess arms 'is the deadliest blow that has been aimed at the Irish nation – more deadly than confiscation, penal laws, land laws, military and legal murder, bribery, corruption, and famine'.[69]

This was a powerful argument that had wider purchase than the Fenian movement, as the writings of John Mitchel and (most strikingly) Isaac Butt reveal. In his major works during the 1850s and 1860s, Mitchel asserted that the legal disarming of the Irish was one of the most potent ways in which British domination over the smaller island was maintained.[70] During his campaigns for land reform in the latter half of the 1860s, Butt frequently drew on the differences in legal rights to possess arms between Ireland and Britain as an indication that the Union did not function as a partnership of equals.[71] Gun control was an issue, then, that spanned the political spectrum in Ireland. The difficulties in acquiring weapons were held up by Mitchel – and, later, the IRB through the *Irish People* – as evidence of a deliberate ploy by the British to inflict a permanent state of slavery on the Irish mind. For Butt, representing a critical unionist perspective, denying the Irish the right to bear arms was evidence that 'the constitution of England is not in force here', thereby highlighting the unwelcome exceptionalism of Irish legislation under the

[67] Breandán MacSuibhne, *The End of Outrage: Post-Famine Adjustment in Rural Ireland* (Oxford: Oxford University Press, 2017), pp. 27–8.

[68] Although the legal right to possess arms was far from unrestricted in England, being subject to various qualifications; see Lois G. Schwoerer, *Gun Culture in Early Modern England* (Charlottesville: University of Virginia Press, 2016), pp. 163–70.

[69] *Irish People*, 20 February 1864.

[70] Mitchel, *Jail Journal*, pp. 146–7; *Last Conquest*, pp. 20–1; *The History of Ireland: From the Treaty of Limerick to the Present Time* (Glasgow: Cameron & Ferguson, 1869), p. 180.

[71] Isaac Butt, *The Irish People and Irish Land: A Letter to Lord Lifford* (Dublin: John Falconer, 1867), p. 183.

Union.[72] Despite their ideological differences regarding the Union, the rhetoric deployed by Mitchel, the IRB, and Butt relating to the legal restrictions on gun ownership was very similar. Indeed, Butt was not averse to deploying the 'slave' mantra of the *Irish People*, equating a 'disarmed nation' with 'an enslaved one'.[73]

Such language was not used within a vacuum. When Frederick Douglass, the famed black abolitionist, toured through Ireland in 1845, he expressed bemusement at the idea that the Irish thought of themselves as 'slaves'. He told an audience in Belfast that the Irish drew on a classical definition of slavery as political oppression, but the term had morphed, carrying a very different (and more horrifying) meaning in the contemporary world.[74] Indeed, Douglass pointed out an important interpretative problem: the word 'slave' carried two distinct definitions during the nineteenth century. One referred to the chattel slavery found most notoriously in the United States; the other was a historicised political form of slavery in which rights were denied but human beings were not legally designated as property. Douglass depicted chattel slavery not as the loss of rights but their annihilation, which cast human beings as little more than animals. This was more grotesque than any form of political oppression that hitherto existed, in Ireland or elsewhere, and could not be likened to the classical form of slavery.[75]

As Douglass's interventions highlight, the language of slavery was slippery, with two very different concepts sharing a common term. Political slavery was an expression of Greco-Roman political philosophy, implying the antithesis of civil freedom. A political slave found themselves governed by an arbitrary power. This metaphorical form of slavery was reinvigorated by Hobbes and Locke in the context of the major dynastic upheavals in seventeenth-century England.[76] Liberty was contrasted in such works with slavery, the latter of which referred to a denial of political rights.[77] This interpretation of slavery was embraced in Ireland by William Molyneux

72 Isaac Butt, *The Parliamentary Policy of Home Rule: An Address Delivered to the Electors of the City of Limerick, 23 September 1875* (Dublin: McGlashan and Gill, 1875), p. 21.

73 Isaac Butt, *Coercion for Ireland: A Speech Delivered in the House of Commons on the Second Reading of the Peace Preservation (Ireland) Bill, March 23rd, 1875* (no publishing details, [1875]), p. 6.

74 Christine Kinealy (ed.), *Frederick Douglass and Ireland: In His Own Words*, 2 vols. (Oxford: Routledge, 2018), i, pp. 23–4.

75 David W. Blight, *Frederick Douglass: Prophet of Freedom* (New York: Simon & Schuster, 2018), pp. 149–50.

76 See Mary Nyquist, *Arbitrary Rule: Slavery, Tyranny, and the Power of Life and Death* (Chicago: University of Chicago Press, 2013) for a penetrating study of slavery in the canonical works of political thought.

77 Quentin Skinner, *Liberty before Liberalism* (Cambridge: Cambridge University Press, 1998), p. 38.

and Jonathan Swift, who deployed the trope to describe England's political dominance over Ireland. Swift, it seems, did not imply any similarity between the metaphorical slavery of the Irish and the experience of enslaved Africans.[78] The American Revolution (and Locke's prominent place within justifications of the colonists to break with Britain) popularised the linguistic binary between liberty and political slavery within Irish Patriot and radical thought from the 1770s to the 1790s, which provided a vocabulary to legitimate the campaigns for legislative independence and ending the penal laws.[79] Indeed, the adopted word for the relief of Catholics – *emancipation* – derived from the language of classical slavery.[80]

Already by this point, however, use of the slavery trope to define a political relationship had become problematic. The Atlantic slave trade flourished at the same time as protestations against political slavery were uttered. Some American writers were accused of hypocrisy for embracing the liberty/slavery dichotomy in depicting British arbitrary rule over the colonies while also defending chattel slavery.[81] What Douglass observed in Ireland was a different but equally dubious set of practices: that there was no distinction between the political slavery of the Irish and the enslavement of Africans, or that the former was *worse* than the latter.

This trend was so prevalent that the Presbyterian clergyman and abolitionist, Isaac Nelson, was forced to denounce any proclaimed similarities between the political status of the Irish and chattel slavery during the 1840s.[82] There were indeed some breathtaking double standards. John Mitchel, a racist of the Carlylean mould, championed chattel slavery in the antebellum South while denouncing the figurative slavery of the Irish under British rule.[83] Mitchel applied the political slavery trope to the Irish because they 'are not citizens in their own land' and are ruled 'by

[78] Ian McBride, *Eighteenth-Century Ireland: The Isle of Slaves* (Dublin: Gill & Macmillan, 2009), pp. 274–5. Professor McBride has further developed the use of the slavery trope in Swift's writings in the introduction to his forthcoming volume in the *Cambridge Edition of the Works of Jonathan Swift*. I am indebted to Professor McBride for sharing this with me.

[79] Stephen Small, *Political Thought in Ireland, 1776–1798: Republicanism, Patriotism and Radicalism* (Oxford: Oxford University Press, 2002), pp. 43, 250. Also see John Phillip Reid, *The Concept of Liberty in the Age of the American Revolution* (Chicago: University of Chicago Press, 1988), pp. 49–50.

[80] McBride, *Isle of Slaves*, p. 277.

[81] Quentin Skinner, *Liberty as Independence: The Making and Unmaking of a Political Ideal* (Cambridge: Cambridge University Press, 2025), pp. 220–1.

[82] Daniel Ritchie, *Isaac Nelson: Radical Abolitionist, Evangelical Presbyterian, and Irish Nationalist* (Liverpool: Liverpool University Press, 2018), p. 50.

[83] John Quinn, *John Mitchel* (Dublin: University College Dublin Press, 2008), p. 56.

the sword'.[84] At the same time, he defended chattel slavery on the basis of a racial hierarchy and the cultivation of a 'respectful' master–servant relationship, thereby (perversely) nurturing a trait of civility in the enslaved.[85] The two forms of slavery met when Mitchel denounced the Irish for passivity during the Famine, choosing to meekly die of hunger rather than revolt against the British, thereby displaying a stereotypical trait of docility that he believed was shared by enslaved people.[86] Mitchel thus damned the Irish for a lack of defiance while justifying the enslavement of Africans as natural order.

Mitchel's handling of the slavery trope was extreme, but he was not an outlier. Many mainstream figures within the world of Irish nationalist journalism shared such a racialised interpretation of the right to liberty.[87] A. M. Sullivan, a more moderate figure than Mitchel, condoned chattel slavery while condemning the 'political slavery' of the Irish during the 1860s.[88] Despite the celebrated pro-abolitionism of Daniel O'Connell, Irish political culture in the years following his death was ambivalent on the question of enslavement.[89] Even within abolitionist activism and writing, there were some questionable comparisons between the enslavement of African people and Irish hardship. The quasi-Fenian *Irishman* was critical of chattel slavery in the US, but believed that the 'white slavery' suffered by the Irish poor was worse and elicited much less sympathy.[90] The slavery idiom in Ireland had deep roots, but the ubiquity of the language within nineteenth-century Ireland is striking for the ability of writers to ignore or downplay the horrors of contemporary enslavement. The *Irish People* was certainly not alone on this. The conflation of political and chattel slavery was a murky part of the Irish political mind.

The *Irish People* brought a new aspect, with the rhetoric of slavery targeting internal forces perceived as equally complicit in Ireland's subjugation. The twin evils of constitutional political agitation and the prominent

84 Mitchel, *Jail Journal*, pp. 5–6.
85 William Dillon, *Life of John Mitchel*, 2 vols. (London: Kegan Paul, Trench & Co., 1888), ii, pp. 113–14.
86 Mitchel, *Jail Journal*, pp. 106–7.
87 David T. Gleeson, 'Failing to "unite with the abolitionists": the Irish nationalist press and US emancipation', *Slavery & Abolition*, vol. 37, no. 3 (2016), p. 634.
88 *Nation*, 8 November 1862, 3 December 1864.
89 Bruce Nelson, *Irish Nationalists and the Making of the Irish Race* (Princeton, NJ: Princeton University Press, 2012), pp. 62–87; Cian T. McMahon, *The Global Dimensions of Irish Identity: Race, Nation and the Popular Press, 1840–1880* (Chapel Hill: University of North Carolina Press, 2015), p. 102.
90 Matthew Kelly, 'Irish nationalist opinion and the British Empire in the 1850s and 1860s', *Past & Present*, no. 204 (2009), p. 148.

role of the clergy in politics were cited as factors that contributed to the crushing of the Irish aspiration to political independence. The O'Connellite commitment to a 'no-drop-of-blood doctrine' surrendered the Irish right to arms to resist tyranny, thus creating 'a nation of helots'.[91] The view of the *People* was that O'Connell propagated such an approach to ensure clerical support, but in doing so, created another suffocating layer that smothered political expression. The *People* frequently championed the idea that national liberty was not the business of the priest; 'submission to certain Irish bishops, in political matters, is equivalent to slavery'.[92] The political priest, speaking out against revolutionary conspiracy and embracing constitutional action, did 'the work of the enemy' in subduing the people.[93] In this reading, Britain was not the only cause of the misery of the Irish people. 'False teaching, and false consciences do more to keep us down than the bayonet of the Saxon.'[94] Part of the remit of the *Irish People* was an explicit desire to liberate the Irish mindset from the nefarious effects of constitutional and clerical domination, twin barriers to waging a successful revolutionary war against Britain.

Despite the formal 'republican' aims of the IRB, the *People* did not provide much insight into what the hallowed Irish Republic would look like. Indeed, the paper stated categorically that national independence was the desired outcome of the revolution, and until this was secured, 'it is of little use to discuss forms of government'.[95] While there was a reluctance to sketch out the blueprints of an independent Ireland, the *People* made occasional overt references to republicanism, which belied a fusion of classical and modern influences. In early 1865, the *People* proclaimed that there were two forms of governing philosophy that have dominated conceptions of power since time immemorial, namely 'despotism and republicanism'. Despotism was defined as the arbitrary rule of an individual; republicanism, on the other hand, was defined by the primacy of laws designed by the 'people'. The law represented the sovereign will of the people and could not be overturned by individuals. Quotes from Livy and Algernon Sidney were brandished to salute a definition of liberty rooted in the authority of law and freedom from external domination.[96] But republicanism in a more radical Paineite form was also articulated by the *People*.

[91] *Irish People*, 16 January 1864. [92] *Irish People*, 14 May 1864.
[93] *Irish People*, 16 September 1865. [94] *Irish People*, 5 November 1864.
[95] *Irish People*, 1 April 1865.
[96] 'Imperia legum potentiora fuerunt quam hominum', which the *People* gave as 'the authority of the laws was more potent than human authority': Livy, *History of Rome*, II, 1.1. Sidney was unnamed in the editorial, but the quote is from his *Discourses Concerning Government*, 2 vols. (Edinburgh:

A later editorial equated republicanism with opposition to hereditary privilege, especially in the form of monarchy, and combined this with a democratic idiom that suggested that legitimate power sprang from the people.[97]

The argument was consistently presented through the pages of the *People* that such republicanism could not be realised in Ireland through the constitutional mechanisms that existed under the Union. While the *People* conceded that the mixed form of government of the hated enemy carried some aspects of republican thought, given the restrictions of the franchise, it was far from democratic. Members of parliament did not truly represent the people: power resided in the hands of a select and wealthy few.[98] In Ireland, this power was monopolised by a 'bastard aristocracy' that personified and perpetuated conquest. The story of the British constitution in Ireland was a tale of oppression by 'bad laws' that ran contrary to Irish interests. Ireland appeared to enjoy the apparatus of constitutional rule – elections, the rule of law, and a free press – but these forms masked the oppression of the British connection. Indeed, this veil over the truth ensured that Ireland suffered more than it otherwise would have under straightforward despotism.[99] Such an analysis explained the *People's* deep-rooted hostility to the norms of constitutional political life. Irish politicians only deluded themselves, and the wider population, about the ability to change Ireland's course from within the British system. Petitioning parliament was merely a form of 'whining'.[100] The *People* took a hardline stance against elections, declaring that it was 'criminal' for the Irish to take any interest in choosing representatives to a foreign parliament.[101] When the 1848 veteran, John Blake Dillon, declared an intention to stand for election to parliament, the Fenian organ was incensed, depicting him as a useful idiot in legitimising British rule. 'No man will be more heartily welcomed to London than Mr Dillon', bemoaned the *People*. 'An ex-rebel leader is the very worst enemy Ireland could have in the foreign parliament.'[102] The Fenian impulse that found expression in the *People* was untainted by the compromises of everyday political life. The purity of its message thus stands in stark contrast to the later political dalliances of the IRB – Fenian prisoners standing for parliament, cautious support for Home Rule, the 'New Departure' with Charles Stewart Parnell, and the Land League – following its reconstruction after the rebellion of 1867.

G. Hamilton and J. Balfour, 1750), i, p. 17: 'liberty solely consists in an independency upon the will of another'. *Irish People*, 28 January 1865.

[97] *Irish People*, 18 March 1865. [98] *Irish People*, 15 April 1865.

[99] *Irish People*, 28 January 1865. [100] *Irish People*, 14 January 1865.

[101] *Irish People*, 11 February 1865. [102] *Irish People*, 15 July 1865.

## Proclaiming the Republic

The *Irish People* ceased publication in September 1865, after its office in Parliament Street – mere minutes away from Dublin Castle – was raided by the police. The paper left an impressive legacy in disseminating the vocabulary of Fenianism. Its demise was intimately bound up with the perception, shared by many in both the IRB and British intelligence, that 1865 was the year when an insurrection was likely. With the end of the Civil War in the US came the possibility of battle-hardened, demobilised Irish-Americans crossing the Atlantic to wage war on Britain. At the same time, IRB operatives proved successful in infiltrating the British Army and recruiting agents.[103] But while Stephens proclaimed 1865 as the year of action, he dithered, endlessly postponing the insurrection. The Head Centre's hesitation gave the British time to counteract the Fenian threat, including suppressing the *People*. The chief writers were arrested or went on the run, and mass arrests of suspected Fenians continued to cripple the movement through 1865 and 1866. The euphoric rhetoric of 'the year of action' had transformed into despair. Stephens was deposed from the leadership of the IRB by the end of 1866, replaced by his deputy, Colonel Thomas Kelly, a Galway-born immigrant to the US with experience in the Civil War.[104] Kelly shared military authority over the IRB with Gustave Paul Cluseret, a French soldier of fortune who also came to Ireland via the Fenian Brotherhood. The organisation that Kelly and Cluseret inherited was far from ready for insurrection, but given the course of dispiriting events of the preceding year, they felt that the IRB needed to assert itself militarily as a matter of urgency.

The uprising was planned for 11 February 1867, but in a Stephensian twist, the leadership pushed it back to 5 March 1867. The attempted insurrection, which was mostly centred on the hills of Dublin, as well as Cork, Tipperary, and Limerick, was a damp squib.[105] The IRB could call on an impressive number of men, but weapons were pitifully few. Combined with confusion over tactics (a hybrid 'regular' and guerrilla insurrection plan was ditched at the last moment in favour of a full-scale mobilisation) and the arrest of Godfrey Massey, a senior leader who subsequently turned informer, the rebellion petered out after a day.[106]

[103] Patrick Quinlivan and Paul Rose, *The Fenians in England, 1865–1872* (London: John Calder, 1982), p. 6.
[104] Ramón, *Provisional Dictator*, pp. 218–22.
[105] Shin-ichi Takagami, 'The Fenian rising in Dublin, March 1867', *Irish Historical Studies*, vol. 29, no. 115 (1995), pp. 340–62.
[106] Newsinger, *Fenianism*, pp. 55–9; Comerford, *Fenians in Context*, pp. 136–9.

But one of the most notable aspects of the rising was that, unlike the rebellion of 1848, it assumed a literary form with a proclamation of the Irish Republic, which was widely reprinted in newspaper reports.[107] This proclamation received little traction at the time, however, as its stated ambitions were immediately defeated with the quick suppression of the rising. Yet the extraordinary document vividly captures a fleeting moment of Fenian engagement with international radical ideas and associations.

Aspects of the proclamation were familiar to readers of the *Irish People* – the injustices on the land, the slave mindset fostered by decades of British domination – but these were honeycombed with a newly found streak of fraternal radicalism. The legitimacy of violent action came from the 'centuries of outrage, enforced poverty, and bitter misery', and the failure of peaceful methods to bring improvement to Ireland's condition. The oppressor took the form of an 'alien aristocracy' that drove away the 'real owners of the soil'. The appeal to force was 'our last resource', but it was 'better to die in the struggle for freedom than to continue an existence of utter selfdom'. While the proclamation built on aspects of Fenianism as articulated in the *Irish People*, the forceful class-based depiction of agrarian relations in Ireland was a new departure. This was coupled with a radical democratic vision of an Irish Republic that enshrined forms of popular sovereignty. The proclamation affirmed that the Irish were 'unable to endure the curse of monarchical government', and instead offered a blueprint for a republic based on universal suffrage and equality. The new dispensation would return the land to the people, securing 'the intrinsic value of their labour'. The 'war' waged by the IRB was against 'the aristocratic locusts, whether English or Irish, who have eaten the verdure of our fields'. A striking fraternal hope for international support – and, explicitly, an insurrection in *England* – concluded the proclamation:

> Republicans of the entire world, our cause is your cause. Our enemy is your enemy. Let your hearts be with us. As for you, workmen of England, it is not only your hearts we wish, but your arms. Remember the starvation and degradation brought to your firesides by the oppression of labour. Remember the past, look well to the future, and avenge yourselves by giving liberty to your children in the coming struggle for human freedom.[108]

In language, tone, and content, the proclamation thus went far beyond the literary pillars of Fenianism as constructed by the *Irish People*.

[107] *Freeman's Journal*, 6 March 1867; *Irish Times*, 8 March 1867.

[108] Ibid. The proclamation can also be found in Alan O'Day and John Stevenson (eds.), *Irish Historical Documents since 1800* (Dublin: Gill & Macmillan, 1992), pp. 76–7.

Unlike the better-known proclamation of the Irish Republic in 1916, the document associated with the 1867 rising was not signed. The authors were almost certainly Kelly and Cluseret.[109] The Irish Republic was thus invoked by an Irish-American who served during the US Civil War and a French radical who had fought for Garibaldi in Italy: the radical fraternalism of the proclamation comes into sharper focus given the likely authors. The document, then, occupies a curious space within literary manifestations of Irish separatism. It was written by the new leaders of the IRB, but they were not necessarily representative of the IRB; its contents present the Irish mid-Victorian revolutionary movement in a more politically radical and universalist light than previous expressions found in the *Irish People*.

Indeed, the appeal to the 'workmen of England' is one of the most intriguing aspects of the revolutionary strategy of 1867. Its presence in the proclamation of the Irish Republic was the outworking of an attempt by Kelly and Cluseret to secure the support of radicals in Britain. Planning for the rising occurred against the backdrop of political and social unrest in Britain, as a renewed campaign for parliamentary reform, focused on the extension of the franchise, reached its crescendo. The most prominent – and seemingly dangerous – organisation agitating for political change was the Reform League. The League was a mostly working-class organisation and attracted the support of the socialist International Working Men's Association (established in 1864) and many ex-Chartists. It enjoyed a noisy political presence through mass rallies, including the infamous Hyde Park meeting in 1866, in which radical supporters clashed with the police and military for three days. The Hyde Park 'railings' affair (so called because the crowd ripped the railings of the park out) was defused after an astonishing climbdown by the Home Secretary, Spencer Walpole, who gratefully consented to the withdrawal of the forces of law and order. Some of the more radical followers of the Reform League, such as Karl Marx, believed the revolutionary potential was sucked out of the movement when the anticipated heavy-handed state response did not materialise. 'Those stiff-necked John Bulls', Marx lamented to Friedrich Engels, 'will accomplish nothing without a really bloody clash with those in power'.[110] Despite the lack of a radicalising 'Peterloo moment' in 1866, the leadership of the IRB followed the fortunes of the Reform League with

[109] Owen McGee argues that William Halpin, an Irish-American, drafted the proclamation. The only evidence cited is a private account that Halpin's grandson shared with McGee. Even if Halpin did indeed draft the proclamation, the document still had to speak for Kelly and Cluseret. *IRB*, p. 46.

[110] Gareth Stedman Jones, '"Pressure from without": Karl Marx and 1867', *Parliamentary History*, vol. 36, no. 1 (2017), p. 124.

great interest, ultimately reaching out to English radicals to assess the possibility of collaboration.

The exact nature of the dealings between the IRB and the Reform League remains shrouded in mystery. The two organisations were, of course, very different from one another – the IRB was a secret society dedicated to the revolutionary overthrow of the British state in Ireland, while the Reform League was a popular pressure group agitating for parliamentary reform – but they shared a general belief in the virtues of radical democracy. While the *Irish People* preached the need for self-reliance – separatists should not pin their hopes on an invading French or American army and should look to 'ourselves alone' to win independence – aspects of the leadership of the IRB were less dogmatic.[111] In 1866, Cluseret calculated that an alliance between the IRB and the Reform League was feasible, and such a coalition would shake the British establishment to its core. In an extraordinary article for *Fraser's Magazine*, published in 1872, Cluseret detailed his mission on accepting the Fenian brief, stressing his belief that 'the Irish Question could only be settled by English cooperation'. Cluseret admitted that such a strategy divided the hierarchy of the IRB, but he pressed ahead and claimed to have reached 'an agreement between Fenianism and the Reform League'. Had the police and army moved in with force against the Hyde Park protestors in 1866, Cluseret claimed, 'all the Fenians in London' would have come to their aid.[112] This version of events was disputed by John Bedford Leno, who claimed that Cluseret first met with a radical faction of the Reform League in a London pub *after* the Hyde Park meeting, and that no agreement was concluded. Indeed, the English radicals baulked at Cluseret's scheming, which, in Leno's recollection, amounted to a dangerous attempt to 'create civil war'.[113]

Another partnership that Cluseret wished to nurture was with Charles Bradlaugh, the leading English radical and controversial advocate of free thought, secularism, and republicanism. This was a complicated and decidedly murky relationship. Stephens attempted to build links with British republicans in 1865, sending Frank Roney to London for an interview with Bradlaugh. Bradlaugh promised the IRB's envoy the 'practical support of 100,000 men', although in Roney's memoir the scope of

111 *Irish People*, 28 May, 4 June 1864.
112 General Cluseret, 'My connection with Fenianism', *Fraser's Magazine*, July 1872, pp. 40–1.
113 John Bedford Leno, *The Aftermath: With Autobiography of the Author John Bedford Leno* (London: Reeves and Turner, 1892), p. 71.

this backing was not explicit.[114] Stephens was heartened by the support apparently given to the IRB by Bradlaugh, but resisted calling for a rising in 1865, given the damaging splits within the American Fenian movement.[115] Ties with Bradlaugh were rekindled in early 1867, after Stephens was deposed as Head Centre and replaced by Colonel Thomas Kelly. Kelly and Cluseret, the two most senior figures in the IRB, visited Bradlaugh in London in the weeks before the rising of 1867. What transpired behind closed doors is unclear. After Bradlaugh's death, his daughter, Hypatia Bradlaugh Bonner, published an account of her father's life, which drew on his own memoirs. She affirmed that Cluseret and Kelly gave a rather curious reason – the premise of seeking 'legal advice' – for visiting her father. Why Cluseret and Kelly, two seasoned revolutionary soldiers, desired to speak to Bradlaugh about the legalities of insurrection and treason is a moot point. In any case, the proclamation of the Irish Republic formed part of the conversations between the IRB leaders and Bradlaugh. Indeed, two high-ranking informers from the IRB ranks claimed that Bradlaugh himself was the author of the proclamation of 1867.[116] A hostile biography of Bradlaugh published during his lifetime repeated this charge, alleging that Bradlaugh confessed his authorship of the proclamation to John Morrison Davidson, a radical journalist, before publicly denying the charge.[117] Hypatia Bradlaugh Bonner believed that her father was not the author of the document, but did play a substantial role in drafting it. 'I was talking to him in his study one day', she recorded,

> and in the course of our conversation he pulled down a thick green volume – on Irish history – and opening it, put his finger upon this proclamation. 'They say I wrote that', he said with a smile. 'And did you?' I asked. He then told me the draft of the proclamation, as it left his study after being approved, was in his handwriting; but when he saw it in print he found that it had been altered after leaving his hands.[118]

Hypatia did not, alas, ask her father which parts of the proclamation had been altered.

After the rebellion of 1867, Bradlaugh issued a pamphlet that vocally rejected 'any separation of Ireland from England' and the establishment of

114 Frank Roney, *Irish Rebel and Californian Labor Leader: An Autobiography*, ed. Ira B. Cross (Berkeley: University of California Press, 1931), p. 119.

115 Ramón, *Provisional Dictator*, p. 191.

116 Adolphe S. Headingley, *The Biography of Charles Bradlaugh* (London: Remington & Co., 1880), p. 210.

117 Charles R. Mackay, *Life of Charles Bradlaugh* (London: D. J. Gunn and Co., 1888), p. 393.

118 Hypatia Bradlaugh Bonner, *Charles Bradlaugh: A Record of his Life and Work*, 2 vols. (London: T. Fisher Unwin, 1894), i, p. 255.

a republic in Ireland. Republicanism was 'the best form of government possible', Bradlaugh insisted, but it did not follow that a republic was achievable in the short term. The 'people of England and of Ireland', Bradlaugh bemoaned, 'are yet too much wanting in true dignity and independence, and too ignorant of their political rights and duties, to at present make good republicans'. Bradlaugh staked his hopes on the ability of the Reform Act, which received its royal assent five months after the IRB's rising in 1867, to transform the British body politic, enabling legislative interventions to correct the worst abuses of the land system and the Established Church in Ireland.[119] In words that rebuffed the *Irish People*'s assertion of the need for pikes and not pamphlets, Bradlaugh colourfully called for the IRB to renounce violent methods and use arguments to present their case for independence: 'I do not believe in a lasting republic to be formed by pike aid – the pen and printing press best teach the littleness of kings'.[120] Bradlaugh was, then, a complex champion of Fenianism. Despite his association with the proclamation of the Irish Republic, he abhorred revolutionary violence and the idea of Irish separatism. While his atheism and republicanism put him on the fringes of radical society, on the question of Irish governance he was closer to the opinions of his more 'respectable' contemporaries, such as John Stuart Mill or William Gladstone.[121] Sympathy for the IRB from such radical networks was more an attack on the perceived illiberal structures of the British state in Ireland than support for the ideas of Fenianism.

Even still, Bradlaugh's connection to the IRB's revolutionary moment in 1867 offers a tantalising glimpse into the potential of a radically subversive Irish-British coalition. 'It is the English revolution', Cluseret claimed in 1872, 'which will enfranchise Ireland'.[122] Before his disposal as Head Centre in 1866, Stephens looked to the International Working Men's Association for support, while his successor, Colonel Thomas Kelly, was eager to explore Cluseret's ideas. Rumours circulated about IRB sponsorship of a revived Chartist movement, with the aim of renewed agitation in England.[123] Fenianism in the 1860s blossomed as a transatlantic

[119] Charles Bradlaugh, *The Irish Question: What it has been, what it is, and how to deal with it* (London: Austin & Co., [1868]), pp. 7–8.

[120] Ibid., p. 12.

[121] Anthony Daly, '"The true remedy for Irish grievances is to be found in good political institutions": English radicals and Irish nationalism, 1847–1874', *Historical Research*, vol. 86, no. 231 (2013), p. 70.

[122] Cluseret, 'My connection with Fenianism', p. 44.

[123] Thomas Frost, *The Secret Societies of the European Revolution, 1776–1876*, 2 vols. (London: Tinsley Brothers, 1876), ii, p. 285.

phenomenon,[124] but the appeal to English radicalism reveals a lesser-known dynamic, which was, as it played out, not without its problems. Radical leaders in Britain distanced themselves from the IRB because of the divisive nature of the use of violence, particularly after the Clerkenwell explosion in December 1867, which saw the Brotherhood plant a bomb in a London prison in a failed attempt to rescue its incarcerated men.[125] Some within the IRB were not surprised at this turn of events. Back in 1864, before the Reform League agitation, the *Irish People* warned that Fenians could not rely on even 'the most advanced of English reformers', such was the powerful grip of imperialism over the radical mind. Radicals in Britain loudly championed national rights in Belgium, Greece, and Poland, but the *People* sardonically noted that calls for independence within the British Empire were quietly ignored in favour of imperial unity.[126] Following the debacle of 1867, Fenianism retreated from its appeal to the English working class. The radical internationalism hinted at in the proclamation of 1867 would not be repeated in the more famous document that accompanied the Easter Rising of 1916.

The IRB was at a low ebb in the aftermath of the 1867 rising. The attempted revolt was not quite as embarrassing as the battle of the Widow McCormack's cabbage patch in 1848, but the conspiracy was far from the imagined revolution that would liberate Ireland. Following the failed uprising, the IRB restructured its leadership, moving away from the autocratic model that centred on one man at the head of the organisation. A Supreme Council was established in 1868 and expanded the following year, styling itself as the government of the Irish Republic. The new body was unafraid to critically reflect on the IRB's first ten years of existence. A public statement issued by the Supreme Council in 1868 implied that the rising of the previous year was driven by Irish-American vanity, without adequate material support. Ties to the American organisation were thus defiantly severed.[127] A constitution was adopted in 1869 and updated in 1873. With these documents, the IRB turned away from Stephens's vanguardist interpretation of revolutionary action – the secret society leading the insurrection and radicalising the masses in its wake – and adopted a more subtle approach. In a 'time of peace', the constitution of 1873 asserted, the IRB would confine itself to 'the exercise of moral

[124] As expertly sketched out in Whelehan, *Dynamiters*.
[125] Quinlivan and Rose, *The Fenians in England*, p. 81. [126] *Irish People*, 3 September 1864.
[127] 'Message from the Supreme Council of the Irish Republic to the Irish People', in T. W. Moody and Leon Ó Broin, 'Select documents: The IRB Supreme Council, 1868–1878', *Irish Historical Studies*, vol. 19, no. 75 (1975), pp. 300–1.

influences', such as 'the cultivation of union and brotherly love among Irishmen, the propagation of republican principles, and the spreading of a knowledge of the national rights of Ireland'. This was a tacit admittance that preparation for the revolutionary moment was not simply a matter of recruiting soldiers and importing arms: Irish society should be 'Fenianised' to provide a foundation for the struggle. The use of the term 'time of peace' was revealing. Under the leadership of Stephens, the IRB's very existence suggested that Ireland was on a war footing. The *Irish People* routinely stressed the need to maintain the organisation for imminent conflict and dismissed the theory that a rising should only occur when Britain became embroiled in an international war.[128] The post-rising IRB envisaged by the Supreme Council was a rather different body from that which had existed before.

This was confirmed in the most controversial decree in the IRB's constitution, which referred to the movement's relationship with democratic values. 'The IRB shall await the decision of the Irish nation', the third article announced,

> as expressed by a majority of the Irish people, as to the fit hour of inaugurating a war against England, and shall, pending such an emergency, lend its support to every movement calculated to advance the cause of Irish independence, consistently with the preservation of its own integrity.[129]

The IRB thus revised its role as the vanguard of Irish democracy, with the 'general will' replaced by the agency of majority opinion. The mechanism to gauge the revolutionary fervour of the population was not, however, mentioned. In effect, this clause postponed revolutionary activities – as hitherto understood – indefinitely. The IRB moved into a new phase of infiltrating and attempting to direct political, agrarian, and cultural movements that sprang up in Ireland from the 1870s. Fenians were to be found close to the heart of a number of popular bodies, from the Land League to the Gaelic Athletic Association.

As the IRB reorganised after the rising of 1867, the organisation received a boost when a body of 'respectable' Irish opinion began lobbying for the release of Fenian prisoners. The rising did not find much support within the Irish population, but the subsequent state trials shone a sympathetic light on the patriotic character of senior IRB men. The transformation of the leaders of the IRB from failed revolutionaries to dedicated

[128] *Irish People*, 6 February 1864.
[129] 'Amended constitution of the IRB and of the Supreme Council, 17 March 1873', in Moody and Ó Broin, 'IRB Supreme Council', p. 314.

servants of Ireland was confirmed by the publication of the influential *Speeches from the Dock*, an anthology of separatist oratory from the courtroom. Originally compiled by the Sullivan brothers, well-known journalists and writers from Cork, the book went through numerous editions throughout the nineteenth and twentieth centuries. *Speeches from the Dock* included addresses from a range of Fenians who had stood trial through 1865 and 1866, placing them in the same rhetorical and political milieu as the likes of Theobald Wolfe Tone, Robert Emmet, and John Mitchel. The Sullivans' introduction unblushingly legitimised the right of the Irish to insurrection to resist 'oppression', with those on the dock displaying immense 'dignity and patriotism'.[130] Writing only a few years after the first edition, Isaac Butt recorded that *Speeches from the Dock* had already become 'a portion of the national literature of Ireland', and had been instrumental in uniting Irish feeling in favour of an amnesty for IRB prisoners.[131]

The publication of *Speeches from the Dock* was an important milestone in the development of political language in Ireland. The book introduced Irish readers to some of the boldest separatist rhetoric of the past, while doing much to create an accessible 'canon' of revolutionary figures, movements, and ideas.[132] The mass appeal of *Speeches from the Dock* served to sanitise rebellions against the Crown, stripping away the violence and bloodshed – and failure – while affirming the courage of the rebels and the attractive idealism of their politics. In using their courtroom appearances to denounce the British connection and equate Irish patriotism with separatism, the incarcerated IRB men followed a tradition that was given a coherent shape by the Sullivans' enterprise.[133] In this sense, rebellion was secondary to displaying defiance and rhetorical elegance on the dock. Patriotism may have been a pastime for some in Ireland, to use R. V. Comerford's memorable phrase, but patriotism was increasingly equated with challenging British rule.[134]

[130] The first edition was published anonymously, but the names of the Sullivans were included in later editions. A. M. Sullivan and T. D. Sullivan, *Guilty or Not Guilty? Speeches from the Dock, or Protests of Irish Patriotism* (Dublin: no publishing house, 1867), p. 7.

[131] Butt, *Ireland's Appeal for Amnesty*, p. 14.

[132] Colin W. Reid, 'The canon of Irish republicanism: constructing a separatist "tradition"', in Matthew Roberts (ed.), *Memory and Modern British Politics: Commemoration, Tradition, Legacy* (London: Bloomsbury, 2024), pp. 76–7.

[133] See the illuminating discussion of *Speeches from the Dock* in Richard A. Keogh, 'Why, it's like a "98 trial": the Irish judiciary and the Fenian trials, 1865–1866', in Kyle Hughes and Donald M. MacRaild (eds.), *Crime, Violence, and the Irish in the Nineteenth Century* (Liverpool: Liverpool University Press, 2017), pp. 131–2.

[134] R. V. Comerford, 'Patriotism as a pastime: the appeal of Fenianism in the mid-1860s', *Irish Historical Studies*, vol. 22, no. 87 (1981), pp. 239–50.

Despite the failure of the 1867 rising, Fenianism continued to dominate political life in Ireland, as well as in Britain. Gladstone's Liberal government was elected in 1868 under a banner of 'pacifying Ireland', with a programme of constructive Irish policies to tackle the social and religious grievances that Fenianism was presupposed to represent.[135] The disestablishment of the Church of Ireland and a moderate, if symbolically important, land act swiftly followed. But the Gladstonian administration also had to face an active campaign for an amnesty for Fenians in prison, some of whom had been included in the Sullivans' *Speeches from the Dock*. An additional factor that inflamed Irish opinion was the execution of William Philip Allen, Michael Larkin, and Michael O'Brien – the 'Manchester Martyrs' – in November 1867 for their role in the accidental death of Sergeant Charles Brett during an attack on a police van transporting the captured Fenian leaders, Thomas Kelly and Timothy Deasy. Again, it was the subsequent events that followed the rescue mission, rather than the operation itself, that increased sympathy for the IRB: the death sentences were expected to be commuted.[136] When the hangman tied the noose around the necks of Allen, Larkin, and O'Brien, they died in the same grisly manner as condemned criminals, which only intensified the anger and grief felt in Ireland.

The Amnesty Association was established in 1869, then, against a fluid and decidedly unstable political backdrop. The Association was a splinter from the Amnesty Committee, which had been founded a year earlier. The Committee was sympathetic to the Gladstone government and restrained itself to 'respectable' means such as petitioning; the Association grew out of frustration with the mildness of the campaign and represented a notable ratcheting up of political anger in Ireland.[137] Large public demonstrations followed in the summer and autumn of 1869, which heard bitter outbursts against the imprisonment of Fenians, who were held up as men of conviction and sincerity. At a rally at Drogheda in August, A. J. McKenna of the Belfast *Northern Star* proclaimed that the amnesty issue eclipsed all others: even though the disestablishment of the Church of Ireland was a boon, he 'will refuse it and refuse everything else till the prison doors are unbarred'.[138] The make-up of the Association was notable, as it brought together an unlikely alliance of Fenians (John

[135] J. L. Hammond, *Gladstone and the Irish Nation* (London: Frank Cass, 1964), p. 81.
[136] For the Manchester Martyrs, see Mervyn Busteed, *The Irish in Manchester, c.1750–1921: Resistance, Adaptation and Identity* (Manchester: Manchester University Press, 2016), pp. 215–47.
[137] Comerford, *Fenians in Context*, p. 170.
[138] *Freeman's Journal*, 23 August 1869.

Nolan, a member of the IRB's Supreme Council, was the secretary of the Association) and farmers (the Association championed tenant right), under the chairmanship of that most impulsive of Irish Tories, Isaac Butt. Frustrated by the lack of progress on the vital questions of prisoner amnesty and land reform, Butt ultimately used his high profile to push for a new federal relationship between Ireland and Britain called 'Home Rule'.

## Political Revolt, Moral Revolution

In 1870, John Savage, the Chief Executive of the faction-ridden Fenian Brotherhood in the US, published an address. He condemned the Gladstonian reforms in land and education that were occurring in Ireland as distractions from the major grievance that occupied the Irish mind:

> No settlement that can be made of these minor questions will content the people of Ireland, or do away with the necessity of Fenianism, while the right of self-government is denied ... Nationality is the only solution to the Irish political problem, the only method of pacification for Ireland.[139]

Savage was a Young Ireland veteran who, like John O'Mahony, fled Ireland for the US after a failed attack on a police barracks in Waterford in September 1848. After establishing himself as a writer and journalist, he came relatively late to Fenianism, replacing O'Mahony as president in 1867.[140] He soon tired of the splits that engulfed Fenianism in the US and left the movement in 1871. In 1856, he published a book (which was reissued in the 1880s) that sketched out the development of the revolutionary tradition in Ireland, fusing together the rebellions of 1798 and 1848 into one unitary ideological event. Many of the later tropes of Fenianism – the justification for violence, the tyrannical nature of British rule, and the bitter hostility to constitutional politicians – were found through Savage's work. Those who took up arms against the British state were positioned in the book as selfless patriots who were above the partisan interests that animated constitutionalism. The rebels, Savage contended, 'were not enamoured with politics, but they worshipped Ireland'.[141]

[139] John Savage, *Address of the Council of the Fenian Brotherhood* (no publishing details, 1870), p. 2.

[140] The Fenian Brotherhood moved from a presidential to a council-based mode of leadership after 1867, hence the change in Savage's title.

[141] John Savage, *'98 and '48: The Modern Revolutionary History and Literature of Ireland* (New York: Redfield, 1856), p. xiv.

'Politics' here referred to the realm of politicians; the statement explicitly situates separatist struggle as a moral imperative to combat the grotesque clique of self-serving political representatives. Savage believed that the mission of Young Ireland did not end in failure, as theories of resistance had, by the 1840s, become more expansive. Despite the failure of 1848, Young Ireland gave Ireland a 'new literature' to 'warn the old and educate the young generation'. The rise of a separatist literary mindset, according to Savage, created a morally improved country, turning labourers away from the tavern, instilling self-reliance in tenant farmers, and leaving the 'landlord more fearful'.[142] Savage turned again to this theme in his address in 1870. The success of Fenianism should be judged not by the existence or not of an Irish republic, but by whether a revolution had occurred in 'the hearts of the people'. 'The Fenian revolution', Savage concluded, 'is practical because it creates an intellectual revolution as a basis for the political one'.[143]

The idea of militancy as a stimulus to the moral improvement of Ireland was taken seriously by Fenian thinkers across the transatlantic nexus. While some IRB activists were attracted to democratic and republican political institutions as the means to improve Ireland, this did not imply a rigid, top-down political vision.[144] The Fenian press urged individual accountability and reflection on personal lifestyle choices. An early edition of the *Irish People* expressed a desire to 'kindle a spirit of heroism in the young manhood of the country', to 'fire them with the rational ambition of the soldier of liberty'.[145] A later issue celebrated that 'drunkenness and faction-fighting are disappearing' in parts of Ireland where Fenianism was well established. 'Our young men are becoming more intelligent and manly, and, consequently, more moral every day.'[146] The framing of political action through moral improvement, especially the prism of masculinity, permeated Fenian literature. In his memoir, O'Donovan Rossa denounced those who 'say that [Ireland] cannot be freed by force' as 'something that no manly Irishman should say'.[147] 'Manliness' within the ranks of the Fenian movement was associated with resistance against the British state; constitutional political campaigns, which sought reconciliation between Ireland and Britain within the Union, were dismissed as evidence of degenerate effeminacy.[148] The separatist agenda pioneered by

[142] Ibid., p. xv. [143] Savage, *Address*, p. 4. [144] McGee, *IRB*, p. 16.
[145] *Irish People*, 16 January 1864. [146] *Irish People*, 17 June 1865.
[147] Rossa, *Rossa's Recollections*, p. 252.
[148] Patrick Bethel, '"Shrovetide will be a merry time in Ireland yet": Fenian visions of Ireland's future', in Richard J. Butler (ed.), *Dreams of the Future in Nineteenth-Century Ireland* (Liverpool: Liverpool University Press, 2021), p. 44.

the IRB and their transatlantic counterparts was, then, multifaceted. The overthrow of the British state and the creation of an independent Irish polity was at the heart of Fenianism; but the Fenians also positioned themselves at the frontline of a slower, gradual revolution. 'Republican forms of government', as the *Irish People* put it, were attractive not only because they illuminated a pathway to Irish independence, but because they tended 'to foster self-respect and manliness amongst a people'.[149] The earnestness of the Fenian message was a product of the belief that the British state in Ireland must be shattered, but also that the Irish as a nation had to be morally redeemed. The IRB was more than a militant nationalist group: it was a manifestation of Irish popular sovereignty that claimed the allegiance of the Irish, challenged the legitimacy of the state, and attempted to alter the character of the people themselves.

[149] *Irish People*, 18 March 1865.

CHAPTER 6

# Federalism
## *The Acme in the Science of Government*

> If we are not governed according to Irish ideas, we are governed as slaves.[1]
>
> Isaac Butt (1870)

> That, in accordance with the ancient and constitutional rights of the Irish Nation, we claim the privilege of managing our own affairs by a Parliament assembled in Ireland, and composed of the Sovereign, the Lords, and the Commons of Ireland.[2]
>
> The Home Rule League (1873)

In 1861, a young graduate from Trinity College Dublin called William Edward Hartpole Lecky anonymously published a book called *The Leaders of Public Opinion in Ireland.* It was Lecky's first historical work. The book's pointed introduction expressed dismay with the state of Irish political life, bemoaning the sectarian split between 'an English party' (meaning the Protestants of Ireland) and 'an Italian party' (the Catholics). 'We look in vain', he lamented, 'for an Irish party'.[3] Lecky found solace in the eighteenth-century Irish Patriot tradition, the anatomy of which he plotted through character profiles of Jonathan Swift, Henry Flood, and Henry Grattan. Daniel O'Connell, the fourth and final of Lecky's 'leaders', represented a rather different political culture. While Lecky was struck by the 'genius' of O'Connell, he condemned the Liberator for harnessing Catholic, clerical, and democratic sentiments, factors which stoked the 'sectarian and class warfare' that blighted nineteenth-century Ireland.[4] But Lecky also conceded that the underlying reasons for Ireland's problems predated O'Connell.

[1] Isaac Butt, *Ireland's Appeal for Amnesty: A Letter to the Right Hon. W. E. Gladstone, MP* (Glasgow: Cameron and Ferguson, 1870), p. 27.

[2] *The Irish Home Rule League: Resolutions of National Conference* (no publishing details, 1873), p. 1.

[3] [W. E. H. Lecky], *The Leaders of Public Opinion in Ireland* (London: Saunders, Otley, and Co., 1861), p. 3.

[4] Ibid., p. 266.

Like many of his contemporaries, Lecky believed that the nineteenth-century zeitgeist was tending towards 'the universal recognition of the rights of nationalities'.[5] He observed that in most countries since the turn of the century, 'national life' depended on the 'Government', not just as an agent that 'discharged certain business', but as a facilitator of 'political education' and 'a great representative of popular feelings'.[6] Parliaments were institutions that granted a people certain political gravitas, a site that symbolised a mature and nuanced public opinion. National parliaments housed rancorous political debates which ultimately resulted in resolution, ending any 'ill-feeling' that agitated the people. But 'little or nothing of this kind', Lecky lamented, 'is to be found in Ireland':

> Severed from their ancient traditions, and ruled by a Legislature imposed on them contrary to their will; differing essentially in character and in temperament from the nation with whom they are this associated; humiliated by the circumstances of their defeat and by the ceaseless ridicule poured on them through every organ of the press, the Irish people seem to have lost all interest in English politics. Parliament can make their laws, but it cannot control or influence their feelings.[7]

For Lecky, the Union was in crisis. The Acts of 1800 swept away the Irish parliament with the promise of Ireland's incorporation into the British state; but the relationship had grown dysfunctional, with the Irish deprived of a meaningful expression of 'national government'.

Lecky prophesied – correctly – that Irish representatives in Westminster, emboldened by a hatred of Britain, would bring parliament to its knees.[8] The religious sectarianism and poverty that blighted Ireland were symptoms of a disturbing political problem that stemmed from a lack of attachment to the structures of power. Ireland's redemption could only come with the emergence of a man who could combine the virtues of Lecky's four 'leaders' – Jonathan Swift, Henry Flood, Henry Grattan, and Daniel O'Connell – fusing the loyal Patriot tradition of the eighteenth century with the democratic Catholic tradition of the nineteenth century. Whether this leader would unite the Irish people behind a restoration of the Irish parliament or 'complete fusion with England' did not concern

[5] Ibid., p. 293. One such contemporary was John Stuart Mill, who published his *Considerations on Representative Government* in the same year as Lecky's *Leaders*. Mill argued that a successful representative government must give expression to 'national feelings and character'. *Considerations on Representative Government* (London: Parker, Son, and Bourn, 1861), p. 2.

[6] [Lecky], *Leaders of Public Opinion*, p. 268. [7] Ibid., p. 272. [8] Ibid., p. 294.

Lecky: the point was that a public mind cleansed of sectarianism 'will eventually triumph', 'whatever direction it may act'.[9]

Much had changed when Lecky returned to *Leaders of Public Opinion* for a second edition ten years later in 1871. The threat from the Irish Republican Brotherhood (IRB) had manifested itself in open revolt in 1867, and the coming of William Gladstone's Liberal administration the following year profoundly altered the possibilities of Irish politics. Lecky despaired of Fenianism, privately claiming that clandestine conspiracy tended to prove how 'absolutely incapable' the Irish were of self-government.[10] When the second edition of *Leaders of Public Opinion* appeared, a new organisation called the Home Government Association was lobbying for a form of federal self-government christened 'Home Rule'. Lecky rewrote the introduction to take account of these changes. He looked to Gladstone as the leader of the future, the man with the capacity to unite the Irish people one way or another: Lecky believed that the government's remedial Irish policy would result in either 'extinguish[ing] the desire of the people for national institutions' or making self-government irresistible.[11] Lecky repeated his belief that the institution of government should be a focal point for the national self. The problem with the British government was the perception that it was a government *of* Ireland rather than a genuine *Irish* government.[12] For Lecky, this did not necessarily mean 'Home Rule'; indeed, he did not believe that the political conditions were in place in Ireland for responsible self-government.[13] Nevertheless, he challenged the governing classes to empower the political talent of Ireland by expanding Irish influence over the imperial legislative programme and increasing the role of local government.[14] His argument was that a genuine *United* Kingdom should fulfil the Irish craving for self-government. Existing constitutional arrangements were not static but could be remoulded and improved if the political will – and, crucially, the understanding – were there.[15]

[9] Ibid., p. 308.
[10] Donal McCartney, 'Lecky's *Leaders of Public Opinion in Ireland*', *Irish Historical Studies*, vol. 14, no. 54 (1964), p. 125.
[11] W. E. H. Lecky, *The Leaders of Public Opinion in Ireland*, 2nd ed. (London: Longmans, Green, and Co., 1871), p. xxiv.
[12] Ibid., pp. xviii–xix.
[13] Elizabeth Lecky, *A Memoir of the Right Hon. William Edward Hartpole Lecky* (London: Longmans, Green, and Co., 1909), p. 88.
[14] Lecky, *Leaders of Public Opinion*, 2nd ed., p. xix.
[15] Donal McCartney, *W. E. H. Lecky: Historian & Politician, 1838–1903* (Dublin: Lilliput Press, 1994), p. 59.

Lecky entered the parliamentary fray in 1895 as the member for Dublin University. By this time, he was a firm liberal opponent of Home Rule, having equated the agitation by the Parnellites during the late 1870s and 1880s with agrarian lawlessness and political extremism. An older and more pessimistic Lecky tied himself more firmly to the Union: the third and final edition of *Leaders of Public Opinion* was published in 1903, with a notable toning-down of the national sentiment of the previous versions.[16] The direction of Irish politics since 1871 increased his hostility to the principle of Home Rule, as political influence had 'passed into the hands of men who have proved during a long succession of years their disloyalty to the Crown [and] their hatred of the Empire'.[17] For Lecky, the Union had failed to accommodate Irish national sentiment, but by the end of the nineteenth century, the political mood in Ireland had become so warped that solace could only be found in the constitutional connection with Britain. The government of Ireland had, in Lecky's eyes, become an insurmountable puzzle.

The three editions of the *Leaders of Public Opinion* chart Lecky's political journey from an ambition to resurrect the Irish Protestant Patriot tradition to liberal unionism. His biographer has opined that Lecky was 'never quite in step with his contemporaries'.[18] But another way of viewing Lecky's body of work is as a window into the fluidity of political life before the Home Rule crisis of the 1880s. It was possible to argue from the vantage points of 1861 and 1871 that the constitutional framework of the Union could yet provide the material and symbolic benefits of self-government for Ireland. Moreover, it was not a political oddity to find an Irish Protestant calling for the greening of British governmental practices in Ireland to match a rising expectation for 'soft' forms of self-government. To return to the first edition of *Leaders of Public Opinion*: the 'master-curse of Ireland' was 'sectarian animosity'. The challenge was to find forms of political discourse that eradicated this evil.[19] For Lecky, the most appropriate constitutional status of Ireland was that which contributed most to an anti-sectarian common good. But the shape of such an arrangement eluded even Lecky.

## Federalism and the Union

However uncertain Lecky was about the future constitutional shape of Ireland, one lost historical opportunity can be gleaned from his work.

[16] McCartney, 'Lecky's *Leaders*', pp. 133–4.

[17] W. E. H. Lecky, *Leaders of Public Opinion*, 3rd ed., 2 vols. (London: Longmans, Green, and Co., 1903), i, p. xii.

[18] McCartney, 'Lecky's *Leaders*', p. 141.

[19] [Lecky], *Leaders of Public Opinion*, pp. 275–6.

Lecky's overview of Henry Grattan's career in *Leaders of Public Opinion* contained a powerful critique of the constitutional architecture adopted by the Acts of Union in 1800. 'The conditions of Irish and English politics are so extremely different', observed Lecky, 'and the reasons for preserving in Ireland a local centre of political life are so powerful, that it is probably a federal Union would have been preferred'.[20] Federalism, as envisaged by Lecky, would have instilled the virtues of self-government into the Irish; a parliament in Dublin had the potential to act as a conductor for national sentiment, fostering responsible governing practices within the broader rubric of the Union. A small number of writers who contributed to the pamphlet debate over the Union from 1798 to 1800 raised the prospect of federalism as the constitutional basis for the United Kingdom, but generally dismissed the concept as too complex and potentially unstable.[21] Lecky's perspective was, of course, coloured by its retrospective nature. He positioned the decisions taken in 1800 as a missed opportunity to reconcile Ireland to the British imperial project, casting federalism as the means to balance responsive local government and the need for a strong, unified administration to provide guidance on matters of war, peace, and empire. With some seventy years of operating the alternative path of federalism, the Union in Ireland, in Lecky's view, might have retreated as a contemporary political issue.

Despite his historical vindication of federalism's applicability in Ireland, Lecky was not an advocate for the federal idea when it reappeared on the Irish political scene in 1870. Federalism, for Lecky, was a road not taken by a previous generation, not a realistic solution to contemporary problems. Under an incorporating Union, Lecky asserted, the Irish lost the prestige and tempering influence of a parliament; political argument had been replaced by appeals to passions, reasonable compromise jettisoned in favour of sectarianism.[22] In the third edition of *Leaders of Public Opinion*, published in 1903, Lecky asserted that the rhetoric of Home Rule had injected disloyalty into the Irish body politic, paradoxically heightening the sense that the Irish were unable to operate a responsible form of self-government.[23] The moment for self-government, Lecky pessimistically suggested, had long since passed.

[20] Lecky, *Leaders of Public Opinion*, 2nd ed., p. 196.

[21] For example, see Anon., *Necessity of an Incorporate Union Between Great Britain & Ireland Proved From the Situation of both Kingdoms: with a Sketch of the Principles upon which it Ought to be Formed* (London: J. Wright, 1799), pp. 46–8; and Sir John Jervis, *A Letter Addressed to the Gentlemen of England and Ireland: on the Inexpediency of a Federal-Union Between the Two Kingdoms* (Dublin: John Whitworth, 1798).

[22] McCartney, *W. E. H. Lecky*, p. 62.

[23] Lecky, *Leaders of Public Opinion*, 3rd ed., i, p. viii.

This argument was countered with much force during the 1870s. Federalism – or 'Home Rule', as it was christened – gained traction as a constitutional idea in an influential pamphlet written by Isaac Butt in 1870. The publication helped to popularise a Dublin-based political society called the Home Government Association, which was established several months before. In 1873, the Association was replaced by a parliamentary movement called the Home Rule League, which put federalism – and later, more nebulous definitions of Irish self-government – onto the high political agenda. Butt was a key figure in popularising the notion of 'Home Rule' and played a crucial (if uneasy) role in expanding the campaign beyond the drawing rooms of Dublin during the 1870s. At first glance, he was an unusual candidate as a 'national leader', with his previous history within the ranks of Irish Toryism. As his writings during the Famine demonstrated, however, Butt's support for the incorporating Union was conditional; added to the sense of fluidity in his constitutional thought was his celebrated legal defence of several high-profile Young Irelanders in 1848, which placed Butt in the forefront of the Irish popular imagination. Butt's standing within Catholic Ireland was further enhanced during the 1860s through the publication of several influential texts advocating tenant rights and (echoing his earlier courtroom work) assuming the defence brief for several IRB men on trial. He was, in many ways, the natural candidate as president of the Amnesty Association, a body created in 1869 that lobbied for the release of IRB prisoners on the grounds that their actions were driven by patriotic and not criminal sentiment. Butt was by 1870, then, an esteemed and popular figure throughout much of Catholic Ireland.[24] But the old Tory in him persisted, not least in his ambition, nurtured as the editor of the *Dublin University Magazine* in the 1830s, of building a space within Irish political life for Protestants to partake in 'national' issues.

Butt unquestionably undertook an unorthodox political journey, but there was a striking degree of consistency underpinning his shifting constitutional thought. Despite this, the first historians of early Home Rule portrayed Butt's advocacy of federalism as a political conversion from firebrand Protestant Toryism to 'moderate' nationalism.[25] The fact that

[24] R. V. Comerford, *The Fenians in Context: Irish Politics and Society, 1848–82* (Dublin: Wolfhound Press, 1998; first published 1985), pp. 170–1.

[25] David Thornley, *Isaac Butt and Home Rule* (London: MacGibbon & Kee, 1964), p. 125; Lawrence J. McCaffrey, 'Isaac Butt and the Home Rule movement: a study in conservative nationalism', *Review of Politics*, vol. 22, no. 1 (1960), p. 75; Terence de Vere White, *The Road of Excess* (Dublin: Browne and Nolan Ltd., 1946), p. 183.

Butt's early reputation was built on his celebrated retort to Daniel O'Connell's Repeal of the Union motion at the Dublin Corporation in 1843 appears to give credence to the idea of a sudden conversion from unionism to 'nationalist' ideas of self-government.[26] While the conversion thesis is compelling, such a perspective overlooks the inherent *unionism* of Butt's federalist project and the wider rationale for Home Rule. As Butt personified, Irish constitutional thought was not a binary choice between incorporating unionism and self-governing nationalism: 'Home Rule', as defined by Butt, was an ambitious political programme that sought a historic compromise between these two positions by reimagining the Union. As one pamphleteer put it in 1870, federalism plotted a middle way between the constitutional endpoints of incorporating Union and O'Connellite Repeal.[27] Butt's vision of a federal union held the ambitious promise of reconciling the respective competing British and Irish aspirations of centralisation and self-government.

What had changed, then, in Butt's constitutional thinking between 1843 and 1870 was not a belief in unionism itself, but which form the Union should take. The path to federalism was signposted in Butt's increasingly vehement writings on land reform and prisoner amnesty during the 1860s, issues that he framed as test cases of the health of the Union.[28] In 1870, Butt published his most significant statement on the amnesty question as an open letter to the Prime Minister, William Gladstone. He elevated the government's response to the Fenian prisoner issue as a watershed moment. 'Its decision determines', Butt asserted, 'whether we are admitted into a partnership with England on equal terms, or whether we are to be governed as a conquered country'.[29] If the government behaved in a manner that was dismissive of Irish perspectives, then the conclusion was that the incorporating Union was not fit for purpose. Returning to a mantra that appeared in the *Dublin University Magazine* during his editorship in the 1830s, Butt surmised that 'If we are not governed according to Irish ideas, we are governed as slaves'.[30]

Butt's articulation of a federal union in 1870 as the ideal constitutional framework to link Britain and Ireland would not, therefore, have surprised his more careful observers. Federalism had the attraction of enshrining

[26] For Butt's speech at the Dublin Corporation, see Chapter 4, p. 173.
[27] 'Protestant Celt', *Irish Nationality in 1870*, 2nd ed. (Dublin: E. Ponsonby, 1870), p. 35.
[28] Colin W. Reid, '"A voice for Ireland": Isaac Butt, environmental justice, and the dilemmas of the Irish land question', in Matthew Kelly (ed.), *Nature and the Environment in Nineteenth-Century Ireland* (Liverpool: Liverpool University Press, 2019), p. 57.
[29] Butt, *Ireland's Appeal for Amnesty*, p. 7. [30] Ibid., p. 27.

Irish participation in the imperial parliament while also creating a responsive assembly in Dublin to legislate for Irish domestic issues. In the face of decades of British legislative indifference to 'Irish ideas', Butt hypothesised that restructuring the Union on federal principles was the only method to secure representative government for Ireland within a unionist framework. This had become a time-sensitive matter. Like many British and Irish contemporaries, Butt interpreted Fenianism as primarily a manifestation of social grievances, to which the government response was inadequate. If these injustices were not addressed, he warned, the more doctrinal separatism of the IRB would gain traction rapidly. Centralised and unrepresentative government had poisoned Irish political culture, Butt lamented, breeding a 'passive disloyalty' within the Catholic population. 'They are not ready, nor do they intend, to take arms against the English Government. But they have a respect and a regard for those who have done so.'[31] Ireland was, in other words, a land of O'Connellites, eager to achieve good government through constitutional reform; but separatism remained an alluring alternative and stood to benefit most from legislative inertia. Home Rule was Butt's solution to the Irish problem, creating a federal constitution to reset the Union settlement based on equality, while satisfying the Irish national yearning for self-government. Federal Home Rule also had another glorious purpose: the resurrection of the ethos of patriotic Toryism and the demonstration that unionism was not incompatible with leading the 'national' movement.

## The Utility of Federalism

Federalism was something of a vogue topic for European political thinkers during the nineteenth century. Interest was piqued by Alexis de Tocqueville's coverage of federal constitutional arrangements in his *Democracy in America* (1835 and 1840). Tocqueville's analysis concluded that a federal constitution fitted the United States but was wholly inappropriate for most European countries.[32] This set the tenor of mid-Victorian discussions about federalism in Britain. Two of the most notable engagements with the idea came in the form of John Stuart Mill's *Considerations on Representative Government* (1861) and Edward A. Freeman's *History of Federal Government from the Foundation of the Achaean League to the*

[31] Ibid., p. 21.
[32] Alexis de Tocqueville, *Democracy in America*, trans. George Lawrence, ed. J. P. Mayer (London: Fontana Press, 1994), pp. 163–70.

*Disruption of the United States* (1863). Mill suggested that several factors were required to ensure such a federal arrangement was successful, such as a shared political identity and equality of power between the contracting states.[33] Freeman historicised the concept in his work, hypothesising that federalism was a compromise political constitution, holding the ground between two 'widely distant extremes'.[34] Through these writings, and the debates they prompted, the principles of federalism became embedded into political discussions about potential constitutional change within the United Kingdom during the 1860s and 1870s. The argument over the applicability, or otherwise, of federalism in Britain and Ireland illuminates how sovereignty was conceptualised within a multinational political union by contemporaries. But as the Home Rulers quickly realised in the early 1870s, the political and intellectual mood in Britain was decisively against radical constitutional tinkering.

Butt's definition of Irish Home Rule followed Freeman's logic in positioning federalism as a compromise between imperial unity and Irish self-government. While Butt was not explicit about this, his scheme rendered the term *Irish Home Rule* a misnomer, as he framed constitutional reform as a United Kingdom-wide ambition. The original definition of Home Rule as a federal arrangement during the 1870s marked a turning point in conceptions of Ireland's place within the Union and, as such, deserves scrutiny as a form of nationally minded unionism. The federal ideal as promoted by Butt placed an emphasis on 'normalising' the Irish experience of Union through the creation of regional parliaments across the two islands. Early Home Rulers envisaged the United Kingdom as the political entity to be reformed; Home Rulers after 1880 placed the focus more exclusively on Ireland. As this shift in constitutional focus suggests, the political language of Home Rule moved dramatically from the early 1870s to the 1880s, assuming a more separatist edge.[35]

Butt's conception of federal Home Rule was, then, very different from the more aggressive form it took from the 1880s. If J. W. Good's decision to include Butt and the early Home Rule movement as a variation of Irish *unionism* in 1920 now seems paradoxical, this is because of the prevailing assumption that schemes for self-government must be nationalist-inspired

[33] Mill, *Considerations*, pp. 298–300.

[34] Edward A. Freeman, *History of Federal Government, from the Foundation of the Achaean League to the Disruption of the United States* (London: Macmillan, 1863), p. 2. Freeman's book was billed as the first of several volumes, but it was the only volume that appeared.

[35] This is a major theme of Matthew Kelly, *The Fenian Ideal and Irish Nationalism, 1882–1916* (Woodbridge: Boydell Press, 2006).

and thus anti-unionist. Good, who was the literary editor of the *Freeman's Journal* in 1920 and future assistant editor at George Russell's *Irish Statesman*, was one of the few observers who accurately positioned Butt within the spectrum of Irish political thought, describing the Home Rule leader's modus operandi as 'an experiment in constructive Unionism'.[36] For some drawn to the resurrected ideal of self-government, however, that was precisely the problem. The discontent with Butt's leadership that escalated in the second half of the 1870s within Home Rule circles was as much a negative reaction against his ambition to harmonise Ireland's place within the Union as frustration at a lack of parliamentary progress under his polite and 'moderate' leadership.

The first organisation that championed Home Rule was the Home Government Association. It drew strongly from Protestant and Conservative ranks, as many from this fold rebelled against Gladstonian Liberalism's assault on the Church of Ireland.[37] Explanations for the genesis of Home Rule tend to stress the immediate context; indeed, the rise of Home Rule alarmed some contemporary unionist observers. Thomas MacKnight, the editor of the Belfast liberal daily, the *Northern Whig*, later recalled the 'strange language' of 'Tory Fenianism', highlighting the unstable nature of political thought during the early 1870s.[38] Appreciating the fluid political boundaries of nineteenth-century Irish political thought is crucial to any understanding of the emergence and rationale of the Home Rule idea. As the trials and tribulations of the 1830s and 1840s revealed, there was a history of patriotic thought within Irish conservative circles that predated the immediate origins of Home Rule.[39] Federalism, as offered by Butt as the first definition of Home Rule, can be viewed as the logical destination of nationally minded Irish Toryism of the *DUM* hue, and not solely as a cynical leap by a class reacting to the Gladstonian attack.

This was the context in which Butt's *Irish Federalism! Its Meaning, its Objects, and its Hopes* was published in 1870. The pamphlet quickly went

[36] J. W. Good, *Irish Unionism* (Dublin: Talbot Press, 1920), p. 148.

[37] See, for example, J. J. Golden, 'The Protestant influence on the origins of Irish Home Rule, 1861–1871', *English Historical Review*, vol. 128, no. 535 (2013), pp. 1483–516; K. T. Hoppen, *Elections, Politics, and Society in Ireland, 1832–1885* (Oxford: Oxford University Press, 1984), p. 327; Alvin Jackson, *Home Rule: An Irish History, 1800–2000* (London: Weidenfeld & Nicolson, 2003), pp. 19–21; Jennifer Regan-Lefebvre, *Cosmopolitan Nationalism and the Victorian Empire: Ireland, India and the Politics of Alfred Webb* (Basingstoke: Palgrave, 2009), p. 73.

[38] Thomas MacKnight, *Ulster As It Is: or Twenty-Eight Years' Experience as an Irish Editor*, 2 vols. (London: Macmillan and Co., 1896), i, p. 225.

[39] See Chapter 4, and also Joseph Spence, 'Isaac Butt, Irish nationality and the conditional defence of the Union, 1833–1870', in D. G. Boyce and A. O'Day (eds.), *Defenders of the Union: A Survey of British and Irish Unionism since 1801* (London: Routledge, 2001), p. 71.

through three editions that year, with a fourth and final edition appearing in 1874 as the result of a popular upsurge in favour of the Home Rule cause.[40] The federal underpinnings of Butt's proposal represented a fervent critique of the operation of the incorporating Union, while advocating Ireland's right to participate as an equal within the structures of the United Kingdom and wider empire.[41] Federalism was driven by a desire to create more effective representative institutions, which ultimately would strengthen the Union. The young polymath George Sigerson argued in 1868 that 'Ireland has not yet fully received the benefit of institutions analogous to those of England, that is to say, of institutions which harmonize with the popular sentiment, and are not imposed on the people against their will'.[42] This was, in essence, the same criticism of the Union that Butt articulated from the mid 1860s until his death in 1879.

Butt's federalism emerged from a fevered period of activism, thinking, and publishing since the mid 1860. His powerful pamphlet from 1866, *Land Tenure in Ireland; A Plea for the Celtic Race*, made the case that Fenianism represented a war on 'the institutions of landed property' for a very good reason: 'landlordism and the land system was the impersonation of English dominance and misrule'.[43] He believed that reform of the landed system would weaken the appeal of Fenianism, rationalising that the Irish sought agrarian justice, not an overthrow of the state or the abolition of property. Butt outlined this conundrum in a striking manner. 'If the rights of property are to be exercised for the extinction of the people', he powerfully affirmed, 'we must not wonder if the people begin to think that their only hope of safety lies in the extinction of all rights of property in land'.[44] The logic of this stance pushed Butt into articulating an early justification of Home Rule, based on the idea that 'laws and institutions are gradually moulded to the wants and wishes of the people' in 'self-governed nations'.[45] Implicit in this argument was a rejection of the centralisation of the incorporated Union, which denied the Irish a constructive outlet to shape British policy, with disastrous consequences *in*

[40] J. P. McAlister to Isaac Butt, 19 September 1874, Home Rule League Letter Book, Public Record Office of Northern Ireland (PRONI), D213/94.

[41] Isaac Butt, 'Advertisement to First Edition, August 1870', *Home Government for Ireland: Irish Federalism! Its Meanings, its Objects, and its Hopes*, 4th ed. (Dublin: Irish Home Rule League, 1874; first published 1870), p. iv.

[42] 'An Ulsterman' [George Sigerson], *Modern Ireland: Its Vital Questions, Secret Societies, and Government* (London: Longmans, Green, Reader, and Dyer, 1868), p. viii.

[43] Isaac Butt, *Land Tenure in Ireland; A Plea for the Celtic Race*, 3rd ed. (Dublin: John Falconer, 1866), p. 9.

[44] Ibid., p. 65. [45] Ibid., pp. 71–2.

Ireland. By 1871, Butt was critiquing the operation of the Union state with a strain of separative language: 'The whole system of Irish government is one of neglect of Irish interests and contempt and defiance of Irish opinion.'[46] Despite the powerful rhetorical flourishes deployed by Butt, however, he was far from rejecting the principle of Union itself.

The preface of Butt's first edition of *Home Government for Ireland* was dated August 1870, several months after the founding of the Home Government Association. The advancement of federalist ideas was made within the wider context of renewed disaffection with the structure of government in Ireland. In 1869, Jeremiah O'Donovan Rossa topped a by-election in Tipperary while in prison, signalling the popular sympathy for the incarcerated IRB men and anger at the government's refusal to concede an amnesty. The result was deemed void, and in February 1870 another Fenian, Charles Kickham, came within four votes of holding the seat. In July 1870, the *Nation* carried a snapshot of the national mood, delivered with a rhetorical clout reminiscent of the Young Ireland generation: 'If our experience of that Parliament has taught us any political truth more clearly than another in the course of the last seventy years, it is that there is to the rational judgement no medial stage, between the absolute fact of provincialism we suffer, and the absolute fact of autonomy we claim.'[47]

Butt was central in channelling this anti-government sentiment and moulding it into the language of Home Rule. Indeed, one of his most notable successes was convincing the leadership of the IRB to adopt a position of benevolent neutrality towards the parliamentary campaign during the mid 1870s.[48] Butt was respected by Fenians because of his past defences of IRB prisoners and his powerful rhetoric in favour of self-government; but what was overlooked (ironically) was that the federal formula for self-government aimed to *strengthen* the Union. He had previously argued that the application of 'justice and liberality' in Ireland would create loyalty and contentment with the British connection.[49] By 1870, Butt had moved to the belief that only an Irish legislature offered the means to reach this end. Butt's conception of federalism provided the means to dampen the separatist impulse of Irish nationalism, channelling its restless energy constructively through the creation of national and imperial political spaces.[50]

[46] Isaac Butt, *The Irish Deep Sea Fisheries: a Speech, Delivered at a Meeting of the Home Government Association, 1871* (Dublin: Irish Home Rule League, 1874), p. 5.
[47] *Nation*, 23 July 1870. [48] Comerford, *Fenians in Context*, p. 188.
[49] Isaac Butt, *The Irish Querist: a Series of Questions Proposed for the Consideration of All Who Desire to Solve the Problem of Ireland's Social Condition* (Dublin: John Falconer, 1867), p. 30.
[50] Butt, *Irish Federalism*, pp. viii–ix.

Butt rejected the O'Connellite idea of Repeal of the Union, which was still prevalent within Irish discourse after the Famine. For Butt, Repeal was anti-imperial and hence damaging to Ireland's standing in the empire. Repeal implied a return to the pre-1800 political landscape, with the second coming of 'Grattan's Parliament'.[51] Critically, this conception of Irish self-government surrendered Irish representation at Westminster, which threatened (in Butt's eyes) to relegate Ireland's status as an integral component of the imperial metropole, turning the clock back to the provincial eighteenth-century conception of 'colonial-national' independence. As we have seen, Butt's strain of Irish Toryism rejected Repeal on these grounds during the 1830s and 1840s; his convictions were as strong during the 1860s and 1870s. '[I]n a Federal Union', Butt asserted in 1870, 'Ireland would take a higher place, and would exercise a greater influence that she did so, or ever could do, under the Constitution of 1782'.[52] The task pursued by Butt was, therefore, doubly ambitious: part of his target audience was Irish Repealers who were not only sceptical of the *performance* of the Union but, in several notable cases, of the *principle* of Union. He conceded that it was also necessary to convince 'thoughtful and intelligent Englishmen' of the virtues of federal reform, as this was the group who would ultimately pass legislation.[53] It would prove a difficult balancing act.

In moving towards the federal ideal, Butt categorically rejected the notion that Gladstonian Liberalism could sufficiently reshape the Union in a manner that would promote harmony across the three kingdoms. The Liberal assault on the pillars of what remained of the Protestant Ascendancy – most notably, the Church of Ireland – was, for Butt, a sufficient demonstration of the corruption of the original ethos of Union. 'We are not now governed by a Parliament administering a treaty of Union', Butt declared, 'but by a supreme Parliament claiming and exercising the supreme control and absolute power of legislation, exactly as if Ireland and England had always been one country, as if an Irish Parliament had never existed, and a treaty of Union never had been made'.[54] If Union implied partnership, the British had corrupted this ethos through an avalanche of exceptional legislation. Federalism offered the means to restore the original unionist ideal of 1800, creating a political chamber to scratch the itch of Irish distinctiveness while contributing to the greater imperial project.

*Irish Federalism* made a compelling case in many regards, but the pamphlet is strangely lacking in analysing historical and contemporary federal examples. Discussion of the 'real-life' experiences of federalism was relegated to a few pages and centred on the Achaean League, the

[51] Ibid., p. iv. [52] Ibid., p. v. [53] Ibid., p. iv. [54] Ibid., p. 18.

Dominion of Canada, and the Swiss Cantons. The federal system of the United States, which formed a crucial component within the worldview of other intellectuals who wrote about constitutional reform during the 1860s and 1870s, such as Walter Bagehot and Freeman, received only one sentence. Readings of American federalism were viewed through the prism of the Civil War, a cautionary tale to British observers of the instability of peculiar constitutional arrangements that divided sovereign power.[55] When the Civil War broke out in 1861, Walter Bagehot wearily recorded that 'it is impossible for Englishmen not to observe that the whole mischief has been, not caused but painfully exacerbated by the unfortunate mixture of flexibility and inflexibility in the United States Constitution'.[56] Butt may have strategically left out the high-profile example for fear of (further) antagonising educated opinion. The only reference to the American example in Butt's pamphlet is a single colourless sentence referring to the United States as 'only another illustration of the universality of the instinct which teaches men that nations as well as individuals may combine, and that there is no inconsistency between the existence of a legislature regulating the internal affairs of each portion of the confederation and a central legislature, directing with efficiency and unity the combined power of all'.[57] The shadow of the Civil War loomed large, to the extent that the American example of federalism, in Butt's reading, potentially presented more problems than virtues.

Other Home Rulers, such as John George MacCarthy, did, however, embrace the American model.[58] The federal system in the US informed a large part of the contributions of Thaddeus O'Malley, the self-styled 'father of federalism in Ireland', who had edited the *Federalist* newspaper during the 1840s.[59] O'Malley emerged from his retirement in 1873 to publish a substantial pamphlet, *Home Rule on the Basis of Federalism*, which offered a sustained expansion of Butt's ideas. O'Malley pressed the case that the American constitutional experiment, which divided sovereignty between the states and the centre, empowered a 'small people' and a 'great nation' simultaneously.[60] Individual states, regardless of their

[55] J. W. Burrow, *Whigs and Liberals: Continuity and Change in English Political Thought* (Oxford: Oxford University Press, 1988), p. 123.

[56] *Economist*, 20 April 1861. [57] Butt, *Irish Federalism*, p. 16.

[58] John George MacCarthy, *A Plea for the Home Government of Ireland* (London: Longmans, Green, and Co., 1871), p. 42.

[59] Alfred Webb, *A Compendium of Irish Biography: Comprising Sketches of Distinguished Irishmen, and of Eminent Persons Connected with Ireland by Office or by their Writings* (Dublin: M. H. Gill & Son, 1878), p. 403. For O'Malley's arguments during the O'Connellite era of Repeal, see Chapter 3, pp. 112–13.

[60] Thaddeus O'Malley, *Home Rule on the Basis of Federalism* (London: Wm. Ridgeway, 1873), p. 31.

size or population, were treated as equals: Delaware and New Jersey had the same political worth as Pennsylvania and New York.[61] The distribution of power within the US prevented the growth of tyranny and unaccountable government; this sharply contrasted with the lopsided nature of the incorporating Union, which left English interests dominant over Irish, Scottish, and Welsh concerns. In balancing the interests of the states and the central government, O'Malley saluted federalism as the high point of constitutional design, 'the acme in the science of government'.[62]

It is therefore telling that Butt chose not to pursue this line of argument in his own writings on the subject. His dismissal of the United States as 'only another illustration' of federalism, rather than the model *par excellence*, represented an effort to play down the negative connotations of federalism and democracy within *British* (quite apart from Irish) political thought. It is no coincidence that the beacon of the federal ideal according to Butt was Canada, which, unlike its North American neighbour, was an integral component of the British Empire. Butt reasoned that federal self-government transformed Canadian attitudes, channelling potential rebellion into responsible government, while strengthening the transatlantic bonds of empire. Given that this example also highlighted a precedent for federalism within the British Empire, it was unsurprising that Butt chose to exploit it. Indeed, the Canadian parallel became a staple of Home Rule discourse during the 1870s and remained in use by imperially minded nationalists throughout the Edwardian period.[63] The nature of the comparison, however, altered over time. Butt interpreted Ireland as a Quebec to the United Kingdom's Canada, while a later generation of Home Rulers saw Ireland as Canada itself, an important shift in perception. There were also some more concrete connections between Butt's movement and Canada. While the organisational spread of the Home Rule League (the body that superseded the Home Government Association in 1873) remained patchy through the 1870s, there were various efforts to cultivate Canadian links: surviving correspondence reveals the existence of sympathetic expatriate associations in Quebec and Montreal. These associations championed Butt's cause in North America, explicitly deploying the example of Canada to explain the fundamental principles and goals of the Home Rule project.[64]

Butt's cautious attitude to US federalism also showcased his wider anxiety about the development of democratic mass politics during the

[61] Ibid., p. 43. [62] Ibid., p. 43.

[63] For example, see Colin W. Reid, *The Lost Ireland of Stephen Gwynn: Irish Constitutional Nationalism and Cultural Politics, 1864–1950* (Manchester: Manchester University Press, 2011), pp. 95–6.

[64] Rev. J. Galbraith to Edward Murphy, 13 August 1875; J. P. McAlister to T. Moloney, 5 April 1876, Home Rule League Letter Book, PRONI, D213/130–4 and D213/192–3.

1860s and 1870s. Home Rule in later years became intertwined with democratic rights, but it should not be forgotten that the brand was popularised by an Irish Tory unionist who viewed the involvement of the masses in politics with deep suspicion.[65] The colours that Butt wore politically may have changed from his *Dublin University Magazine* days, but his underlying philosophy had not. His hostility to democracy and fears of a tyranny of the unenlightened majority formed a central component of his argument for federalism in 1870. Butt reasoned that the Irish Reform and Franchise Acts of 1832, 1850, and 1868 had inadvertently amplified the problems inherent within the British-Irish connection.[66] By expanding the political nation through the increased franchise from the 1830s to the 1860s, nationalist sentiment became a more significant factor in shaping electoral culture in Ireland as the century progressed. 'The moment the Irish vote appeared as a distinct power', argued Butt in 1870,

> detached from, and uninterested in, the questions of English policy, that moment the system of intrigue and bargains, and compacts, became the inevitable result – and from that moment the House of Commons was incapable of fulfilling, even for England, the true functions of the representation of the people.[67]

The United Kingdom was, in other words, threatened by the expansion of the franchise: democratic passions, powered by national grievances, threatened to outgrow the structures of the incorporated Union state.

In this context, federalism was a logical shift for the United Kingdom to make. Butt surmised that it made sense for England to have a parliament that represented only English affairs, as much as it did for Ireland to have its own assembly. There was no 'representative system' of government within the United Kingdom because the existing centralised structures of executive power indirectly encouraged competition and disunity, rather than union and harmony, between the component countries. The logic of Butt's point was that only through substantially redrawing the constitutional map of the United Kingdom could long-term stability be achieved.

There were additional benefits to a federal model. Butt posited that a new constitution would require new leaders, which offered the possibility for the redemption of the Irish landed class. He was greatly attracted to the idea of fusing aristocratic responsibility with democratic sentiment.

65 See, for example, Eugenio F. Biagini, *British Democracy and Irish Nationalism, 1876–1906* (Cambridge: Cambridge University Press, 2007).

66 For an outline of the main features of these acts, see Hoppen, *Elections*, pp. 1, 31–3, and Colin Barr, 'The Irish Reform Act of 1868', *Parliamentary History*, vol. 36, no. 1 (2018), pp. 97–116.

67 Butt, *Irish Federalism*, p. 48.

If democracy is the future, reasoned Butt, its populism can be checked in the upper houses across the various parts of the United Kingdom. Federalism thus presented the upper orders in Ireland with the means to contribute to national politics, a sphere that had been largely removed in 1800 with the abolition of the parliament in Dublin. Butt feared that the political, religious, and property rights of Irish Protestants could not be guaranteed within the current system (as the Liberals' Irish agenda demonstrated) but could be protected within a federal constitution that claimed their allegiance. Despite such an appeal, Butt was certain that federalism offered more than protection of the old Protestant order from which he came: it represented nothing less than the means to re-assume the leadership of the nation. He warned of the grave consequences if the 'natural leaders' shirked from the challenge. 'It is the duty of the upper class of Irish society to place themselves in the front of a national government for self-government. It is the opportunity of a reconciliation with the people which they may never have again.'[68]

Butt's wish to inspire the Irish aristocratic and landed classes to assume a leadership role within the national movement remained one of the most enduring ambitions of the Home Government Association and its successor body, the Home Rule League. Andrew Kettle, a key agrarian activist, described Butt's desire to 'lead all the inhabitants of Ireland', including the landlords, as 'unique and herculean'.[69] In a revised form, the attempt to coax landlords into their 'natural' leadership position was also a component of Charles Stewart Parnell's political thought during the Land War.[70] William Shaw, the Protestant Liberal MP for Bandon and a notable convert to the Home Rule cause, expressed his belief to Butt in April 1870 that while 'the great body of the people' will support a Home Rule organisation because of nationalist sentiment, 'it will be essential to get the better class well with it'.[71]

This desire to win over the 'better class' was a cornerstone of the emerging language of federal Home Rule. This was often rooted in conservatism. At the meeting of the Home Government Association in September 1870, Shaw affirmed the movement's non-revolutionary

[68] Ibid., pp. 54–6, quote on p. 56.

[69] Andrew J. Kettle, *The Material for Victory*, ed. Laurence J. Kettle (Galway: Open Press at the University of Galway, 2023; first published 1958), p. 23.

[70] Paul Bew, *Enigma: A New Life of Charles Stewart Parnell* (Dublin: Gill & Macmillan, 2011), pp. 68–9.

[71] William Shaw to Butt, 23 April 1870, Isaac Butt Papers, National Library of Ireland (NLI), MS 8692(6).

objectives.[72] Those most able advocates of federalism within the Home Government Association, Thaddeus O'Malley and John George MacCarthy, both highlighted the need to blend new ideas with old traditions. They supported the concept of a bicameral Irish parliament, with a strong hereditary element in the upper house: for O'Malley, this would ensure that as much as possible from the past constitution was kept running 'in the old grooves'; for MacCarthy, federalism would 'conserve ancient rights and local institutions', while constructing 'a bulwark against revolution'.[73] This, of course, referred to the potential of federalism to dampen the spirit of Fenianism through the patriotic appeal of a local parliament. Butt also saw the new constitution as a buffer to resist the spread of *English* socialism into Ireland, protecting the Irish from the excesses of increasing democratic fervour in other areas of the United Kingdom. Federalism, as articulated by Butt and his supporters, was a radical yet conservative idea – a framework to create representative government across the two islands, while enhancing aristocratic political power and offering protection against democratic despotism. It was one of the boldest political proposals to emerge from Ireland during the nineteenth century.

## The Turn against Federalism

The problem with Home Rule as a political idea that combined self-government and unionism with an anti-democratic tinge was that it appeared too cautious from an Irish nationalist perspective, and too radical from a conservative vantage point. Butt also failed to connect his constitutional plan to wider ambitions for imperial federation which, given the contemporary British interest in such thinking, was a significant omission.[74] The success that the Home Rule movement enjoyed under Butt's command as the 1870s progressed also cannot be read as popular advocacy of federalism. For all of Butt's careful formulations in connecting Irish self-government with the wider scheme of a federal United Kingdom, many enemies – and, even more damagingly, friends – of Home Rule saw it merely as the return of 'old fashioned' Repeal.

Misunderstandings of federalism were amplified by political incoherence within the Home Rule movement. One of its more senior figures was

72 *Freeman's Journal*, 2 September 1870.

73 O'Malley, *Home Rule on the Basis of Federalism*, p. 48; MacCarthy, *Plea for the Home Government of Ireland*, pp. 160–1.

74 For emerging ideas of imperial federation, see Duncan Bell, *The Idea of Greater Britain: Empire and the Future of World Order, 1860–1900* (Princeton, NJ: Princeton University Press, 2007).

the Repeal activist William O'Neill Daunt, who in private correspondence pressed that members should not raise any issues other than Home Rule in formal discussions. 'If dissension is to be avoided we must as an Association look to Home Rule and it alone as our business', he told an English supporter. 'On nearly every other subject the members utterly disagree'.[75] But even the very definition of Home Rule was far from certain. The Home Government Association attracted former Repealers and Young Irelanders, including the 1848 rebel John Martin, who won a by-election in Meath in 1871. At his victory banquet, Martin declared that he was elected on the principles of 'simple Repeal, and restoration of the national constitution suppressed by the Act of Union'. The only difference between his Young Ireland roots and the new politics of Home Rule, Martin implied, was merely the latter's absolute commitment to non-violent means.[76]

Home Rule as nationalist Repeal, rather than the unionist federalism articulated by Butt, surfaced repeatedly within political circles and printed works connected to the Home Government Association. This trend is most starkly highlighted in the short-lived weekly newspaper founded in September 1870, the *Federalist*. The *Federalist* was not the official organ of the Home Government Association, but an independent advocate of the federal movement. This is, however, not to say that the newspaper consistently championed the political idea of the newspaper's title. Addressing the question 'what is federalism?' in February 1871, the *Federalist* replied that it was 'the Repeal of the Legislative Union between Great Britain and Ireland'. A subsequent question, 'what is meant by Federal Repeal?' was answered by 'Simple Repeal accompanied by such securities against Ministerial craft and English usurpation, base and treacherous representatives, and political subserviency'.[77] Throughout the *Federalist's* six-month existence, there was not one discussion of the form of United Kingdom-wide federalism that Butt advocated; similarly, there was a profound lack of imperially minded discourse that harmonised with the sentiment of the federalist ideal. The *Federalist* insisted that 'our programme is the same as O'Connell's – simple Repeal', thus flattening out the nuances of Butt's articulation of federalism.[78] The stark difference between the rhetoric of Repeal and the imperial concerns of Irish Tories such as W. Foster Vesey-

[75] William O'Neill Daunt to J. Gleeson, 19 June 1873, Home Rule League Letter Book, PRONI, D213/9.

[76] *Freeman's Journal*, 7 February 1871.

[77] *Federalist*, 18 February 1871.

[78] *Federalist*, 25 February 1871.

Fitzgerald, who stressed above all else that 'there is no safety for the empire except in well-arranged federation', was obvious to contemporary observers.[79] The *Times* took an accurate snapshot of the confused nature of political culture in Ireland in 1871: 'Home Rule is in danger of being pulled in pieces between the advocates of Federalism, Separation, and simple Repeal.'[80]

This confusion was the price that Home Rule paid for rapid electoral success as a protest movement. On founding the Home Rule movement, Butt's working hypothesis was that it would assume the form of a small but significant pressure group, inspired by, and drawing energy from, national ideals, but ostensibly led by 'respectable' figures from Irish society. He warned Irish readers of his federalist pamphlet that patience was required, as the 'time may be far distant' when the ambition of constitutional reform would be realised. Indeed, in the first edition of *Irish Federalism*, he implied that he did not want to take Home Rule into the formal political arena.[81] The success of a number of individuals who adopted the banner of Home Rule to win by-elections from 1871 to 1873, coinciding with the collapse of Gladstone's constructive Irish policy, however, dramatically accelerated the timeline, forcibly shifting the new self-governing idea from the drawing rooms into parliament. This process occurred much quicker than Butt would have hoped, given (as he was aware) the lack of support for his scheme in Britain and the sense of confusion regarding the definition of Home Rule. Although he won a seat at a by-election in 1871, Butt was careful not to identify himself as a formal candidate sponsored by the Home Government Association; instead, he stood as an independent Home Ruler. During 1871, when other candidates preaching Irish self-government were winning parliamentary seats, Butt insisted to A. M. Sullivan that 'the Home Rule organisation as a body ought not to interfere at present in any election'.[82] His instinct was to demarcate the work of the Home Rule organisation and the parliamentarians – to separate the national movement from the political movement.

This cautious approach, however, quickly broke down as the idea of Irish self-government, if not of federalism, gained in popularity during the 1870s. After a handful of by-election victories in 1871 and 1872, the impatient John Martin pressured Butt to press for a Home Rule debate in parliament, a course of action the leader wished to avoid, as he was aware it

[79] *Freeman's Journal*, 24 January 1873. [80] *Times*, 19 October 1871.

[81] Butt, *Irish Federalism*, pp. iv, vi, 65.

[82] Butt to A. M. Sullivan, [1871], Butt Papers, NLI, MS 831.

would result in a demoralising defeat.[83] Thus, when he found himself leading a group of (nominally) fifty-nine Home Rule MPs after the 1874 general election, Butt was caught between Irish expectation for change and British hostility to it, which culminated in the heavy defeat of his self-government motion in the House of Commons. The failure to secure substantial concessions for Ireland in terms of land and education reform – still less federalism or any form of administrative devolution – left Butt's long-term conception of political change dangerously open to criticism from the more impatient activists in Ireland.

This was the context for the rise of obstructionism as a parliamentary weapon by an increasingly vocal wing of the Irish party. The obstructionists represented a grave threat not only to Butt's leadership of the movement, but also to his desire to articulate a constructive and 'loyal' political vocabulary in relation to Home Rule. The filibustering actions of Charles Stewart Parnell and Joseph Biggar from 1875 captured the Irish imagination in a way that Butt could not, and ultimately split the party.[84] The theatrical performances of Parnell and Biggar in the House of Commons also fatally undermined Butt's proselytising mission by raising the hackles of the British political classes. By 1878, the damage was such, in the context of Parnell's ascent, that the Irish Protestant historian Richard Bagwell proclaimed that 'Mr Butt's once notorious pamphlet is ancient history now'.[85] Parnell abandoned the last vestiges of federalism in favour of a 'simpler' Home Rule scheme on assuming the leadership of the Irish party in 1880. It is not a coincidence that this was a demand made by John Devoy, a leading figure in Clan na Gael, now the leading militant Irish-American association, as part of the 'New Departure' programme of combining constitutional and revolutionary strategies into a single national movement.[86]

These developments indicate the limited impact which Butt's 'notorious pamphlet' of 1870 achieved. His proposal for federalism was read widely throughout Britain, provoking comment pieces in many leading contemporary journals. Opinion was, however, staunchly against the profound constitutional change advocated by Butt. Reviews typically dwelt on the

[83] John Martin to Butt, 12 April 1872, Butt Papers, NLI, MS 8694(4).
[84] *Nation*, 8 and 15 July 1876.
[85] Richard Bagwell, 'Home Rulers at home', *Dublin University Magazine*, vol. 1, no. 2 (February 1878), p. 212.
[86] Michael Keyes, 'Parnellism: the role of funding in the journey from the semi-revolutionary to the purely constitutional', in Caoimhe Nic Dháibhéid and Colin W. Reid (eds.), *From Parnell to Paisley: Constitutional and Revolutionary Politics in Modern Ireland* (Dublin: Irish Academic Press, 2010), p. 16.

conjunctional and ideological obstacles to federalism: the alliance between Irish Tories and Repealers was believed to be temporary, meaning that the demand for Home Rule would collapse when Orange and Green would (inevitably) revert to form; moreover, the constitutional traditions that had evolved in the United Kingdom rendered federal schemes impossible to implement. Another important theme was the perception that there existed an incompatibility between the vices of Irish civil society and the responsibility of government, with the inherent danger of a clergy-driven oligarchy masquerading as democratic will in Ireland.[87] The Irish problem, from the vantage point of British observers, lay in the barbarous and utterly discordant political culture. Anthony Trollope hysterically dismissed the political lineage between O'Connell and Butt as 'the natural declension of a political disease'.[88] With its 'monster meetings', successive rebellions, and the lure of Fenianism, Ireland was, from an English perspective, an alien political place. British commentators spoke time and time again of the need for a more 'complete', 'equal', and 'real' Union between Great Britain and Ireland, but without any concrete ideas on how to achieve this aim.[89] The *unionist* underpinnings of Butt's proposal, and the potential benefits of institutionalising Irish sentiment within a redesigned Union, were largely overlooked by British reviewers, who maintained that federalism was an inappropriate framework for the United Kingdom.

Much to Butt's chagrin, his proposal was also rejected by the two foremost theorists of federalism in Britain, John Stuart Mill and Edward A. Freeman. As the politico-philosophical weight of these two thinkers was considerable, this posed an immense intellectual challenge to Butt's ambitious federal scheme, indirectly fuelling the rise of more 'simpler' notions of Irish self-government during the 1870s. Mill's *Considerations on Representative Government* (1861) contained a detailed discussion of the practicability of federalism, but he stopped far short of advocating such a scheme for the United Kingdom. There was, however, a marked change in his tone on Irish matters before and after the Fenian rebellion. While *Considerations* claimed that 'there is next to nothing', bar the 'memory of the past' and the outrageous position of the established church in Ireland to divide the British and Irish, his pamphlet from 1868, *England and*

87 'A review of Isaac Butt's *Irish Federalism*', *Edinburgh Review*, vol. 133 (April 1871), pp. 523, 525.

88 Anthony Trollope, *An Autobiography*, ed. Charles Morgan (London: Williams and Norgate Ltd., 1946; first published 1883), p. 79.

89 'Irish federalism', *Spectator*, 3 September 1870, p. 1057; 'The past and future relations of Ireland to Great Britain', *Macmillan's Magazine*, vol. 24 (May 1871), p. 43; 'The Irish temper', *Examiner*, 18 November 1871, p. 1134.

*Ireland*, was a tour de force in righteous anger directed at British policy in Ireland.[90] Despite this shift, Mill's hostility to federalism within the United Kingdom was unshakeable. For all of *England and Ireland's* rage against the injustice of the 'foreign' Irish land system, Mill refused to consider any tinkering with the structures of the Union. 'Separation would be disastrous', he argued: 'an attempt at federal union would be unsatisfactory while it lasted, and would end either in reconquest or in complete separation'.[91]

Such a rejection did not stop John George MacCarthy from drawing on Mill's oeuvre to make the point that Home Rule was not an unprecedented measure within the context of the empire. Mill's outline of the varieties of colonial self-governments in *Considerations* was utilised by MacCarthy to counter the British argument that federalism was a step into the unknown.[92] MacCarthy also exploited a perceived inconsistency in Mill's application of federalism. Mill's theory of representative government rested on the ideal of the nation-state: 'Where the sentiment of nationality exists in any force', he argued in *Considerations*, 'there is a prima facie case for uniting all the members of the nationality under the same government'. Later, in the same work, Mill describes the Irish as being 'sufficiently numerous to be capable of constituting a respectable nationality by themselves'.[93] MacCarthy struggled to square these assertions with Mill's refusal to consider granting Ireland a form of self-government within a larger federal framework.[94] MacCarthy failed to note, however, that Mill had several exceptions to the rule:

> Experience proves, that it is possible for one nationality to merge and be absorbed in another: and when it was originally an inferior and more backward portion of the human race, the absorption is greatly to its advantage. Nobody can suppose that it is not more beneficial to a Breton, or a Basque of French Navarre, to be brought into the current of the ideas and feelings of a highly civilised and cultivated people – to be a member of the French nationality . . . The same remark applies to the Welshman or the Scottish Highlander, as members of the British nation.[95]

Mill included the Irish in this category, too, believing that Ireland's political imagination had become diseased through decades of British misrule. The English-Scottish Union worked well, according to Mill,

[90] Mill, *Considerations*, p. 296.
[91] John Stuart Mill, *England and Ireland* (London: Longmans, Green, Reader, and Dyer, 1868), p. 36.
[92] MacCarthy, *Plea for the Home Government of Ireland*, p. 46.
[93] Mill, *Considerations*, pp. 289, 295.
[94] MacCarthy, *Plea for the Home Government of Ireland*, pp. 173–5.
[95] Mill, *Considerations*, p. 293.

because it enshrined Scottish cultural distinctiveness while promoting legislative unity of purpose.[96] What was needed was to address Irish grievances in a similar way: Irish ideas should play a prominent role in decision-making, but within the parameters of the existing United Kingdom. Mill believed that Ireland was not politically or culturally mature enough for any form of self-government, ensuring that the Union state must be proactive in tackling Irish problems before they became serious grievances. 'The difficulty of governing Ireland lies entirely in our own minds', Mill asserted in *England and Ireland*, 'it is an incapability of understanding'.[97] While Butt saluted Mill's regenerative economic ideas in relation to Ireland,[98] there was no common ground on the question of Home Rule.

While Mill found his work cited – and distorted – by Home Rulers, he did not actively participate in debate with the Irish constitutional reformers. In contrast, the other leading expert on federalism in Britain, the historian Edward A. Freeman, publicly condemned Butt's scheme. Freeman, who later presided over the Oxford University Home Rule League in the 1880s when Parnell was at his pomp,[99] delivered a series of devastating blows against federal Home Rule in 1873 and 1874. In an article in the *Fortnightly Review* in 1873 that reflected on developments in contemporary European federalist thought, Freeman concluded that a 'Federal union may be looked on as the half-way house between total separation and perfect union'. He added, however, a significant caveat to this potentially creative constitutional arrangement: 'it is the nature of a half-way house that people should meet at it whose faces are turned different ways. And it often makes all the difference in the world as to success or failure in which way a man's face is turned'.[100] Freeman did not address the notion of Irish and British federalism in the article, but it was clear that he believed that Ireland and Britain were facing different ways. The following year, after Butt had unsuccessfully moved a motion in the House of Commons to create a committee to investigate the 'present parliamentary relations between Great Britain and Ireland',[101] Freeman launched an assault on Irish ideas of federalism, dismissing Butt's plan as 'wild and impracticable'. What greatly animated Freeman, however, was MacCarthy's selective use of his work on federalism to buttress the Irish

[96] Ibid., p. 310. [97] Mill, *England and Ireland*, p. 42. [98] Butt, *Irish Deep Sea Fisheries*, p. 10.

[99] *Oxford University Home Rule League: List of Members, 1891* (Oxford: Alden and Co., [1891]), p. 3.

[100] E. A. Freeman, 'The growth of commonwealths', *Fortnightly Review*, vol. 14, no. 82 (October 1873), p. 455.

[101] *Hansard*, 30 June 1874, vol. 220, cols. 700–17.

case. As with his treatment of Mill, MacCarthy ignored Freeman's negative views on the utility of federalism in a British and Irish context, focusing instead on lines written by the historian that could be interpreted to philosophically support the Home Rule case. MacCarthy was returned to Westminster as the Member of Parliament for Mallow in 1874. In a parliamentary speech advocating Home Rule in July of that year, he cited a passage from Freeman's *History of Federal Government*: 'Federalism is the true solvent. It gives as much union as the members need, and not more than they need.' MacCarthy argued that this sanctioned the Home Rule case, more so when the present structure of centralised government – one that 'forces a system suitable only for one homogeneous community on two communities which are clearly not homogeneous' – was considered.[102]

Freeman rejected this reading of his work, referring MacCarthy to his theory that federalism only thrived in cases where the desired outcome was further unity, not a deeper sense of detachment. This was the besetting flaw in the Irish scheme when applied to the unified British state, and one that made references to the US model by Home Rulers intellectually redundant. 'I have always held that a Federal system is the right thing when it is a step in advance', Freeman asserted, 'but that it is a wrong thing when it is a step backwards'.[103] British and Irish understandings of how federalism might be applied to the United Kingdom were, in essence, fundamentally different: Home Rulers desired to split a unitary state to create a federal structure, a constitutional pattern that Mill, Freeman, and, later, A. V. Dicey viewed as destructive. For these thinkers, federalism only had utility as a unifier of small states, not a divider of a single polity, and was therefore not applicable to the United Kingdom. But this rebuttal did not stop MacCarthy, who drew on Freeman's own writings to advance the case that federalism was the only viable bridge to harmonise Ireland's relations with the wider Kingdom. He deployed a quote from Freeman's work that suggested that Ireland 'is too far off for the same perfect incorporation which unites the three parts of Great Britain', which MacCarthy read as an argument for a federal union.[104] The *Spectator*, which was sympathetic to the Irish cause during the 1870s, was impressed by MacCarthy's adroit use of Freeman's ideas to support an idea that the historian opposed, but delivered a grim judgement on the chances of

[102] Ibid., 2 July 1874, vol. 220, col. 878.
[103] E. A. Freeman, 'Federalism and Home Rule', *Fortnightly Review*, vol. 16, no. 92 (August 1874), p. 212.
[104] *Nation*, 12 September 1874.

bringing the federal project to fruition: 'The truth is, that unhappy as the relations between the two countries are, they are far too close to admit of the kind of separation implied in Federalism ... History has gone beyond the point where federalism is possible'.[105] That Freeman ended his life as an advocate for Gladstonian Home Rule, a very different concept to the first definition articulated by Butt and his circle, appeared to bear out the *Spectator's* gloomy forecast for federalism.

Federalism slipped off the Irish political agenda after Butt's failure to move a Home Rule motion in the House of Commons in 1874. By that year, P. J. Smyth, an influential old Repealer and Home Rule MP, was delivering blistering attacks on federalism, condemning the idea as a national heresy. He escalated this campaign from 1876 as the more radical Parnellite wing of the Irish party stepped up its campaign of parliamentary obstruction – a tactic that was strongly opposed by Butt.[106] The defeat of federal Home Rule, and its replacement with a simpler, more Irish-focused notion of self-government, marked an important demarcation in the evolution of political life in Ireland. By defining Home Rule as federalism rather than parliamentary devolution (as the scheme later became in British legislation during the 1880s), Butt's conception of the political nation lay within a United Kingdom greater than, but still representative of, its component parts. Home Rule as devolution undermined this cosmopolitan ideal, emphasising instead Ireland's uniqueness within the Union and its historical sense of grievance. Butt's abhorrence of this provincialism manifested itself in his firm opposition to 'simple' Repeal throughout the 1870s, a point that split the Home Rule movement before Parnell formally dropped the federalist baggage on assuming the leadership of the Irish party in 1880. The early 1870s represented something of a turning point, when ideas of federalism – and thus of cementing Ireland's place within the Union – were mainstream within Irish political culture; from 1880, this was resolutely not the case, as the rhetoric of self-government assumed a more exclusive and Ireland-centred form.

The exchanges between federal Home Rulers such as Butt, John George MacCarthy, and Thaddeus O'Malley, and the opponents of a federal United Kingdom, reveal much about contemporary ideas about the state, unitary sovereignty, and Ireland's place within the United Kingdom. The impossibility of federalising the United Kingdom was stressed by Mill and Freeman, and, later, Dicey, on the grounds that federalism was a tool to

105 *Spectator*, 12 September 1874. MacCarthy's letter to the *Nation* also appeared in this issue.

106 *Nation*, 6 June 1874; *Spectator*, 16 September 1876.

permit diverse states to achieve a sense of structured unity, rather than to allow a unified state to divide sovereignty and potentially follow the path of separatism. Reflecting on Butt's *Irish Federalism* pamphlet in 1882, Dicey believed the scheme to be the most revolutionary ever submitted to the British parliament.[107] Federalism, for Dicey, could only be successful when the component regions were driven by the need for unity, not the separatism which he believed underpinned the Irish demand. 'If there be no desire to unite', Dicey argued, 'there is clearly no basis for federalism'.[108] Even so, it is striking how unionist political thinkers from a variety of backgrounds returned to what was, in essence, Butt's federalist vision during the Home Rule crises in 1886 and 1912–14.[109] Moreover, Butt's influence stretched beyond his death in 1879. While the Parnellite strand of John Redmond's political leanings has received attention, his overlooked Buttite inheritance was equally a prominent aspect of his political personality, shaping his conciliatory rhetoric, imperial sensibilities, and openness to a federalist solution.[110]

Butt's federal ideal struggled to capture the hearts and minds of Irish nationalists for several reasons. There were considerable misunderstandings over the definition of Home Rule, with the unionism of Butt's political ideas undermined by the assumption that the new project of the 1870s was a resurrection of O'Connellism. Time and again, supposed advocates of federalism championed a 'return' to an old form of Irish government (such as Repeal of the Union), rather than a genuinely federal constitutional structure. This internal contradiction shaped the evolution of Irish nationalist discourse and actions from the mid 1870s through to the introduction of the first Home Rule Bill in 1886; the reaction against the conservative Buttite conception of the Irish future, which was born from frustration with its limited progress, subsequently radicalised the Parnellite agenda. By the early 1880s, the political landscape had changed, with federalism scrapped in favour of a version of Home Rule that was more imbued with a separatist sentiment. The Irish Tories, whom Butt had hoped to inspire to assume the leadership of the nation, fled the Home Rule movement,

[107] A. V. Dicey, 'Home Rule from an English point of view', *Contemporary Review*, vol. 42 (July 1882), p. 75.

[108] A. V. Dicey, *Introduction to the Study of the Law of the Constitution*, 3rd ed. (London: Macmillan and Co., 1889), p. 132.

[109] See, for example, John Kendle, *The Round Table Movement and Imperial Union* (Toronto: University of Toronto Press, 1975).

[110] Colin W. Reid, 'Isaac Butt's legacy: the Irish Parliamentary Party, 1879–1918', in Martin O'Donoghue and Emer Purcell (eds.), *John Redmond and Irish Parliamentary Traditions* (Dublin: UCD Press, 2024), pp. 20–31.

frightened by the spectre of a new nationalism that fused liberalism, Catholic democracy, and land agitation. Indeed, politics took a rather different turn after 1880, becoming increasingly bitter and polarised; the ideologies that shaped Ireland into the late nineteenth and twentieth centuries became more unconditional and uncompromising.

## The Centrality of Constitutionalism

One of the great ironies about Isaac Butt's political career was that he pioneered some of the more 'muscular' stances subsequently adopted with much aplomb by his successor, Charles Stewart Parnell. Butt's remarkable success in courting the IRB – which led to the Brotherhood acquiescing in a three-year trial of the parliamentary campaign – was a precursor of the 'New Departure', signalling the willingness of elements of the post-1867 Fenian leadership to explore the use of constitutional means. By the 1860s, Butt had established himself as one of the most prominent – and radical – writers urging a reform of the structures of land ownership, foreshadowing the rise of the Land League.[111] While Butt was firmly wedded to a federal solution to resolve the problems created by an overly centralised executive in the United Kingdom, the rhetorical concept of 'Home Rule', explicitly as a form of Irish self-government, dominated the political imagination across Ireland and Britain for almost forty years after his death.

For all of Butt's energetic and ground-breaking political activism, however, it was Parnell who reaped the successes. While Butt was eager to avoid combining the struggles for land reform and Home Rule for fear of merging the 'national' question with a class issue (and thus alienating landlords), Parnell had no such inhibition. Under Parnell's leadership of the Irish Parliamentary Party and the Land League during the early 1880s, the campaigns for Home Rule and radical land reform were fused, granting the otherwise abstract idea of self-government a distinctly material underpinning.[112] While Butt was proactive in seeking the tacit support of the IRB to demonstrate the potential of constitutional means to address the grievances represented by Fenianism, Parnell exploited militant sentiment to (occasionally) instil the unflinching rhetoric of separatism into the vocabulary of Home Rule.[113] In what would have been an astonishing

[111] For Butt's contributions to the debate on Irish land, see Reid, 'A voice for Ireland', pp. 55–74.

[112] Philip Bull, *Land, Politics and Nationalism: A Study of the Irish Land Question* (Dublin: Gill & Macmillan, 1996), pp. 97–8.

[113] Kelly, *Fenian Ideal*, p. 3.

act for the undisputed leader of constitutional nationalism, Parnell may have taken the IRB oath in 1882, days before the Phoenix Park murders, in which a Fenian splinter group assassinated two British officials.[114] Parnell played a dangerous game, but in many ways he was merely expanding on the rules sketched out by Butt during the 1860s and 1870s.

While Butt and Parnell were both unable to secure any form of Home Rule during their lifetimes, the posthumous reputation of the latter leader unquestionably eclipsed that of the former. Parnell was the romanticised, independent-minded national leader, revered even by many who favoured militant separatism such as Patrick Pearse.[115] Butt, in contrast, lingered in historical obscurity. An insightful coda to Butt's life, however, was made by Michael Davitt in his classic *The Fall of Feudalism in Ireland*, published in 1904. Davitt was a former member of the IRB and founder of the Land League. He was also a disciple of the influential American political economist Henry George, who advocated the nationalisation of land, which became a powerful undercurrent within the radical fringes of the Land League.[116] Davitt dedicated a chapter to Butt's career as a skilled polemicist on the land question in *The Fall of Feudalism*, recalling his importance in articulating the idea of fixity of tenure, which became vital Land League doctrine. 'If James Fintan Lalor was the prophet of Irish revolutionary land reform', opined Davitt, 'Isaac Butt was its immediate if more moderate precursor'. He was, in Davitt's reading, the 'reforming link' between the Tenant League of the 1850s and the Land League.[117] While Davitt emphasised the centrality of Fenianism in explaining the origins and organisational development of the Land League, his veneration for Butt as an intellectual father of the movement in *The Fall of Feudalism* was genuine.[118]

Despite his admiration for Butt, Davitt's own thinking on the land question greatly eclipsed the reputation of the old Home Rule chief. Indeed, Davitt is widely regarded as one of the most important social

114 Patrick Maume, 'Parnell and the IRB Oath', *Irish Historical Studies*, vol. 29, no. 115 (1995), pp. 363–70.

115 Pádraic H. Pearse, 'Ghosts', *in Collected Works of Pádraic H. Pearse: Political Writings and Speeches* (Dublin: Phoenix Publishing Co., Ltd., 1924), pp. 244–5.

116 For George's influence in Ireland, see Andrew Phemister, *Land and Liberalism: Henry George and the Irish Land War* (Cambridge: Cambridge University Press, 2023).

117 Michael Davitt, *The Fall of Feudalism in Ireland: Or the Story of the Land League Revolution* (London: Harper & Brothers, 1904), p. 79.

118 Ibid., p. 83. Owen McGee, *The IRB: The Irish Republican Brotherhood from the Land League to Sinn Féin* (Dublin: Four Courts Press, 2007), pp. 66–102, details the Fenian influence on the Land League.

thinkers in late nineteenth-century Ireland, a leading light of progressive agrarian and labourist causes who enjoyed a global status.[119] As Davitt's social radicalism was such a prominent component of his political identity, it is possible to overlook the centrality of constitutionalism – a belief in the inherent importance of the design of the polity – within his wider thought. In 1881, while incarcerated at Portland Prison in Dorset following a state crackdown of the Land League, Davitt penned a lengthy essay entitled 'Ireland's share of the British constitution: as seen in its government and parliamentary franchise'. It was a striking piece of work. Davitt argued that landlordism deprived the people across the United Kingdom of their 'natural rights' to the land, resulting in incredible privilege for a small group and poverty and hardship for the masses. The triumph of the landlord 'Monopoly' was, for Davitt, the 'one grand defect of English civilization and the principal flaw in the British Constitution'.[120] Davitt was well aware of the connections between land and political power; he explicitly argued several years later that a 'more equitable distribution of wealth' would result in a 'more real and just distribution of political power'.[121] But an understated premise of Davitt's reflections was a belief that the British constitution was, in abstract, an admirable construct. The House of Commons acted as an authentic British national convention, and Davitt believed that despite the propertied character of the representatives, 'its functions are probably as democratic and its powers as great as that of any assembly of any republic in the world'.[122] It did not, however, operate equitably for all its representatives.

One of Davitt's central aims in 'Ireland's share of the British constitution' was to demonstrate the constitutional inequalities in the design of the United Kingdom. The typical Englishman, according to Davitt, was able to enjoy substantial political freedoms, such as an extended franchise, equality before the law, unfettered movement throughout the Kingdom, the ability to possess a firearm, and stable government regardless of the party in power.[123] The liberties of the Englishman's Irish counterpart were, on the other hand, according to Davitt, drastically curtailed by a quasi-colonial form of governance that perceived the population as unfit for British rights. 'The Castle' – meaning Dublin Castle, the seat of

119 Vikram Visana, *Uncivil Liberalism: Labour, Capital and Commercial Society in Dadabhai Naoroji's Political Thought* (Cambridge: Cambridge University Press, 2022), p. 123.
120 Michael Davitt, *Jottings in Solitary*, ed. Carla King (Dublin: UCD Press, 2003), p. 41.
121 Michael Davitt, *Leaves from a Prison Diary; or, Lectures to a 'Solitary' Audience* (London: Chapman & Hall, 1885), p. 277.
122 Davitt, *Jottings in Solitary*, p. 38.
123 Ibid., pp. 35–6.

government in Ireland – symbolised the institutionalisation of conquest. This 'singular institution', for Davitt, was 'a Depot of centralised despotism without parallel in the government of any other civilized country'. 'The Castle', in other words, tarnished the British constitutional tradition. It resembled an authority 'situated at the mouth of the Yang-tse Kiang river' that 'was identified with the rule of the Celestial Empire, instead of standing on the banks of the Liffey and the representative of the British Constitution'.[124] Ireland's government was not accountable to Irish opinion: the legislative, executive, and judiciary elements of the polity were hostile to the political claims of the majority of people on the island.[125] An oddity of the British constitution, for Davitt, was the widespread assumption that its liberal form was found everywhere in the British world.[126] 'English opinion', Matthew Arnold recorded in 1882, 'attributes Irish misery to the faults of the Irish themselves', and not to the manifestation of poor government.[127] Much Irish political writing, Davitt included, can be interpreted as a plea to an *English* readership to engage with the problems inherent in the structures of Irish governance. Davitt imagined something like Dublin Castle in operation in England and concluded that the English people would overthrow such a tyrannical form of authority, as it represented the antithesis of the British constitution.[128] If the Union was a genuine partnership, why did such an imbalance in the structure of government continue indefinitely in Ireland?

Davitt's argument was that despite sending representatives to Westminster, the Irish were unrepresented in the upper echelons of public life. They were excluded from the levers of power and hostage to the agenda of others. While the United Kingdom resembled a liberal multinational polity, Davitt depicted Irish governance as tyrannical. He warned of the dangerous consequences if the Irish were denied control of their own political destiny:

> There never *can* be anything like peace or regard for the administration of Law in Ireland, while the sensitive people of that country see their fatherland in the clutches of such a gang and themselves and their rights as civilized men maligned, insulted and trampled upon by those who flaunt the stigmas of official, race, class, and religious ascendancy before their face in almost every transaction of Irish government.[129]

Davitt believed that when British statesmen learned 'to do full justice to Ireland, then and not till then will our people be contended or satisfied'.

[124] Ibid., p. 52. [125] Ibid., pp. 66–9. [126] Ibid., p. 51.
[127] Matthew Arnold, *Irish Essays and Others* (London: Smith, Elder, and Co., 1882), p. 12.
[128] Davitt, *Jottings in Solitary*, p. 66. [129] Ibid. Emphasis in original.

But this was not an O'Connellite choice between justice *or* the Repeal of the Act of Union; Davitt defined 'justice' explicitly *as* Repeal. The colonial structure of government – which Davitt likened to India in another essay – could not continue indefinitely for Ireland.[130] The Irish agitated for a parliament in Dublin not because of an unfulfilled national aspiration, Davitt concluded, but because Home Rule offered the only path to meaningful representative government.[131] Irish discontent with the British connection may have drawn from the well of nationalism, but it was, firmly and consistently, political at heart. It is telling that the first line of the introduction to Davitt's *The Fall of Feudalism in Ireland* centred on this theme: 'The genius of misgovernment has never been more wilfully blind in its methods or more persistent in the folly of political unwisdom than in the ways and means of England's rule in Ireland'.[132] The impulse for responsive, accountable, and fundamentally good government was a prominent component of Irish political thought, even in the mind of the agrarian agitator *par excellence* of the early 1880s.

130 Davitt, *Leaves from a Prison Diary*, p. 282.
131 Davitt, *Jottings in Solitary*, pp. 81–2.
132 Davitt, *Fall of Feudalism in Ireland*, p. xv.

# *Conclusion*

In 1879, Archibald Dobbs promoted the idea of proportional representation (PR) in Irish elections as 'the best method of ascertaining the depth and breadth of political opinion'. Dobbs was a barrister from a prominent Protestant family in Co. Antrim that claimed a rich heritage in national and local politics stretching back centuries.[1] Part of his advocacy of PR was connected to an effort to stymie 'agitators' gaining electoral success. '[Charles Stewart] Parnell and the Obstructionists are the worst foes of the men who could be responsible statesmen, of the able members of the Home Rule party', proclaimed Dobbs. He continued:

> I cannot take the point of view and attitude of the Home Rulers, so far as I know it, nor can I take the English point of view. But my present task is to endeavour to obtain a full and free and real representation for Ireland, believing as I do in the great fund of good stored up in the hearts of her people.[2]

Dobbs's plea for PR laid bare the central crisis of the Union: even its defenders desired to reform a system that had failed to represent Ireland's political realities.

When Dobbs wrote these words, straddling the middle ground between the Home Rulers and the 'English point of view' was becoming increasingly untenable. The 'agitators' in Westminster became a disciplined parliamentary party under the leadership of Parnell, which in turn inspired pro-union representatives to organise on a more professional basis.[3] This

[1] Samuel McSkimin, *The History and Antiquities of the County of the Town of Carrickfergus. From the Earliest Records till 1839*, new ed., with notes by E. J. McCrum (Belfast: Mullan & Son, James Cleeland, Davidson & McCormack, 1909), p. 487.

[2] Archibald E. Dobbs, *Representative Reform for Ireland* (London: Spottiswoode & Co., 1879), pp. 3, 55, 60, 68.

[3] Conor Cruise O'Brien, *Parnell and His Party, 1880–1890* (Oxford: Oxford University Press, 1957). Alvin Jackson, *The Ulster Party: Irish Unionists in the House of Commons, 1884–1911* (Oxford: Oxford University Press, 1989).

renewed parliamentary activism mirrored the increasing antagonism within Irish (and British) political culture more generally into the 1880s. The principle of Irish self-government gained a radical agrarian edge through the Land War of the early 1880s; the introduction of Home Rule legislation in 1886 drove liberal unionists into the ranks of the Conservatives; and support for the Union in the north of Ireland manifested itself in militant forms. Politics in Ireland adopted an air of intractability. As Dobbs feared, the first-past-the-post electoral system exaggerated the strength of regionalised majority interests, contributing to the geographical (north-south) and confessional (Protestant-Catholic) polarisation that increasingly defined Irish politics from the 1880s.

The question of Home Rule dominated Irish and British politics from the 1880s to the First World War. For many people in Ireland, the scheme was the expected future of Irish governance.[4] Home Rulers won the majority of the Irish seats in Westminster in every election from 1874 to 1910, before being replaced by the separatist Sinn Féin party in 1918. The nature of representative politics within the multi-union polity that was the United Kingdom frayed from the late nineteenth century: if representative government required the consent of a parliamentary majority for legitimacy, how were competing national majorities – Irish and British – to be reconciled?[5] There was no constitutional mechanism recognising the status of Home Rule as the majority opinion within Ireland, rendering representative politics a frustrating pastime for champions of Irish self-government.

An important criticism of the British parliamentary model made by the Repealers in the 1830s and 1840s was that the numerical imbalance of seats across the four countries of the United Kingdom effectively locked Irish MPs out of government. For John O'Connell, this constitutional truth ensured that the parliamentary representation of Ireland was 'indisputably defective'.[6] Given the additional problem of the colonial dimensions of the Irish administration, it proved difficult to make a case that the Union provided Ireland with a representative government. Erskine Childers developed this argument in 1911, likening the Irish government to 'a British Crown Colony where the Executive is outside popular control, and the Legislature is only partially within it'.[7] The structure of

[4] James McConnel, *The Irish Parliamentary Party and the Third Home Rule Crisis* (Dublin: Four Courts Press, 2013), p. 222.

[5] Bernard Manin, *The Principles of Representative Government* (Cambridge: Cambridge University Press, 1997), p. 190.

[6] John O'Connell, *An Argument for Ireland* (Dublin: John Browne, 1844), pp. 3–4.

[7] Erskine Childers, *The Framework of Home Rule* (London: Edward Arnold, 1911), p. 188.

government and the nature of representation thus continued to be potent issues animating the Home Rule debates. The context from the 1880s was, however, different from the pre-Parnell age: land became more explicitly connected to the campaign for self-government, and Irish political communities became more rigidly defined and guided by majoritarianism in their arguments, culminating with the Ulster unionists claiming a democratic right to self-determination outside any Home Rule settlement.[8]

The revolution in Irish nationalist and unionist party politics from the 1880s – more professional parliamentary movements and a focus on building grassroots organisations – was underpinned by attempts to create rival monolithic blocs, unified through the adoption of a pro- or anti-Home Rule stance. This is not to say there were singular unionist and nationalist ideological visions for the Irish constitution – on the contrary, there remained considerable dissension within these blocs[9] – but 'party' became the dominant paradigm for the articulation of political ideas. This process was also occurring in Britain and elsewhere: the independently minded representative in Westminster was becoming obsolete, replaced by party men.[10] A trickle-down effect was the weakening of the non-party-aligned pamphleteer, as printed material assumed a more partisan identity. Both the Home Rule movement and their Irish unionist rivals created press agencies for the dissemination of political ideas: party-sponsored pamphlets, leaflets, and tracts were produced in vast amounts throughout the late Victorian and Edwardian periods.[11] These remain a vibrant set of political works, but the core messages were heavily refracted through the prism of the organised parties. Much of the published material examined in this book displayed a more independent streak, reflecting the lack of stable parliamentary blocs. While the history of Irish politics is typically one of crisis and drama involving two seemingly binary perspectives, the

[8] Margaret O'Callaghan, *British High Politics and a Nationalist Ireland: Criminality, Land and the Law under Forster and Balfour* (Cork: Cork University Press, 1994), p. 4; Colin W. Reid, 'Democracy, sovereignty and unionist political thought during the revolutionary period in Ireland, c.1912–1922', *Transactions of the Royal Historical Society*, vol. 27 (2017), pp. 211–32.

[9] Richard Bourke, 'Introduction', in Richard Bourke and Niamh Gallagher (eds.), *The Political Thought of the Irish Revolution* (Cambridge: Cambridge University Press, 2022), p. xxx.

[10] William Selinger, *Parliamentarism: From Burke to Weber* (Cambridge: Cambridge University Press, 2019), p. 196.

[11] Patrick Maume, *The Long Gestation: Irish Nationalist Life, 1891–1918* (Dublin: Gill & Macmillan, 1999), p. 9; Margaret O'Callaghan, 'Franchise reform, "first past the post", and the strange case of unionist Ireland', *Parliamentary History*, vol. 16, no. 1 (1997), p. 97; Colin W. Reid, *The Lost Ireland of Stephen Gwynn: Irish Constitutional Nationalism and Cultural Politics, 1864–1950* (Manchester: Manchester University Press, 2011), p. 79.

fluidity of thought and range of rhetorical influences evident in the published arena before 1880 is striking. O'Connellites such as Thomas Wyse found space to articulate a desire for closer union with Britain, while Tories such as Samuel Ferguson critiqued the British connection and called for the restoration of Irish self-government.[12]

Returning to Archibald Dobbs: the merits or otherwise of PR was an issue that was debated in Britain during the nineteenth century, and Dobbs offers a distinctly Irish perspective.[13] His proposal for PR was a wish to see a *different* kind of Irish representative returned to Westminster, weakening the influence of what he termed the 'caucus' element that had gained an electoral stronghold.[14] Electoral reform was a path, according to Dobbs, to secure the representation of the 'fullness and variety in political life' in Ireland, which would indirectly imbue the Union with a stronger sense of legitimacy.[15] But while Dobbs believed in the potential transformative impact of a different electoral system, this would not, in itself, alter the structures of representative government as understood by several generations of writers who favoured the restoration of a parliament in Ireland. Even with PR, the ability of Irish MPs, as *Irish* MPs, to effect change in Westminster would remain as elusive as ever. What Dobbs did not record was that part of the rationale for ongoing parliamentary obstructionism was the hopelessness felt on the Home Rule benches in realising their primary political goal, despite representing a majority of Irish constituencies.

While the recklessness of obstructionism frustrated and alienated many observers in Ireland – not least Isaac Butt, the leader of the Home Rule League – the tactic highlighted the limitations of parliamentarianism in Ireland by the late 1870s. Three to four generations of Irish representatives had gone to Westminster since the Union became operational, and the powerlessness of these parliamentarians had become internalised. The period of the Union is often depicted in historiography as the era of 'British rule in Ireland'.[16] For late nineteenth-century critics, this was

[12] Thomas Wyse, *Historical Sketch of the Late Catholic Association of Ireland*, 2 vols. (London: Henry Colburn, 1829), ii, pp. 120–1; Mary Catherine Ferguson, *Sir Samuel Ferguson in the Ireland of his Day*, 2 vols. (Edinburgh: William Blackwood and Sons, 1896), i, p. 246.

[13] The debates over PR form a major part of Gregory Conti's *Parliament the Mirror of the Nation: Representation, Deliberation, and Democracy in Victorian Britain* (Cambridge: Cambridge University Press, 2019).

[14] Dobbs, *Representative Reform*, pp. 3, 10.

[15] Ibid., p. 11.

[16] The term is ubiquitous. See, for example, Stephen Howe, *Ireland and Empire: Colonial Legacies in Irish History and Culture* (Oxford: Oxford University Press, 2000), p. 90; D. George Boyce, *Nationalism in Ireland*, 3rd ed. (London: Routledge, 1995), p. 197. Also see Ciaran O'Neill, *Power and Powerless in Union Ireland: Life in a Palliative State* (Oxford: Oxford University Press, 2024), p. 9, for a discussion of similar phrasings.

precisely the problem: it was British rule *in* Ireland, with little scope for Irish political influence over decision-makers. This rationalisation aided a shift in political language, away from the 'justice, or Repeal' mantra of the O'Connellites from the 1830s. One of the most prominent obstructionists, Frank Hugh O'Donnell, recorded that 'it was not the misgovernment of Ireland which troubled us, but its government, good, bad, or indifferent, by anyone but the Irish nation'.[17] O'Connell had emphasised 'good' government above 'Irish' government; O'Donnell represented the changed national zeitgeist that reversed the formula in the later nineteenth century.

While O'Donnell increasingly became an erratic presence in political and cultural life following his stint in parliament – his colleague, Tim Healy, christened him 'Crank' Hugh O'Donnell – he personified a palpable shift in Irish thinking regarding the constitutional connection between Ireland and Britain.[18] Home Rule – and later, the political independence desired by Sinn Féin – stressed the primacy of *Irish* government over all other concerns in imagining the ideal constitutional framework for Ireland. The language of national right and the illegitimacy of a more imperially framed model of government had become enshrined in Irish political culture. 'Even if a country were prospering under foreign rule', stressed Stephen Gwynn in a pro-Home Rule pamphlet in 1911, 'its honour and its dignity should force it to demand the privilege of freedom, which is the right to manage its own affairs'.[19] In some ways, the logic was closer to the mid-Victorian IRB than Daniel O'Connell's Repeal movement, despite the latter's apparent constitutional nationalist kinship with the Home Rulers. The evolution of constitutional thinking in Ireland was not as linear as it appears on the surface.

Irish thinkers, whether radical, Tory, or republican, grappled with one of the Enlightenment's unanswered questions: how the political freedom of a small country can survive within a multinational state. The answers varied dramatically. O'Connell's restorative Repeal movement invoked an Irish 'ancient constitution' of sorts, while Young Ireland embraced popular sovereignty. Federalists attempted to reconcile Irish autonomy with imperial unity, and Fenians rejected both in favour of revolutionary democracy. What united these visions was a shared insistence that a legitimate

[17] F. Hugh O'Donnell, *A History of the Irish Parliamentary Party*, 2 vols. (London: Longmans, Green, and Co., 1910), i, p. 175.
[18] Paul A. Townend, *The Road to Home Rule: Anti-Imperialism and the Irish Nationalist Movement* (Madison: University of Wisconsin Press, 2016), p. 183.
[19] Stephen Gwynn, *The Case for Home Rule: With an Introduction by John E. Redmond* (Dublin: Maunsel and Co., [1911]), p. 5.

government required mechanisms to translate Irish voices into power. The structures of incorporating Union ultimately proved unable to meet this challenge.

While the Union and the perceived problems of governing Ireland framed Irish political thinking, this was never static. Ideological perspectives changed over time, meaning that the arguments of, say, the 1840s were not the same as those of the 1870s. While the neatness of a singular 'Irish Question' is appealing, it assumes an unchanging ideological context. Concepts changed, even if words did not. 'Self-government', for example, could imply a restoration of the pre-1800 Irish parliament, a new federal constitution for the United Kingdom, or an independent Irish republic. A parliament in Dublin could, therefore, be imagined as a nationalist, unionist, and republican aspiration; we cannot assume that advocates of 'self-government' shared the same rationale for their respective positions. The Union acutely shaped Irish political debate, but the responses it generated were not necessarily rooted in zero-sum identity politics. The variety and richness of constitutional ideas articulated in Ireland across the nineteenth century go some way to liberating Irish history from the expectation that the political cultures on the island were rooted in stationary, binary blocs.

While religion was unquestionably a central component of Irish political thought, this again should not be reduced to preconceived and rigid assumptions. The Union was passed in 1800 despite significant opposition from the Anglican elite in Ireland; and while Catholic exclusion politicised denominational identity, a number of Protestants rallied to the banner of equal civic rights in Ireland. Political goals associated with Irish Catholics – the Repeal of the Union and Home Rule, for example – attracted the support of Protestants at various points. While it made sense for William McComb to polemically assert that Repeal 'is essentially a Roman Catholic interest' in 1841, the emergence of the religiously diverse Young Ireland the following year, and the Protestant Repeal Association during the Famine, complicates such a denominationally predetermined reading of Irish politics.[20]

There was another, more subtle dynamic at play within religious politics in Ireland. Irish Tory political arguments during the era of O'Connell often drew on a reading of history that equated liberty with Protestantism, with the counter-image of Catholicism as despotism.[21] These arguments

[20] William McComb, *The Repealer Repulsed! A Correct Narrative of the Rise and Progress of the Repeal Invasion of Ulster*, ed. Patrick Maume (Dublin: UCD Press, 2003; first published 1841), p. 4.

[21] See, for example, T. D. Gregg, *Free Thoughts on Protestant Matters*, 2nd ed. (Dublin: W. Curry, Jr., & Co., 1847), p. 43; *Dublin University Magazine*, October 1844, p. 443.

were not, of course, uniquely Irish – Linda Colley cited Protestantism and the othering of Catholicism as forms of political glue that held together British constitutional identity in the eighteenth century – but they persisted longer and with more intensity in Ireland.[22] That Protestants were a minority in Ireland explains this phenomenon. If Protestantism was equated with liberty, then schemes that potentially empowered Catholics in Ireland – Emancipation, Repeal, Home Rule – represented a grave existential threat to that liberty. The clericalism of the O'Connellite movement, the first mass democratic movement in Ireland, only confirmed the fears of its enemies – Irish Tories and, later, the Fenians – that its ambition was to create a new Catholic political ascendancy. But while nineteenth-century Irish Protestant politics retained its seventeenth-century fear of Jacobitism, the state moved on. The idea of a 'Protestant constitution' came under increasing stress as the United Kingdom liberalised its civic restrictions on non-Anglican denominations during the 1820s, which contributed to the palpable sense of abandonment and the renewed call for self-reliance within Irish Tory ranks in the 1830s and 1840s.

The connection between Protestantism and liberty was also challenged from another source, as the Catholic Association and later Repeal associations increasingly embraced progressive languages to confront the injustice of political exclusion. In contrast to its European counterparts, the Catholic Church in Ireland gained a radical political image through its association with the O'Connellite movements.[23] Daniel O'Connell explicitly fused Catholicism with the language of political liberty, in a direct rebuff to his Irish Protestant critics. In denouncing the Corn Laws in 1842, for example, O'Connell recorded that the taxes were 'unchristian and uncatholic, because they are unjust and oppressive'.[24] This rhetorical dynamic helps to explain some of O'Connell's apparently crass statements relating to religion, such as the Irish people being 'morally superior' to the English on account of their Catholicism. While this can be read as an unsavoury form of bigotry, O'Connell was rather clumsily depicting Catholicism as a political identity imbued with the virtues of dignity,

[22] Linda Colley, *Britons: Forging the Nation, 1707–1837* (New Haven, CT: Yale University Press, 1992).

[23] K. Theodore Hoppen, 'Riding a tiger: Daniel O'Connell, reform, and popular politics in Ireland, 1800–1847', *Proceedings of the British Academy*, vol. 100 (1999), p. 122.

[24] Daniel O'Connell, *Observations on Corn Laws, on Political Pravity and Ingratitude, and on Clerical and Personal Slander, in the Shape of a Meek and Modest Reply to the Second Letter of the Earl of Shrewsbury, Waterford, and Wexford* (Dublin: Samuel J. Machen, 1842), p. 15.

patriotism, and justice.[25] Denominational differences were, therefore, an essential component of nineteenth-century Irish life but not in a narrow sectarian manner: religious ideas informed political thought in more profound ways.

The Irish political imagination of the nineteenth century was, then, a contested arena where unionists, anti-unionists, republicans, and federalists grappled with the question of how a people (however defined) could achieve meaningful representative government. Rather than settling Ireland's place in the United Kingdom, the theory and practice of the Acts of Union ignited an unending crisis of representation, one that British policy exacerbated through indifference, coercion, and legislative half-measures. Catholic Emancipation conceded rights without the ability to influence power; conciliatory government ventures ignored the rationale for self-rule; and federalism, the most creative attempt to reconcile Irish autonomy with imperial unity, was dismissed out of hand within British opinion. The limitations of these responses contributed to the slow decline of the legitimacy of the Union within Ireland. The rupture, when it came in the twentieth century, was not a complete surprise.

The tragedy of Irish political thought is that its richest debates briefly flourished precisely when the future seemed most open. Many of the more ideologically fluid positions investigated in this book – Repealers seeking the importation of British liberties into Ireland, Tory federalists making the case for Irish self-government – found their positions increasingly untenable by the later nineteenth century. With the Land War, the rise of Parnell, and the hardening of nationalist and unionist orthodoxies during the Home Rule crisis of the 1880s, the grey zone within Irish political thought was profoundly reduced, but not eliminated altogether. New political ambitions emerged, but the questions raised between 1798 and 1879 did not completely vanish. Many nineteenth-century insights – the possibility of multiple parliaments within a polity, the appropriate constituent power(s), and the language of self-government – resurfaced in later constitutional crises over Home Rule, partition, and independence. The Good Friday Agreement's revision of the Union, its fragile balancing of sovereignty, and recognition of the legitimacy of competing ideological platforms also drew from the well of nineteenth-century Irish political thinking.

The ideological perspectives examined in this book left powerful legacies. The appeal of repealing the Union lay not in nostalgia for Grattan's

[25] *First Letter of Daniel O'Connell, Esq., on the Repeal of the Union* (Dublin: T. O'Flanagan, 1830), pp. 1, 3.

Parliament, but in the stark reality that Ireland's voice went unheard in Westminster: this informed the later Home Rule struggle. Republicanism gained force in the twentieth century not because the Irish were 'destined' for separation, but because the Union, as practised, offered neither dignity nor democracy. Federalism remains an attractive proposition to observers eager to provide a regulatory framework for the United Kingdom's devolved administrations in the twenty-first century. If there were few British adherents of the idea during the era of Isaac Butt, the contemporary constitutional challenges of devolution, secessionist nationalism, and Brexit have focused minds on ways and means to keep the United Kingdom together. As David Armitage has mischievously quipped, '[w]e are all federalists now'.[26]

The development of representative government in Ireland was never a linear progression, but a contested and contingent process, shaped as much by ideological creativity as by the constraints of sectarianism and national conflict. These debates transcend their time and place, offering important insights into the complexities of sovereignty within multinational states.[27] At their core, Irish political thinkers reimagined several fundamental relationships, such as between people and their representatives, and between local autonomy and centralised power.

Irish grievance in the period covered in this book was articulated powerfully through the language of exclusion: a Protestant political nation that denied Catholic participation; the disenfranchisement of the forty-shilling freeholder and restrictions on Irish suffrage; Irish MPs rendered powerless in the face of the British majority in Westminster; policymaking detached from local accountability; and, ultimately, the denial of the dignity of self-government, a classical trait that was recast in the age of nationalism. Each exclusion slowly eroded the Union's legitimacy while enabling constitutional innovation, as the marginalised in each of these scenarios developed new ways to imagine political inclusion. Ideas of representative government in Ireland sheds light on how political exclusion was experienced and how the excluded redefined power.

[26] David Armitage, 'Conclusion: we have always been federal', in Robert Schütze and Stephen Tierney (eds.), *The United Kingdom and the Federal Idea* (Oxford: Hart Publishing, 2018), p. 277.

[27] Natasha Wheatley, *The Life and Death of States: Central Europe and the Transformation of Modern Sovereignty* (Princeton, NJ: Princeton University Press, 2023), p. 2. Also see Alvin Jackson, *United Kingdoms: Multinational Union States in Europe and Beyond, 1800–1925* (Oxford: Oxford University Press, 2023).

# *Select Bibliography*

## Primary Sources

### *Contemporary Pamphlets, Books and Collected Correspondence*


'A.N.', *Thoughts on the Constitutional Rights of Parliament, Respecting the Power of Surrendering the Legislative Independence of Ireland* (Dublin: V. Dowling, 1798).

Anon., *A Loyal Subject's Thoughts on an Union between Great Britain and Ireland* (Dublin: J. Milliken, 1799).

*Necessity of an Incorporate Union Between Great Britain & Ireland Proved From the Situation of both Kingdoms: with a Sketch of the Principles upon which it Ought to be Formed* (London: J. Wright, 1799).

*A Report of the Debate in the House of Commons of Ireland, on Tuesday and Wednesday the 22nd and 23rd of January, 1799, on the Subject of an Union* (Dublin: James Moore, 1799).

*A Report of the Debate of the Irish Bar, on Sunday, the 9th of December, 1798, on the Subject of an Union of the Legislatures of Great Britain and Ireland* (Dublin: J. Moore, 1799).

*To Be, or Not To Be, a Nation: That is the Question?* (Dublin: Joseph Mehain, 1799).

*An Exposition of the Principal Terms of Union, and its Probable Effects on Ireland* (Dublin: J. Milliken, 1800).

*A Report of the Debate in the House of Commons of Ireland, on Wednesday and Thursday the 15th and 16th of January, 1800 on an Amendment to the Address Moved by Sir Laurence Parsons, on the Subject of An Union* (Dublin: James Moore, 1800).

*Catholic Emancipation: An Accurate Report of the Speeches Delivered in both Houses of the Imperial Parliament of Great Britain, on the Subject of the Petition of the Roman Catholics of Ireland, for a Repeal of the Existing Penal Laws* (Liverpool: W. Jones, 1805).

*State of Ireland Considered, with an Enquiry into the History and Operation of Tithe; and a Plan for Modifying that System, and Providing an Adequate Maintenance for the Catholic and Presbyterian Clergy*, 2nd ed. (Dublin: Downes and Reilly, 1810).

*Prudence True Patriotism; or, an Exposure of the Arts, Views and Characters of the Catholic Directory* (Dublin: John Barlow, 1815).
*Review of the Conduct of the Orange Party, during the Election for the City of Dublin* (Dublin: no publishing house, 1820).
*Triumph of Justice and Liberty over Tyranny and Oppression, Through the Influence of the Catholic Clergy* (London: W. E. Andrews, [1826]).
*The Repeal of the Legislative Union of Great Britain and Ireland, Considered* (London, James Ridgeway, 1830).
*Cursory Observations on the State of Ireland* (Dublin: printed for the author, 1831).
*Ireland. Ignorance. 'Repeal'* (London: James Ridgway, 1833).
*Plain and Practical Hints, for the Serious Consideration of all Protestants, and Particularly of Conservatives, by a Member of that Society* (Dublin: Richard M. Tims, 1833).
*Ireland. Ignorance. 'Repeal'* (London: James Ridgway, 1833).
*The Address of the Metropolitan Conservative Society of Ireland to the Protestants of Great Britain, Along with a Speech Delivered by Doctor Meyler* (Dublin: W. Warren, 1840).
*Repeal, or No Repeal: Repeal of the Union Considered in its Practical Bearings* (London: James Ridgway and Sons, 1833).
*Instructions for the Appointment of Repeal Wardens and Collectors of the Repeal Fund* (Dublin: J. Browne, 1843).
*Essays on the Repeal of the Union, to which the Association Prizes were Awarded; with a Supplemental Essay, Recommended by the Judges* (Dublin: James Duffy, 1845).
*Catalogue of the Law and Miscellaneous Library of the Late Daniel O'Connell, Esq, MP, which will be Sold by Auction, by Order of the Executors, by John F. Jones* (Dublin: no publishing house, 1849).
Arnold, Matthew, *Irish Essays and Others* (London: Smith, Elder, and Co., 1882).
Auckland, Lord, *Substance of the Speech of Lord Auckland, in the House of Peers, April 11, 1799, on the Proposed Address to His Majesty, Respecting the Resolutions Adopted by the Two Houses of Parliament, as the Basis of an Union Between Great Britain and Ireland* (Dublin: J. Milliken, 1799).
'Atticus', *To the People of Ireland* (no publishing details, [1800]).
'Author of the *Necessity of an Incorporate Union between Great Britain and Ireland*', *Competency of the Parliaments of Great Britain and Ireland to Incorporate their Legislatures; With Some Remarks Upon the Debate in the Irish House of Lords upon the Address* (Dublin: J. Milliken, 1799).
Ball, Charles, *An Union Neither Necessary or Expedient for Ireland: Being an Answer to the Author of* Arguments For and Against an Union, Between Great Britain and Ireland, Considered (Dublin: William Porter, 1798).
Barnes, George, *The Rights of the Imperial Crown of Ireland Asserted and Maintained, Against Edward Cooke, Esq., Reputed Author of a Pamphlet, Entitled* 'Arguments For and Against an Union, &c' (Dublin: W. Gilbert, 1799).
Barrington, Jonah, *Rise and Fall of the Irish Nation* (Dublin: James Duffy, 1833).
Battersby, W. J., *The Repealer's Manual or, the Union Reconsidered*, 3rd ed. (Dublin: T & J Coldwell, 1837).

de Beaumont, Gustave, *Ireland: Social, Political and Religious*, ed. and trans. W. C. Taylor (Cambridge, MA: Harvard University Press, 2006; first published 1839).

Bethal, Isaac Burke, *A Reply to the Gentleman who has Published a Pamphlet Entitled* Arguments For and Against an Union, *in which Mr McKenna's* Memoire *is Taken into Consideration* (Dublin: W. Gilbert, 1799).

Bonner, Hypatia Bradlaugh, *Charles Bradlaugh: A Record of his Life and Work*, 2 vols. (London: T. Fisher Unwin, 1894).

Boyton, Charles, *Speech Delivered by the Rev. C. Boyton, FTCD, at a Meeting of the Protestant Conservative Society, on Tuesday, the 10th July, 1832* (Dublin: J. Hoare, 1832).

*Observations on the Church; its Relation to the State; the Authority of its Governors; and the Duties and Obligations of its Ministers* (Dublin: Milliken and Son, 1838).

Bradlaugh, Charles, *The Irish Question: What it has been, what it is, and how to deal with it* (London: Austin & Co., [1868]).

Brougham, Henry, Lord, *Historical Sketches of Statesmen who Flourished in the Time of George III, to which are added Remarks on the French Revolution*, third series (London: Charles Knight and Co., 1843).

Bullen, Edward (ed.), *Five Reports of the Committee of the Precursor Association* (Dublin: Richard Grace, 1839).

Burke, Edmund, *A Letter from the Right Hon. Edmund Burke, MP in the Kingdom of Great Britain, to Sir Hercules Langrishe, MP, on the Subject of Roman Catholics of Ireland, and the Propriety of Admitting Them to the Elective Franchise Consistently with the Principles of the Constitution Established at the Revolution* (Dublin: J. Byrne, 1792).

[Bushe, Charles Kendal], *The Union: Cease Your Funning, or the Rebel Detected*, 4th ed. (Dublin: James Moore, 1798).

Butt, Isaac, *Repeal of the Union: the Substance of a Speech Delivered in the Corporation of Dublin, on 28th February, 1843, on Mr O'Connell's Motion to Petition for a Repeal of the Legislative Union* (Dublin: William Curry, Jr. and Co., 1843).

*A Voice for Ireland, the Famine in the Land: What Has Been Done and What is to be Done* (Dublin: J. McGlashan, 1847).

*Land Tenure in Ireland; a Plea for the Celtic Race*, 3rd ed. (Dublin: John Falconer, 1866).

*Fixity of Tenure: Heads of a Suggested Legislative Enactment*, 2nd ed. (Dublin: John Falconer, 1867).

*The Irish People and Irish Land: A Letter to Lord Lifford* (Dublin: John Falconer, 1867).

*The Irish Querist: a Series of Questions Proposed for the Consideration of All Who Desire to Solve the Problem of Ireland's Social Condition* (Dublin: John Falconer, 1867).

*Ireland's Appeal for Amnesty: A Letter to the Right Hon. W. E. Gladstone, MP* (Glasgow: Cameron and Ferguson, 1870).

*Home Government for Ireland: Irish Federalism! Its Meanings, its Objects, and its Hopes*, 4th ed. (Dublin: Irish Home Rule League, 1874; first published 1870).

*The Irish Deep Sea Fisheries: a Speech, Delivered at a Meeting of the Home Government Association, 1871* (Dublin: Irish Home Rule League, 1874).

*Coercion for Ireland: A Speech Delivered in the House of Commons on the Second Reading of the Peace Preservation (Ireland) Bill, March 23rd, 1875* (no publishing details, [1875]).

*The Parliamentary Policy of Home Rule: An Address Delivered to the Electors of the City of Limerick, 23 September 1875* (Dublin: McGlashan and Gill, 1875).

[Carey, William], *The Warning Protest of an Irish Roman Catholic, Against Every Interference, Change, or Arrangement in the Discipline and Constitution of the Roman Catholic Church in Ireland, as a Compromise or Barter for Catholic Emancipation, Respectfully Addressed to the Members of the Two Houses of Parliament*, 5th ed. (Dublin: Richard Coyne, 1813).

Carlyle, Thomas, *Chartism* (London: James Frazer, 1840; first published 1839).

*Past and Present* (London: Chapman & Hall, 1843).

Castlereagh, Lord, *The Speech of the Right Hon. Lord Viscount Castlereagh, Upon Delivering to the House of Commons of Ireland, His Excellency the Lord Lieutenant's Message on the Subject of an Incorporating Union with Great Britain, with the Resolutions Containing the Terms on which it is Proposed to Carry that measure into Effect, 5 February 1800* (Dublin: J. Milliken, 1800).

Childers, Erskine, *The Framework of Home Rule* (London: Edward Arnold, 1911).

'Civis', *Thoughts on the Repeal of the Union* (Dublin: Richard Moore, 1831).

Colquhoun, J. C., *The Uses of the Established Church to the Protestantism and Civilization of Ireland*, 2nd ed. (London: Hatchards, 1839).

Collis, John, *An Address to the People of Ireland, on the Projected Union* (Dublin: James Moore, 1799).

Connor, William, *The True Political Economy of Ireland: or, Rank-Rent the One Great Cause of all her Evils: with its Remedy* (Dublin: W. F. Wakeman, 1835).

[Cooke, Edward], *Arguments For and Against an Union, Between Great Britain and Ireland, Considered*, 2nd ed. (Dublin: J. Milliken, 1799).

[Croker, J. W.], *A Sketch of the State of Ireland, Past and Present* (Dublin: M. N. Mahon, 1810).

Daunt, William J. O'Neill, *Mr Daunt's Speech at the Repeal Association, in Refutation of the Anti-Repeal Fallacies Adopted from Spring Rice and Others by Lord Shrewsbury, also Mr Daunt's Speech at the Meeting Held in Edinburgh for Repeal* (Dublin: J. Browne, 1843).

*Ireland and Her Agitators* (Dublin: John Browne, 1845).

*Repeal of the Union: A Letter from W. J. O'Neill Daunt, Esq., to the Landlords of Ireland* (Dublin: Loyal National Repeal Association, 1846).

*Personal Recollections of the Late Daniel O'Connell, MP*, 2 vols. (London: Chapman & Hall, 1848).

Davis, Thomas, *The Poems of Thomas Davis: With Notes, Historical Illustrations, etc., and an Introduction by John Mitchel* (New York: P. M. Haverty, 1860).

*Prose Writing of Thomas Davis*, ed. T. W. Rolleston (London: Walter Scott, 1890).

Davitt, Michael, *Leaves from a Prison Diary; or, Lectures to a 'Solitary' Audience* (London: Chapman & Hall, 1885).

*The Fall of Feudalism in Ireland: Or the Story of the Land League Revolution* (London: Harper & Brothers, 1904).

*Jottings in Solitary*, ed. Carla King (Dublin: UCD Press, 2003).

Denieffe, Joseph, *A Personal Narrative of the Irish Revolutionary Brotherhood* (New York: Gael Publishing Co., 1906).

Devoy, John, *Recollections of an Irish Rebel* (New York: Chase D. Young Co., 1929).

Dewar, Daniel, *Observations on the Character, Customs and Superstitions of the Irish; and on Some of the Causes which have Retarded the Moral and Political Improvement of Ireland* (London: Gale and Curtis, 1812).

Dicey, A. V., *Introduction to the Study of the Law of the Constitution*, 3rd ed. (London: Macmillan and Co., 1889).

Dillon, Henry Augustus, *Letter to the Noblemen and Gentlemen, who composed the Deputation from the Catholics of Ireland, on the Subject of their Mission* (Dublin: H. Fitzpatrick, 1805).

[Dillon, John Joseph] 'A Barrister', *The Question, as to the Admission of Catholics to Parliament, Considered, upon the Principles of Existing Laws* (London: W. & C. Spilsbury, 1801).

*Two Memoirs upon the Catholic Question, with an Essay upon the History and Effect of the Coronation Oath* (Bath: Meyler and Son, 1810).

Dillon, William, *Life of John Mitchel*, 2 vols. (London: Kagan Paul, Trench & Co., 1888).

Dobbs, Archibald E., *Representative Reform for Ireland* (London: Spottiswoode & Co., 1879).

Doheny, Michael, *The Felon's Track: or, a History of the Late Attempted Outbreak in Ireland* (New York: H. Holbrooke, 1849).

Douglas, Sylvester, *Speech of the Right Honourable Sylvester Douglas, in the House of Commons, Tuesday, April the 23rd, 1799, on Seconding the Motion of the Rt. Hon. The Chancellor of the Exchequer, for the House to Agree with the Lords in an Address to His Majesty, Relative to a Union with Ireland* (Dublin: John Milliken, 1799).

[Doyle, James Warren] 'J. K. L.', *A Vindication of the Religious and Civil Principles of the Irish Catholics, in a Letter, Addressed to his Excellency, the Marquis Wellesley, K. G.* (Dublin: Richard Coyne, 1823).

*A Defence by J. K. L. of his Vindication of the Religious and Civil Principles of Irish Catholics* (Dublin: Richard Coyne, 1824).

*Letters on the State of Ireland; Addressed by J. K. L. to a Friend in England* (Dublin: Richard Coyne, 1825).

*An Essay on the Catholic Claims, Addressed to the Right Honourable the Earl of Liverpool, K.G.* (Dublin: Richard Coyne, 1826).

Drennan, William, *A Letter to the Right Hon. William Pitt* (Dublin: James Moore, 1799).

Duffy, Charles Gavan, *Young Ireland: A Fragment of Irish History, 1840–45* (London: T. Fisher Unwin, 1896; first published 1881).

*Four Years of Irish History, 1845–1849: A Sequel to 'Young Ireland'* (London: Cassell, Petter, Galpin, and Co., 1883).

*The League of North and South: An Episode in Irish History, 1850–54* (London: Chapman & Hall, 1886).

*Thomas Davis: The Memoirs of an Irish Patriot* (London: Kegan Paul, Trench, Trübner, and Co., 1890).

*Conservations with Carlyle* (New York: Charles Scribner's Sons, 1892).

*Short Life of Thomas Davis, 1840–1846* (London: T. Fisher Unwin, 1895).

*My Life in Two Hemispheres*, 2 vols. (London: T. Fisher Unwin, 1898).

Duigenan, Patrick, *A Fair Representation of the Present Political State of Ireland; In a Course of Strictures on Two Pamphlets, One Entitled* The Case of Ireland Reconsidered*; the Other Entitled* Consideration on the State of Public Affairs in the Year 1799 – Ireland (London: J. Wright, 1799).

Edgeworth, Maria, *Castle Rackrent*, ed. George Watson (Oxford: Oxford University Press, 2008; first published 1800).

Edgeworth, Richard Lovell, *The Substance of Three Speeches, Delivered in the House of Commons of Ireland, February 4, March 6, and March 21, 1800, Upon the Subject of an Union with Great Britain* (London: R. Johnson, 1800).

*Memoirs of Richard Lovell Edgeworth, Esq.: Begun by Himself and Concluded by his Daughter, Maria Edgeworth*, 2 vols. (London: R. Hunter, 1820).

*Poetry Explained for Young People*, new ed. (London: R. Hunter, 1821).

Edwards, John, *Interests of Ireland: a New Method: with Confident Hopes to Attach the Lower Classes to the Laws and Constitution* (Dublin: William Watson, 1814).

Elly, Sandham, *Potatoes, Pigs and Politics, the Curse of Ireland, and the Cause of England's Embarrassments* (London: Kent and Richards, 1848).

Ensor, George, *Anti-Union: Ireland as She Ought to be* (Newry: Morgan and Dunlop, 1831).

Fagan, William, *The Life and Times of Daniel O'Connell*, 2 vols. (Cork: John O'Brien, 1847).

Falkland, Charles, Viscount, *Considerations on the Competency of the Parliament of Ireland to Accede to an Union with Great Britain* (London: J. Wright, 1799).

Farnham, Right Hon. Barry, Earl, *An Examination into the Principles Contained in a Pamphlet, Entitled* The Speech of Lord Minto, *with some Remarks upon a Pamphlet, Entitled* Observations on that Part of the Speaker's Speech with Relates to Trade (Dublin: James Moore, 1800).

Fitzgibbon, John, *The Speech of the Right Hon. John, Earl of Clare, Lord High Chancellor of Ireland, in the House of Lords of Ireland, on a Motion made by the Earl of Moira, Monday 19 February 1798*, 4th ed. (Dublin: J. Milliken, 1798).

*The Speech of the Right Hon. John, Lord Baron Fitzgibbon, Lord High Chancellor of Ireland: Delivered to the House of Peers on the Second Reading of the Bill for the Relief of His Majesty's Roman Catholic Subjects, 13 March 1793* (Dublin: J. Milliken, 1798).

*The Speech of the Right Hon. John, Earl of Clare, Lord High Chancellor of Ireland, in the House of Lords of Ireland, on a Motion Made by Himself, on Monday 10 February 1800* (Dublin: J. Milliken, 1800).

Fitzpatrick, William John, *The Life, Times and Correspondence of the Right Rev. Dr Doyle, Bishop of Kildare and Leighlin*, 2 vols. (Dublin: James Duffy, 1861).

(ed.), *Correspondence of Daniel O'Connell: The Liberator*, 2 vols. (New York: Longmans, Green and Co., 1888).

Fogarty, L. (ed.), *James Fintan Lalor, Patriot and Political Essayist, 1807–1849* (Dublin: Talbot Press, 1918).

Foster, John, *Speech of the Right Honourable John Foster, Speaker of the House of Commons of Ireland, Delivered in Committee, on Thursday the 11th Day of April, 1799* (Dublin: James Moore, 1799).

'A Freeman', *Observations on Mr Bousfield's Letter, etc.* (Cork: Cork Advertiser Office, 1799).

'A Freeman of Dublin', *An Appeal to the Loyal Citizens of Dublin* (Dublin: John Milliken, 1800).

Freeman, Edward A., *History of Federal Government, from the Foundation of the Achaean League to the Disruption of the United States* (London: Macmillan, 1863).

Frost, Thomas, *The Secret Societies of the European Revolution, 1776–1876*, 2 vols. (London: Tinsley Brothers, 1876).

[Gamble, John] 'Protestant Dissenter', *Brief Observations on the Present State of Ireland* (Dublin: Thomas Courtney, 1811).

Gammage, R. G., *History of the Chartist Movement, 1837–1854* (Newcastle-On-Tyne: Browne & Browne, 1894; first published 1854).

Godkin, Rev. J., *Third Prize Repeal Essay: The Rights of Ireland* (Dublin: James Duffy, 1845).

Goold, Thomas, *An Address to the People of Ireland, on the Subject of the Projected Union* (Dublin: James Moore, 1799).

Grattan, Henry, *An Answer to a Pamphlet Entitled,* The Speech of the Earl of Clare, on the Subject of a Legislative Union, Between Great Britain and Ireland, 5th ed. (Dublin: J. Moore, 1800).

*The Speech of Henry Grattan, Esq, on the Subject of a Legislative Union with Great Britain* ... (Dublin: J. Stockdale, 1800).

*The Speech of Mr Grattan in the House of Commons, on the Catholic Question* (Dublin: J & J Carrick, 1806).

[Grattan Jr., Henry], *Faction Unmasked: or a Letter to the Roman Catholics of Ireland, on the Conduct of Certain Men who Compose the Catholic Junta* (Dublin: Richard Miliken, 1815).

[Gregg, T. D.] 'M. S. G.', *Letters to J. E. Gordon, Esq., MP* (London: L. B. Seeley and Son, 1832).

*Protestant Ascendancy Vindicated, and National Regeneration, Through the Instrumentality of National Religion, Urged; in a Series of Letters to the Corporation of Dublin* (Dublin: D. R. Bleakley, 1840).

*Free Thoughts on Protestant Matters*, 2nd ed. (Dublin: W. Curry, Jr. & Co., 1847).

Griffith, Arthur, *Meagher of the Sword: Speeches of Thomas Francis Meagher in Ireland, 1846–1848* (Dublin: M. H. Gill & Son, Ltd., 1916).

Guizot, François, *History of the Origin of Representative Government in Europe*, trans. Andrew R. Scoble (London: Henry G. Bohn, 1852).

Gwynn, Stephen, *The Case for Home Rule: with an Introduction by John E. Redmond* (Dublin: Maunsel and Co., [1911]).

Hamilton, John, *A Letter to Theobald McKenna, Occasioned by a Publication Entitled* A Memoire on Some Questions Respecting the Projected Union (Dublin: James Moore, 1799).

'Hibernicus', *English Union is Ireland's Ruin! Or an Address to the Irish Nation* (Dublin: James Moore, 1799).

'H. N.', *An Address to the People of Ireland on the Repeal of the Legislative Union Between Great Britain and Ireland* (Dublin: Richard Milliken and Son, 1831).

Hodges, John George, *Report of the Trial of John Mitchel for Felony* (Dublin: Alexander Thom, 1848).

[Holmes, Robert], 'A Philosopher', *A Demonstration of the Necessity of a Legislative Union of Great Britain and Ireland, Involving a Refutation of Every Argument which has been or can be Urged Against that Measure* (Dublin: no publishing house, 1799).

*The Case of Ireland Stated*, 5th ed. (Dublin: James McGlashan, 1847).

Huish, Robert, *Memoirs of the Late William Cobbett, Esq., MP for Oldham*, 2 vols. (London: John Saunders, 1836).

'An Irish Catholic', *An Argument for Independence, in Opposition to an Union, Addressed to all his Countrymen* (Dublin: J. Stockdale, 1799).

*The Irish Home Rule League: Resolutions of National Conference* (no publishing details, 1873).

'An Irish Logician', *An Union to be Subjection, Proved from Mr C's Own Words in his* Arguments For and Against. *In Two Parts. Part I* (Dublin, J. Rice, 1799).

'An Irishman', *The French Revolution and the Repeal of the Union: an Address to the People of Ireland* (Dublin: Mullen, Corbet, and Co., 1848).

Jebb, Richard, *A Reply to a Pamphlet, Entitled,* Arguments For and Against a Union (Dublin: William Jones, 1798).

Jennings, Louis J. (ed.), *The Croker Papers: The Correspondence and Diaries of the Late Right Honourable John Wilson Croker*, 2 vols. (New York: Charles Scribner's Sons, 1884).

Jervis, Sir John, *A Letter Addressed to the Gentlemen of England and Ireland: on the Inexpediency of a Federal-Union Between the Two Kingdoms* (Dublin: John Whitworth, 1798).

[Johnson, William], *Reasons for Adopting an Union between Ireland and Great Britain* (Dublin: J. Milliken, 1799).

[Kelly, John] 'An Irishman', *Reasons Against a Union, in which* 'Arguments For and Against a Union', *Supposed to Have Come From a Person in High Station, are Particularly Considered* (Dublin: G. Folingsby, 1798).

[Kenny, Arthur Henry], *The Dangers with which Great Britain and Ireland are Now Menaced, by the Demands of Irish Roman Catholics* (London: F. C. and J. Rivington, 1817).

Kettle, Andrew J., *The Material for Victory*, ed. Laurence J. Kettle (Galway: Open Press at the University of Galway, 2023; first published 1958).

Kinealy, Christine (ed.), *Frederick Douglass and Ireland: In His Own Words*, 2 vols. (Oxford: Routledge, 2018).

Lalor, James Fintan, *'Faith of a Felon' and Other Writings*, ed. Marta Rámon (Dublin: UCD Press, 2012).

Larkin, Emmet (ed.), *Alexis de Tocqueville's Journey in Ireland, July–August 1835* (Washington, DC: Catholic University of America Press, 1990).

Lecky, Elizabeth, *A Memoir of the Right Hon. William Edward Hartpole Lecky* (Longmans, Green, and Co., 1909).

[Lecky, W. E. H.], *The Leaders of Public Opinion in Ireland* (London: Saunders, Otley, and Co., 1861).

Lecky, W. E. H., *The Leaders of Public Opinion in Ireland*, 2nd ed. (London: Longmans, Green, and Co., 1871).

*Leaders of Public Opinion*, 3rd ed., 2 vols. (London: Longmans, Green, and Co., 1903).

Lees, Sir Harcourt, *The Rehearsal: King and Constitution, or Pope and Catholic Emancipation. Recommended to the Attention of the Most Stupid of the Protestant Advocates for Unrestricted Civil Liberty* (Dublin: W. Underwood, 1820).

*The Seventh Edition of the Antidote; or, 'Nouvelles a la Main.' Recommended to the Serious Attention of every Protestant in the Empire, in those days of Political and Religious Apostasy, Military and Naval Evangelicalism, Papal Intolerance, and Popish Bigotry* (Dublin: W. Underwood, 1820).

Leno, John Bedford, *The Aftermath: With Autobiography of the Author John Bedford Leno* (London: Reeves and Turner, 1892).

Levy, John (ed.), *A Full and Revised Report of the Three Days' Discussion in the Dublin Corporation, on the Repeal of the Union* (Dublin: James Duffy, 1843).

Linton, W. J., *Ireland for the Irish: Rhymes and Reasons against Landlordism* (New York: American News Company, 1867).

Lovett, William and John Collins, *Chartism: A New Organization of the People, Embracing a Plan for the Education and Improvement of the People, Politically and Socially* (London: J. Watson, 1840).

MacCarthy, John George, *A Plea for the Home Government of Ireland* (London: Longmans, Green and Co., 1871).

MacKnight, Thomas, *Ulster as it is: or Twenty-Eight Years' Experience as an Irish Editor*, 2 vols. (London: Macmillan and Co., 1896).

Madden, Daniel Owen (ed.), *The Select Speeches of the Right Hon Henry Grattan; to which is added his Letter on the Union, with a Commentary on his Career and Character* (Dublin: James Duffy, 1845).

*Revelations of Ireland in the Past Generation* (Dublin: James McGlashan, 1848).

Madden, R. R., *The Life and Times of Robert Emmet, Esq.* (Dublin: James Duffy, 1847).

Martin, J. C., *Authentic Reports of Special Meetings of the Irish Metropolitan Conservative Society: on the Policy of the Church of Rome in this Country in her Advocacy of the Voluntary System: a Lecture Delivered by Rev. J. C. Martin* (Dublin: IMCS, 1837).

Martin, R. Montgomery, *Ireland Before and After the Union with Great Britain* (London: Wm. S. Orr and Co., 1843).

McComb, William, *The Repealer Repulsed! A Correct Narrative of the Rise and Progress of the Repeal Invasion of Ulster*, ed. Patrick Maume (Dublin: UCD Press, 2003; first published 1841).

McCrea, J. B., *The Cause of Irish Protestant Orphans the Cause of Godliness and Loyalty* (Dublin: Richard Moore, [1833]).

*Education Board of Ireland*, 2nd ed. (Dublin: J. Hoare, 1833).

*The Lord's Spirit the Spirit of Liberty: A Discourse to the Orange Institution of Dublin, on the Twelfth of July, to Commemorate the Revolution by William the Third* (Dublin: William Warren, 1835).

McKenna, Theobald, *Political Essays Relative to the Affairs of Ireland, in 1791, 1792, and 1793; With Remarks on the Present State of that Country* (London: J. Debrett, 1794).

*A Memoire on Some Questions Respecting the Projected Union of Great Britain and Ireland* (Dublin: John Rice, 1799).

*Constitutional Objections to the Government of Ireland by a Separate Legislature: In a Letter to John Hamilton, Esq., Occasioned by his Remarks on* A Memoire on The Projected Union (Dublin: H. Fitzpatrick, 1799).

*Sketch of the Construction of the Statue Passed in 1793, for the Relief of His Majesty's Popish or Roman Catholic Subjects* (Dublin: M. Fitzpatrick, 1806).

Meagher, Thomas Francis, *Speeches on the Legislative Independence of Ireland* (New York: Renfield, 1853).

Melvelle, Lewis (ed.), *The Life and Letters of William Cobbett in England and America: Based upon Hitherto Unpublished Family Papers*, 2 vols. (London: John Lane, 1913).

Meyler, Anthony, *Observations on Ventilation, and on the Dependence of Health on the Purity of the Air which we Respire* (London: Longman, Hurst, Rees, Orme, and Brown, 1818).

*Irish Tranquillity Under Mr O'Connell, my Lord Mulgrave, and the Romish Priesthood* (Dublin: Wm. Carson, 1838).

*A Speech, Delivered by Doctor Meyler, at the Great Meeting of the Irish Metropolitan Conservative Society, on a Petition to the House of Commons, Praying that the Annual Grant Hitherto Voted to the Roman Catholic College at Maynooth may be Discontinued* (Dublin: Joshua Porter, 1839).

*Six Letters Addressed to Lord Stanley, on the Political and Religious Condition of Ireland* (Dublin: William Carson, 1841).

Mill, John Stuart, *Considerations on Representative Government* (London: Parker, Son, and Bourn, 1861).

*England and Ireland* (London: Longmans, Green, Reader, and Dyer, 1868).

'A Mimber', *Unconnected Hints, and Loose Ideas Upon the Union, with Two Propositions* (Dublin: Marchbank, 1799).
Minto, Lord, *The Speech of Lord Minto, in the House of Peers, April 11, 1799, on a Motion for an Address to His Majesty, to Communicate the Resolutions of the Two Houses of Parliament, Respecting an Union between Great Britain and Ireland* (London: John Stockdale, 1799).
Mitchel, John (ed.), *Irish Political Economy, by Jonathan Swift, Dean of St Patrick's and George Berkeley, Bishop of Cloyne* (Dublin: Irish Confederation, 1847).
*Jail Journal: or, Five years in British Prisons* (New York: *The Citizen*, 1854).
*An Apology for the British Government in Ireland* (Dublin: O'Donoghue and Co., 1905; first published 1860).
*The Last Conquest of Ireland (Perhaps)* (Glasgow: Cameron & Ferguson, 1861).
*The History of Ireland: From the Treaty of Limerick to the Present Time* (Glasgow: Cameron & Ferguson, 1869).
Moody, T. W., R. B. McDowell and C. J. Woods (eds.), *The Writings of Theobald Wolfe Tone*, 3 vols. (Oxford: Oxford University Press, 2001).
Morris, Patrick, *Six Letters, Intended to Prove that the Repeal of the Act of Union, and the Establishment of a Local Legislature in Ireland, are Necessary to Cement the Connection with Great Britain and Containing a Short View of the Trade, Manufactures, and Agriculture of Ireland: Addressed to the Right Honourable Sir John Newport* (Waterford, 1831).
Musgrave, Sir Richard, *Memoirs of the Different Rebellions in Ireland, From the Arrival of the English* (Dublin: John Milliken, 1801).
*Strictures Upon an* Historical Review of the State of Ireland*; by Francis Plowden, Esq. or, a Justification of the Conduct of the English Governments in that Country, From the Reign of Henry the Second to the Union of Great Britain and Ireland* (London: F. C. and J. Rivington, 1804).
O'Brien, William and Desmond Ryan (eds.), *Devoy's Postbag, 1871–1928*, 2 vols. (Dublin: C. J. Fallon, 1948).
O'Brien, William Smith, *Speeches of William Smith O'Brien, Esq., on the Causes of Discontent in Ireland*, 2nd ed. (Dublin: J. Browne, 1843).
O'Connell, Daniel, *First Letter of Daniel O'Connell, Esq., on the Repeal of the Union* (Dublin: T. O'Flanagan, 1830).
*Second Letter of Daniel O'Connell, Esq., on the Repeal of the Union* (Dublin: T. O'Flanagan, 1830).
*Third Letter of Daniel O'Connell, Esq., on the Repeal of the Union* (Dublin: T. O'Flanagan, 1830).
*Fourth Letter of Daniel O'Connell, Esq., on the Repeal of the Union* (Dublin: T. O'Flanagan, 1830).
*Repeal of the Union: Mr O'Connell's Address to the Jury in the Case of the King vs Barrett, Proprietor of the Pilot; Delivered in the Court of King's Bench. On Tuesday, November 26th, 1833* (Dublin: P. Byrne, 1833).
*The Speech of Daniel O'Connell, Esq., MP, at a Public Dinner in Edinburgh, on Thursday, September 17th, 1835* (London: John Limbird, 1835).

*First Series of Reports, of the Loyal National Repeal Association of Ireland, with a Dedication to the People of Ireland* (Dublin: J. Browne, 1840).

*Irish Parliament: Report of the Committee of the National Repeal Association of Ireland, to who, it was Referred to Suggest a Proposal, to be Converted into a Law, for the Reconstruction of the House of Commons of Ireland* (no publishing details, 1840).

*Observations on Corn Laws, on Political Pravity and Ingratitude, and on Clerical and Personal Slander, in the Shape of a Meek and Modest Reply to the Second Letter of the Earl of Shrewsbury, Waterford, and Wexford* (Dublin: Samuel J. Machen, 1842).

*A Memoir on Ireland: Vol. 1:1172–1660* (Dublin: Charles Dolman, 1843).

O'Connell, John, *Letters to Friends in Connaught, Respectfully Addressed to Various Parties in that Province* (Dublin: J. Browne, 1843).

*An Argument for Ireland* (Dublin: John Browne, 1844).

*Repeal Dictionary, Part One* (Dublin: J. Browne, 1845).

(ed.), *The Life and Speeches of Daniel O'Connell, MP*, 2 vols. (Dublin: James Duffy, 1846).

*Recollections and Experiences from a Parliamentary Career from 1833 to 1848*, 2 vols. (London: Richard Bentley, 1849).

(ed.), *Select Speeches of Daniel O'Connell, MP*, 2 vols. (London: James Duffy, 1867).

O'Connell, Maurice R. (ed.), *The Correspondence of Daniel O'Connell*, 8 vols. (Dublin: Irish Manuscripts Commission, 1977).

O'Connor, Arthur, *The State of Ireland*, ed. James Livesey (Dublin: Lilliput Press, 1998; first published 1798).

O'Day, Alan, and John Stevenson (eds.), *Irish Historical Documents since 1800* (Dublin: Gill & Macmillan, 1992).

O'Donnell, F. Hugh, *A History of the Irish Parliamentary Party*, 2 vols. (London: Longmans, Green, and Co., 1910).

O'Flanagan, J. Roderick, *The Irish Bar: Comprising Anecdotes, Bon-Mots, and Biographical Sketches of the Bench and Bar of Ireland* (London: S. Low, Marston, Searle, and Rivington, 1879).

O'Leary, John, *Recollections of Fenians and Fenianism*, 2 vols. (London: Downey & Co., Ltd., 1896).

O'Mara, S. D., *Repeal, or Ruin! Addressed to the People of Ireland* (Dublin: James Byrn, [1810]).

[O'Malley, Thaddeus] 'A Minister of Peace', *The Federalist: or a Series of Papers Showing how to Repeal the Union, so as to Avoid a Violent Crisis, and at the Same Time, Secure and Reconcile all Interests, no. 1* (Dublin: the author, 1831).

*Home Rule on the Basis of Federalism* (London: Wm. Ridgeway, 1873).

O'Neill, John Augustus, *Opening of the Conciliation Hall, on Monday, 23rd October, 1843: Speech of John Augustus O'Neill* (Dublin: J. Browne, 1843).

O'Sullivan, Mortimer, *A Guide to an Irish Gentleman in his Search for a Religion* (Dublin: William Curry, Jr., and Co., 1833).

*Case of the Protestants of Ireland, Stated in Addresses Delivered at Meetings in Dublin, Liverpool, Bristol, and Bath, in the Year 1834* (London: John Hatchard & Son, 1836).

Orr, Robert, *A Review of the Speech of the Right Hon. William Pitt, in the British House of Commons, on Thursday, January 31st, 1799* (Dublin: J. Stockdale, 1799).

Paine, Thomas, *Rights of Man, Common Sense and Other Political Writings*, ed. M. Philp (Oxford: Oxford University Press, 1998).

[Parnell, William], 'An Irish Country Gentleman', *An Inquiry into the Cause of Popular Discontents in Ireland* (London: J. Wallis, 1804).

*An Historical Apology for the Irish Catholics*, 2nd ed. (Dublin: H. Fitzpatrick, 1807).

Pearse, Pádraic H., *Collected Works of Pádraic H. Pearse: Political Writings and Speeches* (Dublin: Phoenix Publishing Co., Ltd., 1924).

[Phelan, William], *The Case of the Church of Ireland, Stated, in a Second Letter, Respectfully Addressed to his Excellency the Marquess of Wellesley, and in Reply to the Charges of J.K.L.* (Dublin: Richard Milliken, 1824).

Phillpotts, Henry, *A Letter to the Right Honourable George Canning, on the Bill of 1825, for Removing the Disqualifications of his Majesty's Roman Catholic Subjects*, 4th ed. (London: John Murray, 1827).

Pigott, Richard, *Personal Recollections of an Irish National Journalist*, 2nd ed. (Dublin: Hodges, Figgis & Co., 1883).

Pitt, William, *Speech of the Right Hon. William Pitt, in the House of Commons, Thursday 31 January 1799, on Offering to the House the Resolutions which he Proposes as the Basis of a Union between Great Britain and Ireland* (Dublin: John Exshaw, 1799).

Plowden, Francis, *A Short History of the British Empire During the Last Twenty Months; Viz. from May 1792 to the Close of the Year 1793* (Dublin: P. Byrne, 1794).

*The Constitution of the United Kingdom of Great Britain & Ireland: Civil and Ecclesiastical* (London, T. Sutton, 1802).

*An Historical Review of the State of Ireland, from the Invasion of that Country Under Henry II to its Union with Great Britain on the 1st of January 1801*, 2 vols. (London: T. Egerton, 1803).

*The History of Ireland, From its Union with Great Britain in January 1801, to October 1810*, 3 vols. (Dublin: John Boyce, 1811).

Porter, J. G. V., *Ireland: The Union of 1801 . . . A Federal (The Only Fair) Union between Great Britain and Ireland Inevitable, and most Desirable for Both Islands*, 2nd ed. (London: Fisher, Son & Co., [1844]).

'Protestant Celt', *Irish Nationality in 1870*, 2nd ed. (Dublin: E. Ponsonby, 1870).

'A Protestant of the Established Church', *The Repeal of the Union Considered* (Dublin: Richard Milliken and Son, 1831).

'R. B. G.', *A Repeal of the Union: The Ruin of Ireland* (Dublin: William Curry, 1831).

Read, Charles and T. P. O'Connor (eds.), *The Cabinet of Irish Literature: Selections from the Works of the Chief Poets, Orators, and Prose Writers of Ireland*, 4 vols. (London: Blackie and Son, 1880).

Recchia, Stefano and Nadia Urbinati (eds.), *A Cosmopolitanism of Nations: Giuseppe Mazzini's Writings of Democracy, National Building and International Relations* (Princeton, NJ: Princeton University Press, 2009).

Redfoord, Archibald, *Union, Necessary to Security: Addressed to the Loyal Inhabitants of Ireland* (Dublin: J. Archer, 1800).

*Report of the Proceedings at the First Public Meeting of the Irish Metropolitan Conservative Society, Held at their House, 19 Dawson Street, on the 16th of November, 1836* (Dublin: Irish Metropolitan Conservative Society, 1836).

*Report of the Speeches and Proceedings at the Belfast Society's Fourth Anniversary Dinner, Held on Tuesday, December 20, 1836, in the Conservative Hall, Belfast*, 2nd ed. (Belfast: G. Phillips, 1837).

Roney, Frank, *Irish Rebel and Californian Labor Leader: An Autobiography*, ed. Ira B. Cross (Berkeley: University of California Press, 1931).

Rossa, Jeremiah O'Donovan, *Rossa's Recollections, 1838 to 1898* (New York: Mariners Harbor, 1898).

Rudd, Pemberton, *An Answer to the Pamphlet Entitled* Arguments For and Against an Union, *in a Letter Addressed to Edward Cooke* (Dublin: J. Milliken, 1799).

Russell, William, *Catholic Emancipation Contended for, and Justified from the Words of Eminent Statesmen, and the Plain Deductions of Justice and Common Sense* (London: the author, 1807).

Rutherford, John, *The Secret History of the Fenian Conspiracy: its Origin, Objects, and Ramifications*, 2 vols. (London: C. Kegan Paul & Co., 1877).

Ryan, John, *Reflections on an Important Subject, Respectfully Addressed to the Roman Catholics of Ireland* (Dublin: R. Coyne, 1809).

Saurin, William, *An Accurate Report on the Speech of William Saurin, Esq., in the Irish House of Commons, on Friday, the 21st of February, 1800, on the Question of a Legislative Union with Great Britain* (Dublin: J. Moore, 1800).

Savage, John, *'98 and '48: The Modern Revolutionary History and Literature of Ireland* (New York: Redfield, 1856).

*Address of the Council of the Fenian Brotherhood* (no publishing details, 1870).

Scrope, George Poulett, *How is Ireland to be Governed? A Question Addressed to the New Administration of Lord Melbourne in 1834, with a Postscript, in which the same question is addressed to the Administration of Sir Robert Peel in 1846* (London: James Ridgway, 1846).

Scully, Denys, *Statement of the Penal Laws, which Aggrieve the Catholics of Ireland*, 2 vols. (Dublin: H. Fitzpatrick, 1812).

Sheehy, P., *Union a Plague: In Answer to Counsellor McKenna's* Memoire on the Projected Union (Dublin: J. Hill, 1799).

Sheffield, Lord, *Substance of the Speech of the Right Honourable Lord Sheffield, Monday, April 22, 1799, Upon the Subject of Union with Ireland* (Dublin: J. Milliken, 1799).

Sheil, Richard Lalor, *Sketches of the Irish Bar*, 2 vols. (New York: Redfield, 1854).

Shelley, Percy Bysshe, *Essays, Letters from Abroad, Translations and Fragments*, ed. Mary Shelley, 2 vols. (Philadelphia, PA: Lea and Blanchard, 1840).

Sheridan, Richard Brinsley, *Speech of Richard Brinsley Sheridan, Esq., in the House of Commons of Great Britain, on Thursday, January 31st, 1799, in Reply to Mr Pitt's Speech on the Union with Ireland* (Dublin: James Moore, 1799).

[Sigerson, George] 'An Ulsterman', *Modern Ireland: Its Vital Questions, Secret Societies, and Government* (London: Longmans, Green, Reader, and Dyer, 1868).

Smith, William Cusack, *Review of a Publication, Entitled,* The Speech of the Right Honourable John Foster, Speaker of the House of Commons of Ireland*; in a Letter Addressed to Him*, 2nd ed. (Dublin: Marchbank, 1799).

*The Substance of Mr William Smith's Speech on the Subject of a Legislative Union Between this Country and Great Britain, Delivered in the House of Commons, Thursday, January 24th, 1799, and now Reduced to the Form of an Address to the People of Ireland*, 2nd ed. (Dublin: Marchbank, 1799).

*Animadversions on the Speech of Mr Saurin and Mr Bushe etc.* (Dublin: Marchbank, 1800).

*Letter to Henry Grattan, Esq, MP* (Dublin: Marchbank, 1800).

*Recent Scenes and Occurrences in Ireland: or Animadversions on a Pamphlet entitled* 'One Year of the Administration of the Marquess Wellesley' (London: Longman, Hurst, Rees, Orme, and Brown, 1823).

Spencer, Joshua, *Thoughts on an Union* (Dublin: William Jones, 1798).

'A Student of Trinity College', *Observations on a Pamphlet, Supposed to be Written by an Englishman, Entitled* Arguments For and Against an Union (Dublin: J. Milliken, 1799).

Sullivan, A. M. and T. D. Sullivan, *Guilty or Not Guilty? Speeches from the Dock, or Protests of Irish Patriotism* (Dublin: no publishing house, 1867).

[Taylor, William Cooke] 'A Munster Farmer', *Reminiscences of Daniel O'Connell, Esq, MP, during the Agitations of the Veto, Emancipation and Repeal*, ed. Patrick Maume (Dublin: UCD Press, 2005; first published 1847).

Thorpe, Rev. William, *An Address to the Protestants of Great Britain and Ireland on the Subject of Catholic Emancipation, Presenting Facts and Documents Illustrative of the Real Object of Irish Roman Catholic Leaders*, 3rd ed. (Dublin: R. Napper, 1815).

de Tocqueville, Alexis, *Democracy in America*, trans. George Lawrence, ed. J. P. Mayer (London: Fontana Press, 1994).

Torrens, Robert, *Thoughts on the Catholic Question*, 2nd ed. (London: Gale, Curtis, and Fenner, 1813).

Townsend, William C., *Modern State Trials: With Essays and Notes*, 2 vols. (London: Longman, Brown, Green, and Longmans, 1850).

Townshend, Thomas, *Consideration on the Theoretical Spirit of the Times: on the Inefficacy of Theory to the Formation of Civil Government; on the Doctrines of Liberty and Equality; on the different Kinds of Government; and also, on the Pre-Eminent Merits of the British Constitution* (Cork: A. Edwards, 1793).

*A Summary Defence of the Right Hon. Edmund Burke* (London: A. Edwards, 1796).

*General Opinions on the Conduct of Ministers with Respect to the Past and Present State of Ireland, and Inculcating the Justice and Policy of Catholic Emancipation* (London: Oriental Press, 1801).

*Part of a Letter to a Noble Earl: Containing a Very Short Comment on the Doctrines and Facts of Sir Richard Musgrave's Quarto; and Vindicatory of the Yeomanry and Catholics of the City of Cork* (Dublin: P. Fitzpatrick, 1801).
*Transactions of the Protestant Colonisation Society of Ireland, Reported at a Public Meeting of Subscribers, in the Dublin Institution, on Thursday, May 24, 1832* (Dublin: J. Hoare, 1832).
Trollope, Anthony, *An Autobiography*, ed. Charles Morgan (London: Williams and Norgate Ltd., 1946; first published 1883).
Trotter, John Bernard, *Five Letters to an Eminent Character on Catholic Relief, the Affairs of Ireland, and the Conduct of the New Parliament* (Dublin: C. Crookes, 1813).
'A Voice from the North', *To the Orangemen of Ireland* (Belfast: Stuart & Gregg, 1835).
Wakefield, Edward, *An Account of Ireland, Statistical and Political*, 2 vols. (London: Longman, Hurst, Rees, Orme, and Brown, 1812).
[Wallace, Thomas] 'A Protestant', *The Orange System Exposed; and the Orange Societies Proved to be Unconstitutional, Illegal and Seditious, in a Letter to the Marquess Wellesley* (Dublin: Richard Milliken, 1823).
[Walmesley, Charles] 'Pastorini', *The General History of the Christian Church from her Birth to her Final Triumphant State in Heaven, Chiefly Deduced from the Apocalypse of St John the Apostle*, 5th ed. (Dublin: P. Wogan, 1812; first published 1771).
Webb, Alfred, *A Compendium of Irish Biography: Comprising Sketches of Distinguished Irishmen, and of Eminent Persons Connected with Ireland by Office or by their Writings* (Dublin: M. H. Gill & Son, 1878).
Weld, Matthew, *No Union! Being an Appeal to Irishmen*, 4th ed. (Cork: J. Haly, M. Harris and J. Connor, 1798).
Whiteside, James, *Italy in the Nineteenth Century*, 3 vols. (London: Richard Bentley, 1848).
*Whiteside's Defence of Wm. S. O'Brien, Esq., MP: On His Trial for High Treason at Clonmel, on Thursday and Friday, 5th and 6th, October, 1848* (Dublin: no publisher details, [1848]).
*The Life and Death of the Irish Parliament: A Lecture* (Dublin: Hodges, Smith and Co., 1864).
Wyse, Thomas, *Historical Sketch of the Late Catholic Association of Ireland*, 2 vols. (London: Henry Colburn, 1829).
*The Political Catechism, Explanatory of the Constitutional Rights and Civil Disabilities of the Catholics of Ireland* (London: James Ridgway, 1829).
Yelverton, Lord Barry, *The Speech of the Right Honourable Barry, Lord Yelverton, Chief Baron of His Majesty's Court of Exchequer, in the House of Lords of Ireland, on Saturday, March 22, 1800; in the Debate on the Fourth Article of a Legislative Union Between Great Britain and Ireland* (Dublin: J. Milliken, 1800).

## *Newspapers, Magazines and Periodicals*

*Anti-Union*
*Anti-Unionist*
*Belfast Monthly Magazine*
*Belfast Newsletter*
*Citizen*
*Dublin Examiner*
*Dublin Review*
*Dublin University Magazine*
*Economist*
*Edinburgh Review*
*Examiner*
*Federalist*
*Fortnightly Review*
*Frazer's Magazine*
*Freeman's Journal*
*Gentleman's Magazine*
*Irish Book Lover*
*Irish Felon*
*Irish People*
*Irish Rush-Light*
*Irish Times*
*Macmillan's Magazine*
*Morning Chronicle*
*Morning Post*
*Nation*
*National Magazine*
*Northern Star*
*Political Register*
*Quarterly Review*
*Spectator*
*Times*
*United Irishman*

## *Manuscript and Digital Archival Material*

Broadside Ballads Online, Bodleian Library, Oxford.
Home Rule League Letter Book, Public Record Office of Northern Ireland (PRONI), Belfast.
Isaac Butt papers, National Library of Ireland (NLI), Dublin.
William Smith O'Brien papers, NLI.
Thomas Ray papers, John J. Burns Library, Boston, MA.

### *Parliamentary and Legal Papers*

*Evidence of the Right Rev. James Doyle, DD. Roman Catholic Bishop of Kildare and Leighlin, given before the Committee of the House of Lords, on the State of Ireland, March 21st, 1825* (London: W. E. Andrews, 1825).
*Hansard*
*The Queen against John Mitchel* (1848), 6 St Tr NS 599.
*The Queen against O'Doherty* (1848), 6 St Tr NS 831.
*The Queen against O'Brien, and the Queen against Meagher* (1848), 6 St Tr NS 571.
*The Queen against Smith O'Brien* (1848), 7 St Tr NS 1.
*Repeal of the Union: Report of the Debate in the House of Commons on Mr O'Connell's Motion, and its Proceedings in the House of Lords on Earl Gray's Motion for Concurring in the Address of the Commons, April, 1834* (London: William Clowes, 1834)
'Union with Ireland Act' (1800), 39 & 40 Geo 3.

### *Historical Writings*

Blackstone, William, *Commentaries on the Laws of England*, 4 vols. (Oxford: Oxford University Press, 1765; first published 1763).
Cicero, Marcus Tullius, *On Duties*, ed. M. T. Griffin and E. M. Atkins (Cambridge: Cambridge University Press, 1991).
Hamilton, Alexander, James Madison and James Jay, *The Federalist Papers*, ed. Ian Shapiro (New Haven, CT: Yale University Press, 2009).
Hume, David, *Essays: Moral, Political and Literary* (New York: Longmans, Green and Co., 1898).
Locke, John, *Two Treatises of Government*, ed. Peter Laslett (Cambridge: Cambridge University Press, 1988).
*Political Writings*, ed. David Wootton (Indianapolis, IN: Hackett Publishing Co., 2003).
Sidney, Algernon, *Discourses Concerning Government*, 2 vols. (Edinburgh: G. Hamilton and J. Balfour, 1750).
Smith, Adam, *An Inquiry into the Nature and Causes of the Wealth of Nations*, 2 vols. (London: W. Strahan, 1776).
Temple, John, *The Irish Rebellion: or a History of the Attempts of the Irish Papists to Extirpate the Protestants in the Kingdom of Ireland, Together with the Barbarous Cruelties, and Bloody Massacres which Ensued Thereupon* (London: White, Cochrane and Co., 1812; first published 1646).

## **Secondary Sources**

Andrews, Ann, *Newspapers and Newsmakers: The Dublin Nationalist Press in the Mid-Nineteenth Century* (Liverpool: Liverpool University Press, 2014).

Andrews, Stuart, *Irish Rebellions: Protestant Polemic, 1798–1900* (Basingstoke, Palgrave Macmillan, 2006).

Armitage, David, 'Conclusion: we have always been federal', in Robert Schütze and Stephen Tierney (eds.), *The United Kingdom and the Federal Idea* (Oxford: Hart Publishing, 2018), pp. 277–84.

Auchmuty, James Johnston, *Sir Thomas Wyse, 1791–1862: The Life and Career of an Educator and Diplomat* (London: P. S. King & Son, Ltd., 1939).

Bailyn, Bernard, *The Ideological Origins of the American Revolution* (Cambridge, MA: Harvard University Press, 2017; first published 1967).

Baker, Keith Michael, *Inventing the French Revolution: Essays on French Political Culture in the Eighteenth Century* (Cambridge: Cambridge University Press, 2012; first published 1990).

Barclay, Katie, *Men on Trial: Performing Emotion, Embodiment and Identity in Ireland, 1800–45* (Manchester: Manchester University Press, 2019).

Barker, Chris, 'Mass and elite politics in Mill's *Considerations on Representative Government*', *History of European Ideas*, vol. 41, no. 8 (2015), pp. 1143–63.

Barnard, T. C., 'The uses of 23 October 1641 and Irish Protestant celebrations', *English Historical Review*, vol. 106, no. 421 (1991), pp. 889–920.

*Irish Protestants Ascents and Descents, 1641–1770* (Dublin: Four Courts Press, 2004).

Baronowski, Donald Walter, *Polybius and Roman Imperialism* (London: Bloomsbury, 2011).

Barr, Colin, 'The Irish Reform Act of 1868', *Parliamentary History*, vol. 36, no. 1 (2018), pp. 97–116.

Bartlett, Thomas, *The Fall and Rise of the Irish Nation: The Catholic Question, 1690–1830* (Dublin: Gill & Macmillan, 1992).

Bell, Duncan, *The Idea of Greater Britain: Empire and the Future of World Order, 1860–1900* (Princeton, NJ: Princeton University Press, 2007).

Benson, Charles and Siobhán Fitzpatrick, 'Pamphlets', in James Murphy (ed.), *The Oxford History of the Irish Book, vol. iv: the Irish Book in English, 1800–1891* (Oxford: Oxford University Press, 2011), pp. 139–43.

Bethel, Patrick, '"Shrovetide will be a merry time in Ireland yet": Fenian visions of Ireland's future', in Richard J. Butler (ed.), *Dreams of the Future in Nineteenth-Century Ireland* (Liverpool: Liverpool University Press, 2021), pp. 37–54.

Bew, John, *The Glory of Being Britons: Civic Unionism in Nineteenth-Century Belfast* (Dublin: Irish Academic Press, 2009).

*Castlereagh: Enlightenment, War and Tyranny* (London: Quercus, 2011).

Bew, Paul, *Conflict and Conciliation in Ireland, 1890–1910* (Oxford: Oxford University Press, 1987).

*Enigma: A New Life of Charles Stewart Parnell* (Dublin: Gill & Macmillan, 2011).

*Ancestral Voices in Irish Politics: Judging Dillon and Parnell* (Oxford: Oxford University Press, 2023).

Biagini, Eugenio F., *British Democracy and Irish Nationalism, 1876–1906* (Cambridge: Cambridge University Press, 2007).

Black, R. D. C., *Economic Thought and the Irish Question, 1817–1970* (Cambridge: Cambridge University Press, 1960).

Blackstock, Allan, *Loyalism in Ireland, 1789–1829* (Woodbridge: Boydell Press, 2007).

Blight, David W., *Frederick Douglass: Prophet of Freedom* (New York: Simon & Schuster, 2018).

Bolton, G. G., *The Passing of the Irish Act of Union: A Study in Parliamentary Politics* (Oxford: Oxford University Press, 1966).

Bourke, Marcus, *John O'Leary: A Study of Irish Separatism* (Tralee: Anvil Books, 1967).

Bourke, Richard, *Peace in Ireland: The War of Ideas* (London: Pimlico, 2003).

*Empire and Revolution: The Political Life of Edmund Burke* (Princeton, NJ: Princeton University Press, 2015).

Bourke, Richard and Niamh Gallagher (eds.), *The Political Thought of the Irish Revolution* (Cambridge: Cambridge University Press, 2022).

Bourke, Richard and Ian McBride (eds.), *The Princeton History of Modern Ireland* (Princeton, NJ: Princeton University Press, 2016).

Bourke, Richard and Quentin Skinner (eds.), *Popular Sovereignty in Historical Perspective* (Cambridge: Cambridge University Press, 2016).

Bowen, Desmond, *The Protestant Crusade in Ireland, 1800–1870* (Dublin: Gill & Macmillan, 1978).

Boyce, D. George, *Nationalism in Ireland*, 3rd ed. (London: Routledge, 1995).

Boylan, Thomas A. and Timothy P. Foley, *Political Economy and Colonial Ireland: The Propagation and Ideological Function of Economic Discourse in the Nineteenth Century* (London: Routledge, 1992).

Brogan, Hugh, *Alexis de Tocqueville: A Life* (New Haven, CT: Yale University Press, 2006).

Brown, Malcolm, *The Politics of Irish Literature: From Thomas Davis to W. B. Yeats* (Seattle: University of Washington Press, 1972).

Brown, Michael 'The injured lady and her British problem', in Michael Brown, Patrick M. Geoghegan and James Kelly (eds.), *The Irish Act of Union: Bicentennial Essays* (Dublin: Irish Academic Press, 2003), pp. 37–49.

*The Irish Enlightenment* (Cambridge, MA: Harvard University Press, 2016).

Brown, Michael, Patrick M. Geoghegan and James Kelly (eds.), *The Irish Act of Union: Bicentennial Essays* (Dublin: Irish Academic Press, 2003).

Bruce, James P., *Ireland's Hope: The 'Peculiar Theories' of James Fintan Lalor* (Wilmington, DE: Vernon Press, 2020).

Brundage, David, *Irish Nationalists in America: The Politics of Exile, 1798–1998* (Oxford: Oxford University Press, 2016).

Bull, Philip, *Land, Politics and Nationalism: A Study of the Irish Land Question* (Dublin: Gill & Macmillan, 1996).

Burrow, J. W., *Whigs and Liberals: Continuity and Change in English Political Thought* (Oxford: Oxford University Press, 1988).

Busteed, Mervyn, *The Irish in Manchester, c.1750–1921: Resistance, Adaption and Identity* (Manchester: Manchester University Press, 2016).

Campbell, Fergus, *Land and Revolution: Nationalist Politics in the West of Ireland* (Oxford: Oxford University Press, 2005).

Chase, Malcolm, *Chartism: A New History* (Manchester: Manchester University Press, 2007).

Chatterjee, Partha, *The Nation and Its Fragments: Colonial and Postcolonial Histories* (Princeton, NJ: Princeton University Press, 1993).

Claeys, Gregory, *The French Revolution Debate in Britain: The Origins of Modern Politics* (Basingstoke: Palgrave Macmillan, 2007).

Clark, J. C. D., *English Society, 1688–1832* (Cambridge: Cambridge University Press, 1985).

*The Language of Liberty, 1660–1832: Political Discourse and Social Dynamics in the Anglo-American World* (Cambridge: Cambridge University Press, 1994).

*Thomas Paine: Britain, America & France in the Age of Enlightenment and Revolution* (Oxford: Oxford University Press, 2018).

Clyde, Tom, *Irish Literary Magazines: An Outline History and Descriptive Biography* (Dublin: Irish Academic Press, 2002).

Colantonio, Laurent, '"Democracy" and the Irish people, 1830–48', in Joanna Innes and Mark Philp (eds.), *Re-Imagining Democracy in the Age of Revolutions: America, France, Britain, Ireland, 1750–1850* (Oxford: Oxford University Press, 2013), pp. 162–73.

Colley, Linda, *Britons: Forging the Nation, 1707–1837* (New Haven, CT: Yale University Press, 1992).

Comerford, R. V., 'Patriotism as a pastime: the appeal of Fenianism in the mid-1860s', *Irish Historical Studies*, vol. 22, no. 87 (1981), pp. 239–50.

*The Fenians in Context: Irish Politics and Society, 1848–1882* (Dublin: Wolfhound Press, 1998; first published 1985).

Connolly, S. J., *Religion, Law and Power: The Making of Protestant Ireland, 1660–1760* (Oxford: Oxford University Press, 1992).

(ed.), *Political Ideas in Eighteenth-Century Ireland* (Dublin: Four Courts Press, 2000).

*Divided Kingdom: Ireland, 1630–1800* (Oxford: Oxford University Press, 2008).

'The limits of democracy: Ireland 1778–1848', in Joanna Innes and Mark Philp (eds.), *Re-Imagining Democracy in the Age of Revolutions: America, France, Britain, Ireland, 1750–1850* (Oxford: Oxford University Press, 2013), pp. 174–90.

Conti, Gregory, *Parliament the Mirror of the Nation: Representation, Deliberation, and Democracy in Victorian Britain* (Cambridge: Cambridge University Press, 2019).

Craig, David, and James Thompson (eds.), *Languages of Politics in Nineteenth-Century Britain* (Basingstoke: Palgrave Macmillan, 2013).

Curtis, L. Perry, *Apes and Angels: The Irishman in Victorian Caricature*, revised ed. (Washington, DC: Smithsonian Institution Press, 1996; first published 1971).

Daly, Anthony, '"The true remedy for Irish grievances is to be found in good political institutions": English radicals and Irish nationalism, 1847–1874', *Historical Research*, vol. 86, no. 231 (2013), pp. 53–75.

Davis, Michael T., Emma Macleod and Gordon Pentland (eds.), *Political Trials in an Age of Revolutions: Britain and the North Atlantic, 1793–1848* (London: Palgrave Macmillan, 2019).

Davis, Richard, *The Young Ireland Movement* (Dublin: Gill & Macmillan, 1988).

Deane, Seamus, *Strange Country: Modernity and Nationhood in Irish Writing since 1790* (Oxford: Oxford University Press, 1997).

Dickey, Laurence, 'Power, commerce and natural law in Daniel Defoe's political writings, 1698–1707', in John Robertson (ed.), *A Union for Empire: Political Thought and the Union of 1707* (Cambridge: Cambridge University Press, 1995), pp. 63–96.

Donnelly, Jr., James S., *Captain Rock: The Irish Agrarian Rebellion of 1821–1824* (Madison: University of Wisconsin Press, 2009).

Dungan, Myles, *Conspiracy: Irish Political Trials* (Dublin: Prism, 2009).

Dunn, John, *Setting the People Free: The Story of Democracy* (London: Atlantic, 2006; first published 2005).

Dwan, David, *The Great Community: Culture and Nationalism in Ireland* (Dublin: Field Day, 2008).

'Romantic nationalism: history and illusion in Ireland', *Modern Intellectual History*, vol. 14, no. 3 (2017), pp. 717–45.

Dyck, Ian, *William Cobbett and Rural Popular Culture* (Cambridge: Cambridge University Press, 1992).

Elliott, Marianne, *Wolfe Tone: Prophet of Irish Independence* (New Haven, CT: Yale University Press, 1989).

*Robert Emmet: the Making of a Legend* (London: Profile, 2003).

Epstein, James, 'The constitutional idiom: radical reasoning, rhetoric and action in early nineteenth-century England', *Journal of Social History*, vol. 23, no. 3 (1990), pp. 553–74.

Evans, Eric J., *William Pitt the Younger* (London: Routledge, 1999).

Fawcett, Edmund, *Conservatism: The Fight for a Tradition* (Princeton, NJ: Princeton University Press, 2020).

Ferguson, Mary Catherine, *Sir Samuel Ferguson in the Ireland of his Day*, 2 vols. (Edinburgh: William Blackwood and Sons, 1896).

Fitzpatrick, David, *Irish Migration, 1801–1921* (Dundalk: Dundalgan Press, 1984).

*Descendancy: Irish Protestant Histories since 1795* (Cambridge: Cambridge University Press, 2014).

Foster, R. F., *Charles Stewart Parnell: The Man and His Family* (Hassocks: Harvester Press Ltd., 1979; first published 1976).

*Words Alone: Yeats and His Inheritances* (Oxford: Oxford University Press, 2011).

Gash, Norman, *Politics in the Age of Peel: A Study in the Technique of Parliamentary Representation, 1830–1850* (London: Longman's, 1966; first published 1953).

Geoghegan, Patrick M., *The Irish Act of Union: A Study in High Politics, 1798–1801* (Dublin: Gill & Macmillan Ltd., 1999).

*King Dan: The Rise of Daniel O'Connell, 1775–1829* (Dublin: Gill & Macmillan, 2008).
*The Liberator: The Life and Death of Daniel O'Connell, 1830–1847* (Dublin: Gill & Macmillan, 2010).
'"An act of power & corruption"? The Union debate', in John Gibney (ed.), *The United Irishmen, Rebellion and the Act of Union, 1791–1803* (Barnsley: Pen & Sword Books, 2018), pp. 120–9.
Geoghegan, Vincent, 'The emergence and submergence of Irish socialism, 1821–51', in D. George Boyce, Robert Eccleshall and Vincent Geoghegan (eds.), *Political Thought in Ireland Since the Seventeenth Century* (London: Routledge, 1993), pp. 100–23.
Gibney, John, *The Shadow of a Year: The 1641 Rebellion in Irish History and Memory* (Madison: University of Wisconsin Press, 2013).
Gibson, Josh, 'The Chartists and the constitution: revisiting British popular constitutionalism', *Journal of British Studies*, vol. 56, no. 1 (2017), pp. 70–90.
Gillen, Ultán, 'Ascendancy Ireland, 1660–1800', in Richard Bourke and Ian McBride (eds.), *The Princeton History of Modern Ireland* (Princeton, NJ: Princeton University Press, 2016), pp. 48–73.
'Blackstone and Ireland', in Anthony Page and Wilfred Priest (eds.), *Blackstone and His Critics* (London: Bloomsbury, 2018), pp. 97–115.
Gleeson, David T., 'Failing to "unite with the abolitionists": the Irish nationalist press and US emancipation', *Slavery & Abolition*, vol. 37, no. 3 (2016), pp. 622–37.
Golden, J. J., 'The Protestant influence on the origins of Irish Home Rule, 1861–71', *English Historical Review*, vol. 128, no. 535 (2013), pp. 1483–516.
Good, J. W., *Irish Unionism* (Dublin: Talbot Press, 1920).
Goodrich, Amanda, *Debating England's Aristocracy in the 1790s: Pamphlets, Polemics and Political Ideas* (Woodbridge: Boydell Press, 2005).
Gordon, Daniel, 'From act to fact: the transformation of suicide in western thought', *Historical Reflections*, vol. 42, no. 2 (2016), pp. 33–51.
Gray, Peter, *Famine, Land and Politics: British Government and Irish Society, 1843–1850* (Dublin: Irish Academic Press, 1999).
Gurney, Peter. *Wanting and Having: Popular Politics and Liberal Consumerism in England, 1830–70* (Manchester: Manchester University Press, 2015).
Gwynn, Stephen, *Henry Grattan and His Times* (Dublin: Browne and Nolan Ltd., 1939).
Hall, Gerard, *Ulster Liberalism, 1778–1876* (Dublin: Four Courts Press, 2010).
Hall, Wayne E., *Dialogues in the Margin: A Study of the Dublin University Magazine* (Gerrards Cross: Colin Smythe Ltd., 2000).
Hammond, J. L., *Gladstone and the Irish Nation* (London: Frank Cass, 1964).
Harling, Philip, 'Parliament the state, and "Old Corruption": conceptualizing reform, *c.* 1790–1832', in Arthur Burns and Joanna Innes (eds.), *Rethinking the Age of Reform: Britain 1780–1850* (Cambridge: Cambridge University Press, 2003), pp. 98–113.

Hawkins, Angus, *Victorian Political Culture: 'Habits of Heart & Mind'* (Oxford: Oxford University Press, 2015).

Headingley, Adolphe S., *The Biography of Charles Bradlaugh* (London: Remington & Co., 1880).

Henriques, U. R. Q., 'The Jewish Emancipation controversy in nineteenth-century Britain', *Past & Present,* no. 40 (1968), pp. 126–46.

Hill, Jacqueline, *From Patriots to Unionists: Dublin Civic Politics and Irish Protestant Patriotism, 1660–1840* (Oxford: Oxford University Press, 1997).

Holmes, Andrew R., *The Irish Presbyterian Mind: Conservative Theology, Evangelical Experience, and Modern Criticism, 1830–1930* (Oxford: Oxford University Press, 2018).

Hont, Istvan, *Politics in Commercial Society: Jean-Jacques Rousseau and Adam Smith,* ed. Béla Kapossy and Michael Sonenscher (Cambridge, MA: Harvard University Press, 2015).

Hoppen, K. Theodore, *Elections, Politics, and Society in Ireland, 1832–1885* (Oxford: Oxford University Press, 1984).

'Riding a tiger: Daniel O'Connell, reform, and popular politics in Ireland, 1800–1847', *Proceedings of the British Academy,* vol. 100 (1999), pp. 121–43.

*Governing Hibernia: British Politicians and Ireland, 1800–1921* (Oxford: Oxford University Press, 2016).

Howe, Stephen, *Ireland and Empire: Colonial Legacies in Irish History and Culture* (Oxford: Oxford University Press, 2000).

Huggins, Michael, 'John Mitchel and his biographers', *Irish Historical Studies,* vol. 38, no. 150 (2012), pp. 249–68.

'A strange case of hero-worship: John Mitchel and Thomas Carlyle', *Studi Irlandesi,* no. 2 (2012), pp. 329–52.

The *Nation* and Giuseppe Mazzini', *New Hibernia Review,* vol. 17, no. 3 (2013), pp. 15–33.

Hughes, Kyle and Donald R. MacRaild, *Ribbon Societies in Nineteenth-Century Ireland and Its Diaspora: The Persistence of Tradition* (Liverpool: Liverpool University Press, 2018).

Innes, Joanna, Mark Philp and Robert Saunders, 'The rise of democratic discourse in the reform era', in Joanna Innes and Mark Philp (eds.), *Re-Imagining Democracy in the Age of Revolutions: America, France, Britain, Ireland, 1750–1850* (Oxford: Oxford University Press, 2013), pp. 114–28.

Israel, Jonathan, *Revolutionary Ideas: An Intellectual History of the French Revolution from The Rights of Man to Robespierre* (Princeton, NJ: Princeton University Press, 2014).

Jackson, Alvin, *The Ulster Party: Irish Unionists in the House of Commons, 1884–1911* (Oxford: Oxford University Press, 1989).

*Home Rule: An Irish History, 1800–2000* (London: Weidenfeld & Nicolson, 2003).

*The Two Unions: Ireland, Scotland, and the Survival of the United Kingdom, 1707–2007* (Oxford: Oxford University Press, 2012).

*United Kingdoms: Multinational Union States in Europe and Beyond, 1800–1925* (Oxford: Oxford University Press, 2023).

Janis, Ely M., *A Greater Ireland: The Land League and Transatlantic Nationalism in Gilded Age America* (Madison: University of Wisconsin Press, 2015).

Jennings, Jeremy, *Revolution and the Republic: A History of Political Thought in France since the Eighteenth Century* (Oxford: Oxford University Press, 2011).

Jones, Emily, *Edmund Burke and the Invention of Modern Conservatism, 1830–1914* (Oxford: Oxford University Press, 2017).

Jones, Gareth Stedman, *Languages of Class: Studies in English Working-Class History, 1832–1982* (Cambridge: Cambridge University Press, 1984).

'"Pressure from without": Karl Marx and 1867', *Parliamentary History*, vol. 36, no. 1 (2017), pp. 117–30.

Judge, David, *Representation: Theory and Practice in Britain* (London: Routledge, 1999).

Kanter, Douglas, *The Making of British Unionism, 1740–1848: Politics, Government and the Anglo-Irish Constitutional Relationship* (Dublin: Four Courts Press, 2009).

'The politics of Irish taxation, 1842–1853', *English Historical Review*, vol. 127, no, 528 (2012), pp. 1121–155.

Kavanaugh, Ann C., *John Fitzgibbon, Earl of Clare: Protestant Reaction and English Authority in Late-Eighteenth-Century Ireland* (Dublin: Irish Academic Press, 1997).

Kelleher, Margaret, '*The Cabinet of Irish Literature*: a historical perspective on Irish anthologies', *Éire-Ireland*, vol. 38, no. 3 (2003), pp. 68–89.

Kelly, James, 'The origins of the Act of Union: an examination of unionist opinion in Britain and Ireland, 1650–1800', *Irish Historical Studies*, vol. 25, no. 99 (1987), pp. 236–63.

'Popular politics in Ireland and the Act of Union', *Transactions of the Royal Historical Society*, vol. 10 (2000), pp. 259–87.

'The Act of Union: its origins and background', in Dáire Keogh and Kevin Whelan (eds.), *Acts of Union: The Causes, Contexts and the Consequences of the Act of Union* (Dublin: Four Courts Press, 2001), pp.46–66.

'The failure of opposition', in Michael Brown, Patrick M. Geoghegan and James Kelly (eds.), *The Irish Act of Union: Bicentennial Essays* (Dublin: Irish Academic Press, 2003), pp. 108–28.

'The historiography of the Act of Union', in Michael Brown, Patrick M. Geoghegan and James Kelly (eds.), *The Irish Act of Union: Bicentennial Essays* (Dublin: Irish Academic Press, 2003), pp. 5–36.

*Sir Richard Musgrave, 1746–1818: Ultra-Protestant Ideologue* (Dublin: Four Courts Press, 2009).

Kelly, Matthew, *The Fenian Ideal and Irish Nationalism, 1882–1916* (Woodbridge: Boydell Press, 2006).

'Irish nationalist opinion and the British Empire in the 1850s and 1860s', *Past & Present*, no. 204 (2009), pp. 127–54.

'The *Irish People* and the disciplining of dissent', in Fearghal McGarry and James McConnel (eds.), *The Black Hand of Republicanism: Fenianism in Modern Ireland* (Dublin: Irish Academic Press, 2009), pp. 34–54,

Kelly, Patrick, 'Perceptions of Locke in eighteenth-century Ireland', *Proceedings of the Royal Irish Academy*, vol. 89c (1989), pp. 17–35.

Kendle, John, *The Round Table Movement and Imperial Union* (Toronto: University of Toronto Press, 1975).

*Federal Britain: A History* (London: Routledge, 1997).

Kenna, Shane, *War in the Shadows: The Irish-Americans Fenians Who Bombed Victorian Britain* (Dublin: Irish Academic Press, 2014).

Kennedy, B. A., 'Sharman Crawford's federal scheme for Ireland', in H. A. Cronne, T. W. Moody and D. B. Quinn (eds.), *Essays in British and Irish history in Honour of James Eadie Todd* (London: Frederick Muller Ltd., 1949), pp. 235–55.

Kenny, Kevin, 'The Irish in the Empire', in Kenny (ed.), *Ireland and the British Empire* (Oxford: Oxford University Press, 2004), pp. 90–122.

Keogh, Richard A., 'Why, it's like a "98 trial": the Irish judiciary and the Fenian trials, 1865–66', in Kyle Hughes and Donald M. MacRaild (eds.), *Crime, Violence, and the Irish in the Nineteenth Century* (Liverpool: Liverpool University Press, 2017), pp. 131–48.

Kerr-Richie, Jeffrey R., 'Black abolitionists, Irish supporters, and the brotherhood of man', *Slavery & Abolition*, vol. 37, no. 3 (2016), pp. 599–621.

Keyes, Michael, 'Parnellism: the role of funding in the journey from the semi-revolutionary to the purely constitutional', in Caoimhe Nic Dháibhéid and Colin W. Reid (eds.), *From Parnell to Paisley: Constitutional and Revolutionary Politics in Modern Ireland* (Dublin: Irish Academic Press, 2010), pp. 15–32.

*Funding the Nation: Money and Nationalist Politics in Nineteenth-Century Ireland* (Dublin: Gill & Macmillan Ltd., 2011).

Kidd, Colin, *Unions and Unionisms: Political Thought in Scotland, 1500–2000* (Cambridge: Cambridge University Press, 2008).

Kinealy, Christine, '"Brethren in bondage": Chartists, O'Connellites, Young Irelanders and the 1848 uprising', in Dónal Ó Drisceoil and Fintan Lane (eds.), *Politics and the Irish Working Class, 1830–1945* (Basingstoke: Palgrave Macmillan, 2005), pp. 87–112.

*Repeal and Revolution: 1848 in Ireland* (Manchester: Manchester University Press, 2009).

Kinzer, Bruce L., *England's Disgrace? J. S. Mill and the Irish Question* (Toronto: University of Toronto Press, 2001).

Kloppenberg, James T., *Toward Democracy: The Struggle for Self-Rule in European and American Thought* (Oxford: Oxford University Press, 2016).

Knight, Denis (ed.), *Cobbett in Ireland* (London: Lawrence and Wishart, 1984).

Knight, Matthew, 'The *Irish Republic*: reconstructing liberty, right principles and the Fenian Brotherhood', *Éire-Ireland*, vol. 52, nos. 3&4 (2017), pp. 252–71.

Lane, Fintan and Andrew G. Newby (eds.), *Michael Davitt: New Perspectives* (Dublin: Irish Academic Press, 2009).

Leaney, Enda, 'Provincial science lectures in nineteenth-century Ireland', *Irish Historical Studies*, vol. 34, no. 135 (2005), pp. 266–88.

Leerssen, Joep, *Remembrance and Imagination: Patterns in the Historical and Literary Representation of Ireland in the Nineteenth Century* (Cork: Cork University Press, 1996).

Legg, Marie-Louise, *Newspapers and Nationalism: The Irish Provincial Press, 1850–92* (Dublin: Four Courts Press, 1998).

Livesey, James, 'The fall of the Catholic cosmopolitan: Charles O'Connor and the Catholic debate on the Act of Union', *Britain and the World*, vol. 6, no. 2 (2013), pp. 152–70.

LoPatin, Nancy D., *Political Unions, Popular Politics and the Great Reform Act of 1832* (London: Macmillan, 1998).

Lynch, Niamh, 'Defining Irish nationalist anti-imperialism: Thomas Davis and John Mitchel', *Éire-Ireland*, vol. 42, nos. 1–2 (2007), pp. 94–103.

MacDonagh, Oliver, *The Hereditary Bondsman: Daniel O'Connell, 1779–1829* (London: Weidenfeld and Nicolson, 1986).

*The Emancipist: Daniel O'Connell, 1830–1847* (London: Weidenfeld and Nicolson, 1989).

Mackay, Charles R., *Life of Charles Bradlaugh* (London: D. J. Gunn and Co., 1888).

MacSuibhne, Breandán, *The End of Outrage: Post-Famine Adjustment in Rural Ireland* (Oxford: Oxford University Press, 2017).

Manin, Bernard, *The Principles of Representative Government* (Cambridge: Cambridge University Press, 1997).

Mansergh, Daniel, 'The Union and the importance of public opinion', in Dáire Keogh and Kevin Whelan (eds.), *Acts of Union: The Causes, Contexts and the Consequences of the Act of Union* (Dublin: Four Courts Press, 2001), pp. 126–39.

Mansergh, Danny, *Grattan's Failure: Parliamentary Opposition and the People in Ireland, 1779–1800* (Dublin: Irish Academic Press, 2005).

Mansergh, Nicholas, *The Irish Question, 1840–1921*, 3rd ed. (Toronto: University of Toronto Press, 1975).

Margerison, Kenneth, *Pamphlets & Public Opinion: The Campaign for a Union of Orders in the Early French Revolution* (West Lafayette, IN: Purdue University Press, 1998).

Maume, Patrick, 'Parnell and the IRB Oath', *Irish Historical Studies*, vol. 29, no. 115 (1995), pp. 363–70.

*The Long Gestation: Irish Nationalist Life, 1891–1918* (Dublin: Gill & Macmillan, 1999).

'Unionists and patriots: James Whiteside, the Irish bar and the dilemmas of the Protestant nation in Victorian Ireland', in Allan Blackstock and Frank O'Gorman (eds.), *Loyalism and the Formation of the British World, 1775–1914* (Woodbridge: Boydell Press, 2014), pp. 145–62.

McBride, Ian, *Scripture Politics: Ulster Presbyterians and Irish Radicalism in the Late Eighteenth Century* (Oxford: Oxford University Press, 1998).

*Eighteenth-Century Ireland: The Isle of Slaves* (Dublin: Gill & Macmillan, 2009).

McCaffrey, Lawrence J., 'Isaac Butt and the Home Rule movement: a study in conservative nationalism', *Review of Politics*, vol. 22, no. 1 (1960), pp. 72–95.

*Daniel O'Connell and the Repeal Year* (Lexington: University of Kentucky Press, 1966).

McCartney, Donal, 'Lecky's *Leaders of Public Opinion in Ireland*', *Irish Historical Studies*, vol. 14, no. 54 (1964), pp. 119–41.

*The Dawning of Democracy in Ireland, 1800–1870* (Dublin: Helicon Ltd., 1987).

*W. E. H. Lecky: Historian & Politician, 1838–1903* (Dublin: Lilliput Press, 1994).

McConnel, James, *The Irish Parliamentary Party and the Third Home Rule Crisis* (Dublin: Four Courts Press, 2013).

McCormack, W. J., *The Pamphlet Debate on the Union between Great Britain and Ireland, 1797–1800* (Dublin: Irish Academic Press, 1996).

*Sheridan Le Fanu*, 3rd ed. (Stroud: Sutton Publishing Ltd., 1997).

McDonough, Terrence (ed.), *Was Ireland a Colony? Economics, Politics and Culture in Nineteenth Century-Ireland* (Dublin: Irish Academic Press, 2005).

McDowell, R. B., *Irish Public Opinion 1750–1800* (London: Faber and Faber, 1944).

McGee, Owen, *The IRB: The Irish Republican Brotherhood from the Land League to Sinn Féin* (Dublin: Four Courts Press, 2005).

McGovern, Bryan P., *John Mitchel: Irish Nationalist, Southern Secessionist* (Knoxville: University of Tennessee Press, 2009).

McGrath, Thomas, *Politics, Interdenominational Relations and Education in the Public Ministry of Bishop James Doyle of Kildare and Leighlin, 1786–1834* (Dublin: Four Courts Press, 1999).

*Religious Renewal and Reform in the Pastoral Ministry of Bishop James Doyle of Kildare and Leighlin, 1786–1834* (Dublin: Four Courts Press, 1999).

McMahon, Cian T., *The Global Dimensions of Irish Identity: Race, Nation and the Popular Press, 1840–1880* (Chapel Hill: University of North Carolina Press, 2015).

McMahon, Richard, *Homicide in Pre-Famine and Famine Ireland* (Liverpool: Liverpool University Press, 2013).

McSkimin, Samuel, *The History and Antiquities of the County of the Town of Carrickfergus: From the Earliest Records till 1839*, new ed., with notes by E. J. McCrum (Belfast: Mullan & Son, James Cleeland, Davidson & McCormack, 1909).

Miller, Kerby, *Emigrants and Exiles: Ireland and the Irish Exodus to North America* (Oxford: Oxford University Press, 1985).

Moody, T. W. and Leon Ó Broin, 'Select documents: the IRB Supreme Council, 1868–78', *Irish Historical Studies*, vol. 19, no. 75 (1975), pp. 286–332.

Morash, Christopher, *Young Ireland: A Global Afterlife* (New York: New York University Press, 2023).

Morrow, John, 'Thomas Carlyle, "Young Ireland" and the "condition of Ireland question"', *Historical Journal*, vol. 51, no. 3 (2008), pp. 643–67.

Murphy, James H., *Abject Loyalty: Nationalism and Monarchy in Ireland during the Reign of Queen Victoria* (Cork: Cork University Press, 2001).

Nally, David P., *Human Encumbrances: Political Violence and the Great Irish Famine* (Notre Dame, IN: University of Notre Dame Press, 2011).

Nelson, Bruce, *Irish Nationalists and the Making of the Irish Race* (Princeton, NJ: Princeton University Press, 2012).

Nelson, Eric, 'Prerogative, popular sovereignty and the American founding', in Richard Bourke and Quentin Skinner (eds.), *Popular Sovereignty in Historical Perspective* (Cambridge: Cambridge University Press, 2016), pp. 187–211.

Newsinger, John, *Fenianism in Mid-Victorian Britain* (London: Pluto Press, 1994).

Nic Dháibhéid, Caoimhe et al., 'Round table: decolonising Irish history? Possibilities, challenges, practices', *Irish Historical Studies*, vol. 45, no. 168 (2021), pp. 303–32.

Nootens, Geneviéve, *Popular Sovereignty in the West: Polities, Contention, and Ideas* (London: Routledge, 2013).

Novak, Rose, 'Ellen O'Leary: a bold Fenian poet', *Éire-Ireland*, vol. 43, nos. 3&4 (2008), pp. 58–84.

Nowlan, Kevin B., *The Politics of Repeal: A Study in the Relations between Great Britain and Ireland, 1841–50* (London: Routledge & Kegan Paul, 1965).

Nyquist, Mary, *Arbitrary Rule: Slavery, Tyranny, and the Power of Life and Death* (Chicago: University of Chicago Press, 2013).

O'Brien, Conor Cruise, *Parnell and His Party, 1880–1890* (Oxford: Oxford University Press, 1957).

O'Callaghan, Margaret, *British High Politics and a Nationalist Ireland: Criminality, Land and the Law under Forster and Balfour* (Cork: Cork University Press, 1994).

'Franchise reform, "first past the post", and the strange case of unionist Ireland', *Parliamentary History*, vol. 16, no. 1 (1997), pp. 85–106.

Ó Ciosáin, Niall, *Print and Popular Culture in Ireland, 1750–1850* (Dublin: Lilliput Press, 2010; first published 1997).

O'Day, Alan, *Irish Home Rule* (Manchester: Manchester University Press, 1998).

'Isaac Butt and neglected political economists, in Noel Thompson and Nigel Allington (eds.), *English, Irish and Subversives among the Dismal Scientists* (Bingley: Emerald, 2010), pp. 375–401.

O'Donoghue, David (ed.), *The Life of William Carleton*, 2 vols. (London: Downey & Co., 1896).

O'Dowd, Mary. 'O'Connell and the lady patriots: women and O'Connellite politics, 1824–1845', in Allan Blackstock and Eoin Magennis (eds.), *Politics and Political Culture in Britain and Ireland, 1750–1850: Essays om Tribute to Peter Jupp* (Belfast: Ulster Historical Foundation, 2007), pp. 283–303.

Ó Gráda, Cormac, *Ireland: A New Economic History, 1780–1939* (Oxford: Oxford University Press, 1994).

O'Keeffe, C. M., *Life and Times of Daniel O'Connell, with some Sketches of his Contemporaries*, 2 vols. (Dublin: John Murray, 1864).

O'Neill, Ciaran, *Power and Powerless in Union Ireland: Life in a Palliative State* (Oxford: Oxford University Press, 2024).

Ó Síocháin, Séamus (ed.), *Social Thought on Ireland in the Nineteenth Century* (Dublin: UCD Press, 2009).

O'Sullivan, T. F., *The Young Irelanders* (Tralee: Kerryman Ltd., 1944).

Oakley, Francis, *The Conciliarist Tradition: Constitutionalism in the Catholic Church, 1300–1870* (Oxford: Oxford University Press, 2003).

Okin, Susan Moller, *Women in Western Political Thought* (Princeton, NJ: Princeton University Press, 1979).

Parssinen, T. M., 'Association, convention and anti-parliament in British radical politics, 1771–1848', *English Historical Review*, vol. 88, no. 348 (1973), pp. 504–33.

Pašeta, Senia, 'Feminist political thought and activism in revolutionary Ireland, *c.*1880–1918', *Transactions of the Royal Historical Society*, vol. 27, (2017), pp. 193–209.

Patten, Eve, *Sir Samuel Ferguson and the Culture of Nineteenth-Century Ireland* (Dublin: Four Courts Press, 2004).

Patterson, James G., *In the Wake of the Great Rebellion: Republicanism, Agrarianism and Banditry in Ireland after 1798* (Manchester: Manchester University Press, 2008).

Pettit, Philip, *Republicanism: A Theory of Freedom and Government* (Oxford: Oxford University Press, 1997).

Phemister, Andrew, *Land and Liberalism: Henry George and the Irish Land War* (Cambridge: Cambridge University Press, 2023).

Philp, Mark, *Reforming Ideas in Britain: Politics and Language in the Shadow of the French Revolution, 1789–1815* (Cambridge: Cambridge University Press, 2014).

Pitkin, Hanna Fenichel, *The Concept of Representation* (Berkeley: University of California Press, 1967).

Pocock, J. G. A., *The Machiavellian Moment: Florentine Political Thought and the Atlantic Republican Tradition* (Princeton, NJ: Princeton University Press, 2003; first published 1975).

*Political Thought and History: Essays on Theory and Method* (Cambridge: Cambridge University Press, 2009).

Popper, Karl, *The Open Society and Its Enemies* (Abingdon: Routledge, 2011; first published 1945).

Portsmouth, Robert, *John Wilson Croker: Irish Ideas and the Invention of Modern Conservatism* (Dublin: Irish Academic Press, 2010).

Power, Thomas P., *The Apocalypse in Ireland: Prophecy and Politics in the 1820s* (Oxford: Peter Land, 2023).

Prest, Wilfred, *William Blackstone: Law and Letters in the Eighteenth Century* (Oxford: Oxford University Press, 2008).

Quinlivan, Patrick and Paul Rose, *The Fenians in England, 1865–1872* (London: John Calder, 1982).

Quinn, James, 'John Mitchel and the rejection of the nineteenth century', *Éire-Ireland*, vol. 38 (2003), pp. 90–108.

*John Mitchel* (Dublin: UCD Press, 2008).
*Young Ireland the Writing of Irish History* (Dublin: University College Dublin Press, 2015).
'The *Nation*, history, and the making of national citizens', in Rebecca Anne Barr, Sarah-Anne Buckley and Muireann O'Cinneide (eds.), *Literacy, Language and Reading in Nineteenth-Century Ireland* (Liverpool: Liverpool University Press, 2019), pp. 53–65.
Rabin, Dana Y., *Britain and Its Internal Others, 1750–1800: Under Rule of Law* (Manchester: Manchester University Press, 2017).
Ramón, Marta, *A Provisional Dictator: James Stephens and the Fenian Movement* (Dublin: UCD Press, 2007).
Regan-Lefebvre, Jennifer, *Cosmopolitan Nationalism and the Victorian Empire: Ireland, India and the Politics of Alfred Webb* (Basingstoke: Palgrave, 2009).
Reid, Colin W., *The Lost Ireland of Stephen Gwynn: Irish Constitutional Nationalism and Cultural Politics, 1864–1950* (Manchester: Manchester University Press, 2015; first published 2011).
'Citizens of nowhere: longing, belonging and exile among Irish Protestant writers in Britain, *c.*1830–1970', *Irish Studies Review*, vol. 24, no. 3 (2016), pp. 255–74.
'Democracy, sovereignty and unionist political thought during the revolutionary period in Ireland, *c.*1912–22', *Transactions of the Royal Historical Society*, vol. 27 (2017), pp. 211–32.
'"A voice for Ireland": Isaac Butt, environmental justice, and the dilemmas of the Irish land question', in Matthew Kelly (ed.), *Nature and the Environment in Nineteenth-Century Ireland* (Liverpool: Liverpool University Press, 2019), pp. 55–74.
'The canon of Irish republicanism: constructing a separatist "tradition"', in Matthew Roberts (ed.), *Memory and Modern British Politics: Commemoration, Tradition, Legacy* (London: Bloomsbury, 2024), pp. 67–92.
'Isaac Butt's legacy: the Irish Parliamentary Party, 1879–1918', in Martin O'Donoghue and Emer Purcell (eds.), *John Redmond and Irish Parliamentary Traditions* (Dublin: UCD Press, 2024), pp. 20–31.
Reid, John Phillip, *The Concept of Liberty in the Age of the American Revolution* (Chicago: University of Chicago Press, 1988).
Ritchie, Daniel, *Isaac Nelson: Radical Abolitionist, Evangelical Presbyterian, and Irish Nationalist* (Liverpool: Liverpool University Press, 2018).
Roberts, Matthew, *Popular Movements in Urban England, 1832–1914* (London: Macmillan, 2009).
'Daniel O'Connell, Repeal and Chartism in the age of Atlantic revolutions', *Journal of Modern History*, 90 (2018), pp. 1–39.
*Chartism, Commemoration and the Cult of the Radical Hero* (Abingdon: Routledge, 2020).
*Democratic Passions: The Politics of Feeling in British Popular Radicalism, 1809–1848* (Manchester: Manchester University Press, 2022).

Romani, Roberto, 'British views on Irish national character, 1800–1847: an intellectual history', *History of European Ideas*, vol. 23, nos. 5–6 (1997), pp. 193–219.

Roszman, Jay R., '"Ireland as a weapon of warfare": Whigs, Tories, and the problem of Irish outrages, 1835 to 1839', *Historical Journal*, vol. 60, no. 4 (2017), pp. 971–95.

*Outrage in the Age of Reform: Irish Agrarian Violence, Imperial Insecurity and British Governing Policy, 1830–1845* (Cambridge: Cambridge University Press, 2022).

Rubinelli, Lucia, *Constituent Power: A History* (Cambridge: Cambridge University Press, 2020).

Saunders, Robert, *Democracy and the Vote in British Politics, 1848–1867: The Making of the Second Reform Act* (Farnham: Ashgate, 2011).

Schwoerer, Lois G., *Gun Culture in Early Modern England* (Charlottesville: University of Virginia Press, 2016).

Scott, Geoffrey, '"The times are fast approaching": Bishop Charles Walmsley OSB (1722–1797) as a prophet', *Journal of Ecclesiastical History*, vol. 36, no. 4 (1985), pp. 590–604.

Selinger, William, *Parliamentarism: From Burke to Weber* (Cambridge: Cambridge University Press, 2019).

Sewell Jr., William H., *A Rhetoric of Bourgeois Revolution: The Abbé Sieyès and What Is the Third Estate?* (Durham, NC: Duke University Press, 1994).

Shields, Andrew, *The Irish Conservative Party, 1852–1868: Land, Politics and Religion* (Dublin: Irish Academic Press, 2007).

Skinner, Quentin, *The Foundation of Modern Political Thought*, 2 vols. (Cambridge: Cambridge University Press, 1978).

*Liberty before Liberalism* (Cambridge: Cambridge University Press, 2012; first published 1998).

*Visions of Politics*, 3 vols. (Cambridge: Cambridge University Press, 2002).

*Liberty as Independence: The Making and Unmaking of a Political Ideal* (Cambridge: Cambridge University Press, 2025).

Skjönsberg, Max, 'The history of political thought and parliamentary history in the eighteenth and nineteenth centuries', *Historical Journal*, vol. 64, no. 2 (2021), pp. 501–13.

Sloan, Robert, *William Smith O'Brien and the Young Ireland Rebellion of 1848* (Dublin: Four Courts Press, 2000).

Small, Stephen, *Political Thought in Ireland, 1776–1798: Republicanism, Patriotism and Radicalism* (Oxford: Oxford University Press, 2002).

Smyth, Jim, 'Anti-Catholicism, conservatism, and conspiracy: Sir Richard Musgrave's *Memoirs of the Different Rebellions in Ireland*', *Eighteenth-Century Life*, vol. 22, no. 3 (1998), pp. 62–73.

'The Act of Union and "public opinion"', in Smyth (ed.), *Revolution, Counter-Revolution and Union: Ireland in the 1790s* (Cambridge: Cambridge University Press, 2000), pp. 146–60.

Spence, Joseph, 'The philosophy of Irish Toryism, 1833–1852: a study of the reactions to liberal reformism in Ireland in the generation between the first

Reform Act and the Famine, with especial reference to expressions of national feelings among the Protestant Ascendancy' (University of London PhD thesis, 1991).
'Isaac Butt, Irish nationality and the conditional defence of the Union, 1833–1870', in D. G. Boyce and A. O'Day (eds.), *Defenders of the Union: A Survey of British and Irish Unionism Since 1801* (London: Routledge, 2001), pp. 65–89.
Stafford, James, *The Case of Ireland: Commerce, Empire and the European Order, 1750–1848* (Cambridge: Cambridge University Press, 2022).
Steinbach, Susie L., *Understanding the Victorians: Politics, Culture and Society in Nineteenth-Century Britain*, 2nd ed. (Abingdon: Routledge, 2017).
Takagami, Shin-ichi, 'The Fenian rising in Dublin, March 1867', *Irish Historical Studies*, vol. 29, no. 115 (1995), pp. 340–62.
Thompson, Dorothy, *The Chartists* (London: Temple Smith, 1984).
Thornley, David, *Isaac Butt and Home Rule* (London: MacGibbon & Kee, 1964).
Thursfield, J. R., *Peel* (London: Macmillan and Co., 1891).
Todd, David, *Free Trade and its Enemies in France, 1814–1851* (Cambridge: Cambridge University Press, 2015).
Townend, Paul A., *The Road to Home Rule: Anti-Imperialism and the Irish Nationalist Movement* (Madison: University of Wisconsin Press, 2016).
Tribe, Keith, *Strategies of Economic Order: German Economic Discourse, 1750–1950* (Cambridge: Cambridge University Press, 1995).
Tuck, Richard, *The Sleeping Sovereign: The Invention of Modern Democracy* (Cambridge: Cambridge University Press, 2015).
Vieira, Mónica Brito and David Runciman, *Representation* (Cambridge: Polity Press, 2008).
Visana, Vikram, *Uncivil Liberalism: Labour, Capital and Commercial Society in Dadabhai Naoroji's Political Thought* (Cambridge: Cambridge University Press, 2022).
Whatmore, Richard, *Terrorists, Anarchists and Republicans: The Genevans and the Irish in Time of Revolution* (Princeton, NJ: Princeton University Press, 2019).
Wheatley, Natasha, *The Life and Death of States: Central Europe and the Transformation of Modern Sovereignty* (Princeton, NJ: Princeton University Press, 2023).
Whelan, Fergus, *May Tyrants Tremble: The Life of William Drennan, 1754–1822* (Dublin: Irish Academic Press, 2020).
Whelehan, Niall, *The Dynamiters: Irish Nationalism and Political Violence in the Wider World, 1867–1900* (Cambridge: Cambridge University Press, 2012).
*Diaspora Activism and the Irish Land War* (New York: New York University Press, 2021).
White, R. J., *The Conservative Tradition*, 2nd ed. (London: Adam & Charles Black, 1964).
White, Terence de Vere, *The Road of Excess* (Dublin: Browne and Nolan Ltd., 1946).

Whyte, J. H., *The Independent Irish Party, 1850–1859* (Oxford: Oxford University Press, 1958).

Wilkinson, David, 'How did they pass the Union? Secret service expenditure', *History*, vol. 82, no. 266 (1997), pp. 223–51.

Wright, Jonathan Jeffrey, *The 'Natural Leaders' and Their World: Politics, Culture and Society in Belfast, c. 1801–1832* (Liverpool: Liverpool University Press, 2012).

# Index

For EU product safety concerns, contact us at Calle de José Abascal, 56–1°, 28003 Madrid, Spain or eugpsr@cambridge.org.

www.ingramcontent.com/pod-product-compliance
Ingram Content Group UK Ltd.
Pitfield, Milton Keynes, MK11 3LW, UK
UKHW020051100326
468807UK00007BA/1185
*9781009630184*